D0321935

Crowds, Culture, and Politics in Georgian Britain

Crowds, Culture, and Politics in Georgian Britain

Nicholas Rogers

CLARENDON PRESS · OXFORD
1998

Oxford University Press, Great Clarendon Street, Oxford OX2 6DP
Oxford New York
Athens Auckland Bangkok Bogota Buenos Aires Calcutta
Cape Town Chennai Dar es Salaam Delhi Florence Hong Kong Istanbul
Karachi Kuala Lumpur Madrid Melbourne Mexico City Mumbai
Nairobi Paris São Paolo Singapore Taipei Tokyo Toronto Warsaw
and associated companies in
Berlin Ibadan

Oxford is a registered trade mark of Oxford University Press

Published in the United States
by Oxford University Press Inc., New York

First published 1998

British Library Cataloguing in Publication Data
Data available

Library of Congress Cataloging in Publication Data
Rogers, Nicholas.
Crowds, culture, and politics in Georgian Britain / Nicholas
Rogers.
p.   cm.
Includes index.
1. Great Britain—Politics and government—18th century.
2. Political participation—Great Britain—History—18th century.
3. Popular culture—Great Britain—History—18th century.
4. Crowds—Great Britain—History—18th century.   I. Title.
DA480.R64   1998
941.07—dc21   98–13096

ISBN 0–19–820172–9

1 3 5 7 9 10 8 6 4 2

Typeset by Graphicraft Limited, Hong Kong
Printed in Great Britain
on acid-free paper by Biddles Ltd., Guildford & King's Lynn

For Nini

Acknowledgements

In writing this book I have incurred many debts. The Faculty of Arts at York University awarded me a leave fellowship to begin and consolidate this project a decade ago, and having spent a number of years chairing my department in an era of cuts in post-secondary education in Ontario, I returned to the task on sabbatical leave. The book has consequently taken a longer time to write than I had hoped. I thank Anna Illingworth of Oxford University Press for smoothly guiding the manuscript to production.

A different kind of material assistance was provided by archivists and librarians in three countries. They include: in Britain, the Avon Reference Library, Bristol, the Bodleian Library, Oxford, the Bristol Record Office, the British Library, the Corporation of London Record Office, the Gloucester Library, the Greater London Record Office, the Guildhall Library, London, the Institute of Historical Research, London, the Manchester Central Library, the National Library of Wales, the Newcastle Central Library, the Newspaper Library at Colindale, the Norfolk and Norwich Record Office, the Norwich City Library, the Public Record Office (both at Chancery Lane and Kew), the Suffolk Record Office, and the Worcester Library; in Canada, the Mills Library, McMaster University, Hamilton, the Robarts Library at the University of Toronto, and the Osgoode Hall and Scott Libraries at York University; in the United States of America, the Huntington Library, San Marino, California, and the William L. Clements Library at the University of Michigan, Ann Arbor. I thank all for their help, particularly the librarians at Robarts Microtext, who handled my inquiries with unfailing courtesy and efficiency, even when their own department had to do more with less.

Earlier versions of some chapters in this book, namely chapters 3, 5, and 8, were printed as articles and as a chapter in *Jack Tar In History*, Colin Howell and Richard Twomey (eds.) (Fredericton, New Brunswick, 1991). I should like to thank the editors of *left history*, the *Journal of the*

Canadian Historical Association, and Acadiensis Press for permission to reprint materials first published there.

Every chapter of this book has also been presented in an abbreviated form to some academic audience: to various meetings of the Conference of British Studies; to the Jack Tar in History conference at Halifax, Nova Scotia; to the Early Modern British History group in the Greater Toronto area; to historians at the University of Berkeley, California; to the Lamarsh Centre for Violence and Conflict Resolution at York University; to the History Research group in my own department. I would like to thank all who gave me helpful advice and criticism on those occasions. In particular, I should like to express a debt to a number of historians of eighteenth-century Britain who happen to live in my own city. These include Donna Andrew, John Beattie, Douglas Hay, and Jeanette Neeson. They have constantly pushed references my way and probed my own lines of inquiry.

Other historians have also been generous with their time and criticism in the making of this book. I would like to single out Joanna Innes of Somerville College, Oxford, who has not only been unfailingly hospitable to me when I visited Oxford but has generously given me the benefit of her encyclopaedic knowledge of the eighteenth century and constructive commentary of my own arguments about crowds. Needless to say, she, too, has given me some useful references, as have Jeff Chamberlain, Eveline Cruickshanks, Fred Donnelly, Jim Epstein, Susan Foote, Benjamin Klein, Virginia McKendry, and Andrea McKenzie.

In writing a book spanning over a century and drawing on a pretty wide range of sources, I have also benefited from some graduate assistance. I should like to thank Catherine Thompson, Adele Perry, Stephen Moore, Brett Cohen and Suzanne Le May-Sheffield for tracking down references for me, and sometimes laboriously scanning newspapers for the illumin-ating festival or riot.

I should like to acknowledge three more debts. The first is to my sister Sally Powell and her partner Iain Coleman, whose hospitality, good cheer, and support have always made my trips to London so memorable.

The second is to two towering historians of the eighteenth century, George Rudé and Edward Thompson. They were both enormously gen-erous with their time and support as I navigated the already charted but still choppy waters of popular political history. They did not live long enough to see the final product, and I am not sure what they would have made of it. All I know is that I have constantly engaged their ideas on crowds as I have tried to find a space for my own.

Finally, I should like to thank my partner, Nicole Tellier, who has always been supportive of this project amid her own busy, legal career. This book is dedicated to her, with love and affection.

Contents

List of Illustrations

Introduction
Crowds in History

The 'Crowd' is, at best, an evanescent theme. Like the Cheshire Cat it is there, it is almost there, then it is not there, and then it is there again.

([Richard Cobb,] 'Overcrowding', *Times Literary Supplement* (30 Dec. 1965), 1205)

Over the past thirty years the study of collective protest has been a major point of departure for students interested in the history of the lower classes, especially those of pre-democratic societies. Admittedly, the subject was not ignored by earlier generations of historians. In France there existed a long tradition of left-wing historiography which addressed the question of popular ferment in the revolutionary era. In Britain and America popular unrest constituted a minor theme outside orthodox academic circles and, indeed, commanded some sympathetic attention from within the academy itself. But the examination of popular movements 'from below', in terms of the common people's own experiences and aspirations, expanded considerably in the late 1950s and 1960s to establish itself as a major tributary of the new social history. Evanescent or not, the crowd's status in historical discourse is hardly ephemeral, as even a brief glance at mainstream journals will testify. In fact, the history of popular disturbances has become an indispensable feature of the early modern era in particular, disclosing new facets of popular consciousness and highlighting, often in dramatic form, the broad structures of authority and power.

In spite of the welter of empirical explorations on the crowd in history, there have been relatively few attempts to explore its methodological and theoretical ramifications. Those that have been offered tend to focus upon the contributions of specific historians rather than upon this particular genre of history. What I propose to do here, as an introduction to my own contribution to crowd studies, is to trace the changing problematic of the crowd,

the issues, both contemporary and historiographical, which shaped its formulation, beginning with the early pioneers of collective psychology and
the way in which their notions of collective behaviour were challenged by
practising historians. Special attention will be given to the British Marxist
school of historians, notably Hobsbawm, Rudé, and Thompson, because
their redefinitions of popular history have been theoretically important and
influential. Their work has the merit of focusing, in quite central ways, upon
the difficulties of reconstructing the 'popular' in history.

Crowd studies have never been the exclusive province of historians, even
to this day. The subject has always engaged the attention of social psychologists and sociologists. In fact it was among the early practitioners of these
disciplines that the concept of the crowd was first conceived. The particular
moment when this definition took place was the political and social crisis
of the French Third Republic and, more generally, the emergence of a more
militant labour movement whose socialist aspirations challenged existing
social formations. Confronted with the resurgence of popular militancy and
class conflict after the Paris Commune of 1871, conservative intellectuals
articulated their fears about the breakdown of social order and the threat
of socialism in a series of studies on crowd behaviour. The historical evidence for this theory of the crowd came from Hippolyte Taine's *Les Origines
de la France contemporaine*, a profoundly anti-democratic work written in
the immediate aftermath of the 1871 revolt. According to Taine, the *philo-
sophes* of the French Revolution had poisoned the people, undermined tradition, and, with the ensuing collapse of monarchical authority, had unleashed
a bestial, irrational mob that quickly fell into the hands of criminal elements.[1] Unlike earlier historians such as Michelet, who had been generally
apologetic about the popular excesses of the first revolutionary era, Taine
saw crowd interventions as symptomatic of the inadequacies and dangers
of revolutionary politics. In his eyes, the French Revolution had generated forces of a pathological dimension which it proved incapable of
controlling.

Social psychologists quickly picked up on this work and sought to cre-
ate a new science of collective behaviour to address the problems of what
Gustave Le Bon termed 'the new era of crowds'.[2] In the writings of Tarde,
Sighele, and Fournail, a basic analogy was made between individual and

---

[1] See Susanna Barrows, *Distorting Mirrors: Visions of the Crowd in Late Nineteenth-Century
France* (New Haven, 1971), ch. 3.
[2] See Robert A. Nye, *The Origins of Crowd Psychology: Gustave Le Bon and the Crisis of
Mass Democracy in the Third Republic* (London, 1975), and Serge Moscovici, *The Age of the
Crowd: A Historical Treatise on Mass Psychology* (Cambridge, 1985), esp. part II.

collective pathology, between the crowd and the criminal mind. The prevailing interest in hypnotism was brought into service to verify the irrational, imitative aspects of crowd action and its basic malleability, even though there was some debate about the general applicability of mesmerism to collective behaviour. Eugenics was also used to equate racial and collective mentalities so that the crowd came to reflect primordial sentiments deeply embedded in the heritage of the race. According to Gustave Le Bon, who provided a popular synthesis of these ideas in his *The Crowd*, first published in 1895, crowd sentiments represented the 'atavistic residuum of the instincts of the primitive man' in which reason was paralysed and momentary passions held sway.[3] In sum, the crowd was conceived as a pyschological phenomenon, symptomatic of a broader social malaise in industrial society characterized by rootlessness, want, and anomie, and prone to atavistic brutality, fanaticism, and frenzied intolerance. Not surprisingly, it was relegated to the bottom of the ladder of social evolution. 'By the mere fact that he forms part of an organized crowd,' claimed Le Bon, 'a man descends several rungs in the ladder of civilization.'[4]

This extremely negative definition of the crowd was deployed to discredit both the motives and legitimacy of left-wing movements. Although some sociologists like Gabriel Tarde sought to distinguish spontaneous crowds from the activities of more organized collectivities, the distinction was often lost in more popular discourse. Le Bon, for example, saw crowds on the same continuum as other popular associations, a correlation that fuelled his scepticism about all forms of participatory democracy. Unlike Taine, however, he did not simply mourn the passing of an older aristocratic order. Recognizing the inevitability of democracy, this 'Macchiavelli of mass societies'[5] devoted his energies towards formulating strategies to save the people from socialism. Greatly impressed by General Boulanger, he placed his faith in the powers of charismatic leadership and patriotic militarism, and towards the end of his life in the educative possibilities of the visual media in inculcating appropriate notions of order and hierarchy. It is no accident that his ideas were taken up by the École de Guerre prior to the First World War and by Mussolini afterwards. It has even been suggested that *Mein Kampf* reveals a familiarity with Le Bon's *Crowd*.[6]

---

[3] Gustave Le Bon, *The Crowd: A Study of the Popular Mind* (2nd edn., Dunwoody, Ga., 1968), 34.

[4] Ibid. 12.   [5] The phrase is from Serge Moscovici.

[6] On the appropriation of Le Bon's ideas by the fascists, see Nye, *Origins*, 177–80, and Moscovici, *The Age of the Crowd*, 62–4.

Even so, the influence of European crowd psychology was not confined exclusively to right-wing circles. It attracted a remarkably wide range of political and scientific opinion. Freud believed Le Bon had drawn a 'brilliantly executed picture of the group mind' and commended his equation of crowd with primitive mentalities.[7] In Britain Le Bon's ideas were taken up by conservative eugenicists like William McDougall and Sir Martin Conway as well as by the liberal-radical psychologist and surgeon Wilfred Trotter, who in the first issue of the *Sociological Review* used Le Bon as a springboard for his speculations on the herd instinct.[8] Even Sorel accepted the trance-like unconscious nature of crowd action and its mimetic proclivities, while Zola's insurgents in *Germinal* were governed by instinct and blood lust.[9]

In a less lurid fashion crowd psychology also entered American social thought by way of Robert Park and the Chicago school. To be sure, Park, like Trotter, played down the pathological and racial dimensions of collective unrest so pronounced in European thought. For both writers, crowd actions denoted a groping for a new order however crudely such aspirations were formulated, and it was the business of the sociologist to analyse the social problems which popular upheavals both posed and addressed and to bring them before an informed public.[10] Even so, Park, like Trotter, drew heavily on Le Bon's characterization of the crowd as an impulsive, malleable, and ephemeral phenomenon, rootless and regressive. Differentiating it from a 'public' where interaction took the form of reasoned discussion and debate, he consistently saw the crowd as a very imperfect expression of the general will, promising at best 'to reveal the secret of the social, the general influence of human contagion on rational behaviour'. Within this liberal context collective unrest was regarded as more regrettable than reprehensible. But it was still viewed as a sickness or dysfunction, capable of diagnosis or cure. To this day this perspective constitutes one important

---

[7] Nye, *Origins*, 67, 173; see also Moscovici, *The Age of the Crowd*, part VI.

[8] Wilfred Trotter, 'The Herd Instinct and its Bearing on the Psychology of Civilized Man', *Sociological Review*, 1 (1908), 227–48; Martin Conway, *The Crowd in Peace and War* (London, 1915); Robert M. Farr, 'The Social Psychology of William McDougall', in Carl F. Graumann and Serge Moscovici (eds.), *Changing Conceptions of Crowd Mind and Behavior* (New York, 1986), 83–96.

[9] Unlike Le Bon, Sorel did not believe that crowds were intrinsically conservative, believing that the power of revolutionary faith and mythology could mobilize the masses against capitalism. See Nye, *Origins*, 105. On Zola, see Barrows, *Distorting Mirrors*, ch. 4.

[10] Wilfred Trotter, 'Sociological Application of the Psychology of Herd Instinct', *Sociological Review*, 2 (1909), 36–54; Robert Park, *Masse und Publikum* (1904), translated into English several years later as *The Crowd and the Public, and Other Essays*, ed. Henry Elsner, Jr. (Chicago, 1972).

strain in American sociology as the work of Neil Smelser, among others, testifies.

Park's theory went some way towards modifying the negative image of European sociologists. It was not suffused with racial associations, nor was it coloured with any overriding obsessions with the herd instinct and hypnotism. But it did assume that collective unrest was the product of the atomizing effects of modern urban life and consequently denied crowd action any real history or cultural identity. This problem was taken up in the 1930s by the French historian Georges Lefebvre. In a series of discrete and detailed studies of the revolutionary peasantry, of which *La Grande Peur* is the best-known example, Lefebvre reconstructed the actions and mental world of the populace in ways that challenged the prevailing assumptions of collective pyschology.[11] Contrary to Le Bon, Lefebvre argued that crowds were not involuntary and ephemeral aggregates of individuals devoid of any collective mentality beyond an inherited residuum of instincts, desires, and prejudices, but quintessentially cultural phenomena whose form and outlook were shaped by everyday habits and associations. In other words, the very existence of crowds presumed a prior collective mentality, whose bonds and shared experience served as the touchstone for popular intervention. From this perspective Lefebvre showed that the seemingly irrational character of peasant protest in 1789, its millenarian temper, its sensitivity to rumours of an impending aristocratic reprisal, could not be ascribed to the primacy of the psychic element in collective life and the hypnotic sway of leaders. Rather, it obeyed a logic and autonomy derived from the quotidian. Rumours of reprisals travelled along the well-trodden routes of the countryside. Peasants assembled at everyday rendezvous. Their primitive egalitarianism was not the product of repressed impulses activated by temporary hardships and manipulative agitators. It expressed a deep-rooted hatred of the seigniory, stored in the collective memory over many decades. Only through an investigation of the communal bases of popular protest and its 'collective unconscious', nurtured through an oral tradition, could one begin to decode the meaning of peasant unrest.

Lefebvre thus called for a deeper contextualization of popular life, a profounder understanding of the submerged history of the common people of which riots were but one manifestation. In this way the underlying rationality of crowd action could be disclosed, however limited or visionary its aspirations might appear to be. By attending to the myths and symbols

[11] Georges Lefebvre, *The Great Fear*, trans. Joan White (London, 1973); id., 'Revolutionary Crowds', in Jeffrey Kaplow (ed.), *New Perspectives on the French Revolution* (New York, 1965), 173–90.

which fired the insurgents' imagination, to the targets of their militancy, and to the particular conjunctures which triggered popular action, one might probe the limits and divergent temporalities of popular consciousness (between peasant and artisan, for example) as well as the sources of their organizational strength. Hence it was possible to move beyond a definition of crowd action as pathological disorder to one which saw it as essentially belonging to the same continuum as other forms of collective behaviour, as an aspect of power struggles between and within organized groups in society.

Lefebvre's pioneering forays into popular protest at the inception of the French Revolution set important precedents for what became known as 'history from below'; that is, the reconstruction of the lives of the common people in terms of their own standards, expectations, and experience. 'If there is a single historian who anticipates most of the themes of contemporary work [in this field]', wrote Eric Hobsbawm, 'it is Georges Lefebvre, whose "Great Fear", translated into English after forty years, is still remarkably up-to-date.'[12] To be sure, 'history from below' encompassed a broader range of studies than simply the 'crowd'. As Edward Thompson's early reflections on the genre revealed,[13] it involved an exploration of popular culture beyond the confines of orthodox labour history and, inevitably, a reconstruction of forms of popular intervention outside the ambit of crowd studies strictly defined: peasant revolts, secret societies, seditious rumours, social banditry, and so on. Yet, in the context of the eighteenth and early nineteenth centuries, the crowd became central to this new venture. In France, Cobb, Rudé, and Soboul followed in Lefebvre's footsteps by exploring the diverse forms of popular militancy and resistance spawned by the Revolution. In America the new interest in crowds reopened the debate about the Progressivist interpretation of the American Revolution, notably the theme of home rule and who ruled at home. In Britain it served to prise open the prehistory of the labour movement, the patterns of resistance to agrarian capitalism, and the apparent caesura of popular protest between the Civil War and Chartism. By the early 1970s, partly through the influence of journals like *Past and Present*, specifically founded to explore themes and methodologies outside the mainstream of orthodox political and economic history, the study of the crowd and other forms of collective resistance had become a major international preoccupation of the new social history.

[12] E. J. Hobsbawm, 'History from Below: Some Reflections', in Frederick Krantz (ed.), *History from Below: Studies in Popular Protest and Ideology* (Oxford, 1988), 15.

[13] E. P. Thompson, 'History from Below', *Times Literary Supplement* (7 Apr. 1966), 279–80.

Although the resurgence of interest in 'history from below' owed much to the expansion of post-secondary education after the war and to the quest for new historical horizons, it was also a political intervention. 'History from below' was not simply intended to complement Great Man's history or to correct the elisions of a Whig historiography which rummaged the past for presentist origins; it sought to recover the long struggle for popular rights and liberties in terms that would stress the creative possibilities of the common people in class struggle. In Britain, in particular, many of its leading practitioners were Marxists anxious to revivify historical materialism in non-reductionist ways, to reassert the primacy of agency in popular history, and to redress the imbalance of historical orthodoxies which tended to subsume the popular experience within national or institutional contexts. Deeply involved in the popular front against fascism, they were anxious to rescue the 'people' from reactionary folklore and Churchillian notations of the 'national-popular'. Thus Christopher Hill recast the myth of the Norman Yoke as a pre-industrial ideology of liberation which differentiated the 'people' from the 'nation' and reaffirmed the resilience of the radical popular tradition in the protracted era of agrarian capitalism.[14] In this and other ways, 'history from below' might serve as a source of inspiration for an ascendant labour movement confronted with the patriotic blandishments of post-war conservatism, Cold War polarities, and the class-muted, technocratic, ideology of consumerism. Within the international sphere, it could offer some historical pointers about Third World struggles. Hobsbawm's *Primitive Rebels*, for example, was a historical lesson of how traditional forms of protest might or might not contribute towards the creation of a socialist or communist movement, and in what circumstances strong party leadership might prove decisive. It was no accident that the book was prompted by an interest in colonial revolt and the Italian 'Southern question'.[15]

Sharpened by the break with Stalinism and the emergence of the New Left in Europe and America, this radical vision shaped the agenda of 'history from below'. Within the territory of crowd studies the initiative was taken by George Rudé. In British Marxist circles Rudé was the first to engage in the study of popular disturbance.[16] As a protégé of Lefebvre,

---

[14] Christopher Hill, 'The Norman Yoke', in *Puritanism and Revolution* (London, 1969), 58–125, first published in John Saville (ed.), *Democracy and the Labour Movement* (London, 1954).

[15] 'Interview with E. J. Hobsbawm', *Radical History Review*, 19 (Winter 1978–9), 155. See also MARHO, *Visions of History* (New York, 1984), 32–3.

[16] Eric Hobsbawm, 'The Historians' Group of the Communist Party', in Maurice Cornforth (ed.), *Rebels and their Causes: Essays in Honour of A. L. Morton* (London, 1978), 37.

he had followed hard in his mentor's footsteps, once more challenging
Le Bon's characterization of the crowd and also the abstract images of
liberal-Whig historians such as Michelet. Through a painstaking examination of the police or judicial records, Rudé was able to repudiate the notion
that the Parisian and London crowds were composed of riff-raff, or the
migratory poor.[17] In both capitals he showed that the participants in the
major, late eighteenth-century riots and demonstrations were drawn from
the settled rather than marginal sections of the population: journeymen,
small masters, and shopkeepers, very few of whom had criminal records.
Moreover, he was able to throw further light on the local, disciplined pattern of collective action; in the Parisian context, how traditional demands
for cheaper bread fused with revolutionary aspirations as the political crisis
of the *ancien régime* intensified. From this perspective it became increasingly difficult to see urban riot as a collective pathology, a frenzied protest
of the uprooted.

Rudé's own findings on this score were quickly incorporated into the
burgeoning research on the crowd and his pioneering exploration of the
social anatomy of the crowd and its targets set important guidelines for
further study. Yet his overall approach did pose some difficulties as his
broader generalizations about crowd action revealed. His first and arguably predominant interest had always been in the emergence and evolution of popular revolutionary activity, particularly in the relationship between
traditional forms of mass insurgency and radical action. These preoccu-
pations have inevitably influenced the scope of his explorations into the
crowd. Within his terms of reference the study of the crowd became the
study of riot and, by extension, the most dramatic forms of social and political protest. In his introduction to *The Crowd in History*, Rudé initially
defined the crowd as a 'face-to-face' or 'direct contact' group, but it became
clear that his central focus was devoted to 'political demonstrations and
to what sociologists have termed the "aggressive mob" or the "hostile
outburst"—to such activities as strikes, riots, rebellions, insurrections, and
revolutions'.[18]

Clearly there are some problems with this definition. As it is first formulated it is too inspecific, allowing for the inclusion of groups that Rudé
would wish to exclude from his studies: street gangs, for example, or, in
the early modern context, the rough bands of a *charivari*. It could also

---

[17] George Rudé, *The Crowd in the French Revolution* (Oxford, 1959); id., *Wilkes and Liberty*
(Oxford, 1962); and his collection of essays on crowds republished as *Paris and London in
the Eighteenth Century: Studies in Popular Protest* (London, 1970).

[18] George Rudé, *The Crowd in History* (New York, 1964), 3–4.

accommodate forms of direct action under the heading of social criminality that Rudé has sought to differentiate from crimes of protest: the activities of smuggling gangs, semi-professional poachers, or coastal wreckers.[19] On the other hand, when Rudé specifies what activities might legitimately be classified as crowd history, his focus is too narrow. Electoral crowds are quite explicitly omitted from his definition, although many political demonstrations in eighteenth-century England were a by-product of the electoral process. Indeed, it is hard to make sense of the Jacobite riots of the Hanoverian accession without some knowledge of local and regional rivalries and of the way in which elections, like anniversaries, provided a setting for violent conflict.[20] The same objection applies, though with less force, to the Wilkite disturbances, a subject that Rudé has himself studied. Some of the riots associated with Wilkes's name began as pre-electoral processions or post-electoral triumphs, with supporters demanding that the inhabitants illuminate their windows to honour the hero of the hour, demarcating radical territory with the number '45'.[21]

Just as electoral crowds are excluded from the parameters of Rudé's history, so, too, are crowds assembled on 'purely ceremonial occasions'.[22] The decision would bother many anthropologists as well as historians. They might legitimately ask in the first instance what constitutes a '*purely* ceremonial occasion'. Anthropologists, in particular, have given a great deal of attention to the function of ceremony, how it dignifies important *rites de passage* in a society's development, dramatizes a social order, reinforces a particular heritage. To be sure, the structural-functionalist camp within anthropology has tended to look at ceremony as a mechanism or expression of consensus; to follow Durkheim in arguing that 'there can be no society which does not feel the need of upholding and reaffirming at regular intervals the collective sentiments and collective ideas which make its unity and personality'.[23] But even if one rejects the underlying assumptions behind this approach, one is still left with what Clifford Geertz calls 'the

---

[19] George Rudé, *Protest and Punishment* (Oxford, 1978), 3–6.

[20] Nicholas Rogers, 'Riot and Popular Jacobitism in Early Hanoverian England', in Eveline Cruickshanks (ed.), *Ideology and Conspiracy: Aspects of Jacobitism 1689–1759* (Edinburgh, 1982), 70–88. For brief remarks on the importance of elections and holidays in the promotion of the demonstration as a form of collective action, see Charles Tilly, *From Mobilization to Revolution* (Reading, Mass., 1978), 167–8.

[21] John Brewer, *Party Ideology and Popular Politics at the Accession of George III* (Cambridge, 1976), ch. 9.

[22] Rudé, *The Crowd in History*, 4.

[23] Émile Durkheim, *The Elementary Forms of Religious Life* (London, 1915), 427, cited by Robert J. Holton, 'The Crowd in History; Some Problems of Theory and Method', *Social History*, 3 (May 1978), 222.

symbolics of power', the way in which ritual or ceremony contributes to social integration or conflict, becomes a metaphor of differentiation or solidarity. In an age on the threshold of literacy, the symbolic aspects of politics were especially important. In eighteenth-century Britain, America, and France, festivals frequently shaped popular political activity, just as the rituals of authority defined the form they took. One has only to look at the highly ritualized behaviour of the eighteenth-century crowd with its oaths, symbols, parades, mock executions, and effigy-burnings to recognize this was so.

One final aspect of Rudé's definition must be discussed: this is his tendency to look for the lineaments of the 'revolutionary crowd' in his studies, to concentrate on those dramatic confrontations that presaged radicalism. Indeed, this quest for a radical potential underscored his definitional priorities. Hence Rudé's readiness to distinguish crowds from 'mobs' that were explicitly manipulated from above, and, within the tradition of a more autonomous plebeian politics, crowds that tended to follow a party line (and were accessories to major political feuds) from those which were more obviously independent. In practice, such distinctions are not easy to maintain. Client crowds were sometimes involved in a complex reciprocity with their patrons that allowed them some degree of autonomy. In mid-eighteenth-century Bristol, for example, where the un-enfranchised participated vigorously in a system of venal politics, they did so on their own terms. Neither faction in this city found it could build up a permanent interest by purchasing favour alone.[24] Contrariwise, independent crowds were not necessarily radical, or even configurations of the 'revolutionary crowd'. The Gordon rioters are a case in point, as I shall attempt to show in Chapter 5. Although the popular supporters of the Protestant Association quickly lost touch with their official leaders, their demonstrations were politically counter-productive and deeply embarrassing to a radical camp who, with few exceptions, deplored their excesses. For the 1780 rioters highlighted the ambiguities of the Englishman's birthright, its proto-nationalist, sectarian dimensions as much as its libertarian. From an ideological point of view their protests anticipated the loyalist, anti-Gallican effusions of the revolutionary era, not the democratic aspirations of the Painite radical. Their experience underlines the dangers of looking for the origins of the 'revolutionary crowd' without some attention to the ideological complexities of popular history.

---

[24] Nicholas Rogers, *Whigs and Cities: Popular Politics in the Age of Walpole and Pitt* (Oxford, 1989), ch. 8.

Rudé's definition of the crowd was, thus, too exclusive, too inattentive to the conventions of popular assembly, too teleological. His methodological strategies posed some problems as well. By concentrating upon those dramatic interventions which promised to reveal the social composition of the rioters, Rudé's studies tended to become an episodic history of disturbance with little discussion of those aspects of popular political culture that did not bear directly upon the riots themselves. In some of his monographs, it is true, this imbalance was less apparent. *The Crowd in the French Revolution*, for example, contained a brief but informative chapter on the organization of the revolutionary *journées* and the sources of collective action. Similarly his joint venture with Eric Hobsbawm, *Captain Swing*, threw rays of light on the pattern of agrarian disturbance in 1830 and the crucial mediating role of the village craftsman, the only link between the agricultural labourer and the outside world. But these insights were not sustained in Rudé's more general work, nor curiously in *Wilkes and Liberty*, where there is little mention of political clubs, pubs, markets, festivals, nor of political balladry and the rich symbolism of protest.

The result was that popular interventions were too frequently explained in straightforwardly reactive terms: in the context of either economic hardship or rough justice against the rich. Little attention was paid to their ideological configurations or indeed to the crowd's own relations with authority beyond the coercive instrumentalities of order. As Gwyn Williams complained in a review of *The Crowd in History*, there was too much concentration upon 'the mechanics of the crowd at the expense of its mystique',[25] and, by extension, at the expense of popular experience. In this work, in particular, Rudé's reliance upon the classic sociological dyads of pre-industrial/industrial, traditional/modern was particularly damaging, for it underplayed the force of custom and law in shaping popular interventions and simplified the complex repertoire of collective action of which 'riot' was only a part. It also led to an unfortunate eclecticism. Rudé's endorsement of Neil Smelser's notion of 'generalised beliefs', for instance, was intellectually disabling for a 'history from below'. Such a notion was associated with a lack of rationality in collective behaviour, with the crowd's susceptibility to rumour, hearsay, and fantasy, with anxieties that were the product of 'structural strain'. This perspective harked back to Le Bon, to a tradition that Rudé and his colleagues officially sought to dispel, and it is instructive that the whole notion of 'generalised beliefs' was dropped

---

[25] Review in *New Society* (27 May 1965), 30.

from *Ideology and Popular Protest*, where the formation of popular ideology is addressed in more sophisticated terms.[26]

Rudé's methodology, then, tended at times to divorce the crowd from its deeper historical context, from the ensemble of relations in which it might be situated. By focusing upon the phenomenon of riot in its most confrontationalist mode, he frequently marginalized the symbolic language of popular remonstrance and foreclosed a broader discussion of the patterns of collective action which ought legitimately to have included non-violent as well as violent forms of popular negotiation. Within the last decade or so, this emphasis has been redressed. Historians who have followed Rudé's expansive venture into popular protest, most notably the Tillys, have become increasingly sceptical of narrowing its focus to a discussion of collective violence alone, seeking rather to chart the varied repertoire of collective action in response to large-scale changes in the economy, the state, and society.[27] Among other things they have shown how capitalist relations and state centralization nibbled away at the communal bases of collective action upon which tax revolts and bread riots were based, promoting in their wake more proactive (but not necessarily less violent) forms of protest in the shape of the strike, the petition, and the mass demonstration.

More typically, historians have shied away from such large-scale, longitudinal comparisons, largely because they have remained sceptical of the possibilities of measuring such changes over time; especially from such sources as newspapers, whose political bias mediated coverage of riots and other forms of political contention.[28] Rather they have sought to situate the phenomenon of popular disturbance within precise regional or national contexts. This has brought tangible gains. It has stimulated an interest in modes of plebeian resistance that fell outside the ambit of crowd studies; seditious rumours, threatening letters, rural incendiarism, for example, forms of protest that existed in societies whose collective resources were weak. And it has prompted an exploration of the geographical incidence of protest and the capacities for collective action, why some areas exhibited a

---

[26] George Rudé, *Ideology and Popular Protest* (New York, 1980).

[27] Charles Tilly, Louise Tilly, and Richard Tilly, *The Rebellious Century 1830–1930* (Cambridge, Mass., 1975); see also Charles Tilly, *Popular Contention in Britain 1750–1830* (Cambridge, Mass., 1995), where closer attention is given to the broadening and changing repertoire of collective action in the half-century prior to 1830.

[28] In the British literature there has been a vigorous debate about the usefulness of newspapers as a window to riot and popular contention. See Roger Wells, 'Counting Riots in Eighteenth-Century England', *Bulletin of Labour History Society*, 37 (1978), 68–72. I share Wells's scepticism about the hazards of counting riots and demonstrations. In my own studies I have been particularly struck by the erratic coverage of such phenomena in London and provincial newspapers. Much depended upon the discursive salience of political contention in particular conjunctures.

proclivity to riot and others did not; or, as in the case of John Bohstedt's work, how local and national politics shaped the form and frequency of collective action.[29] Above all, it has led to a profounder understanding of the relation between rulers and ruled, of the role that the law has played in eliciting assent to a social order, reproducing deference, and legitimizing popular protest.[30] These insights have pushed social historians further towards the quotidian, towards a more comprehensive picture of the prevailing structures of power and their complex resolution, and towards an appreciation of the uneven rhythms of socio-economic change.

One consequence of these developments has been the recognition that crowds frequently operated under conventions that were implicitly sanctioned by authority. As Colin Lucas has recently sought to re-emphasize,[31] there was a series of well-defined occasions when the people-as-the-community was invited to occupy public space to endorse the public acts of state power, whether to celebrate political anniversaries, to witness royal or civic inaugurations, to hear royal proclamations, to sanction criminal sentences, or to approve as well as participate in the practices of the open market. Consequently the crowd, as representative of the community, was 'a definable actor' in the drama of early modern politics.[32] Indeed, it was a necessary actor in the enforcement and enactment of public authority, however contumacious and reproving its presence happened to be, for the majesty of power required popular endorsement. By extension, the crowd sometimes functioned as an extra-legal enforcer of community norms, whether its actions were sanctioned from above or not.[33] It was from these sources, as a policing agent and as an essential component in the symbolic

[29] John Bohstedt, *Riots and Community Politics in England and Wales 1790–1810* (Cambridge, Mass., 1983). Even Bohstedt's impressive study is vulnerable to the charge that his 'sample' of riots is problematic, as a comparison between his findings and those of Roger Wells in *Wretched Faces: Famine in Wartime England 1763–1803* (Stroud, 1988) reveals.

[30] On these questions, see especially Douglas Hay, 'Property, Authority and the Criminal Law', in Douglas Hay, Peter Linebaugh, and E. P. Thompson (eds.), *Albion's Fatal Tree: Crime and Society in Eighteenth-Century England* (London, 1975), 17–63; E. P. Thompson, *Whigs and Hunters: The Origin of the Black Act* (London, 1975), esp. ch. 10; John Brewer and John Styles (eds.), *An Ungovernable People: The English and their Law in the Seventeenth and Eighteenth Centuries* (London, 1980).

[31] Colin Lucas, 'The Crowd and Politics between *Ancien Regime* and Revolution in France', *Journal of Modern History*, 60/3 (Sept. 1988), 432–9; see also Michel Foucault, *Discipline and Punish: The Birth of the Prison*, trans. Alan Sheridan (New York, 1977), 57–65 and Dirk Hoerder, *Crowd Action in Revolutionary Massachusetts 1765–1780* (New York, 1977), 44–56.

[32] Lucas, 'Crowd and Politics', 439.

[33] This has especially been emphasized by historians of revolutionary America. See Pauline Maier, 'Popular Uprisings and Civil Authority in Eighteenth-Century America', *William and Mary Quarterly*, 27 (1970), 3–35; id., *From Resistance to Revolution: Colonial Radicals and the Development of American Opposition to Britain 1765–1776* (New York, 1972), ch. 1; and Hoerder, *Crowd Action*, chs. 1 and 2.

transmission of authority, that the crowd drew much of its legitimizing power. As we shall see in the next and in subsequent chapters, the legitimacy of political regimes was intimately bound up with the way in which crowds intervened in public space, and how those interventions were represented in contemporary discourse.

To suggest that the crowd often acted as an enforcer of community norms is not, it should be stressed, to suggest that it necessarily shared the values and objectives of the social élite. Much depended upon precisely how the 'community' was defined. While some crowd actions could be seen as justifiable extensions of magisterial authority, purging society of unwanted outsiders or safeguarding it from moral transgressors, others revealed sharp divisions within society and conflicting claims of custom and law. In eighteenth-century Europe and America this was particularly the case over market practices, tax priorities, land claims and perquisites, smuggling and the informal economy of coastal communities, as well as recruitment to the armed forces; that is, over issues that directly affected the living standards of the labouring classes. Even official holidays could generate social discord, not simply because they often endorsed institutionalized ridicule and the rites of inversion, but because they provided the occasion, resources, and symbolic space for a dramatic airing of popular grievances.

These collective actions, their timing, form, and symbolic content, have pushed historians to a closer examination of popular culture. The influences propelling historians in this direction have come from both outside and within the discipline. Edward Thompson's study of the English working class, with its strong literary resonances and its insistence that class formation is as much a cultural as a political and economic process 'embodied in traditions, value-systems, ideas, and institutional forms', has been extremely influential.[34] So, too, in the early modern context, at least, has been the *Annalesiste* notion of *mentalité*, the taken-for-granted habits, presumptions, and structures which shape the mental horizons of an age.[35] Anthropologists such as Clifford Geertz and Victor Turner and literary critics such as Mikhail Bakhtin have also engaged the attention of historians for their insights into ritual, festival, and the strategies of ethnographic description. As a result historians have begun to re-explore the links between riot and carnival, the cultural derivations of collective protest, its rich symbolic repertoire, and the ways in which customary forms of community

[34] E. P. Thompson, *The Making of the English Working Class* (Harmondsworth, 1968), 10.
[35] On this notion, see Patrick H. Hutton, 'The History of Mentalities: A New Map of Cultural History', *History and Theory*, 20 (1981), 237–59.

sanction such as the charivari could be adapted to different social contexts.[36] This has enormously enriched our understanding of the ramified language of collective action and has enabled historians to move beyond the ingrained behaviourism and reductionism that characterized early ventures in the field.

This is not to suggest that the cultural perspective has been free of problems. An obsession with symbolism and ritual can breed its own exoticisms, a fascination with the 'otherness' of past societies to the detriment of analyses of power. The work on carnival and the carnivalesque, for example, has usefully disclosed the parodic, profane, topsy-turvy dimensions of popular culture, its antinomies to officialdom. It has also highlighted the ambiguities of the rites of inversion, that seasonal, liminal, upside-down world whose revels might prove to be subversive rather than simply cathartic reinforcements of the social order. But this has led at times to a cosmic populism, an exaltation of irreverent counter-cultures whose historical significance is ultimately elusive, paradoxical, and indeterminate. The application of the concept of *mentalité* to areas of political and social conflict has also been rather problematic. Originally it was associated with slow-moving, often timeless mental structures; what Jacques Le Goff called 'the gradual in history'. As such, it was principally concerned with those shared and taken-for-granted systems of belief which defined a society's cosmos. The result was that it remained a rather static concept, useful in analysing the limits of consciousness and habit, the mental inertia of an age, but inattentive to the dynamics of change and to what Steven Lukes has termed the 'mobilization of bias'. For this reason it remains debatable whether the notion of *mentalité* can usefully recapture the complexities of power struggles in eras of dramatic political mobilization.[37]

British historians have generally been sceptical of importing the concept, impressed as they have been by the range of themes it might encompass. They have preferred a more engaged, dialectical notion of culture, a study of how social and material life is handled, shaped, and interpreted

[36] Natalie Zemon Davis, 'The Reasons of Misrule', *Past and Present*, 50 (1971), 41–75; id., 'The Rites of Violence: Religious Riot in Sixteenth-Century France', *Past and Present*, 59 (May 1973), 51–91; Emmanuel Le Roy Ladurie, *Carnival in Romans*, trans. Mary Feeney (New York, 1979); Yves-Marie Bercé, *Fête et révolte: Des mentalités populaires du XVIe au XVIIIe siècle* (Paris, 1976); Peter Burke, *Popular Culture in Early Modern Europe* (New York, 1978); E. P. Thompson, '"Rough Music": Le Charivari anglais', *Annales ESC* 18 (1972), 285–312; Bryan D. Palmer, 'Discordant Music: Charivari and Whitecapping in North America', *Labour/Le Travailleur*, 1 (1978), 5–62.

[37] Michael A. Gismondi, '"The Gift of Theory": A Critique of the *Histoire des mentalités*', *Social History*, 10/2 (May 1985), 211–30; Steven Lukes, 'Political Ritual and Social Integration', *Sociology*, 9 (1975), 289–308.

within and between classes. Within the context of crowd studies, Edward Thompson, in particular, has made an important contribution to this notion. Developing arguments first sketched out in *The Making of the English Working Class*, Thompson has situated the eighteenth-century crowd within a societal 'field of force' constrained within the parameters of gentry hegemony.[38] Unlike Rudé, who tended to see crowd actions as either backward- or forward-looking, Thompson saw the crowd as rebellious, but traditional, resisting economic innovation in defence of custom, defending its rights as free-born Englishmen, contesting the symbolic authority of a self-assured patriciate. The resilient and robust character of crowd interventions, Thompson argued, was predicated upon the libertarian inheritance of the seventeenth century, itself a source of gentry rule, and upon plebeian control of the labour process within a vigorous manufacturing sector. It was this space of self-regulation, untrammelled by the intrusions of church and state, that allowed for a relatively autonomous and vibrant plebeian culture.

Thompson's model has the merit of relating the diverse forms of collective action to the formative experiences in plebeian life and to the prevailing structures of dominance in eighteenth-century English society. But the crowd actions which he privileges are those that resonate the full pulse of customary definitions and expectations; the skimmington, for example, or the bread riot, with its legitimizing notion of the moral economy. Alternatively, he focuses upon those forms of direct action which illustrate the demystifying potential of plebeian protest, such as Jacobite or proto-republican 'counter-theatre'. The choice appears legitimate given Thompson's prime objective: the exploration of the class 'field of force', the equilibrium of social relations, within which plebeian interventions might be situated. But it does lead to a displacement of more subaltern crowd formations, what Thompson termed licensed or gentry-manipulated crowds, which fit uneasily into his framework.[39]

Two consequences follow from this. One is Thompson's tendency to reify the crowd as an explicitly plebeian phenomenon. It is true, of course, that contemporaries generally understood the crowd (or mob) to be a 'horizontal sort of beast', composed, as one MP declared in 1737, 'of

---

[38] The three key articles on this theme are E. P. Thompson, 'The Moral Economy of the English Crowd in the Eighteenth Century', *Past and Present*, 50 (Feb. 1971), 76–136; id., 'Patrician Society, Plebeian Culture', *Journal of Social History*, 7 (1974), 382–405; and id., 'Eighteenth-Century English Society: Class Struggle without Class?', *Social History*, 3 (1978), 133–66. Thompson's earlier reflections on the crowd are to be found in *The Making*, ch. 3.

[39] Thompson was certainly aware of this problem. See Thompson, 'Eighteenth-Century English Society', 163 n. See also his comments in *The Making*, 67, and in the postscript to the 1968 edition, 916.

the lowest class of the people'.[40] But one needs to be reminded that crowds were not necessarily 'a homogeneous social bloc', but, as Perry Anderson has pointed out, 'a changeable coalition composed of different categories of urban and rural wage earners, small producers, petty traders, and unemployed, whose frontiers could vary according to the successive conjunctures that crystallized it'.[41] Those conjunctures could involve situations in which the gentry and middling sort had an important share and in which the boundaries among actual participants, spectators, and orchestrators were very small and arguably unimportant. Within the political terrain, these considerations are weighty enough to qualify, if not seriously question, Thompson's central context for crowd action, the polarity between patricians and plebs.

In what ways, then, does this study address some of the central issues surrounding the historiography of the crowd? What are the substantive themes that I plan to cover in this dense and complex field of study?

In the first instance I must emphasize that this is a series of essays about the role of crowds in Georgian politics. It is not intended to be a comprehensive account of all crowd interventions in the Georgian era, nor even of all political interventions. The riots and demonstrations that grew out of John Wilkes's flamboyant career, for example, are not covered in this book, principally because they have already been extensively examined elsewhere;[42] although they inevitably inform my narrative on how crowds might open up public space for a more radical, libertarian politics and form an important counterpoint to the subsequent repossession of political space by loyalist forces at the end of the century.

Central to this study is the recognition that crowd interventions were a constituent element in the rich and ramified demotic political culture of the Georgian era. In this context crowds were very much a product of a seventeenth-century inheritance whose aversion to military rule and ongoing politics of commemoration allowed them considerable public space for making political claims upon the state or even affirming or questioning the legitimacy of successive political regimes. As I suggested in the final chapter of *Whigs and Cities*, crowd interventions were routinely synchronized to a calendar of public anniversaries, or to political events of

---

[40] *Gentleman's Magazine*, 7 (Aug. 1737), 457. The phrase 'horizontal sort of beast' is Thompson's. See 'Patrician Society, Plebeian Culture', 397.

[41] Perry Anderson, *Arguments with English Marxism* (London, 1980), 42.

[42] Most notably by Rudé, *Wilkes and Liberty*, and Brewer, *Party Ideology and Popular Politics*, ch. 9.

some importance, such as general elections, trials, or victories of the armed forces; to occasions in which all members of the political nation had some stake and some opportunity to influence the course of events or how those events might be represented in the expansive public press. As a result, crowd actions in politics constituted a contested terrain in which power, ideology, and class interest intersected. They were more mediated actions than the plebeian–patrician polarity of E. P. Thompson allows, an equation that is fundamentally built around popular interventions in the marketplace concerning the distribution and price of grain. They also generated a heated debate as to where the 'sense of the people' might be drawn; whether they might be regarded as genuine signifiers of popular sentiment, or marginalized as mindless rabbling that illustrated either the political ignorance of the un-enfranchised or their gullibility to appeals from more malevolent forces. Such a debate informed all the important political crises of the eighteenth century, from the Hanoverian accession to the popular mobilizations of the French revolutionary era, and even influenced the more class-based interventions of the mass platform in the aftermath of the French wars, when radicals sought to revamp the constitutional importance of the people assembled in a new idiom.

These considerations, then, provide some unity to the chapters that follow, although all of them can be read as discrete interventions in an already dense historiography. In Chapter 2, I develop Thompson's insight that popular Jacobitism was a demystifying solvent of Whig political hegemony, sometimes expressing a Tory territorialism that was shared by disaffected gentlemen as well as plebeian revellers, but on other occasions generating an idiom of defiance that could be annexed to more plebeian concerns. In Chapter 3, I suggest that the food riots of 1756–7, which occurred at the outset of the Seven Years War, can usefully be situated in a broader and specifically political discourse about the national interest in which grain speculators were excoriated along with 'unpatriotic' admirals and politicians by a volatile coalition of interests that included middling Tory-radicals as well as hungry wage-earners. In Chapter 4, in the first detailed examination of the opposition to impressment during the mid-century wars, I again suggest that the plebs–patrician polarity is too reductive a formulation to account for the lines of confrontation that pitted seafaring communities against the government. Rather these conflicts ought to be framed within a tripartite struggle between the government, merchants, and plebeians over the coercion of maritime labour and its anti-libertarian implications, with urban radicals encouraging legal challenges to the government's regulatory policy with a new urgency after 1770.

In the last five chapters of this book I explore a theme addressed by a host of historians: the role of crowds in the popular politics of the era of the American and French Revolutions and beyond. At the outset I depict the remarkable success of the Opposition Whigs in co-ordinating popular anti-ministerialism around the trial of Admiral Keppel, noting in particular the critical role that the press took in elevating a naval feud into a high political drama. In the next chapter I show how this unstable coalition of interests collapsed during the Gordon riots of 1780, generating deep divisions within the Whig-radical camp and a new scepticism among radicals about the political capabilities of the crowd and its negative effects upon new modes of political association. Thereafter, I shall suggest, bourgeois radicals attempted to frame a new politics of commemoration that marginalized the crowd, vacating a space that their opponents readily seized by revamping loyalism in a popular idiom. Only in the postwar decades was the political potential of the crowd-as-people reintegrated into the radical lexicon, and then in the shape of the more orderly parades and demonstrations of the mass platform. Here women played a significant role, not as proto-feminists nor as fully accredited political citizens, but as the moral guardians of class-based community standards, drawing upon a tradition of collective action that stretched back into the eighteenth century.

In the final chapter I investigate the agitation surrounding the Queen Caroline affair of 1820, an event that has frequently been noted for its populist resonances, most recently by historians writing from a postmodern perspective. Here I cavil at the attempt to write class out of the episode, suggesting that the demonstrations in Lancashire and London can usefully be decoded in class terms and situated within a context that foregrounds the struggle for political space. Indeed, although recent historians have attempted to stress the continuities of popular radicalism from the 1790s to 1848, focusing principally upon the formal language of popular constitutionalism,[43] the Queen Caroline affair appears to me to have been a significant watershed in popular politics, pointing to new modes of remonstration with clear class signifiers, as well as to more traditional and transgressive responses that harked back to the topsy-turvy revels of eighteenth-century crowds. The year 1820 represents a turning point in popular political contention in which crowd action is reconfigured within a more complex repertoire of collective action.

---

[43] Gareth Stedman Jones, *Languages of Class: Studies in English Working-Class History 1832–1982* (Cambridge, 1983), ch. 3; James Vernon, *Politics and the People* (Cambridge, 1993).

One final remark must be made about the terms 'mob' and 'crowd' used in this book. The late George Rudé was very insistent upon avoiding the term 'mob' in his pioneering studies because of its pejorative connotations, in terms of both the disreputable status of the participants and the illegitimacy of their activity. The point is well taken, for examples of such usage litter the contemporary literature. On the other hand, the noun 'mob' was not always used pejoratively. Sometimes it simply denoted, harking back to its Latin derivation, a mobile gathering of people, a jostling throng, in juxtaposition to the word 'crowd' (or 'croud' in most eighteenth-century renditions) which, in festive contexts especially, often represented a static or passive group of spectators. In other words, there are some objections to using 'crowd' because of its eighteenth-century resonances, especially if one seeks to stress the agency or militancy of popular interventions. For this and for stylistic reasons, I have sometimes used the terms interchangeably, well aware of the force of Rudé's objections. In the later decades of the Hanoverian era, contemporaries sometimes used the terms interchangeably too. Witnesses examined at the bar of the Commons on the alleged attack upon the King in 1795 did so, as did Benjamin Haydon in his account of the Edinburgh jubilations in support of Queen Caroline. I should add that radicals very occasionally deployed the term 'mob' with an in-your-face irreverence that mirrored the crowd's own confrontation with authority, just as they named their periodicals *Hog's Wash* or *Pig's Meat* as an ironical retort to Burke's 'swinish multitude'. The term had a more complex signification than historians have allowed.

I

Seditious Words, Subversive Laughter
Popular Jacobitism in Hanoverian England

In 1749 a 'poor lame Fiddler' came from Redruth to Truro and holed up in a barn just outside town. He was not there long, the *Whitehall Evening Post* reported, 'before he was alarmed with a Gentleman and a Lady, who were to meet there that Night, agreeable to some former Assignation'.[1] The fiddler held his peace while the couple discussed 'the Preliminaries, the Chief of which was, that the Lady should lay aside her Hoop-Petticoat . . . as well as sundry other Articles' before 'they proceeded to the Ceremony'. Just as 'they had accomplished their Desires agreeable to their Satisfaction', the fiddler struck up the tune of 'The King shall enjoy his own again'. The intrusion prompted the couple to beat a hasty exit and amid the 'Hurry and Confusion, the Lady left her Hoop behind'. The fiddler 'cry'd' the petticoat in 'the public Market-Place' the following day, the story continued, but since nobody claimed it, he auctioned it off for 3 shillings, a nice return on a fortuitous encounter.

This might seem a frivolous tale to begin an essay on popular Jacobitism, yet it is instructive for what it tells us about the appropriation of Jacobite ideology in the eighteenth century and the plural meanings that could be derived from it. 'The King shall enjoy his own again' was the Jacobite ballad of the eighteenth century. Originally the song which sang in the Stuart restoration of 1660, it was adopted by Monmouth's supporters during the Western rising of 1685, and subsequently repossessed by the Jacobites after 1688 to express the hope of a second Stuart restoration. A statement of hereditary right to the royal succession, it focused upon the legitimacy or illegitimacy of the rival houses of Stuart and Hanover. In the Cornish context of 1749, it celebrated an illicit, but successful, sexual

---

[1] *Whitehall Evening Post*, 3–5 Jan. 1749.

encounter; from a patriarchal perspective the 'gentleman-King' would, no doubt, enjoy his 'own' again. It was also a jocose, plebeian intervention at a gentle couple's expense, recalling many plebeian renderings of the same tune on the anniversaries of the Restoration (29 May) and the Pretender's birthday (10 June), ones that often unnerved the gentry, particularly those of a Whig disposition. Whether the story in the *Whitehall Evening Post* was apocryphal or not, its multiple meaning was clear. Few would have not understood its polysemy.

Recent accounts of Jacobitism would find such an incident difficult to accommodate within their analytical structures, so riveted are they to literal interpretations of the Jacobite phenomenon. Jacobitism is seen as synonymous with hereditary right and *jure divino*, with a deep-seated reverence for social hierarchy and sacred monarchy, with élite politics and conspiracy. To suggest that popular Jacobitism was sometimes profane and blasphemous is to commit its own kind of blasphemy against the seriousness of Jacobite politics and the capacity of the plebs to understand its treasonable implications.[2] Yet if one examines the cultural context in which popular Jacobitism grew and of which it was an expression, such profanity becomes entirely explicable. Jacobitism emerged out of a world of oaths, portents, riddles, revels, and anniversaries; in an often carnivalesque atmosphere of seditious laughter and ritual inversion. Profanity and blasphemy were part of the language of this marketplace, at once grotesque, sensuous, satirical, and transgressive. As a language of dissent and defiance in this revelrous world, Jacobitism could generate meanings beyond political orthodoxy, including, somewhat paradoxically, a scabrous disrespect for élite politics and monarchy itself. Popular Jacobitism, I shall suggest, proved too local, too volatile, to engender a sustained and politically integrated challenge to the Hanoverian regime. But at the same time it was not subordinate to élite politics in quite the way historians imagine. What made it an unpredictable, and sometimes subversive, force was its roots in plebeian culture; a culture that the better sort strove fitfully to engage, marshal, and contain.

In order to understand popular Jacobitism, it is important to map out the conventions of street politics within which it took place. Although aspirations for the return of the exiled house of Stuart were often voiced in alehouse conversations and quarrels, the most politically damaging expressions

---

[2] Paul Kléber Monod, *Jacobitism and the English People, 1688–1788* (Cambridge, 1989), 195–6.

of Jacobitism, and the ones that caught the public eye, tended to occur upon fairly predictable occasions such as royal and national anniversaries. The development of this calendar was a long-term process. It grew out of the nation's confrontations with the Catholic powers of Europe during the sixteenth century and the internal struggles that so beset the seventeenth. By 1700 state services were held to commemorate the accession and coronation of the reigning monarch, the martyrdom of Charles I (30 January), the restoration of the monarchy in 1660 (29 May), and the discovery of the Gunpowder Plot and William's landing at Torbay in 1688 (5 November), England's double deliverance from popery.[3] These occasions were celebrated with bells, sermons, and, for the joyous anniversaries at least, festivity and good cheer. They were not the only ones to be so. Until 1730, and in some parishes even later, Queen Elizabeth's accession day (17 November) was celebrated as a symbol of Britain's Protestant destiny.[4] The same was true of William III's birthday, an anniversary that recalled Britain's libertarian credentials and her rise to first-class European status.

Public anniversaries were essentially designed to sanctify the political order, to observe the memorable events in its creation, and by extension to provide opportunities for ruling-class liberality and spectacle. The populace was invited to occupy public space on these occasions, to share in the jubilation of a polity's creation and regeneration, to reverence its legitimacy. Without a public the festivals themselves would have been meaningless. Within the conventions of political commemoration, crowds were critical in the sense that they were emblematic of the community at large, despite the fact that they were not, in other contexts, accorded the status of political citizens. To have denied them their holidays would have been tantamount to admitting the unpopularity of the regime if not undermining its legitimacy. George I, whose accession rested upon parliamentary mandate and whose coronation medals portrayed Britannia crowning him beneath the motto 'Proceribus et Populis Consentientibus', the 'Nobles and People Consenting',[5] could hardly have done this. He had to live with the political calendar he inherited.

That calendar was shaped by three important developments. First, the unparalleled frequency of general elections in the years 1694–1715

---

[3] For the long-term development of the calendar, see David Cressy, 'The Protestant Calendar and the Vocabulary of Celebration in Early Modern England', *Journal of British Studies*, 19 (1990), 31–52, and id., *Bonfires and Bells: National Memory and the Protestant Calendar in Elizabethan and Stuart England* (London, 1989).

[4] For evidence of the celebration of Queen Elizabeth's accession in the 1750s, see Bristol Record Office, All Saint's parish, churchwardens' accounts.

[5] John Doran, *London in the Jacobite Times*, 2 vols. (London, 1877), i. 21–2.

broadened the geographical range of political contention as well as sustaining popular interest in national politics on a more regular basis. Second, the development of the London and provincial press arguably enhanced the importance of anniversaries as a potential barometer of popular opinion, bringing their observance across the country to a growing audience; judging from Stamp Duty returns and readership conventions, to perhaps one in ten of all adults. Third, the political calendar itself became denser as the dynastic struggle once more absorbed British politics. By 1715, no less than thirteen royal and state anniversaries were routinely observed in the parishes of the leading towns and cities, leaving only July, September, and December free from commemorative events. The year began with the solemn observance of Charles I's martyrdom, to be followed by three anniversaries celebrating Queen Anne's birthday (6 February), accession (8 March), and coronation (23 April), still observed in some London parishes as late as 1730. May brought George I's birthday and the state-endorsed commemoration of the Restoration; June the unofficial and potentially explosive celebration of the Pretender's birthday. Then there was a brief hiatus until 1 August, the Hanoverian accession, and a further crop of Hanoverian and Protestant-cum-libertarian holidays in October and November. In 1715 these included George I's coronation day (20 October), his first son's birthday (30 October), William of Orange's birthday (4 November), his landing at Torbay (5 November), and Queen Elizabeth's birthday. In this busy calendar Whigs and Tories competed for public space, mobilizing the vocabulary of celebration to their own advantage. Generally speaking, the spring anniversaries privileged the Tories; the autumnal the Whigs. But every anniversary was susceptible to crossed meanings: to muffled bells, lacklustre bonfires, ambiguous toasts, contentious processions, and controversial oaths. The Highgate cobbler who dressed in mourning on George I's birthday (28 May) and donned his finery to celebrate the Restoration the following day knew precisely the message he was transmitting; to emphasize the point on 29 May he 'insulted several Gentlemen and Ladies' and demanded 'money for the bonfire . . . to drink to the damnation of Whigs and Dissenters'. So, too, did the Shoreditch housekeeper who ridiculed rather than reverenced the same Stuart high holiday by placing an owl in an oak-leaved egg-basket over his door, together with a crucifix and a pair of wooden shoes, the symbols of Catholicism and impoverished despotism.[6]

As this last example suggests, political loyalties were expressed through a rich repertoire of signs. The royal oak had long recalled Charles Stuart's

---

[6] *The Shift Shifted, or Robin's Last Shift*, 28 July 1716.

miraculous escape from the battle of Worcester in 1651, and oak sprigs and green ribbons were regularly sported by the Tory clans, especially on Restoration day. The party's favourite song appears to have been 'The King shall enjoy his own again'; as I have suggested, the song that sang in the return of the Stuart dynasty in 1660 but inevitably connoted its possible return after 1688. Those who disapproved of its seditious connotations could simply have whistled it, for the Whigs revamped it with pro-Hanoverian doggerel in 1714 and inadvertently gave it plausible legality. Several ballad singers and fiddlers argued this out with incensed Londoners in 1717 and again in 1723.[7] By contrast, orange was the favourite Whig colour, much in evidence on 4 or 5 November, sweet William its seasonal emblem, and 'Lillibullero' its favourite tune, the one that sang out James II in England and Ireland. Jacobites were often indistinguishable from Tories save for indiscreet songs such as 'Jemmy, dear Jemmy' and the flaunting of white roses on the Pretender's birthday. On Whiggish anniversaries, however, they would have to put up with the provocative parading of warming pans, recalling the rumour that the Old Pretender was really a plebeian child that had been smuggled into the Queen's bedchamber to serve as a legitimate male heir for a court that was politically bankrupt and sexually impotent.[8] On 30 January Tories might even have had to stomach the more radical calf's head, which denied Charles I his martyrdom. In reply Tory-Jacobites might burn the effigies of Jack Presbyter or Oliver Cromwell, symbols that tarnished Whiggery with religious fanaticism and republic-anism; or they might flourish a turnip or a pair of horns, scorning King George's regality and revelling in his well-reported cuckoldry at the hands of Count Königsmarck.

Popular Jacobitism surfaced within this contentious political context; within a context that was both revelrous and interlocutory, or what Mikhail Bakhtin would have called dialogic. Popular Jacobitism was the product of intense party rivalry, of Whig and Tory battles for public space and popular loyalty, with each side indulging in malicious caricature and rhetorical overkill. Yet at the same time it was also the product of a dia-logue between élite and popular culture, with party ideologues continu-ally revamping politics in a popular idiom and the populace appropriating

---

[7] *Weekly Journal, or Saturday's Post*, 6 July 1717, 29 June 1723.

[8] On the warming-pan legend, see J. P. Kenyon, 'The Birth of the Old Pretender', *History Today*, 13 (1963), 418–26 and Rachel J. Weil, 'The Politics of Legitimacy: Women and the Warming-Pan Scandal', in Lois G. Schwoerer (ed.), *The Revolution of 1688–1689: Changing Perspectives* (Cambridge, 1992), 65–82. Weil notes (p. 72) that the early pamphlets of the legend were reprinted in 1715 and 1745 and that between 1688 and 1745 over fifty works made significant reference to it.

its motifs for its own purposes. This inevitably complicated its meanings. On coronation day 1714, for example, a crowd disrupted the loyalist procession of Frome clothiers by parading a fool, whose turnip-topped wand mimicked the insignia of their superiors, crying out all the while, 'here's our George, where's yours?'[9] Was this lords-of-misrule counter-procession genuinely Jacobite? Was it anti-Whig? Or a droll commentary on the town leaders' pomposities? It is difficult to tell. It is similarly difficult to determine the import of a Cambridge street demonstration two years later on the King's birthday and the anniversary of the Restoration the following day. Irritated by the loyalist festivities at Clare Hall, a mob of 'hundreds of townsmen and scholars' broke loose from the traditional mayings to smash the windows of the college and also those of well-known Whig churchmen and Dissenters. Egged on by scholars at the Three Tuns tavern, the crowd 'clad in Black and Russet' denounced Hanover and the 'Rump', burnt the pews of the local meeting-house, and, as a festive climax, proclaimed the Pretender in the marketplace.[10] Was this impudent act of insurrectionary import? Did it register a substantive commitment to the house of Stuart or the smouldering tensions between Whig and Tory within the university, which had earlier expelled a scholar for drinking the Pretender's health?[11] And to what degree was the episode leavened by youthful high spirits? Once again we are confronted with an intervention in street politics that was revelrous, evanescent, seditious, laughable, and distinctly ambiguous.

Popular Jacobitism did not imprint itself dramatically on the political scene in England in the immediate years following the coup of 1688. Whiffs of disaffection could surface on royal anniversaries, when the bold or foolhardy might toast the exiled house or strike up strains of 'The King shall enjoy his own again'. In 1691, Jacobite supporters in London countered the celebrations for the surrender of Limerick by building fresh bonfires for the exiled King's birthday.[12] Three years later, further celebrations of James II's birthday came to the attention of the government as the long war with France took its human toll, and on 10 June 1695, in the wake of an anti-impressment riot, Jacobite ex-officers erected a bonfire outside the

---

[9] *Flying Post*, 30 Oct.–2 Nov. 1714.

[10] Ibid. 7–9 June 1716. Monod dates this riot as 28 May, the King's birthday, as does the *Political State of Great Britain*, 11 (May 1716), 647–8. See Monod, *Jacobitism and the English People*, 205. The *Flying Post* suggests the main action took place on 29 May.

[11] For the expulsion, see *Weekly Packet*, 11–18 June 1715.

[12] *The Portledge Papers*, ed. Russell J. Kerr and Ida C. Duncan (London, 1928), 122–3.

Dog tavern in Drury Lane and drank the Pretender's health to the rattle of 'kettle drums and other military music'. Yet on this occasion, one writer noted, 'the mob soon got about them and broke the vintner's windows and would have done more damage had not money been given them to prevent it'.[13] Popular passions, as Narcissus Luttrell's diary reveals, were politically volatile in the 1690s and were as likely to be in favour of the new regime as agin it. Or at least loyalist enough to partake of the festive doles of victory celebrations and birthdays.

Despite the plots and sham plots of the 1690s and the growing un-certainties surrounding the succession in the next decade, it was not until 1710 that popular sympathies seemed formidably disaffected to the post-revolutionary regime. In that year Dr Henry Sacheverell and his clerical allies mobilized the frustrations of militant Toryism against the political establishment. In the wake of his trial for a provocative sermon on the ini-quities of Whiggery, nonconformity, and Whig definitions of 1688, one which led him to be charged with 'high crimes and misdemeanours' against the state, London erupted with an attack upon six of the best-known meeting-houses in the City and its out-parishes and a planned assault upon the Bank of England.[14] The following year the Whigs revived the huge anti-Catholic processions of the Exclusion era in a bid to win back a popular following, underscoring their own commitment to the Protestant succes-sion and the subversive loyalties of their opponents. On this occasion the Tory government intervened by confiscating the effigies, but from 1712 onwards the politics of the succession regularly informed public annivers-aries, filling the day and night with seditious cries and revelries. King Billy's birthday saw Tory mobs attack Whig revellers and denounce Hanover; Queen Anne's saw mock processions of devils, popes, and pretenders in the teeth of Tory carousing for a legitimate Stuart; and the Pretender's birthday brought a flurry of white roses, and very occasionally, as at Ipswich in 1713, a maypole revel amid fireworks and 'other Demonstrations of Joy'.[15] Even those holidays whose dynastic connotations were slight, such as Queen

---

[13] Ibid. 205; see also *Calendar of the State Papers Domestic: William and Mary, 1694–5*, v (London, 1906), 494; Narcissus Luttrell, *A Brief Historical Relation of State Affairs from September 1678 to April 1714*, 6 vols. (Oxford, 1862), iii. 207.

[14] Geoffrey Holmes, 'The Sacheverell Riots: The Crowd and the Church in Early Eighteenth-Century London', *Past and Present*, 72 (1976), 55–85, reprinted in Paul Slack (ed.), *Rebellion, Popular Protest and the Social Order in Early Modern England* (Cambridge, 1984), 232–62; see also Geoffrey Holmes, *The Trial of Doctor Sacheverell* (London, 1973), ch. 7.

[15] *Flying Post*, 4–6 Nov. 1712, 7–10 Feb., 18–20 June 1713; Abel Boyer, *Political State of Great Britain*, 7 (1713), 184–6.

Elizabeth's accession day, became the scene of effigy-burnings of Pope and Pretender and partisan quarrels over the ringing of bells.[16] Predictably, the expiration of Dr Sacheverell's sentence in 1713 was celebrated with bells, white flags, burnt wigs, and further strains of 'The King shall enjoy his own again'.[17] Two months later, the same tune was played at Farnham in Surrey during the celebrations of the Peace of Utrecht. Twenty miles away, the daughter of a Surrey landowner had her father's estate ransacked for calling the Tory-inspired treaty 'a scandalous, shitten, Jacobite peace' and for refusing to give money for a celebratory junket. According to one account, the mob 'broke down fences, pales, gates, trod down standing corn and grass', and 'did all the mischief they could invent'.[18]

The smouldering tensions of partisan politics were evident at the proclamation of the new reign in London, where Bolingbroke was hissed and Harley had halters thrown into his coach. They broke out dramatically in the provinces on coronation day. Disturbances of some sort were reported in thirty towns across the country, from Dorchester and Chichester in the south to York in the north, from several West Country towns to Norwich in East Anglia.[19] Many of these involved scuffles at the marketplace bonfires, or attacks upon taverns where the coronation festivities were held. A few entailed the disruption of coronation processions by armed mobs. At Bristol, amid rumours that the Whigs intended to burn Dr Sacheverell in effigy, a Tory crowd attempted to search the houses of two zealous Dissenters who were suspected of hatching the plan and broke the windows of the Whig under-sheriff in Temple Street. In the ruckus before Richard Stephen's house, where the effigy was believed to have been hidden, a Quaker cordwainer was killed and several gentlemen were injured before the violence was brought under control.[20]

The coronation-day disturbances were rarely explicitly Jacobite. At Birmingham and Norwich rioters damned King George; at Trowbridge

---

[16] *Flying Post*, 6–8, 18–20 Nov. 1712.

[17] W. B. Ewald, *Rogues, Royalty and Reporters* (Boston, 1956), 77, 79; *Flying Post*, 4–7 Apr. 1713.

[18] *Flying Post*, 11–13 Nov. 1714. The daughter, a Miss Douglas, had attempted to indict the rioters at the Kingston assizes, without success. The charge of sedition against her for vilifying Utrecht was removed to Queen's Bench, and remained unsettled at the Hanoverian accession.

[19] Monod lists twenty-three, to which should be added Chester, Coventry, Ellesmere, Nottingham, Old Sarum, Trowbridge, and York. See Monod, *Jacobitism and the English People*, map 1, p. 175.

[20] *The Annals of George I* (6 vols.; London, 1716–21), i. 257–9; [John Oldmixon], *The Bristol Riot* (London, 1714); [Daniel Defoe], *A Full and Impartial Account of the Late Disorders in Bristol* (London, 1714).

they denounced King William; while at Reading a 'tumultuous and riotous Mob' was said to have shouted 'No Hanover, no Cadogan' and to have 'spoil'd the Mirth of the Night' by crying out 'No Foreign Government'. Yet the predominant cry of crowds was emphatically for Sacheverell or High Church; in other words, for quite traditional Tory signifiers. They were intended to puncture Whig pride in a Hanoverian 'deliverance' and may be seen as a continuation of the party strife of the previous decade.

In fact many of the disorders occurred in open constituencies where the Hanoverian succession was likely to tip the balance in favour of the Whigs. Canterbury, Cirencester, Chichester, Gloucester, Hereford, and Salisbury, for example, all experienced coronation-day affrays, and all had a record of disputed elections during the eighteenth century, sometimes leading to counter-petitions in the Commons. So, too, did Worcester, where the Pakington faction was politically opposed by the mitre and Dissent; and Norwich, where the town leaders and clergy were evenly distributed between the two parties in the years immediately following the Sacheverell trial.[21] In these towns the coronation-day disorders resembled pre-electoral showdowns, orchestrated by Tory élites who resented the Whigs' readiness to transform the coronation-day celebrations into party fanfares. Such was the case at Norwich where the High Church party incited supporters to disrupt the marketplace celebrations to the cry of 'Bene and Berney', the standing members. The same was true of Taunton and Shrewsbury. At the Shropshire town, where the country gentry jostled for power with a predominantly nonconformist group in alliance with Lord Bradford, his lordship's celebration was interrupted by the crowd 'crying High Church and Dr. Sacheverell for ever'. At Taunton, a clothing town deep in Tory country, noted for its Dissenting academy and imposing meeting-house, the Tory mayor's son played a leading role in the disruption of the coronation festivities while his father and the town recorder looked on. Several months later, the mayor himself would admit spurious voters to the hustings in an attempt to sustain the Tories' electoral fortunes.[22]

The coronation-day disorders of 1714 prompted a series of investigations as to why the local authorities had not taken better precautions to curb sedition on this most auspicious of holidays. At Bristol they engendered

[21] Rogers, *Whigs and Cities*, 310–11; BL, Add. MS 38507, fo. 147; Joseph Grego, *A History of Parliamentary Elections* (London, 1892), 72; Alec Macdonald, *Worcestershire in English History* (London, 1943), 125–6. For the contested elections, see W. A. Speck, *Tory and Whig: The Struggle in the Constituencies* (London, 1970), 126–31.
[22] *Journals of the House of Commons* (hereafter *JHC*), 18 (1714–18), 31; PRO, SP 35/11/141, SP 35/74/6–7.

a special commission of oyer and terminer to try the sixteen individuals, principally craftsmen, who were accused of riot or murder. This heavy-handed strategy backfired. The judges entered Bristol to the cry of 'Down with the Roundheads, no Jeffry's, no Western Assizes'; in other words, to slogans that associated Whig law with the Bloody Assizes of 1685. Despite a tough address from the senior judge, local jurymen were sufficiently intimidated by the depth of popular feeling against the commission to turn in relatively lenient bills and verdicts. Eight men were fined 30 nobles and sentenced to three months' imprisonment for riot and misdemeanour; that is, for riots of a private nature rather than of treasonable import. By contrast, the two capital indictments against the rioters (both for murder) failed to stick, much to the delight of Tories as far afield as Chichester.[23] The episode positively reminded the Whigs of the difficulties of securing exemplary justice before unsympathetic juries, and other cases of rioting on coronation day were promptly removed to King's Bench.[24]

The coronation-day disturbances revealed considerable anxiety about the future course of Hanoverian politics and not a little rage from the Tory clans that their leaders had been displaced from power after four years in government. Although the general election of 1715 consolidated the Whigs' hold on power, their decision to impeach the Tory leaders for their purported mishandling of Utrecht brought disaffection to a head. In mid-April a Brentford wool-comber was indicted for maligning the King's speech. Three other men were charged with drinking the Pretender's health, including one who wagered 50 guineas that King George would not reign for more than a year. On the anniversary of Queen Anne's coronation, crowds in the western parishes of the City of London staged a defiantly Tory commemoration for the last Stuart monarch, parading a hoop and a picture of the Queen. They also hassled passers-by for money to toast her health, and attacked the houses of known Dissenters. Six days later, they joyously celebrated the birthday of the Duke of Ormonde, the popular Tory general who had organized the military disengagement from Europe prior to Utrecht and who was a likely target of the Whig-dominated Committee of Secrecy devoted to destroying its enemies.

The Tory rank and file was clearly in a confrontational mood. It was quite prepared to unsettle the Whig élite as it plotted its politics of revenge. The anniversaries of 28 and 29 May predictably saw further demonstrations of

---

[23] *Weekly Packet*, 4–11 Dec. 1714. On the Bristol trial, see [Oldmixon], *The Bristol Riot* and [Defoe], *A Full and Impartial Account*.

[24] The Attorney-General brought informations against fourteen rioters in Reading to King's Bench, for example. See *Weekly Packet*, 27 Nov.–4 Dec. 1714.

Tory solidarity. On the evening of the King's birthday a crowd gathered at the Stock Exchange, the pre-eminent site of Whig financial power, 'armed with great Clubbs and crying out High Church and Ormonde'. At Cheapside it displayed effigies of Cromwell, William III, and Marlborough to shouts of 'Down with the Rump', 'No Hanoverian, No Presbyterian Government'. A French schoolmaster, one John Burnois, even had the temerity to huzza for King James III and to declare King George a 'Usurper to the Crown'.[25] A number of arrests were made on this occasion, including the luckless Burnois, who was later whipped and imprisoned for his sedition. The militia was also called out, but this did not deter Tories from celebrating the Restoration the following day. On this occasion they broke windows that were not illuminated, including those of the Whig Lord Mayor, Sir Charles Peers. At Smithfield market they burnt an effigy of Oliver Cromwell; according to one report, with horns on his head, a signifier of Whig political devilment or of George I's reputed cuckoldry at the hands of Count Königsmarck. In other accounts the crowd burnt a print of William III and effigies of the Devil and Jack Presbyter, which some believed resembled Benjamin Hoadley, one of the more vociferously Whig clergymen in the metropolis.[26]

These London-based demonstrations were provocative enough, but they were more than matched by those in the provinces. At Bristol, Tory-Jacobites wore rue and thyme on King George's birthday and jauntily hummed 'The King shall enjoy his own again' on 29 May and again on the Pretender's birthday.[27] Twenty-five miles away, at Beckington near Frome, bells were rung on 10 June, and at nearby Norton St Philip the Pretender was actually proclaimed.[28] Other parts of the country also experienced defiantly Tory protests, among them Norwich, Cambridge, and Hertford, where the Tory MP Charles Caesar was greeted on his return to his seat at Bennington with cries of 'High Church, No Presbyterian, Caesar and Ormond'.[29] More ominously still, the end of May anniversaries saw a series of attacks upon nonconformist meeting-houses, beginning in Oxford and Manchester, and spreading further afield in June. By the time

---

[25] Corporation of London Record Office (hereafter CLRO), London Sessions papers, depositions, May 1715; PRO, SP 35/74/33–4; CLRO, Lieutenancy Minutes (1714–44), fo. 27; Boyer, *Political State of Great Britain*, 9 (1715), 335.

[26] *Annals of George I*, i. 433; Boyer, *Political State of Great Britain*, 9 (1715), 444–5; *Weekly Journal*, 4 June 1715.

[27] John Latimer, *The Annals of Bristol in the Eighteenth Century* (Bristol, 1893; reprint Bath, 1970), 110–11.

[28] *Flying Post*, 14–16 June 1715.

[29] Ibid. 2–4 June 1715; *Weekly Journal*, 4, 18 June, 12 July 1715; PRO SP 35/3/185–96.

that the Whig Committee of Secrecy had tabled its articles of impeachment against the Tory lords, beginning symbolically on the Pretender's birthday, the country was in the throes of a second Sacheverell fever. From 28 May until 1 August, at least fifty meeting-houses were attacked and sometimes completely gutted, the main swathe of destruction taking place around Manchester and in the West Midlands, where Toryism coexisted uneasily with Dissent.[30] In Staffordshire virtually every conventicle with over 100 hearers was attacked, all of them Presbyterian.

The meeting-house riots of 1715 were a serious affront to the government and a Hanoverian dynasty already incensed by the coronation-day disturbances.[31] They registered Tory rancour at the prosecution of their leaders, and in some cases, certainly, a disposition to settle local political scores. In the West Midlands, in particular, the affluent, imposing meeting-houses of the Presbyterians were the most visible symbol of local Whiggery. It was predictable that angry Tories would single them out for destruction. The Dissenters themselves were well aware this might occur. At Newcastle under Lyme they had parleyed with the mayor about the prospect of Tory mobs pulling down their conventicle, as indeed had happened in 1702 at the accession of Queen Anne. To no avail. All that they could do in the face of unsympathetic magistrates was to drive off the demonstrators themselves. This happened in the Wolverhampton area, where a roving mob heading for the Bromwich meeting-house was beaten off by a large group of armed Dissenters on horse and foot.[32]

Political and religious rivalries undoubtedly fuelled the meeting-house riots of 1715 and sometimes implicated members of the Tory hierarchy. At Newcastle, the ex-MP Ralph Sneyd actively encouraged the rioters and the mayor and two magistrates were bound over for questioning in London for their collusion. At Wrexham the former servant of a

---

[30] Monod, *Jacobitism and the English People*, map 3, lists thirty-nine centres where meeting-houses were attacked between 11 June and 1 August 1715. Two meeting-houses were pulled down in West Bromwich. Meeting-houses were also attacked at London (*Flying Post*, 11–14 June 1715), Cambridge (*Whalley's Newsletter*, 16–22 June 1715), Oxford (two) (*Evening Post*, 31 May–2 June 1715), Oswestry (*Weekly Journal*, 6 Aug. 1715), Cradley and Coseley in Staffordshire (Dr Williams's Lib., London, John Evans MS 24.4), Banbury (two) (*Flying Post*, 26–8 July 1715), Morton (*Flying Post*, 12–14 July 1715). Two meeting-houses were also attacked in unspecified places in Derbyshire (*Weekly Packet*, 30 July–6 Aug. 1715) and there were others in Denbighshire and Montgomeryshire (John Evans MS 24.4). The total damages were in excess of £5,000 (John Evans MS 24.4).

[31] In the King's proclamation to the voters in January 1715 he had urged them to return 'the fittest Persons to redress the present Disorders'. See *JHC* 18 (1714–18), 14.

[32] See J. H. Y. Briggs, 'The Burning of the Meeting House, July 1715: Dissent and Faction in Late Stuart Newcastle', *North Staffordshire Journal of Field Studies*, 14 (1974), 61–79.

Denbighshire gentleman testified that he was virtually conscripted to help in the destruction of the meeting-house by his then master, who, along with a local attorney, actively encouraged the crowd as it warmed to its task. The servant's evidence was not watertight. There is reason to believe he might have implicated his former master in order to exculpate himself, for another witness heard him say, 'Down with ye Rump—now for a Merry Chase . . . —who will fight for King James.'[33] Even so, there is some evidence of gentry complicity at Wrexham as well as elsewhere. At Whitchurch, for example, it was reported that the mob had been encouraged by gentlemen 'of no small quality'. At Birmingham two gentlemen were believed to have given the mob money to rescue the rioters from Stafford gaol. Eight gentlemen, in fact, were indicted at the assizes on the Oxford circuit for their part in the disturbances. Only one was found guilty.[34]

Legal records are an imperfect index of crowd involvement, and George Rudé has been rightly criticized for his undue reliance on this sort of evidence. Yet in view of the widespread rumours of gentlemanly complicity during these disturbances and the very visibility of gentlemen in crowds, it is worth considering the legal evidence in some detail. On the basis of the assize record, gentlemen were under-represented in these riots, for which roughly 500 were indicted. Furthermore, their open involvement was confined to only four of the twenty-four centres within the Oxford circuit that witnessed attacks upon Dissenting meeting-houses. Tory magistrates, of course, might wink at disorders and drag their feet in suppressing them. The Staffordshire JP Sir Henry Gough was reprimanded for taking 'trifling security from those who were bound over' for attacking the meeting-house at West Bromwich and for 'not discouraging' his own servants 'from joyning with the Mobb in disorderly and seditious crys'.[35] Yet if Tory gentlemen sometimes gave covert support to the demonstrations, they seldom led or initiated them. Those that did incite or encourage violence, such as the magistrates of Newcastle under Lyme, soon found themselves in deep trouble with the government.

Judging from the judicial records few of the anti-meeting-house rioters appear to have been agricultural labourers, despite the fact that they accounted for about a third of all occupations at the turn of the century.

---

[33] Nat. Lib. of Wales, Wales 4/41/4. For Sneyd and company, see Briggs, 'Burning of the Meeting House', 72–5, PRO, Assi. 4/18/240. For Sir Watkin Williams Wynn's possible role at Wrexham, see E. D. Evans, *A History of Wales 1660–1815* (Cardiff, 1976), 57.
[34] PRO, Assi. 4/18; Abel Boyer, *A Compleat and Impartial History* (London, 1716), 176–80; *Weekly Journal or British Gazetteer*, 9 July 1715.
[35] PRO, SP 44/117/227–8.

Most of them were involved in the dominant trades of their area: buckle-makers in Walsall and Wolverhampton; nailers in Dudley; scythemakers in Stourbridge; with a broader cross-section of trades emerging from the market towns. The preponderance of metalware workers is none the less the most noteworthy feature of those indicted for riot or seditious words, at least in the industrial heartland of the West Midlands. Few of these men would have been directly dependent for their livelihood upon the employ-ment or goodwill of the gentry; some combined industrial pursuits with farming in what was still a viable dual economy. They were political actors in their own right, led by local men such as Henry Weeks, a Worcester butcher, and the Shrewsbury skinner Henry Webb, alias Captain Rag.[36] Drawn into the fray of contemporary struggles, they were ready, in what was classic Sacheverellite territory, to revive the intimidatory strategy of 1710 when Sacheverell himself was under impeachment. It was no accident that ten of the fifteen towns that Sacheverell visited during his triumphant tour of the Midlands in 1710 were the scene of meeting-house riots five years later. Whether the London riots of March 1710 were responsible for Sacheverell's reduced sentence is perhaps a moot point, but a sus-tained Sacheverellite showdown, of vastly greater proportions, was certainly intended to unsettle a Whig ministry bent on destroying the Tory party. It was also designed to undercut the rising fortunes and political preten-sions of an increasingly bourgeois Dissent, one that was fast becoming a pillar of the new Whig order.

What also fuelled hostility to the new government was the fear of war. The strain of the war years had been considerable, aggravated by a series of poor harvests that pushed some areas of the country to the brink of a subsistence crisis. The price of bread in 1709–10 had reached famine pro-portions and credit had been extremely tight. A Warwickshire parson reported in 1710 that 'Everything is very dear & money very scarce in ye Country & ye poor now in great streights & the Rich scarce able to sup-ply them.' Consequently the drive for peace brought the Tories great popu-larity, at least outside some business circles. Thanksgiving celebrations had been enthusiastically staged throughout the country with maypoles and peace garlands. At Lichfield the populace wore laurel leaves with the motto 'Peace and Plenty' inscribed upon them, while in Bristol, Birmingham, Norwich, and Warwick, the festivities took on an air of a Tory triumph, with mobs demanding illuminations from neighbouring households.[37]

[36] PRO, Assi. 4/18/314; *Flying Post*, 16–19 July 1715; *HMC Townshend MSS*, 158.
[37] *Post Boy*, 12–14, 21–3 May, 11–14, 18–21 July 1713; *Flying Post*, 19–21 July 1713.

The Hanoverian succession raised fears that this policy would be abandoned. The new monarch was known to be hostile to Utrecht, and it was widely believed that his new ministry would embroil the country in further continental campaigns. Such sentiments were widely circulated during the 1715 general election and they surfaced again during the summer of sectarian violence. At the outset of the meeting-house riots, a letter from Staffordshire detailed the anxieties of the populace and the anger that the Tory peacemakers and their general had been tried for high treason. 'If the Ministry and Secret Committee and their Friends will not let the country have Peace and Trade', the rioters threatened, 'the Dissenters shall not have a quiet Toleration.' They looked upon 'these Impeachments as nothing else but a Piece of Spight and Revenge in this military Ministry', the author noted, 'because the Ratification of the Peace took some Bread off their Trenchers'.[38] In Stafford the attack upon the Presbyterian chapel was self-consciously scheduled for 7 July, the day traditionally observed to commemorate Utrecht.[39] At eight other towns attacks commenced on the day following. At Worcester the cry of the crowd was 'down with the roundheads, noe Duke of Marbro, Ormond for ever'. Marlborough, of course, was the pre-eminent general who had grown fat on continental wars; Ormonde, the Tory general who had extricated Britain from them. As late as September 1716 a woman was committed to New Prison, Clerkenwell, for blessing Ormonde and declaring he was 'a better man than the king'.[40]

Jacobite sentiments certainly surfaced in the meeting-house riots, arguably more aggressively than before. At Wolverhampton a labourer, a screwmaker, a locksmith, and several bucklemakers were indicted for drinking the Pretender's health during the disturbances and for forcing onlookers to do the same. One bucklemaker even declared, as he urged fellow rioters to gut the meeting-house, that 'we will have no king but James the third & he will be here in a month and we will drive the old Rogue [George I] into his country again to sow Turnipps'.[41] Similar sentiments were expressed elsewhere; at Walsall and Leek, for example.[42] Yet there is no evidence that the meeting-house riots were a part of a broader plan designed to draw troops away from the West Country where a Jacobite invasion led by the Duke of Ormonde was anticipated. Such a hypothesis, recently

[38] Briggs, 'Burning of the Meeting House', 74.
[39] The choice of 7 July was deliberate, not coincidental. See *Flying Post*, 8–10 Sept. 1715, reporting the trials at the Staffordshire assizes.
[40] Greater London Record Office (hereafter GLRO), MJ/SR 2276, Oct. 1716, gaol calendar; for the Worcester riot, *HMC Townshend MSS*, 158. For a Wolverhampton bucklemaker denouncing Marlborough, see PRO, Assi. 4/18/230.
[41] PRO, Assi. 4/18/231–2.   [42] PRO, Assi. 4/18/230, 248.

advanced by Paul Monod, is pure conjecture.[43] It presumes a level of conspiratorial zeal, unity, and organization on the part of the Tory gentry that was simply lacking in the summer of 1715; and it reduces the rioters themselves to the status of political marionettes. The meeting-house riots, sparked by the government's parliamentary attack upon Tory leaders, focused upon very tangible local rivalries and remained local in orientation, with the disaffected gentry offering sympathetic support rather than leadership. The disturbances petered out in early August, not on any gentlemen's cue as Monod suggests, but because that was the month when the Riot Act came into effect. In fact, two of the rioters who attacked the meeting-house at King's Norton on 1 August, the anniversary of the Hanoverian accession, were hanged under the new statute.[44]

The first wave of popular disaffection to the Hanoverian Whig regime peaked before the Jacobite rebellion of Scotland began. Although at least 700 Englishmen joined the Scottish rebels as they marched south, the bulk of them hailed from a socially select quarter.[45] They were predominantly Northumberland and Lancashire gentlemen and their clients, largely Catholic by religious disposition, and by upbringing and heritage likely Jacobite sympathizers. Certainly, a few rebels had seen active service in the previous disturbances, among them Tom Syddal and William Ward, the leaders of the Manchester mob, who joined the insurrection upon their release from gaol from Lancaster. Yet the remarkable fact is that despite the evident disaffection that informed northern cities like York, Newcastle, and Leeds, and the Sacheverellite fury that engulfed Manchester and the West Midlands, the Jacobite insurrection did not command a popular following beyond attracting some farmers and weavers from the Calder valley and from the villages and townships north and east of the Ribble. In good measure this may be explained by the conservatism of the rebel leaders, who, despite the precedent of the Western rising of 1685, discouraged foot soldiers and thought largely in terms of a gentlemanly army. But it was also a telling reminder that Tory rage did not necessarily translate into

---

[43] Monod, *Jacobitism and the English People*, 185–6.

[44] *Whalley's Dublin Post Man*, 19 Aug. 1715; *Flying Post*, 13–15 Sept. 1715. Curiously there is no record of this in Assi. 4/18. Monod suggests the riots 'abruptly' ended on 1 August because the gentry were not ready for insurrection. In fact the attack upon the Kingswood meeting-house at King's Norton appears to have continued into 2 August, and as late as 1 September 1715 Tories at Burton on Trent disrupted a Dissenting service by driving a bull into the meeting-house. By this time rioters were doubtless aware that pulling down a meeting-house was a capital offence. See Monod, *Jacobitism and the English People*, 187 and *Flying Post*, 13–15 Sept. 1715.

[45] On this theme, see Monod, *Jacobitism and the English People*, 317–27; Patrick Purcell, 'The Jacobite Rising of 1715 and the English Catholics', *English Historical Review*, 44/175 (1929), 418–32.

Jacobite militancy and that the tributaries of disaffection were too diverse and often too volatile for a Tory-Jacobite gentry to mobilize. That gentry was itself ambivalent about taking up arms. Although one can find Tory gentlemen such as James Holkenhull of Shotwich, Cheshire, who swore he would ride his horse 100 miles to serve the Pretender in any way he could,[46] the great majority supported the house of Stuart from their cups rather than their saddles.

The Jacobite rebellion of 1715 and the defection of Bolingbroke and Ormonde to the Stuarts seriously impaired the fortunes of the Tory party and forced disgruntled Tory gentry to keep a very low profile. But it did not silence popular opposition to the Hanoverian Whig regime. The calendar of riot and political profanity continued. In the spring and summer months of 1716, there were Tory-Jacobite demonstrations at Bristol, Cambridge, Dorchester, Marlborough, Norwich, Leeds, and Stafford, some of them sparked by zealously Whig celebrations of royal anniversaries. At Oxford, where a major riot broke out on the Prince of Wales's birthday (30 October) on account of many inhabitants refusing to illuminate their windows, there had been jangled bells on the thanksgiving for the suppression of the rebellion and seditious tunes piped from Tory colleges on Oak Apple day.[47] Further south, at a bull-baiting just outside Shaftesbury, some dragoons of General Carpenter's company were attacked by 'hundreds of Jacobites' who shouted 'Murder the Rogues, they are the Villains that beat the King's army at Preston.'[48] Even in smaller towns such as Ashbourne in Derbyshire, there were sufficient signs of disaffection to trouble the commanding officer stationed there. Major Roberts complained to the government that while the locals ignored his exhortations to celebrate the King's birthday on 28 May, professing ignorance of the anniversary, Restoration day was pointedly commemorated as a Stuart anniversary. This snub so incensed Roberts that on the anniversary of the Hanoverian accession he made sure that inhabitants illuminated their windows.[49]

It was in London that disaffection most troubled the government, for historically London had been critical to the stability of any regime. In order to stem the tide of Jacobite revelry, Whig loyalist societies in London had once again sought to captivate the public by staging a series of mock processions linking the exiled house of Stuart with Catholicism and foreign

---

[46] PRO, Chester 24/152/3.
[47] Abel Boyer, *Political State of Great Britain*, 11 (May 1716), 646, and 12 (Nov. 1716), 505–33; Thomas Hearne, *Remarks and Collections*, ed. D. W. Rannie, 11 vols. (Oxford, 1898–1918), v. 235–7.
[48] *Flying Post*, 31 May–2 June 1716.   [49] PRO, SP 35/6/43–7.

absolutism. The first of these had been planned for the anniversary of the King's coronation in 1715, when the Loyal Society of Young Men and Apprentices planned to parade the familiar trio of Pope, Devil, and Pretender through the streets of London together with the rebels Bolingbroke, Ormonde, and Mar. But an unsympathetic Lord Mayor banned the parade for fear it would end in uproar. His successor, however, proved more receptive to loyalist spectacle and approved one for the anniversary of the Gunpowder Plot, arguably most cherished of anti-Catholic festivals. To the tune of 'Lillibullero', Pope, Pretender, and Tory rebels were drawn backwards with halters over their heads, and an effigy of the infant Pretender in a warming-pan was paraded before them. The effigies were drawn through the streets from Cheapside to St James's, returning by way of the Strand to the Royal Exchange, the centre of Whig banking and wartime finance, where they were burnt with much ceremony.[50]

More elaborate Pope-burning processions were staged in 1716 on the anniversary of the defeat of the rebels at Preston and Dumblane; and again on the return of the King from Hanover early the next year. They featured devils, pretenders, dummy generals, a warming-pan bastard, and mock-cardinals, friars, and a monk whose corpulence connoted 'the voracious and devouring Jaws of the Church of Rome'. Men dressed as clowns and Highland rebels derisively sprinkled 'Holy Water' on the crowd as the procession wound its way to Charing Cross, where the Pope, Pretender, and rebel generals were put to flame in the presence of the King's Champion.

These purgative rites were also accompanied by attempts to contain popular Toryism at the grass roots. With the help of the Duke of Newcastle, the Lord Lieutenant of Middlesex, the sponsors of these parades also organized a series of loyalist mughouses throughout London. These drinking clubs were designed to boost Whig spirits, to animate loyalism, and, in Dyder Ryder's words, eventually to 'gain over the populace'. In the face of uncertainty about the political loyalties of the local militia, they were also designed to provide vigilante squads to disrupt Tory demonstrations and to take up seditious revellers. It is no accident that some of the leading loyalists in the City were closely affiliated with the militia and the Whig caucus in City politics.[51]

---

[50] See Nicholas Rogers, 'Popular Protest in Early Hanoverian London', *Past and Present*, 79 (May 1978), 77–8.

[51] For example, Captain Joseph Bell, president of the Roebuck in 1716, acted as an agent of the Whig caucus in Queenhithe and Aldergate wards. See *London Politics 1713–1717: Minutes of a Whig Club 1714–1717*, ed. H. Horwitz, London Record Society 17 (London, 1981), 130, 134–5, 141–2, and *Weekly Journal*, 3 Nov. 1716. Bell was a member of the Goldsmiths' Company and voted Whig in the 1713 election. Captain Hilliard, the president of the mughouse

The interventionist strategies of the mughouse squads proved, if anything, counter-productive. They generated a series of pitched battles between the 'Jacks' and the 'Mugites' on public anniversaries. Jacks taunted Mugites by attempting to burn Jack Presbyter or Oliver Cromwell on Whig anniversaries; or by disrupting their toasts with profane and seditious cries. Mugites responded by traversing their opponents' territory on Stuart anniversaries, disrupting their bonfires, even thrashing them with oaken staves. This war of nerves continued until July 1716, when the ongoing rivalry between two politically opposed alehouses in Salisbury Court generated a full-scale attack upon Robert Read's mughouse. In this confrontation, one of the ringleaders of the Tory rioters, Daniel Vaughan, a small-coals man and former Bridewell apprentice, was shot dead in the street by the landlord. About thirty other rioters were arrested. Five rioters were hanged at the end of the street under the terms of the new Riot Act; another, a Fleet Street watchmaker, was convicted at King's Bench for 'inciting the Mobb to throw Stones at the Mughouse windows'. He was eventually pardoned. Robert Read, by contrast, was acquitted of murder after a three-hour trial.[52]

The Salisbury Court sentences were bitterly resented. It was widely felt that the provocative actions of the mughouse-men had been condoned by those in authority, while only Tory rioters felt the full force of the law. Yet the strict enforcement of the Riot Act did arrest the momentum of open protest in London, just as it had done a year previously in the West Midlands. It did not eliminate it altogether. Although the government had by 1717 ferreted out some of the obvious sources of disaffection, cracking down on non-juring meeting-houses, policing Tory preachers, harassing Jacobite printers with writs of information and seditious libel, it proved harder to track down the small fry.[53] Riverside coalsmen who plied a trade

in St John's Lane, was linked to the City militia and probably used the mughouse as a recruiting ground for reliable men. See John Dunton, *Royal Gratitude* (London, 1716), 49. Another man linking mughouse politics with the Whig caucus was Colonel Samuel Westal. He stood bail for Robert Read, the landlord of the mughouse in Salisbury Court, having been in charge of the militia troops there in July 1716. Westal was a member of the City Lieutenancy, a colonel of one of the City militia regiments, and prominent in the caucus. He also promoted the candidature of Sir Harcourt Masters in the chamberlain's election of 1718. See *Weekly Journal*, 21 June 1718; City Lieutenancy (1714–44), fos. 11 and 62.

[52] On the Salisbury Court riots, see Rogers, 'Popular Protest', 81–3; for evidence of the rivalry between Read's mughouse and the Tory headquarters, the Swan alehouse at Holbourn bridge, see *Newcastle Courant*, 25–8, 28–30 July, 30 July–1 Aug. 1716; *Political State of Great Britain*, 11 (Aug. 1716), 130, and 12 (Sept. 1716), 217.

[53] On the vicious campaign of the Whigs against Tory-Jacobite printers, see P. B. J. Hyland, 'Liberty and Libel: Government and the Press during the Succession Crisis in Britain, 1712–1716', *English Historical Review*, 101 (Oct. 1986), 863–88. For attempts to control the more elusive ballad trade, see Rocco Lawrence Capraro, 'Political Broadside Ballads in Early Hanoverian London', *Eighteenth Century Life*, 11 (May 1987), 12–21.

in seditious broadsheets proved almost impossible to control; pubs deep in the Tory quarter of the city, such as the Three Tuns, Old Bailey, where one informer reported that 'all cabal with news gazeteers', proved difficult to infiltrate. The government did try, of course. In 1717 the Middlesex bench threatened to withdraw the licences of all victuallers who harboured disaffected persons. Four years later the Secretary of State considered employing ministerial hacks to 'make sevl. Ballads and Storys as might engage the ears of the Mob' and to have them 'sold by proper hands to all persons yt have anything of a retail trade'.[54] But seditious ballads continued to circulate. In 1723 one ministerial sympathizer drew attention to several anti-Hanoverian libels which were 'cryed thorou [gh] our Streets and Sung on every Corner which caused great Lafter and many people gathered together'. Two years later a foreign visitor passing Cranbourne Alley recalled 'a fellow . . . eternally bawling out his Pye-Corner pastorals in behalf of Dear Jemmy, Lovely Jemmy'.[55]

The result was that the government had to live with a continuing undercurrent of Jacobitism that persisted well into the 1720s and periodically surfaced in more dramatic ways. In London the authorities had to tolerate the garlanding of Jacobite printers and preachers pilloried for disaffection. At Tower Hill and St James's Park, the Pretender was again proclaimed.[56] At Bath, the outlaw Ormonde's birthday was celebrated in 1718, much to the consternation of the government, which had already sent rattling letters to the mayor about the political loyalty of his town. In Hertfordshire a carpenter even had the impudence to ride about the county with horns on his head and a fiddler before him, a signal snub to a king ridiculed for his cuckoldry.[57] At Manchester, loyalists had to suffer 'a Rabble of People who went the Rounds all over Town' on coronation day, 'breaking windows, and insulting the Inhabitants in an outrageous manner'. At Ashford, in Kent, they might have witnessed a band of Jacks on a drunken spree,

[54] PRO, SP 35/31/296; Doran, *London*, i. 288. For an example of a constable (of St Leonard Shoreditch) who had his alehouse licence revoked for failing to intervene in a Tory riot, see GLRO, MJ/SBB/750/35.

[55] Doran, *London*, i. 71.

[56] *Berrow's Worcester Post Man*, 18–25 Oct. 1717, 11–18 July 1718; Doran, *London*, i. 319, 353; *Norwich Gazette*, 29 Dec. 1716–5 Jan. 1717; *Weekly Journal, and British Gazetteer*, 22 Dec. 1716.

[57] *Weekly Journal, or Saturday's Post*, 10 Aug. 1717; *Pue's Occurrences* (Dublin), 10–13 May 1718; PRO, SP 44/118, 15 Dec. 1715. The Hertfordshire incident is probably related to the demonstration at Walton on 28 May, for which a gardener was bound over to the quarter sessions. At the Hertfordshire assizes the carpenter was sentenced to two whippings and a year in gaol, his collaborator to one whipping and six months' imprisonment. For the Walton incident, see Monod, *Jacobitism and the English People*, 205.

drinking the Pretender's health on their knees and proclaiming his regality in the marketplace.[58] Such interventions, with their Jacobite airs, riddles, or cockades, continually punctuated the Whig supremacy, reminding the government that its legitimacy was not unquestioned. Indeed, most English towns of any size or importance experienced some kind of Jacobite disorder in the years 1715–22.

The result was that government officials were routinely poring over documents concerning Jacobitism in London and in the provinces. These included Hereford in 1718, where the town crier purportedly proclaimed the Pretender on 10 June; Hull and Halifax in 1719, where there were further pro-Jacobite demonstrations of sympathy on the Pretender's birthday; and Bridgwater in 1721, where the tensions between the troops and the Tories exploded on 10 June. Here the soldiers attempted to restrain the inhabitants of Eastover from wearing white roses, baited them by parading a warming-pan doll through their quarter, and were aggrieved to discover that their opponents had placed a garland of 'Roses, Hornes & Turnipps' over their officers' door. This sort of seditious revelry surfaced dramatically three years later at Harwich, where the accession-day celebration of the Whiggish corporation was disrupted by a band of fishermen who carried about 'a Person Dressed up with Horns and Crying out here is your King George'.[59] The mayor attempted to arrest the 'Mock King', it was reported, but the revellers were protected by the Tory JP and leading shipowner Daniel Smith, whose son not only entertained the band but encouraged them to insult the mayor again two days later, at the bi-annual fishermen's feast. On this occasion a fool dressed up in ribbons 'turned up his Backside' to the mayor and 'Clapt his hand on it' while his fellow fishermen drummed up the tune of the 'roundhead[ed] cuckolds'. The mayor arrested the fool for this insult, but he was challenged by one of Smith's shipowning allies for so doing, who told him 'he did not value him nor his House neither, tho he was a bigger Man'.[60] The mayor demanded redress for this affront and sought to persuade the Secretary of State that the fishermen's revel was in 'contempt of the government'.[61] How far the government was persuaded by this explanation it is difficult to say. Several burgesses sought to defuse the confrontation on the grounds that the fishermen's revel was customarily transgressive and politically harmless. Sir Charles Wager at the Admiralty was informed that the whole

[58] PRO, SP 44/79A/161–3 (Ashford, 10 June 1718); *Weekly Journal, or Saturday's Post*, 26 Oct. 1717 (Manchester, 20 Oct. 1717).
[59] PRO, SP 35/51/16.   [60] PRO, SP 35/54/258–9, 261–4.
[61] PRO, SP 35/54/263–4.

episode was really an underhand attempt by Daniel Smith to discredit the corporation and gain the stewardship of the town. Indeed, Wager felt that Smith, an ally of the London alderman and MP Humphrey Parsons, could be detached from the Tory camp to the government's advantage, provided, of course, that the current friends of the administration on the corporation were not badly compromised.[62] His insider knowledge may well have induced the government to temper their response to this flagrant insult to Whig rule.

The calendar of riot and sedition that so characterized the early years of the Hanoverian succession began to wane in importance in the mid- to late 1720s. Royal anniversaries were noticeably less contentious after 1723, and the coronation of George II passed without any major incident, in marked contrast to that of his father. One reason for this was that the Hanoverian accession did not inaugurate a new era of religious sectarianism and debilitating wars, as was widely predicted. Another was the growing attractiveness of a Country critique of Walpolean politics. Opposition Whigs shared with die-hard Tories a fear that British interests would be subordinated to Hanover. They both opposed the authoritarian thrust of official Whiggery, and were critical of Walpole's cynical deployment of patronage and money in defence of the Protestant succession. Only those Jacobites riveted to passive obedience and hereditary right, and these were largely non-jurors, could not find common ground with other opponents of the existing Hanoverian polity.

The shifting configurations of popular politics can usefully be traced by examining the fortunes of the two major provincial towns, Bristol and Norwich.[63] Both had large, open, politically active electorates, a welter of political clubs and societies, a vibrant press, and a strong tradition of political partisanship. Both cities experienced riots on the first Hanoverian coronation and both were bedevilled with an undercurrent of disaffection thereafter that expressed itself in Jacobite revelry and a continuing crop of cases involving seditious words. In 1718 Bristol magistrates informed a government spy that they feared 'the vulgar in general' were 'two parts in three more inclined to the Pretender than the king'. In Norwich a correspondent reported in September 1722 that the government and King were

[62] PRO, SP 35/52/95–6, 122. Cf. Monod, *Jacobitism and the English People*, 221–2, who wants to link the demonstration to Parsons's Jacobite loyalties and ignores the politics of interest which compromises that explanation.

[63] For a lengthier comparison of these two cities, see Nicholas Rogers, 'Popular Jacobitism in Provincial Context: Eighteenth-Century Bristol and Norwich', in Eveline Cruickshanks and Jeremy Black (eds.), *The Jacobite Challenge* (Edinburgh, 1988), 123–41.

daily ridiculed 'for the Mobb are spirited up to such a Degree . . . that all who are well affected to the Government are hiss'd at, and curst as they go in the streets'. The spirit of disloyalty, he maintained, was buoyed up by 'popish schools' and alehouses 'where all disaffected persons have opportunity to hold Cabals and utter their treason without controul'. He also feared the clergy were a problem, 'abundance of whom are so disaffected that they can seldom give the Government a good word'.[64]

This situation continued on into the 1730s. In 1731, after a frustrating election in Wymer ward, a 'Tory Mobb' went on the rampage in Norwich, 'cursing and abusing such as they knew to be Friends of the Government' and attacking an alehouse whose landlord was known to have discovered and reported a treasonable tract to the authorities. These reprisals were accompanied by threatening and seditious letters to local aldermen, open declarations of Jacobite sentiment on the marriage of the Prince of Orange to George's eldest daughter in 1734, and quite flamboyant refusals of a few Tory voters to take the oaths of allegiance to Hanover.[65] Bristol did not have such a strong non-juring tradition as Norwich, but its street politics remained as contentious. In 1735, a Tory crowd composed of petty craftsmen, miners, labourers, a gentleman, and a surgeon disrupted a loyalist celebration on accession day at Lawford's Gate, where it was rumoured that the weavers planned to burn an effigy of the newly elected Tory MP, Thomas Coster, in conjunction with the Pope and Pretender. They even broke into a house to confiscate the Dragon, Crown, and Orange that loyalists planned to parade in a King George and Dragon show, carrying them about the town in triumph to huzzas of 'Coster for ever'.[66] Four months later, on the King's birthday, another crowd disrupted the corporation's celebrations by destroying the illumination which commemorated the King and the erection of a statue in honour of King William in Queen Square.[67]

The 1730s none the less prove a turning point in Bristolian politics. Whigs and Tories found common ground in opposing Walpole's Excise Bill and his pacific policy towards Spain and from 1735 onwards shared the representation of the City. Although Jacobite sentiments surfaced during the 1745 rebellion they were not taken as seriously as they were in Norwich, where the mayor banned the customary Plough Monday revel for fear it would turn into a full-scale riot. In Bristol, the successful promotion of a Country platform and a workable arrangement between Whigs and Tories had marginalized Jacobitism. In Norwich, where the non-juring tradition

---

[64] PRO, SP 35/33/137, SP 35/15/254–6.
[65] *Norwich Gazette*, 14–21, 21–8 Nov. 1730, 3/10 Apr. 1731, 16–23 Mar. 1734.
[66] *Daily Gazetteer*, 10 July 1735; PRO, KB 33/5/3.   [67] Latimer, *Annals*, 193.

was stronger and where the campaign for a bellicose mercantilism proved less relevant to the city's economy, the old party polarities persisted, despite efforts to foster a Country Toryism and to capitalize upon Admiral Vernon's well-publicized victories against the Spanish.[68] Excluded from local power, Norwich Toryism continued to wear a Jacobite hue, best personified in Henry Crossgrove, the printer of the *Norwich Gazette*, who seldom overlooked an opportunity to rail at Dissent, to enthuse about Stuart anniversaries, and to despise prestigious Country weeklies such as the *Craftsman*, which he regarded as a 'vile republican paper'.[69] Predictably, the vestry of St Peter Mancroft, in the heart of the Tory quarter of the city, refused to celebrate Cumberland's victory over the rebels at Culloden. Five years later, mobs calling themselves 'Hell-Fire Clubbers' or 'Jemmy's Men' protested against the introduction of a Calvinist Methodist meeting-house in the city. When the mayor attempted to disperse them by reading the Riot Act, they behaved 'very rudely' before him, shouting 'Church and King, down with the meetings', slogans which recalled the meeting-house riots of 1715. According to one source, they were heard singing treasonable songs in early 1752, including 'Now is the time, or never, let us throw off George and bring in Jemmy'.[70]

The examples of Bristol and Norwich force us to reconsider the regional persistence of popular Jacobitism in Hanoverian England. The recent revisionist interpretation of Hanoverian politics detracts from that project.[71] In its obsession to discount Whig-Marxist interpretations of the century, it has inflated the overall importance of the dynastic idiom in British politics and failed to consider its regional specificities and the multiple meanings it could engender.

Judging from the reported cases of disaffection in the newspapers and the courts, popular Jacobitism declined nationally after 1722. In London no Tory-Jacobite demonstrations occurred after the trial of Bishop Atterbury

---

[68] Cf. Kathleen Wilson, *The Sense of the People: Politics, Culture and Imperialism in England, 1715–1785* (Cambridge, 1995), 401–4, who believes that the Norwich Tories adapted to the changing political circumstances of the late 1730s and early 1740s.

[69] J. B. Williams, 'Henry Cross-grove, Jacobite Journalist and Printer', *Library*, 3rd ser. 5/18 (Apr. 1914), 218.

[70] Anon., *A True and Particular Narrative of the Disturbances and Outrages that have been Committed in the City of Norwich since November to the Present Time* (London, 1752); Norfolk and Norwich Record Office, PD 26/73 (S), St Peter Mancroft, Churchwardens' Accounts (1707–52), 815.

[71] J. C. D. Clark, *English Society 1688–1832* (Cambridge, 1985), and his 'The Politics of the Excluded: Tories, Jacobites and Whig Patriots, 1715–1760', *Parliamentary History*, 2 (1983), 209–22.

in 1723, although there were whiffs of disaffection during the 'Mother Gin' protests of 1738, when demonstrators were heard to curse the King and threaten 'No gin, no King'.[72] Cases of disaffection resurfaced in 1745; nearly a hundred of them were prosecuted in the courts. But many of those can be identified with the Irish-Catholic minority in London, not with the populace as a whole. Indeed, in what appears to have been a highly successful mobilization of loyalist sentiment in London, many ordinary men and women were prepared to give evidence against those denouncing George and toasting the Pretender. The pattern of disaffection found in the metropolis at the Hanoverian accession, when some of the western parishes of the City were strongly alienated from the new regime, had disappeared.

Other areas of the country where disaffection was rife in 1714–20 gave evidence of their loyalist sentiments in 1745–6. In the Tory West Country, where loyalist associations abounded, prosecutions for seditious words at the assize courts dwindled to the handful.[73] In the north-east, where some of the Tory gentry and their clients contemplated rebellion in 1715, junkets for Culloden abounded and effigies of the Pretender were burnt with gusto. Very few signs of disaffection sullied the festivities. Even the keelmen, suspected of harbouring Jacobite tendencies in 1715, joined loyalist associations and set two mass-houses on fire to provide an 'illumination' for the Duke of Cumberland.[74] Indeed, militant anti-Catholic, and by extension anti-Jacobite, passions were not uncommon in the years 1745–6. Nailers, colliers, and bucklemakers threatened Catholic mass-houses in the Stourbridge area; carpenters and sailors pulled one down in Liverpool. The same happened at Stokesley, where a mob of 200 stripped off all the tiles of the local mass-house, brought down the ceiling, and burnt the contents at the market cross. There one of the crowd donned 'a fine vestment and cross', and, with a mitre in his hand, commended the company for 'the great service they had done to the king and country' and absolved them for 'all their past sins'. The crowd responded to this mockery of Catholic ritual with the words, 'God save king George and down with the mass.'[75]

Anti-Jacobite sentiments were very evident during the 1745 rebellion and its aftermath. Outside East Anglia, it was in Lancashire and the West Midlands that the Jacobite tradition remained the most resilient. In

[72] *HMC Egmont Diary*, iii. 304–5.

[73] Monod, *Jacobitism and the English People*, 252, table 3. For the geography of loyalism in 1745, see Linda Colley, *Britons: Forging the Nation 1707–1837* (New Haven, 1992), appendix 1.

[74] Wilson, *Sense of the People*, 335; *Newcastle Courant*, 12–19, 19–26 Apr., 19–26 July 1746.

[75] *Gentlemen's Magazine*, 16 (1746), 40, cited in Thomas Richmond, *The Local Records of Stockton and Neighbourhood* (Stockton, 1868; reprint 1972), 65; *True Patriot*, 31 Dec. 1745; *Bath Journal*, 2 June 1746.

Lancashire Jacobitism was sustained by a strong hostility to Dissent and a vibrant non-juring community in Manchester which produced a handful of Jacobite martyrs. During the Forty-Five about 200 Catholics gathered at Ormskirk to proclaim the Pretender before being dispersed by a pro-Hanoverian crowd.[76] Even after the suppression of the rebellion, disaffection continued. At Manchester, Jacobites disrupted the celebrations of Cumberland's birthday in 1746, an action that provoked retributions from a loyalist crowd during the thanksgiving for the suppression of the rebellion, when known Jacobites were forced to illuminate their windows and the houses of Thomas Deacon and the widow of Tom Syddal were attacked. These reprisals did not silence the Manchester Jacks. The following year, they provocatively paraded oak leaves on Restoration day. One of their number, Edward Hall, a physician and a member of the Jacobite mock corporation of Ardwick, even had the audacity to steal the heads of the Manchester rebels that hung from the Royal Exchange.[77]

The West Midland counties also nurtured a tradition of Jacobite festival and resistance that survived beyond the Forty-Five. In Shropshire and Staffordshire, in particular, Whigs were routinely vilified on Stuart anniversaries. In 1750 a cornet was told that in Walsall it was customary 'to ridicule the rebellious proceedings of Charles I's time by making a figure to represent Oliver Cromwell or Parson Baxter'. Forty miles away at Shrewsbury, where the populace had a reputation for being 'very bold and given to mobbing', it was reported that the town maypole had been regularly 'decked with garlands of roses on the Pretender's birthday'.[78] This Jacobite symbolism had frequently been visible at the hustings. At the Lichfield by-election of 1718, for instance, supporters of the Whig candidate, William Chetwynd, were confronted by 'a very great mob with papers in their hats resembling white roses'. Jacobite colours were also paraded at the Coventry election of 1722 and at the Cheshire contest twelve years later.[79] The custom was still going strong in 1747, for plaid waistcoats were also spotted at several Midland hustings. In Staffordshire, where the Tories were incensed by the defection of Lord Gower to the ranks of the

---

[76] W. A. Speck, *The Butcher: The Duke of Cumberland and the Suppression of the '45* (Oxford, 1981), 63.

[77] Monod, *Jacobitism and the English People*, 120, 204, 223, 300; W. H. Thomson, *History of Manchester to 1852* (Altrincham, 1967), 185.

[78] PRO, SP 36/113/183–5; SP 36/113/73–86; *A Selection from the Papers of the Earls of Marmont*, ed. Sir George Rose (2 vols.; London, 1831), i. 214. I owe this last reference to Dr Eveline Cruickshanks.

[79] *The History of Parliament: The House of Commons 1715–54*, ed. Romney Sedgwick (2 vols.; London, 1970), i. 319, 340; *VCH Cheshire*, ii. 122; *Northampton Mercury*, 13–20 Nov. 1722.

government, Jacobite favours flourished. Nor did matters end there. At the Lichfield hunt two months after the general election, one spectator recalled the town entry of the Burton contingent, 'most of 'em in Plaid waistcoats, Plaid ribbon round their hats and some with white cockades'. Their Birmingham allies, decked out in the same dress, even 'drank the Pretender's health publicly in the streets, singing treasonable tunes'.[80]

This flagrant affront to the government, flushed with its success in the 1747 election, was soon to be echoed by the Lancashire Tories. In November 1748 Peter Legh and his cronies transformed the annual Newton hunt into a Jacobite revel in which the Pretender was proclaimed at the market cross and money was offered to 'any likely Fellow' who would enlist with Prince Charles. For two days they paraded up and down the town, crying 'a Legh, a Legh, and down with the Rump', accompanied by their servants in plaid waistcoats and with white ribbons in their hats. Eventually a Whig posse from Wigan routed the company, proclaiming King George at the cross to re-establish duly constituted authority.[81]

It is difficult to know what to make of the Newton and Lichfield hunts. They may have been genuine manifestations of Jacobitism, but they were also designed to draw Whig anger, to tease and unsettle the court. To wear tartan in the wake of the Disarming Act, which specifically banned Highland dress in Scotland, was to snub the ministry in a most pointed way; just as the display of white roses in the face of official proscription had been earlier in the century. Yet parading the plaid can also be seen as a defiant vindication of freedom of expression against a background of Jacobite witch-hunting and staged trials, the last of which was concluded only a few months before the general election of 1747. Tartan hunts were in addition a telling reminder of Cumberland's retributive campaign north of the border, especially when the quarry was rumoured to be a red-coated fox! Jacobite theatre, in other words, combined carnival with political commentary, licence with liberty. For the Tory gentry of the Midlands and Lancashire, indeed, for the Welsh gentry who toasted the 'king across the water' from the safety of their mansions and masonic lodges and who occasionally organized a cock-fight to the familiar strains of 'The King shall enjoy his own again', Jacobitism also expressed a sense

---

[80] Lichfield Papers, Mr Hinton to Lord Anson, 26 Sept. 1747. I am indebted to Dr Eveline Cruickshanks for this reference. For other accounts of Jacobite festival 1747–8, see Eveline Cruickshanks, *Political Untouchables: The Tories and the '45* (London, 1979), 106–8; Henry Fielding, *The Jacobite Journal and Related Writings*, ed. W. B. Coley (Oxford, 1974), 93 n., 126, 368–70; BMC 2863–5.

[81] *Whitehall Ev. Post*, 26–9 Nov. 1748; Monod, *Jacobitism and the English People*, 293.

of place, a defence of local traditions, a heritage of anti-Whiggery in a palpably Whig age.[82]

The flurry of disaffection that broke out in Lancashire and the West Midlands in the aftermath of the Forty-Five did not end with the Lichfield and Newton hunts. In 1750 the government encountered other instances of Jacobite revelry that it felt compelled to investigate. In Walsall a trooper witnessed a ritual execution of the Hanoverian monarch at the Hill Top just outside town on Restoration day. According to his and other reports, an effigy of King George I or II[83] with the motto 'Evil to him that Evil think, it is this that makes the Nation stink' was hoisted on a pole to the amusement of hundreds of spectators.[84] Dressed up in a brown paper coat, with hose, shoes, gloves, and periwig, with horns affixed to the barber's block of a head and a bunch of turnips in one hand and an orange in the other, the effigy was ritually abused like a cock-shy and even fired at. In the evening, the effigy was taken down, dragged around the market cross, and afterwards taken to the churchyard, where it was burnt 'with great rejoicing'. According to the testimony of the soldier, the mob paraded the streets until 9 p.m. crying out, 'Down with the Rumps and Down with the Hanover Line.'

Initially the officers at Walsall wrote the episode off as a frivolous affair carried out by 'a parcel of children and boys'. But as rumours began to circulate about this revelrous affair, their superiors pressed for an inquiry. The mayor of Walsall, who had been out of town on business on 29 May, initially seemed willing to co-operate. 'The Hill Top was a bad place to live in,' he assured Captain Hamilton, 'there were thereabouts several disaffected poor low-lived Fellows of bad characters.'[85] Yet he consistently prevaricated, and was thought to 'make lite of the matter'.[86] When a bucklemaker strolled the streets of Walsall singing treasonable tunes in anticipation of the Pretender's birthday,[87] the government sent the

---

[82] For Welsh Jacobitism, see Philip Jenkins, 'Jacobites and Freemasons in Eighteenth-Century Wales', *Welsh Historical Review*, 19 (1979), 391–406; P. D. G. Thomas, 'Jacobitism in Wales', *Welsh Historical Review*, 1 (1960), 279–80; Donald Nicholas, 'The Welsh Jacobites', *Trans. Hon. Soc. Cymmrodorion* (1948), 467–74. For the Jacobite cock-fight, orchestrated by William Lewis of Llanyfnam in 1747, see BL, Add. MS 35602, fo. 299.

[83] Accounts differed as to whether the effigy was George I or II. The turnips and cornuted head would suggest George I; but the motto implied the current King. One witness believed he saw a second paper pinned to the dummy with the words 'George Rex the second' upon it (SP 36/113/119). The effigy was clearly a composite representation of the Hanoverian monarchy.

[84] PRO, SP 36/113/73–86.   [85] PRO, SP 36/113/83.

[86] PRO, SP 36/113/121.   [87] Monod, *Jacobitism and the English People*, 206.

King's Messenger, Nathaniel Carrington, to investigate. The local leather-workers clearly resented this intrusion. When Carrington eventually secured six of the rioters and packed them off to Stafford gaol, he was surrounded by a mob of 500–600 people.[88] No violence was offered, but Carrington feared that the bucklemakers would be joined by local colliers for a future showdown and so he called for more troops. At this point, the already tense situation deteriorated. Six troops of cavalry were called in to deal with 'the Confusion' that had spread to Birmingham and Wednesbury, and clashes between the dragoons and rioters were reported in which several soldiers were killed. Eventually the government thought it advisable to move their prosecutions to King's Bench, away from courts where the accused might win sympathy. Even so, collections were raised in several towns in Staffordshire for the accused, testimony to the bad blood that the episode had drawn in this most Tory of counties.

What frayed the government's nerves on this occasion was the know-ledge that trouble was also brewing at Shrewsbury. Like Walsall, this Shropshire town had a strong legacy of sectarian rivalry; one that in 1715 had manifested itself in the destruction of the local Dissenting meeting-house. During the 1720s the Whigs had only captured the town's political representation by drastically reducing its electorate. Tories responded to this situation with a festive politics that was anti-Whig and anti-Hanoverian. In 1749 inhabitants paraded a white flag around the town on the Pretender's birthday with 'Long Live Prince Charles' written upon it.[89] To prevent such an occurrence in 1750 the local commander ordered troops to police the street on the eve of the 10th. On their rounds they encountered a master bricklayer and his labourers singing 'Charley O', a Scottish ditty commemorating Bonnie Prince Charlie's march to Derby in 1745.[90] The patrol confronted the revellers about this, but was humili-atingly driven down the street for its pains. The troops returned with re-inforcements and a full-scale brawl ensued in which several soldiers and labourers were wounded. The town blamed the soldiers for the disturbance and began a prosecution against them at King's Bench. A paper dropped in the marketplace even urged the 'Honest Lads of Shrewsbury' to take to arms and act 'as Englishmen, as Men of Courage'.[91] The commanding officer, for his part, urged the government to defend the soldiers. If the Tories won this suit through the testimony of 'a parcell of Jacobite Witnesses', he told the Secretary of State, 'there will be no room for any

[88] PRO, SP 36/113/168.   [89] PRO, SP 36/113/157–9.
[90] PRO, TS 11/929/3268.   [91] PRO, SP 36/113/158.

of His Majesty's Troops to live in this Town, nor any one about us'.[92] As it was, his soldiers had been subjected to humiliating taunts to drink the Pretender's health and continually had to stomach the singing of Jacobite songs in the streets.

The Walsall and Shrewsbury episodes cannot be framed within a pattern of conspiratorial politics, as Paul Monod has suggested. To suggest that the Walsall disturbances were a Jacobite 'regional uprising' and that the Shrewsbury revels were part of a 'West Midlands plot' is to indulge in wishful fantasy.[93] It is more plausible to see these confrontations as part of an ongoing culture of Tory resistance to Whig rule, aggravated by the intrusive presence of troops and commanders who wanted to see 'traiterous' riots at every turn.[94] Walsall and Shrewsbury Tories used Jacobite symbolism to tease the Whigs, to reaffirm their own political traditions, to demarcate their territory. In the case of the Hill Top bucklemakers, this territorialism was also directed at the local authorities and was so understood by them. As the government came to realize, neither the mayor nor the town clerk had any wish to meddle in an annual Jacobite revel in 'the most rude and rebellious part of the town'.[95] The Hill Top lads asserted the right to burn in effigy whom they bloody well pleased, and every figure of authority, right down to the meanest common soldier, was advised to lay off.

As an idiom of defiance, Jacobitism could be used in contexts that were not political in the most conventional sense of the term, especially by those outside or on the fringes of the law. As early as 1690, several highwaymen executed at Tyburn called for sack on their way to the gallows and drank King James's health, bidding the Ordinary and the crowd to swear obedience to the exiled monarch. Two years later, highwaymen who robbed fifteen butchers on their way to Thame market 'made them drink King James' health with a bottle of brandy'.[96] One member of the Golden Farmer's gang even told Chief Justice Holt that 'he did not own him for a judge, King

[92] PRO, SP 36/113/159.

[93] Monod, *Jacobitism and the English People*, 206–9, 216–17. There is no conclusive evidence to link the Walsall effigy-burning to the Uttoxeter Bowling Green club. Monod's suggestion that the club was formed 'to incite the disorders that broke out at Walsall on 29 May' (p. 209) ignores (1) the fact that the Hill Top regularly burnt Hanoverian monarchs in effigy on 29 May, and (2) that it was the government inquiry that aggravated the situation.

[94] See the comments of Major Chaban and Captain Hamilton, PRO, SP 36/133/108–9, 157–9.

[95] PRO, SP 36/113/158.

[96] Luttrell, *A Brief Historical Relation*, ii. 103, 610; *The Portledge Papers*, 85.

James being his lawful sovereign', while another tried to plea bargain with the crown by offering to reveal details of a plot to assassinate King William.[97]

As a script to defy the law, Jacobitism was also used by minters hiding out in urban sanctuaries. Southwark minters, driven to find a new hiding-place in Wapping, damned King, justices, and bailiffs in a rollicking Jacobite song.[98] This sort of rhetorical insolence extended to smugglers as well. In 1716 smugglers operating out of Goring, Sussex, were said to have distributed the Pretender's declaration and to have drunk his health. A few years later, a Dorset revenue officer reported that Blackmore Vale abounded 'with great numbers of dangerous rogues, two whereof were . . . committed for declaring themselves for the Pretender'.[99] Successive Smuggling Acts did little to endear the Whig regime to smugglers, and some may even have helped Jacobite emissaries in passing information and money across the Channel. Predictably, in the crackdown against smuggling in the 1740s by the arch-loyalist Duke of Richmond, Jacobite oaths and denunciations of the government surfaced once more. According to one customs officer, the smugglers in Romney Marsh had been 'so impudent as to publically drink to the Pretender and his sons' health, wish success to their arms and confusion to his Majesty King George'.[100] The convention was still alive years later. In 1756 the master of an Irish brig running goods to Ostend damned King George at the Pool in the Scilly Isles and professed his admiration for Charles Stuart, with whom, he bragged, he had had the honour to drink.[101] Over twenty years later, tea-smugglers in Dorset repossessed some of their contraband trade from a house at Palgrave, and sent two threatening letters to the excise officer there, bidding 'Defiance to you and all that belong to you and even your——King George.' What followed, the rector and churchwardens of nearby Diss reported, was 'too shocking and too treasonable' to insert in a public newspaper.[102]

---

[97] Luttrell, *A Brief Historical Relation*, ii. 252, cited by Monod, *Jacobitism and the English People*, 113.

[98] R. L. Brown, 'The Minters of Wapping: The History of a Debtors' Sanctuary in Eighteenth Century East London', *East London Papers*, 14 (1972), 77–86.

[99] Edward Carson, *The Right and Lawful Customs: A History of the English Customs Service* (London, 1972), 64. For Jacobite sentiments voiced by pirates, see David Cordingly, *Under the Black Flag* (New York, 1995), 93.

[100] Cal Winslow, 'Sussex Smugglers', in Douglas Hay, Peter Linebaugh, and E. P. Thompson (eds.), *Albion's Fatal Tree: Crime and Society in Eighteenth-Century England* (London, 1975), 157. See also Paul Monod, 'Dangerous Merchandise: Smuggling, Jacobitism, and Commercial Culture in Southeast England, 1690–1760', *Journal of British Studies*, 30 (Apr. 1991), 150–82.

[101] PRO, 36/136/88, 89. The boast may have been true, for the captain, James Downey, had captained a French privateer out of Dunkirk during the previous war.

[102] *Ipswich Journal*, 27 Feb. 1779.

Jacobitism was clearly a familiar script for those on the margins of the law. It also entered the language of social protest. Deer poachers and commoners at odds with Whig office-holders who were cracking down on the customary perquisites of the royal forests voiced Jacobite sentiments. In 1718, in response to allegations of poaching by Hampshire gentlemen and their tenants, a 'great number' of armed men raided the Bishop of Winchester's park at Farnham, fired at the deer, cattle, and horses, and shouted disrespectful words about the King and government.[103] Five years later, a butcher closely associated with the Waltham Blacks, as the protesters became known, organized a cabbage processional ridiculing the official ceremonies welcoming the King to Winchester. The following year, the bells at nearby Hambleton were rung on the Pretender's birthday. A similar undercurrent of disaffection appeared in the royal parks of Berkshire, where foresters were not only indicted for breaking fish-ponds and poaching deer, but for Jacobite denunciations of the King and his clients.[104] In part these sentiments may have been influenced by the Tory-Jacobite disposition of the neighbouring landlords suspected of protecting them. This was as true of the Waltham Blacks as of those in Berkshire; indeed, some of the former may well have been dejected smugglers recruited to the Jacobite cause by Sir Henry Goring.[105] Yet in the midst of consistent rumours of Jacobite plots fanned by the government, Jacobitism was also the idiom of defiance most likely to enrage the government and to question the legality of their policies in the royal forests. It was to snub the government in the most pointed way.

Jacobite symbolism could also be used to draw attention to social issues and to express frustration at the failure to redress them. In the opening years of the Hanoverian accession Devonshire weavers were locked in a series of struggles with their masters over wages and the customs of the trade and made a great parade of their loyalty to the new regime. By 1724, weavers at Culmstock were angry enough to destroy pictures of George I upon breaking into the house of an unpopular employer, who was not only a nonconformist but also had close ties with the government. Similarly, Newcastle keelmen were quite prepared to destroy portraits of James I and Charles I when they ransacked the town hall during the strike and food riot of 1740. Yet, ten years later, they proclaimed Charles Stuart as 'King

---

[103] *Berrow's Worcester Post-Man*, 27 June–4 July 1718.

[104] E. P. Thompson, *Whigs and Hunters: The Origin of the Black Act* (London, 1975), 164–6.

[105] See Eveline Cruickshanks and Howard Erskine-Hill, 'The Waltham Black Act and Jacobitism', *Journal of British Studies*, 24 (July 1985), 358–65; Monod, 'Dangerous Merchandise', 165–6.

of England, France and Ireland' during another refractory strike.[106] Clearly these episodes belong more properly to a theatre of threat and retribution than to any sustained commitment to the Stuart cause. They were replicated in 1756, when Midland miners, angry at the ruthless actions of Justice Willes in hanging two food rioters and holding a further two as hostages to fortune, warned that 'the Pretender would soon come and head them'. The threat was taken seriously enough by the government to merit an inquiry, but Lord Hardwicke quickly discounted a Jacobite rising as a possibility.[107]

Jacobitism was a mobile script in the eighteenth century. It was deployed in a variety of contexts and could generate multiple meanings. Of course Jacobitism sometimes denoted a genuine commitment to a Stuart restoration, or at least a belief that George of Hanover was a 'usurper', 'an unlawful king', a man without title; a man, as a Bromley yeoman declared in 1716, who was 'not the Lord's appointed king' but was 'brought in by a parcel of Bogtrotters'. There are plenty of prosecutions that reveal these sentiments, just as there are many that expressed that wish that 'Jemmy' would return to take his rightful throne.[108] In the Midland counties, two-thirds of all prosecutions involved Jacobite statements of this kind. In London roughly a third of all prosecutions for disaffection during the opening years of the Hanoverian succession involved quite explicit Jacobite loyalties, with the wealthier sections of society being somewhat over-represented.[109] This figure, it should be added, excludes Jacobites who were indicted for riot rather than for any pro-Stuart slogans they may have voiced in the streets or marketplace.

Yet what was said in the flush of the crowd may well have been jocose, waggish, irreverent. Royal anniversaries, after all, were ready-made occasions for the carnivalesque, for political parody and misrule. In the intoxicating moments of festive revelry, political loyalties always had a tendency to become overcharged, to run to excess, to move to the bottom

---

[106] Monod, *Jacobitism and the English People*, 197, 329; Wilson, *Sense of the People*, 335; SP 35/49/52 (2), SP 35/50/61, SP 36/112/331–3; *Newcastle Courant*, 5 May 1750.

[107] BL, Add. MS 32867, fos. 33, 145–6.

[108] See London prosecutions (1715–16), nos. 36, 52, 127, 128, 145, 167, 175, 176, 179, 204, 217. Add. MJ/SR 2259, gaol calendar no. 54.

[109] Rogers, 'Popular Protest', 86. As his table shows, 89 of 253 cases (35%) involved Jacobite toasts and oaths, or unequivocally Jacobite denunciations of Hanover. For the Oxford circuit, see Monod, *Jacobitism and the English People*, 246–7. Monod's figures do not permit a strict social comparison, for he has divided his cases into the periods 1690–1714 and 1715–52. One suspects, however, that the London pattern holds; that is, that gentlemen and wealthier traders were over-represented in the years 1714–16.

line. The fact that many cases of seditious words were inconclusively prosecuted, that a number were let off with relatively small fines, suggests that contemporaries recognized this.[110] In London, in particular, it is quite conceivable that prosecutors often used the courts to embarrass their political opponents, to temper their zeal with the threat of legal action. All this inevitably complicates one's reading of Jacobitism. How much of it was the product of bitter partisanship between Whig and Tory, which, through prosecuting zeal or festive licence, was translated into a dynastic polarity between Hanover and Stuart? In the end we will probably never know.

What we do know is that the Jacobite rebels failed to muster a sizeable popular following in England despite the seeming ubiquity of disaffection. In the Fifteen, the recruitment in the northern counties was disappointing. In the Forty-Five it was little better. Even in a town as disaffected as Manchester, the rebels could only recruit 200 men out of a population of 30,000. The poor showing in this Jacobite stronghold induced some officers to counsel a retreat to Scotland. As Lord Elcho observed, Prince Charles was deceived by the bells and bonfires.[111]

Those bells and bonfires none the less registered regional political traditions, just as Jacobite oaths, airs, and imprecations were appropriated to other contexts: to register defiance of the law; to protest the intrusive presence of troops, or the predatory actions of Whig grandees in royal forests; to mock the pomposities of Whig rule; even to catch a Whig gentleman with his breeches down.

In view of the salience of the Jacobite repertoire, it is worth considering, finally, what effect it may have had on popular political consciousness. At least one author has interpreted the resilience of the Jacobite idiom as

---

[110] In London (1714–16) only 20% of all cases are known to have gone to trial (of which 60% were found guilty). Others may have, because some were respited to later sessions, but no further record of the cases has been found. In the Oxford circuit and in the Palatine of Lancaster, a third of all cases were inconclusively prosecuted. Of those that were, the conviction rates were lower than for other crimes, averaging 27% for the Oxford circuit and 30% for the Palatine of Lancaster. See Monod, *Jacobitism and the English People*, 247. As for lenient sentences, Anne Savage, a widow, was fined 3s. 4d. for drinking the health of King James and Johannah Hawkins was fined only 12d. for raising a disturbance at the sign of the King's Head in Golden Lane and asking the landlord's wife 'if they [would] Hang his Head there where they would hang his body'. William Crippen was fined 12d. for damning the King and sentenced to several months' hard labour at the Clerkenwell house of correction. John Jonas was fined 12s. for cursing the King and threatening to 'make that Towne smoake'. He was also ordered to be whipped from Westminster Hall gate to Charing Cross. GLRO, WJ/SR 2240 indt. 35; MJ/SR 2248 indt. 53; MJ/SR 2263, unnumbered rec.; MJ/SBB 740/21; MJ/SR 2273 recs. 35–6; MJ/SR 2273 indt. 35.

[111] Frank McLynn, *The Jacobite Army in England, 1745* (Edinburgh, 1983), 98–9.

evidence of the long-term survival of sacred monarchy and an enduring conservatism marked by deference to social superiors.[112] Paradoxically, the converse is true. Jacobite revelry seldom showed much respect for rank. The carnivalesque freedoms of the crowd defined the limits to which people were prepared to be pushed around and signalled even to sympathetic patrons that there were limits to deference. The vilification of George I, moreover, did much to corrode respect for the monarchy. In the banter of the street, George I was nothing more than an uncouth German on the make. He was a 'Turnip man' or turnip-hoer who should be sent packing back to Hanover, a 'turnip dog' who hocus-pocused vast sums of money to Hanover and, according to one shipwright's wife, was responsible for bringing the cattle plague to England. One Middlesex cordwainer simply exclaimed, 'King George, King Turd.'[113]

George was not only criticized for being a bumpkin German unwilling to adapt to English ways but very willing to cash in on his fortuitous succession to the English throne. He was also mocked in the ribald idiom of cuckoldry. Much was made of George's estranged marriage with Sophia Dorothea of Celle, whom he kept under castle arrest at Ahlden for her affair with Count Königsmarck. The King was regularly burnt in effigy with horns on his head, or derided in a mock skimmington ride to the tune of the 'Roundheaded Cuckolds'. In London Restoration-day revellers were known to chant 'make way for the Cuckoldy King and Send him to Hanover'. One ballad described George as a buffoon-like knight who came up to town from Turnipshire, only to discover his wife had committed adultery. 'Upon this, Sir George determined thus, | To padlock up his pretty Puss', so the doggerel ran, only to be cuckolded again by the dashing Sir James King, who had a key to the chastity belt and 'made the Horn to play the Whore'.[114]

If jests were continually made about King George's inability to control his wife, his separation bred rumours not only that she was a whore but that the Prince of Wales was illegitimate, an interesting counterpoint to the Pretender's alleged bastardy. As these rumours circulated they were themselves embellished to provide profane commentaries on the sexual proclivities of the court. In 1715 Leonard Piddock entertained an audience at Ashby de la Zouch by declaring:

---

[112] J. C. D. Clark, *English Society 1688–1832* (Cambridge, 1985), ch. 3.

[113] *Berrow's Worcester Post Man*, 8–15 Aug. 1718; *HMC Stuart MSS*, iv. 275, 303; GLRO, Midd., MJ/SR 2273 rec. 180. For turd (45); turnip king (26); turnip man (163, 205, 208).

[114] PRO, SP 35/24/241. The ballad is entitled 'Sir James King's Key to Sir George Horn's Padlock'; it was probably printed in 1720.

that King George has no more right to the Crown than my arse, that King George has the pox and had pox'd the Court and that the Court had pox'd the prince and princess and that they would pox the nation; that the prince was a shitten dog and run out, and people cry'd how can that be since his coming in was soe very great? but that then the said Mr Leonard Piddock explained himself thus, that the Prince beshitt himself and the Princess every night, and further said that the Prince whored so much that the Princess took him to bed so soon as he had dined; that, when his Nailes were pared he might go where he pleased.[115]

Piddock's embellishments boggled the imagination, but they were not idiosyncratic. In 1716, when one of the princesses gave birth to a stillborn child, London rang with jokes about her 'labour and birth' and 'many reflections' were 'made by the enemies of the government about it'.[116] Two years later, a paper circulated by non-jurors attributed the stillbirth to incest, and suggested that George was irremediably poxed and did not have any legitimate or worthy progeny.[117]

The sexual defamation of kings and their courts was not new, but when it was combined with a rudimentary nationalism that balked at George's unabashed preference for Hanover, it was an intoxicating brew that did much to tarnish the image of monarchy. Of course, committed Jacobites could take solace in a Stuart alternative, but the unswerving Catholicism of the exiled house was an impediment to many. As one Westminster woman, very likely the wife of an artisan, declared in 1716, the Pretender would be the 'lawful heir of ye Crown of England, had he not been a papist'.[118] This explains why Jacobite authors persistently played down James's Catholicism and portrayed him in an idealized fashion as a 'brisk and lordly' British paternalist who would respect the liberties of the people.

In some ways Jacobite writers unwittingly endorsed a libertarian critique of monarchy that squared uneasily with their belief in hereditary right and the illegality of the revolution settlement. Jacobite pamphleteers, after all, advanced the right of resistance to unconstituted authority. They flirted with the idea of elected monarchy on the supposition that James was a preferable alternative for the English people to the Duke of Brunswick, as George was sometimes called. In 1719 one writer disingenuously touted the idea of popular sovereignty in a tract entitled *Vox Populi, Vox Dei*, drawing its inspiration from a radical Whig tract of ten years' standing. At the same time, writers such as Isaac Dalton and Nathaniel Mist highlighted the authoritarian thrust of Hanoverian rule in a manner that

---

[115] PRO, SP 44/117/204–5.   [116] *HMC Stuart MSS*, iii. 272, 275.
[117] Anon., *To a THING they Call the Prince of Wales* (n.p., 1718), 8.
[118] GLRO, WJ/SR 2265 rec. 111.

creditably out-Whigged the Whigs. They were among the first to stress how the Riot and Septennial Acts circumscribed popular activity after two decades of unquestioned political vitality. Mist even penned a constitutional critique of naval impressment, noting its incompatibility with Magna Carta and the Bill of Rights, that would be taken up by radical Whigs later in the century.[119]

Dalton and Mist sailed close to the popular wind. Although their Jacobite libertarianism was a volatile and contradictory ideology, it accorded well with the libertarian instincts of the crowd. It is no accident that they were among the printers most harassed by the ministry. When Dalton stood in the pillory in December 1716 for printing *The Shift Shifted*, one newspaper reported, 'he was so far from being pelted that a Gathering of Money was made for him, and the Standers By gave him repeated Huzzas'. Five years later, Mist was similarly applauded.[120]

As a final indication of how libertarian perspectives could insinuate themselves into Jacobite ideology, one might consider the case of George Cleeve. In 1716, he was committed to the Berkshire assizes for declaring 'the pretender is a true protestant and has been so for three years past and it would be well for the nation if he were king. And King George must have a care what he did otherwise he would lose his head as King Charles had done.'[121] It was an unorthodox thing for a Jacobite to say, not only because it created the fiction that the Pretender was a Protestant, but because it cited the precedent of 1649 in a manner that was Whig rather than Jacobite. Tory-Jacobites normally revered Charles I and solemnly observed his 'martyrdom'. They would not have deployed his execution as a threat to another monarch. That was the sort of thing reserved for the radical Calves Head club. Yet, as we have seen, popular Jacobitism was a protean phenomenon capable of generating subversive meanings and seditious laughter. If other Jacobites would not take Cleeve's cue concerning King George, they might well have applauded the sentiments of a 1722 ballad:

> Put on his bob wig piss burnt with the weather
> And his grog coat in which he came thither
> With his Horns in his head he will look very smart
> And so drive him back in an ould turnip Cart.[122]

---

[119] *Mist's Weekly Journal*, 18 May 1728.
[120] *Norwich Gazette*, 29 Dec.–5 Jan. 1717; Doran, *London*, 353.
[121] PRO, Assi. 4/18/10.   [122] PRO, SP 35/31/270.

2

The Politics of War and Dearth, 1756–1757

On 16 August 1756, 500 men assembled at Wherrybridge, near Walsall, and pulled down a large corn mill belonging to 'a great Engrosser of Corn'.[1] Two days later, Samuel Crosland reported from Tamworth that the Bedworth colliers 'entered this Town about Noon, declaring their intention of pulling down a set of Boulting Mills occupied by Messrs. Englands which they set about directly, destroying the inside of the Mills and taking the Corn and Meal & wasting and destroying more than they carried away'. They later 'returned to this town again', Crosland continued,

and gutted the Quakers Meeting House, and pulled a Part of it down; then they went about the Town from House to House, demanding Money, and threatening, in case of refusal, to plunder and pull down the Houses of the Inhabitants. They collected some money after that manner & quartered themselves in the Town all night, and have not left us . . . There are several Mobs of this Sort up in divers Parts of Warwick & Staffordshire who have done a great deal of damage . . . I hope some Method will be thought of to put a stop to their proceedings, or I fear for the consequences.[2]

Thus began the most serious outbreak of food rioting that eighteenth-century Britain had thus far experienced, beginning in the Midlands and by December 1757 numbering about 140 reported outbreaks in no less than thirty counties.[3]

Bread riots were not the only forms of popular intervention that engrossed the attention of Britons in these two years. In the three weeks preceding the outbreak of violence in the Midlands, crowds had burnt Admiral John Byng in effigy along the south coast and in several northern

---

[1] *Daily Advertiser*, 20 Aug. 1756. [2] BL, Add. MS 32866, fos. 482–3.
[3] See the summary by Jeremy Caple in Andrew Charlesworth (ed.), *An Atlas of Rural Protest in Britain 1548–1900* (London, 1983), 86–8, 111–13.

ports and inland centres, including some that were later to be the scene of extensive food rioting. At the same time the Admiralty was confronting continuing opposition to naval impressment. In June, sixty pressed men on board an Admiralty tender at Harwich had mutinied and engaged in a bloody confrontation with the soldiers of the local garrison. In August, forty whalers seeking protections from the Admiralty resisted a local press gang, stabbing the lieutenant in the thigh and prising out one of his eyes.[4] Two months later, impressed men aboard a tender off Liverpool mutinied and escaped back to port. When two of the deserters were captured, a local mob rescued them, breaking into the watchhouse and carrying one off 'in Triumph'.[5] To these anti-recruitment riots would later be added those pertaining to the militia, which engulfed major parts of the country in the autumn of 1757, including, once again, areas where there had been market riots and attacks upon mills.

The temporal conjunction of these diverse crowd interventions in the opening years of the Seven Years War provide us with a good opportunity to probe the collective protests of the poor in the face of widespread deprivation brought about by poor harvests, the uneven distribution of grain, and military mobilization. Because the crisis of 1756–7 was political as well as social, involving the replacement of a seemingly unassailable ministry by a more popular coalition led by William Pitt, the conjuncture also allows us to chart the manner in which political discourses intersected with those pertaining to food supply and popular entitlements to 'the staff of life'. Such a perspective has seldom been brought to bear on the now extensive literature on bread riots, which has tended to focus, *sui generis*, upon the ongoing struggle between the moral and the market economy and its attendant implications for understanding eighteenth-century power relations, without much reference to notions of patriotism, nationalism, and political partisanship. Here I wish to explore these associations; to address, in particular, whether there were any significant differences within the ranks of the propertied about the legitimacy of popular interventions and their resolution.

In August 1756, when the first food riots broke out in the Midlands, Britain was already at war with France and had suffered a significant setback with the loss of Minorca. In March Admiral John Byng had led an expedition to reconnoitre the Mediterranean and to protect Gibraltar and Minorca

---

[4] *Northampton Mercury*, 9 Aug. 1756; *Whitehall Ev. Post*, 19–22 June 1756.
[5] *Daily Advertiser*, 20 Oct. 1756.

from French incursions. His fleet was small, for the Admiralty had decided to concentrate its ships of the line in home waters to counter an anticipated French invasion; but it proved comparable to the French fleet that Byng encountered off Minorca under the command of the Marquis de la Galissonière. After a confusing and inconclusive battle in which Vice-Admiral West's division bore the brunt of the fighting, Byng retreated to Gibraltar to repair his vessels.[6] His withdrawal cost Britain the island, one strategically important for the protection of her commercial interests in the Mediterranean. It also blighted Britain's naval prestige, which augured badly for war morale.

From the beginning the government attributed the fall of Minorca to Byng's dishonourable actions and abdicated responsibility for it. Before the Admiralty had even received Byng's official dispatch, steps were taken to relieve him of his command. When the dispatch finally did arrive, it was carefully edited to impugn his reputation.[7] By the time the news of the surrender of Minorca broke, Byng's name was a byword for cowardice. Crowds burnt his effigy before his country house in Hertfordshire and at various ports along the south coast. At Southampton Byng's dummy was carried around the town by a mob and hanged from a signpost; at Gravesend, his effigy 'dressed in Blue Grey richly trimmed with Gold', together with bag-wig and sword, was hanged from a jib-boom 40 feet high.[8] In London, Byng's effigy was ceremoniously executed on at least four occasions between early August and mid-September. At Tower Hill, 10,000 people were reported to have watched the effigy-burning, while at Covent Garden the execution was prefaced by a skimmington ride in which the effigy 'was very whimsically exhibited in a Cart, with his back to the Horses', accompanied by chimney sweeps riding donkeys 'with their Faces to the Tails'.[9]

Opposition writers accused the ministry of deliberately fomenting the demonstrations, even to the point of financing the effigies in London.[10]

---

[6] For accounts of the battle, see William Laird Clowes, *The Royal Navy: A History from the Earliest Times to the Present*, 5 vols. (London, 1898), iii. 148–52, and Sir Julian Corbett, *England in the Seven Years' War: A Study in Combined Strategy*, 2 vols. (London, 1918), i. 107–28.

[7] The edited version was published in the *London Gazette*, 26 June 1756. For accessible versions of the whole text, with the omissions italicized, see Clowes, *Royal Navy*, iii. 153–5, and Brian Tunstall, *Admiral Byng and the Loss of Minorca* (London, 1928), 142–8.

[8] *Boddely's Bath Journal*, 2 Aug. 1756.

[9] *Reading Mercury*, 13 Sept. 1756; *Whitehall Ev. Post*, 26–8 Aug. 1756; *Northampton Mercury*, 23 Aug. 1756; *Berrow's Worcester Journal*, 8 July 1756.

[10] *A Collection of Several Pamphlets, Very Little Known, Relative to the Case of Admiral Byng* (London, 1756), 41; *An Appeal to the People, Part I* (London, 1756), 70.

Such a charge is difficult to sustain. It is true that one of the clerks of the Victualling Office was injured by a stage-coach while burning Byng's effigy in Whitechapel, but there is no evidence that the government actively promoted the demonstration.[11] In fact the Admiralty was taken aback by the popular fury against Byng, changing its plans for bringing him to Greenwich for fear he would be torn apart by the hundreds who assembled on the Portsmouth road with pitchforks and clubs in the 'Hopes of paying their Respects'.[12] Certainly the government's selective publication of Byng's dispatch helped fuel the ferment; yet the demonstrations were too general and dispersed to have been carefully co-ordinated and were by no means concentrated in areas where ministerial interests were paramount.

Some of the anti-Byng demonstrations were certainly orchestrated from above. At Southampton it was reported that the effigy-hanging had been sponsored by 'Persons of the best rank'. At Stokesley in the North Riding of Yorkshire, the anti-Byng skimmington was organized by a club of local gentlemen; in North Shields by master mariners.[13] Yet mock executions of Byng undoubtedly had a broad appeal, striking a chord with the bellicose public who had previously supported Admiral Vernon. Not only was Byng unfavourably compared to the hero of Porto Bello in prose and verse, but towns that had enthusiastically commemorated Vernon's triumphs were equally condemnatory of Byng, including Bristol, Birmingham, Leeds, York, and Worcester. At Worcester, Byng's effigy was hung on one of the booths at the local races, where a 'vast Number of People . . . paid their *due Respects* to it with Sticks, Stones &c'.[14] At York, Byng's symbolic execution took place on the birthday of General Blakeney, the commander of Minorca who had honourably surrendered to the French after Byng's retreat. A party of chimney sweeps opened the procession, carrying four black streamers and two flags with the words 'Poltroon' and 'Cowardice unparalleled' upon them. They also paraded a broken admiral's staff and a wooden sword to underscore Byng's singular lack of heroism. The procession was closed by the mob, with hawkers crying 'the last dying Words and Confessions' of the infamous admiral, whose effigy was hoisted from the gallows and consumed in flames, To complete Byng's disgrace, the ashes were dumped in a slaughter-house.[15]

Byng's retreat drew patriotic rancour. It also raised the hackles of those who suffered the dislocations of war. At Exeter and Devizes, towns

---

[11] *An Appeal to the People, Part I*, 70.   [12] *Berrow's Worcester Journal*, 12 Aug. 1756.
[13] *Newcastle Courant*, 11 Sept. 1756; *Salisbury Journal*, 2 Aug. 1756; *Berrow's Worcester Journal*, 5 Aug. 1756.
[14] *Berrow's Worcester Journal*, 5 Aug. 1756.   [15] *York Courant*, 14 Sept. 1756.

dependent upon Spanish wool and dyes for their textile industry, Byng
was execrated as a coward and a traitor.[16] Similarly in East Anglia, where
the worsted industry was disrupted by the loss of Minorca, the 'poor people' denounced Byng 'with bitter imprecations . . . looking on him as the
author of their Misfortunes'.[17] In Cornwall, the Minorca crisis resulted in
the immediate layoff of 10,000 tinners, who expressed their anger by hanging Byng on alehouse and pawnbrokers' signs. At Falmouth, Byng's effigy
was tied to a donkey's tail and dragged around the common before 15,000
spectators. Upon its chest, the dummy wore the motto 'The Friend of
Monsieur Ragout and the Tinners' Scourge'. A few days later, another
effigy of the admiral was paraded around the town by a 'Multitude of
Seamen', this time with the inscription 'THE BRITISH NAVY'S SCORN'.[18]

As this last example reveals, Byng's conduct was perceived as an affront
to naval and national honour, sharpened no doubt by the vigorous impressment that had accompanied the mobilization of the fleets. Since early 1755
the Admiralty had issued press warrants to man the fleet, extending its
reach to the northern ports and even to some inland towns. In the process
it had encountered considerable resistance, particularly from the eastern
and north-eastern ports, where seamen systematically evaded the gangs and
occasionally, as at Bo'ness, threatened to sweep them out of the area.[19] Not
surprisingly, a number of anti-Byng protests emanated from ports where
impressment had been a vexatious issue, such as Newcastle, and can be
readily interpreted as impassioned outbursts against upper-class timidity
when other lives had been so unceremoniously put on the line. As one newspaper noted,[20] the problem of impressment could only be aggravated by
the admiral's 'ignominious Conduct', an ignominy that was constantly
exposed in ballad and couplet. Byng was the professional seaman who, when
'the Engagement was hot . . . wisely kept out of the reach of the shot'; an
'ADMIRABLE admiral', one scornfully noted, who fudged his account of the
battle to save his neck. 'If you believe what *Frenchmen* say,' ran one mocking verse,[21]

> B—— came, was beat, and ran away.
> Believe what B—— *himself* hath said,
> He fought, He conquered, and He fled.

---

[16] *Salisbury Journal*, 16, 23 Aug. 1756.
[17] *Schofield's Middlewich Journal*, 4–11 Jan. 1757.
[18] *London Ev. Post*, 12–14 Aug. 1756.   [19] See next chapter.
[20] *Reading Mercury*, 7 Mar. 1757.
[21] *Berrow's Worcester Journal*, 8 July 1756; *Northampton Mercury*, 2 Aug. 1756.

Although these gibes were unfair to Byng, who was ultimately acquitted of personal cowardice, the stigma of dishonour indelibly stained his conduct. Rumours circulated that his lower deck resented his inactivity in Minorcan waters and had threatened to string him up if he avoided another engagement with the French.[22] Captains openly impugned his conduct, commending those officers who had broken the line to assist Temple West's division. Many openly asserted that Byng might have saved Minorca had he energetically borne down upon the enemy. Even when Byng's culpability was mitigated by the revelation that the government had tinkered with his dispatch to evade its own responsibility for Minorca, few were prepared to exonerate him of all blame. Byng was indelibly cast as a craven naval officer, a man who lacked personal valour and public virtue. Indeed, because it was thought that he owed his promotion to the connections of his father, the prestigious naval commander Sir George Byng (later Viscount Torrington), John Byng was sometimes depicted as a ruling-class scion whose cosmopolitan manners better equipped him for the salon than the upper deck. 'We cannot expect that the hero, who dotes on his lap dog, lolls at ease on his soft couch, and is supported by a court interest,' wrote one writer, 'will risque the hazard of a broadside, much less sail in quest of the enemy.'[23] To underscore the point, demonstrators at Richmond in Yorkshire decked out their effigy of Byng in a 'genteel Navy Dress, *a la Mode de* France'. At Market Harborough, Byng's effigy lolled on a cushion, his wooden sword 'pointing downwards'.[24]

Byng thus served as a butt for the libertarian, chauvinist, and populist sympathies of the public and also as a commentary on the class-bound predicaments of war. Notwithstanding the widespread belief that Byng was to some degree the victim of political artifice, there was a strong demand that the admiral should pay for his misconduct, and a corresponding fear that his rank and influence might shield him from justice and undermine respect for the rule of law. As 'Britannicus' reminded his readers:

Justice ought always to take a fast and impartial Hold of every Offender, and not, like a Cobweb, catch only small Flies, and be broken by great Ones. To take away the Life of the Poor, who break the Laws for Want of Bread, and to suffer great Traitors to truck away a Nation's Territories, and plunder the Publick of Millions with Impunity, is great and manifest Injustice . . . Justice on great and national

---

[22] *Ipswich Journal*, 31 July 1756; *Reading Mercury*, 23 Aug. 1756.
[23] *Monitor*, 12 Mar. 1757, reprinted in the *Salisbury Journal*, 21 Mar. 1757.
[24] *Derby Mercury*, 3–10 Sept. 1756; *Newcastle Journal*, 14–21 Aug. 1756.

Offenders should ever be executed speedily; for deferring it in such Cases always did, in every Kingdom, raise Discontent.[25]

How far these considerations weighed in the decision to execute Byng is difficult to assess. Voltaire believed that Byng was shot on his own quarter-deck 'pour encourager les autres'; in other words, to boost or stiffen naval officer morale.[26] But Thomas Turner thought that Byng was executed to placate 'a clamorous and enraged populace'.[27] This is entirely conceivable, for amid widespread rioting and a lively debate about the need for a regen-erative patriotism to defeat the French, broader issues of public policy inevitably came into play. Without doubt the issues of law, justice, and public welfare helped frame the response to the popular grievances that grew out of the social dislocations of war and scarcity.

The food riots of 1756–7 were unprecedented in a number of respects. To begin with, there were more than three times as many riots in these years as there had been in 1740–1. Those riots had been largely concen-trated in the ports and East Anglia and were principally directed against the transportation and export of corn. The disturbances of 1756–7 were more diverse, involving marketplace interventions to fix the price of corn as well as attacks upon millers and dealers. They were also geographically more extensive, encompassing some of the more densely populated areas of the North, the Midlands, and the West Country. As in 1740–1, they frequently involved well-organized groups of workers with strong tradi-tions of industrial action: tinners, weavers, nailers, and especially colliers. These tough, sooty workers 'all act in League', one anonymous corres-pondent informed the fourth Earl of Holdernesse, '& would stand by one another throughout the Kingdom, & are desperate Fellows'.[28]

The immediate response of the magistrates and country gentlemen to the food riots seems to have been one of panic. There was little sense of any measured strategy of rule on the part of local officialdom. When Justice Willes reached Warwick on his Midland circuit in the summer of 1756, he 'found everyone there in the greatest consternation' concerning the activ-ities of the roving band of colliers who had been sacking mills and Quaker

[25] *Reading·Mercury*, 6 Sept. 1756.

[26] Voltaire, *Candide, ou L'Optimisme*, ch. 23. One newspaper thought that a merciful reprieve of Byng would 'benumb the very Sinews of our Fleets'. See *Schofield's Middlewich Journal*, 1–8 Mar. 1757.

[27] *The Diary of Thomas Turner 1754–1765*, ed. David Vaisey (Oxford, 1984), 93.

[28] PRO, SP 36/135/283–8.

meeting-houses in the vicinity.[29] The sheriff and JPs, he reported, 'seemed greatly intimidated (The Proclamation [i.e. Riot Act] having been read without any Effect)' and it was only by the ruthless expedient of hanging two rioters under the Riot Act and holding two others as hostages to fortune that any semblance of order was restored.[30]

The same was true elsewhere. At Sheffield, where a mob broke into the storehouse of a local corn factor and forced the local constables to take refuge in the church, the 'much affrighted' gentlemen of the town had to appeal to the Marquis of Rockingham to restore order, which he did by bribing the mob and raising a posse of master cutlers to contain it.[31] In Wellington, Shropshire, where 'a large number of Colliers' visited local markets to force dealers to disclose their wares and to sell at a just price, the neighbouring magistrates and gentlemen were paralysed until two well-known squires and the local MP organized their tenants and local farmers into two large posses of 2,500 men.[32] At Nottingham, the local mayor and hosier, Samuel Fellows, had rather more resolve, having arrested several Woolaton colliers who had entered the town intent upon destroying several mills; but he was forced to release them for fear that 'the Town Hall would be pulled down over our Heads'.[33] Three days later he lamented that the rioters had 'gone on from place to place and done damage to Ten Corn Mills in and about this Town'. Only with the appearance of troops was Fellows again prepared to intervene, and then with difficulty, for the justice who endorsed his warrant had 'fled for Fear of the Colliers' and there was 'scarce a Constable' who was prepared to execute it.[34] In the event he was able to arrest seven rioters, including four who had behaved 'with great Insolence' towards him, having dared 'to nose me', he told the Duke of Newcastle, 'with the Name of their Noble Lord'. Yet he was only able to keep them with a conspicuous parade of military force and a tense stand-off with the colliers, a situation that hardly boded well for the peace of the neighbourhood or his own credibility.[35]

The prospect of roving bands of miners ransacking mills and threatening magistrates who attempted to restrain them was deeply troubling to the authorities, and further troops were moved into the Midlands from the south. The situation was further aggravated by the outbreak of food

---

[29] The attack upon Quaker meeting-houses does not appear to have been prompted by religious considerations. As newspapers noted, the meeting-houses were singled out because leading members of their congregations were known to be corn dealers.

[30] BL, Add. MS 32867, fos. 8–11.   [31] *Northampton Mercury*, 6 Sept. 1756.

[32] *Nottingham Mercury*, 22 Nov. 1756.   [33] PRO, SP 36/135/256–7.

[34] PRO, SP 36/135/299.   [35] PRO, SP 36/135/299, 305.

riots in the West Country and by the onset of a major strike along the Stroudwater by weavers who sought to resist wage cuts by invoking the regulatory machinery of a very recent Act governing the trade. With as many as 25,000 weavers out of work in the Gloucestershire woollen industry, the autumn of 1756 threatened to be a very explosive one, especially as there were signs that the struggle might spread into Wiltshire and Somerset. By the end of November 5,000–6,000 troops were stationed in the disaffected areas.[36] This state of affairs was viewed with considerable concern by the government, not only because it feared that news of widespread rioting would come to the attention of the French, but because of the considerable redeployment of troops who might otherwise have contributed to the war effort. The predicament called for alternative strategies to deal with public order.

Magistrates often sought to emphasize the destructive nature of food riots, particularly when they were anxious to solicit troops from the government, and they were quick to highlight any 'levelling' or retributive dispositions on the part of the crowd. Market looting certainly occurred in the riots of 1756 and 1757, and, in the early outbreaks especially, roving colliers extorted food, drink, and sometimes money from farmers, dealers, and local gentlemen, doubtless accompanying these demands with threats and insults. These actions fuelled an underlying fear that the riots would escalate into something more portentous.

Yet it would be unwise to exaggerate the anarchy of the disturbances. Beyond the looting and the attacks upon mills and houses, there was a logic to the crowds' interventions, which was to ensure that local supplies of grain were brought to market. Crowds were not persuaded that the escalating prices of 1756, which reached 6s. 8d. a bushel in mid-August, rising to over 8s. in a matter of months, were simply the product of harvest failure. A wet summer had certainly produced a poor crop in some areas, but not everywhere. Lord Rockingham could report from Yorkshire that fine weather had pulled down prices and placated consumers. The price of oatmeal at Newcastle had by early September fallen by a third. Good harvests were also reported in Oxfordshire, Wiltshire, and Gloucestershire, despite the fact that rioting would occur in all these counties before the crisis was over.[37] What prompted the common people into action was market speculation. In Coventry the Bedworth colliers complained to the

[36] Tony Hayter, *The Army and the Crowd in Mid-Georgian England* (Totowa, NJ, 1978), 87. For troop movements, see table 7.1.

[37] Jeremy N. Caple, 'Popular Protest and Public Order in Eighteenth-Century England: The Food Riots of 1756–7', MA thesis (Queen's Univ., Ontario, 1978), 26; *Northampton Mercury*, 20 Sept. 1756; BL, Egerton MS 3436, fos. 93–4.

mayor that 'the Farmers would sell them Nothing in the Villages on reasonable Terms, & that Corn & cheese had been engrossed & sent abroad, & even the Crops bargained for on the ground'. Such sentiments were general enough to reach the ears of the Secretary of State, the Earl of Holdernesse, for he opened discreet inquiries to determine whether there was any truth to the crowd's accusation that dealers were exploiting harvest failure to their own advantage.[38]

Market speculation was certainly more possible in 1756 than it had been at the beginning of the century; at least it was certainly harder to regulate and control. The century had witnessed the development of a national and international market in grain, encouraged by the bounty of 1689 which shored up prices for farmers (and by extension rents for landlords) in years of bumper harvests. By 1750, English merchants were exporting approximately a million quarters of grain a year, the bulk of the barley, malt, and rye going to the Dutch ports, the bulk of the wheat to the Iberian and Mediterranean.[39] Both the domestic and foreign grain trade was increasingly dominated by a narrow group of merchant factors and dealers; in the case of the domestic market, from the corn exchange at Mark Lane, London. Within the country as a whole, selling by sample, that is, on a wholesale basis, became typical, although the poor still had access to small quantities of grain at the 'pitched' markets and from miller-dealers.[40] Such a system made economic specialization possible and ensured that industrial areas of the country were supplied with grain, although massive grain exports probably raised the price of domestic grain, especially wheat, by approximately 20 per cent.[41] Since the regulatory machinery for controlling grain speculation, most notably the Edwardine statutes against forestalling, engrossing, and regrating,[42] was only intermittently enforced, the country was highly vulnerable to sharp practice in time of dearth. Such

---

[38] BL, Egerton MS 3436, fo. 91; PRO, SP 36/135/283–4.

[39] On grain exports, see J. A. Chartres, 'The Marketing of Agricultural Produce', in Joan Thirsk (ed.), *The Agrarian History of England and Wales*, v. ii (Cambridge, 1985), 450–1, and David Ormrod, *English Grain Exports and the Structure of Agrarian Capitalism 1700–1760*, Occasional Papers in Economic and Social History 12 (Hull, 1985), 25–6.

[40] A 'pitched' market represented an intermediary stage between the traditional open market and the full sample market. At such a market the bulk of grain was delivered to local granaries or inns, but some sacks were 'pitched' at the open market so that poor consumers could buy small quantities of grain. See Chartres, 'Marketing of Agricultural Produce', 472 n.

[41] Ibid. 500.

[42] 5 & 6 Edw. VI c. 6. Forestalling was holding back supplies of grain in order to enhance the price; engrossing was buying up corn in bulk in order to sell again; regrating was buying up corn at the marketplace and reselling the same within 4 miles of that market or fair. The laws were designed to enforce open dealing, to inhibit wholesale, and to ensure consumer accessibility to grain at the open market. Subsequent Acts such as 5 Eliz. I c. 12 and 13 Eliz. I c. 25 allowed for wholesale dealing and distribution under licence.

jobbery could not only drive up the price of grain, it could also affect the size, price, and quality of bread that was officially regulated under the local assize. In 1756–7 adulteration was a particular concern, because the wet weather had produced soggy flour that would neither leaven nor whiten without a good supply of alum.[43]

In the early months of rioting, the targets of the crowd were principally unpopular dealers and millers who were suspected of withholding grain from the market or adulterating flour with inferior or noxious materials. By early November, however, colliers in Shropshire began assembling in local markets and fixing prices themselves. At Much Wenlock a band of miners, 'join'd by a few Watermen and other Labourers', obliged the sellers to sell wheat at 5s. a bushel, barley at 2s. 6d., and oats at 2s. 2d., with 'other necessaries of Life' being proportionately reduced as well. Similar tactics were employed at other Shropshire towns. The same was true of Taunton, where a mob of 'poor people' broke into a local mill, and 'finding near fifty sacks of Wheat and Flour, carried it all upon Corn-Hill, sold the Wheat at 4s. a bushel and the Flour at One Penny per Pound'.[44] This kind of market intervention was not unprecedented. There had been a few incidents of price-fixing in 1740 and again in Somerset in 1753.[45] But the prospect of crowds taking the law into their own hands and acting as magisterial surrogates in the distribution of food was a clear signal that a more constructive response to dearth had to be forthcoming if social order was to be restored.

In a few areas such a response had already taken place. In Worcester and Manchester the laws against hoarding and market abuse had been implemented before the rioting began. At Coventry, where the Bedworth colliers had threatened to fix the price of grain if the farmers did not bring it to market, the mayor, John Hewitt, promptly posted the laws against forestalling and engrossing and enjoined the farmers to comply; although in the interests of social order rather than out of sympathy with the rioters.[46] Such actions became more general after 25 November when the government issued a royal proclamation to enforce the Edwardine statutes. They were soon supplemented by various kinds of voluntary schemes to provide cheaper food for the poor. A number of towns organized public subscriptions

[43] H. Jackson, *An Essay on Bread* (London, 1758), 12–13.

[44] *Manchester Mercury*, 16–23, 23–30 Nov. 1756.

[45] See Charlesworth (ed.), *An Atlas of Rural Protest*, 84, map 22, and BL, Add. MS 32731, fo. 446.

[46] [John Hewitt], *A Journal of the Proceedings of J. Hewitt, Coventry* (London, 1779), 3–16; Caple, 'Popular Protest', 65; SP 36/135/283–4; *Northampton Mercury*, 13 Sept. 1756.

to buy grain so that inhabitants could obtain food below the market rate. At Tring in Hertfordshire a fund was raised to supply the poor with bread three times a week until Mayday.[47] At Gateshead, the authorities made a special effort to relieve the families of impressed seamen.[48] In the country-side gentlemen provided bumper dinners for the poor, or encouraged their tenant farmers to bring their corn to market to sell on reasonable terms. Sir Thomas Whitmore, who was deeply disturbed by the riots in Shropshire, reported to the Earl of Holdernesse that he had ordered his tenants to 'take each of them some Corn to the Market on Saturday as the only means I can think of to prevent greater Outrages, till the government can give orders in the Matter'. According to the newspapers, he promised his co-operative tenants a rebate from their rents.[49]

These were face-saving strategies, designed to reaffirm paternalist authority as much as to address the grievances of the poor. Once parliament met in December 1756, they were accompanied by a series of other Acts intended to bring an explosive situation under firmer control. In early December the Privy Council had issued a temporary embargo on the export of grain and this was given statutory effect within a matter of weeks. In the following months, while food rioting continued, further Acts were implemented to consolidate and improve upon the existing domestic stock of grain. Despite protests from the merchants and maltsters of East Anglia, the distillation of spirituous liquors was temporarily suspended. Grain was also allowed into the country duty free, and the American colonies were ordered to send their wheat only to Britain and its colonies.

The emergency measures passed in the winter and early spring of 1757 prompted a vigorous debate that extended beyond the parliamentary élite. The towns that had borne the brunt of the rioting in 1756 and early 1757 were especially active, presenting their views to parliament in the form of petitions or instructions to their members. Some of these views simply echoed the policy recommendations of the parliamentarians. The Bristol and Gloucester corporations, for example, whose supplies of corn had been cut off by blockages along the rivers Wye and Severn, recommended the prohibition of grain in the distillery industry.[50] Along with other towns, they also pressed for the free importation of grain and a uniform set of weights and measures throughout the country so that the assize of bread could be effectively regulated in the interests of the consumer. Several towns, however, went further. Blaming the dealers for the food shortages, they

[47] *Daily Advertiser*, 24 Jan. 1757.   [48] *Manchester Mercury*, 8–15 Feb. 1757.
[49] *Daily Advertiser*, 18 Nov. 1756.   [50] *JHC* 27 (1754–7), 652, 662.

demanded a tightening of the moral economy: a revision of the laws against hoarding so that engrossers could be more effectively prosecuted; a banning of bolting mills which facilitated the adulteration of flour; and in the case of Stafford, a demand that middlemen sell their grain in the open market rather than by sample.[51]

The towns that petitioned parliament in the early months of 1757 also expressed the view that the middlemen's quest for profit undermined British manufacture. The town of Tamworth, for example, urged that the 'industrious manufacturer' be provided with a modest subsistence so 'that he may afford his Labour at a low price in order that we may be able to sell our manufactures at foreign Markets, at least as cheap as our Rivals and implacable enemies, the French'.[52] This particular complaint was not new. It had been voiced earlier in the decade by Charles Townshend in one of the first open attacks upon the export bounty upon grain. But it was of particular relevance in 1756 to towns whose industries were facing wartime dislocations and heavy competition from the French.

The urban petitions of 1757, however, were by no means unique in their condemnation of the dealers. Such accusations touched a raw nerve, especially with the Tory-radical press. In the bulk of pamphlets and newspaper commentaries, it was the middlemen who were held responsible for what was seen as an 'artificial scarcity'. Their selfish pursuit of profit was viewed as both un-Christian and unpatriotic. They were described as 'Men of Blood', 'Cannibals', 'inhuman Harpies', 'murderers of the Poor', 'Corn-Conspirators' who were starving their 'fellow-citizens' and preventing them from becoming 'useful members of the Community by adding Strength to the State'.[53] No one condoned the rioters' destruction of private property, but some did think that the authorities should be as assiduous in prosecuting the middlemen whose 'combinations' had aggravated rather than relieved food shortages.[54] Relatively few felt that private property should be unconditionally free of state and social responsibilities, especially in the wartime predicament of 1756–7. In the language of patriotic discourse, dealers were routinely described as 'Stockjobbers of Bread'.[55] Like some

[51] *JHC* 27 (1754–7), 656.

[52] Ibid. 665. See also the petition of Newcastle under Lyme, ibid. 639.

[53] *London Ev. Post*, 15–17 Feb., 1–3 Sept. 1757; *Artificial Dearth, or the Iniquity and Danger of Withholding Corn* (London, 1756), 4, 21; Edward Chandler, *A Charge Delivered to the Grand Jury at the Quarter Sessions Held at Durham . . . 16 July 1740* (London, 1756), pp. vi–vii. Chandler's forthright attack upon middlemen in 1740 was reprinted in 1756 at 4*d*. a copy, or 3*s*. 6*d*. a dozen.

[54] *Bath Journal*, 7 Feb. 1757.

[55] Eusebius Silvester, *The Causes of the Present High Price of Corn and Grain* (London, 1757), 16. See also *London Ev. Post*, 3–5 Jan. 1758, where they are described as 'monied men'

politicians and admirals, they were selling the nation short in its time of need: undermining its manufacture; starving its potential soldiers and sailors; promoting public disorder; and even, some thought, selling British grain to the enemy. As one correspondent to the Secretary of State reported from Ross-on-Wye, where barges bound for Bristol had been detained, there was a 'General Opinion prevailing that a great part of the Grain carried down the River was to be put on Board Dutch Ships for the service of the French'. Similar rumours circulated in Warwickshire.[56]

The emergency measures that parliament passed in the opening months of 1757 proved insufficient to contain the crisis. Some grain was exported after the temporary embargo in early December 1756, and although the customs eventually brought these exports to a halt, bread prices remained high. In fact, they continued to rise despite the influx of corn from southern Europe and the Baltic, with wheat reaching as much as 15*s.* a bushel in Sherborne, twice the price that it fetched at Mark Lane in London.[57] In April a report from Cumberland noted that a widow and her two children had starved to death, the children having been discovered with 'Straw in their Mouths'. 'The Cry of Dearth begins to be heard throughout the Land', remarked the *Centinel*, and wondered why the government had not taken further measures to secure a sufficient food supply; a matter that it believed to be of 'more Importance to the Publick than all our foreign Connections'.[58] Three months later, the Warminster clothier George Wansey reflected that the year had been one 'of want and affliction to many by the dearness and scarcity of provisions' and feared that many had 'perished for want or suffered extreme distress'.[59] In the context of regional variations in the price of provisions, higher expectations of relief, and persistent rumours of hoarding, it was predictable that riots would continue.

---

who abused the public by creating monopolies of essential supplies. For demands that private interests be subordinated to national, see *London Ev. Post*, 16–18 Oct. 1756. For arguments supporting the middlemen, especially in supplying areas of the country that were not self-sufficient in grain, see *Newcastle Journal*, 19–26 Feb. 1757 and [Charles Smith], *A Short Essay on the Corn Trade* (London, 1758), 15–16.

[56] PRO, SP 36/135/238–9, 36/137/84. See also the letter from Kidderminster published in *Derby Mercury*, 10–17 Dec. 1756.

[57] *Northampton Mercury*, 9 May 1757. On grain exports, see BL, Add. MS 38387, fos. 45–6. These figures show that whereas 101,936 quarters of wheat was exported from Christmas 1755 to Christmas 1756, 11,226 quarters (roughly 11% of the 1755–6 total) was exported in the following year, most of it presumably in early 1757.

[58] Cited in *London Ev. Post*, 28–30 Apr. 1757, and *Berrow's Worcester Journal*, 5 May 1757. For the Cumberland report, see *Salisbury Journal*, 18 Apr. 1757.

[59] Julia de Lacy Mann (ed.), *Documents Illustrating the Wiltshire Textile Trades in the Eighteenth Century*, Wiltshire Arch. and Nat. History Society 19 (1963; Devizes, 1964), 39.

Indeed, despite the emergency legislation, rioting actually increased, spreading southwards to Dorset, Devon, Sussex, and Hampshire, and eastwards to Cambridgeshire and Norfolk, where villagers north-east of Norwich seized twenty-four sacks of grain bound for Yarmouth. Attacks on mills continued, especially at Frome, where colliers levelled one mill and were only repulsed at another by gunfire.[60] Yet what was noteworthy about the riots of April to June was the high number of blockages and market interventions. Local populations, exasperated by high prices and fearful of local shortages, stopped wagons and barges. At Market Lavington, women prevented a consignment of wheat from travelling to Melksham. At Hereford, the poor seized a wagon load of wheat bound for Bristol, opened the sacks, and emptied them in the marketplace for the benefit of local consumers.[61] A similar occurrence took place at Worcester, where a 'great number of persons, chiefly Women' assembled at the corn market, 'and after a stout Engagement with the Farmers, ripped open several Bags, and carried off the wheat in their Hats, Aprons and Petticoats'.[62] These interventions were accompanied by attacks upon dealers and farmers, leading to violent confrontations at Nuneaton, Hereford, and Cambridge in which several rioters were killed or wounded.[63] Renewed efforts were also made to fix the price of corn. At Bewdley, Sherborne, Yeovil, and Exeter, farmers were forced to sell at below the market rate, in the last instance by the wives of the weavers and woolcombers of St Sidwell's.[64] In situations where troops were absent and the local authorities laggard, rioters sometimes took advantage of the proclamation against hoarding to take the law into their own hands. Thus at Gloucester, where an information had been lodged against a dealer for selling by sample, the 'tumultuous Populace' confiscated his load of grain 'without waiting the Resolution of the Magistrate, and carried it off in spite of all Endeavours to prevent them'.[65]

There were no disturbances in July and August, as a better harvest was anticipated. But rioting resumed in September amid continuing complaints that dealers were speculating on regional scarcities. Mills were attacked, millers and middlemen threatened, and the final months of 1757 saw a further spate of price-fixing by angry crowds. At least ten such incidents were reported in the press. In these circumstances there were demands for further action. 'As the Meeting of Parliament is now approaching near,' wrote 'Britannicus' in the *London Evening Post*, 'we will suppose that the wicked Combination of the Engrossers and Retainers of Corn, who, in spite of

[60] *Derby Mercury*, 3–10 June 1757.
[62] *Derby Mercury*, 13–20 May 1757.
[64] *London Ev. Post*, 23–6 Apr. 1757.
[61] *Northampton Mercury*, 9 May 1757.
[63] *Northampton Mercury*, 6, 13, 27 June 1757.
[65] *Manchester Mercury*, 3–10 May 1757.

Plenty, would starve the Poor, will soon be crushed.'[66] At Liverpool, where a large posse had been assembled to deal with a roving mob of colliers from Prescot market, merchants and burgesses instructed their MPs to demand further regulatory controls upon dealers and the baking of bread. 'The oppression with respect to the high price of Corn', the address insisted, was 'a National Affair' that demanded redress.[67] At Warwick, too, where high prices were attributed to the 'illegal Exportation of Corn', and to the 'mercenary Combinations of Farmers, Corn-factors, Millers and Meal-Men', the mayor, aldermen, and 'other constituents' recommended that the exportation of wheat should be prohibited once the price of wheat reached 5s. a bushel (40s. a quarter), at which time foreign wheat should be allowed into the country duty free. The instructions further recommended that all grain be sold by a standard Winchester measure, that selling by sample be abolished, that 'Collusions in Bargain-making for Corn' be unlawful, that millers should not deal in grain, that dressing mills be destroyed as they were too frequently used to adulterate bread. 'Avaricious Cannibals' had sought to 'devour the Poor', the address claimed, 'imposing their killing Powders for nourishing Wheat Meal'.[68]

The Warwick proposals were not idiosyncratic. Similar arguments had been advanced in the press throughout the year, including a much-publicized proposal to compel farmers and dealers to bring corn to the open market when the price of wheat reached 5 or 6s. a bushel.[69] Together they represented a signal challenge to the prevailing pattern of marketing and distributing grain, a demand for a moral economy of provision that went beyond the old Tudor statutes and arguably restricted the discretionary powers of the magistracy to determine what constituted anti-social hoarding.

The immediate target of the reformers was the Commons select committee formed in December 1756 to consider means to prevent the high price of provisions. It was this large committee, representative of all shades of opinion in the House, that had moved many of the emergency measures put into effect in March 1757. In December 1757, at the time of the Liverpool and Warwick instructions, this committee was expected to bring in further recommendations. But it delayed doing so until February of the following year, when the food crisis had ebbed.

---

[66] *London Ev. Post*, 19–22 Nov. 1757.

[67] *London Ev. Post*, 8–10 Dec. 1757. See also *Northampton Mercury*, 19 Dec. 1757. The Liverpool merchants also petitioned parliament for regulatory controls. See *JHC* 28 (1757–61), 6.

[68] *London Ev. Post*, 17–20 Dec. 1757.

[69] Ibid. 10–12 Feb., 15–17 Sept., 24–6 Nov. 1757; *Derby Mercury*, 16–23 Sept. 1757; *Northampton Mercury*, 26 Sept. 1757; *Berrow's Worcester Journal*, 22 Sept. 1757.

When the recommendations came down they proved to be significantly more modest than those proposed or anticipated in the press. The committee did suggest a uniform set of weights and measures for grain. It also recommended duty-free imports of grain once London prices had reached an unspecified price for three weeks. But neither of these resolutions passed the House.[70] A relatively innocuous proposal to revise the Bounty Act of 1689 did pass, but it never reached the statute book. The other resolution that passed was a telling one. In the committee's opinion, the 'Violences committed by Mobs in many Parts of this Kingdom' were themselves partly responsible for the high price of corn, preventing its proper circulation and distribution. No corresponding indictment of the middlemen was forthcoming.

In the end, then, parliament chose to vindicate the existing structure of marketing grain that had proved such a tonic to agrarian capitalism. No revision of the laws pertaining to wholesaling occurred, nor of those concerning the import and export of grain beyond those set down in 1689. During the dearth of 1756–7, parliament chose to handle the crisis by instituting a series of emergency measures to regulate the domestic and international supply of corn and by encouraging local authorities to use the old laws against hoarding to restrain flagrant cases of speculation. Some dealers were taken to court, usually to placate angry crowds. On balance, the statutes against forestalling, engrossing, and regrating proved inadequate to counter food shortages. As sympathizers of the poor persistently claimed, the laws themselves were difficult to enforce and dealers were adept at evading them.[71] More successful were the voluntary efforts to provide cheaper grain by public subscription. Yet even here, as the experience of Liverpool, Manchester, and Gloucester revealed, charitable gestures of this kind sometimes provided only a temporary respite from market interventions and recriminations by the populace. Confrontations between local authorities and the crowd were frequent, and in the absence of troops, armed posses of landlords and farmers were the order of the day. At least twenty people were killed in the food riots of these years, including five at Manchester where a large crowd of colliers and weavers had demanded a reduction in the price of oatmeal and potatoes from the high sheriff and were only restrained by gunfire.[72] Over 200 were charged with rioting, of

[70] *JHC* 28 (1757–61), 74.
[71] See, for example, *Berrow's Worcester Journal*, 25 Aug. 1757; *London Ev. Post*, 6–8 Oct. 1757; James Manning, *The Nature of Bread* (London, 1757), 44.
[72] *Northampton Mercury*, 21 Nov. 1757; *Derby Mercury*, 18–25 Nov. 1757; Alfred P. Wadsworth and Julia De Lacy Mann, *The Cotton Trade and Industrial Lancashire 1600–1780* (Manchester, 1965), 360.

which 93 were convicted.[73] Only four rioters were eventually hanged, although it took good character references and mitigating circumstances to obtain a reprieve for some of the others. In the case of three rioters, probably colliers from the Forest of Dean, who had been indicted at the Gloucester assizes for stealing corn from a barge at Lydbrook on the river Wye, it was claimed that they had 'as good characters as to Honesty and Peaceable Behaviour as Men of their Rank can have'. They had not taken the corn out of any felonious intent, a further petition claimed; rather, they 'mistakenly' thought they had a right to it 'as being ingrossed or Forestalled'.[74] This was eventually enough to secure them a reprieve, and to have their sentences reduced to seven years' transportation. How they responded to this judicial mercy we do not know. In the end they received the same sentence as three fellow rioters at the Hereford assizes. There is no evidence that they personally grovelled to the authorities for a 'crime' that commanded widespread assent.

Nor, indeed, did Peter Bettely alias Foster, one of the last rioters hanged during the disturbances, in his case for pulling down a mill. At the Chester gallows his behaviour was described as 'very obstinate', and neither the Methodist preacher who accompanied him in the cart, nor the Anglican minister who 'interrogated' him about an associated case of arson, could bring him to repentance or get him to squeal. He refused to answer his worship's questions, and 'died in silence, having made his peace with God'.[75]

As the country braced itself for the final round of food riots in 1757, reports came in of disturbances from another quarter. Throughout the eastern counties, from Norfolk to Yorkshire, and on into the Midlands and the West Country, labourers, colliers, weavers, and a few tenant farmers openly resisted the Militia Act. The Act was the pet project of the patriot programme. It had been vigorously promoted by the Opposition as a necessary response to the Minorca crisis in town and country instructions to MPs. A national militia was viewed as an appropriate answer to a French invasion, arguably better than the volunteer regiments that had been formed during the Forty-Five, and a useful complement, if not counterpoint, to a standing army and to the German mercenaries whose presence on British soil had been greeted with unease and, in some circles, downright hostility. A 'constitutional' militia, it was claimed, would not only serve as an auxiliary source of domestic defence; it would also actively revivify

[73] Caple, 'Popular Protest', 96, 123.   [74] SP 36/137/85, 87.

[75] *Manchester Mercury*, 27 Sept.–4 Oct. 1757. See also the account in the *Salisbury Journal*, 10 Oct. 1757, where Bettely's alias is said to be Forster and the place of execution, Liverpool.

patriotism and counteract the self-interest, corruption, and foppish 'effeminacy' that currently plagued British politics and society. In other words, the militia had a political as well as strategic importance. It was hoped that it would rejuvenate public service as well as defend the nation from French aggression.

Politicians of all camps were taken aback by the popular hostility to the Act. On the face of it, the terms of recruitment were not onerous.[76] The intention was to raise a force of 60,000 men to be levied on a county-by-county basis. The levy was to be determined by taking a census of all able-bodied men between the ages of 18 and 50 and choosing a proportion of them by lot. Each recruit would serve for three years, would drill every Sunday from February to October, roughly twenty days a year, and would be subject to civil discipline unless the militia was called up for emergency service. Only then could the militia be marched out of its county. Those recruited would be exempted from army and naval service, and those rich enough could find substitutes or pay a fine of £10. The officers for the militia would be drawn from the gentry or richer tenant-farmers. Essentially, the structure of the militia was built around the ideal of a model county community, with the chain of command reflecting the 'natural' dependencies and reciprocities of masters and men.

The central problem with the project was the lack of trust between masters and men. In the wake of a poor harvest and continuing shortages in 1757 that were scarcely alleviated by gentry paternalism, the common people were hardly likely to greet the Militia Act with enthusiasm. The situation was aggravated by the fact that the promoters of the bill had not adequately publicized its terms, save conceivably in East Anglia, and on the critical question of pay had remained silent. No provision for pay had been included in the original bill in deference to the Lords, who would not otherwise have been able to amend it and whose co-operation was crucial to its implementation.[77] This was a remarkable oversight given the immiseration of the general population. It was all very well for the political élite to assert that some provision for pay would be forthcoming out of the general finances of the Act. Its absence was deeply damaging to the Act's enforcement.

The resistance to the Militia Act has been largely attributed to a mis-understanding of the law.[78] This was the official, public explanation. The Earl of Hardwicke, who was a critical and attentive commentator on the

---

[76] For the full terms, see J. R. Western, *The English Militia in the Eighteenth Century* (London, 1965), 127–39.

[77] Ibid. 132 n.   [78] Ibid. 290.

militia, confided to Newcastle that it was 'a mistake to say that the common people dislike it because they don't know what it is'. It was true, he went on, 'that they don't comprehend the train of political arguments on which it depends, & never will; but they know what is in it, & profess to dislike it for what is *contain'd in it*, & what is *omitted out of it*'.[79] What, then, was the nature of popular grievances?

In the first place it is clear that the labouring poor saw the Act as a form of selective conscription. In practical terms, very few labouring men could buy their way out of personal service. All were potentially vulnerable to compulsory enlistment. This was not only socially discriminatory, underscoring the power that property and wealth could bring to national service, it was also seen as a repudiation of the Englishman's birthright to equal treatment under the law. As protesters told Nathaniel Cholmley in Yorkshire, 'they would not be slaves'; they 'looked upon the bill as taking their libertys from them'.[80]

The labouring poor were also troubled by the terms and purposes of enlistment. Militia-men could be used to put down domestic disturbances rather than confront an invading army, as they were in 1780 and (though with mixed success) during the food riots at the end of the century.[81] Militia-men could also find themselves in the house of correction for acts of insubordination to their superior officers. Given the tense relations in the countryside over food supply, there was always the possibility that disciplinary action would be taken against men who had stood up to farmers, dealers, or gentlemen during the previous months of riot and arson. Particularly worrying to labourers was the fear they would be drafted abroad, despite disclaimers to the contrary. This was not as alarmist as it might appear. In the year prior to the Act, when new cavalry regiments had been raised in each county on a three-year commission, recruits had been assured that they would remain on domestic soil. Yet in Somerset and Dorset the men raised for Lord Digby's regiment had been ordered on board transports by force, and it was genuinely feared that the same might happen to the militia. Lord Poulett reported to Pitt from Somerset that he found 'the common people outrageously against' the Act 'for fear as they called it of being Digby'd abroad'.[82] Similar concerns were voiced in Lincolnshire,

---

[79] BL, Add. MS 32874, fos. 146–7.   [80] Ibid. 46.

[81] Roger Wells, *Wretched Faces: Famine in Wartime England 1763–1803* (Stroud, 1988), 99–105; Hayter, *Army and the Crowd*, 152–9. Walter Shelton notes that the militia were not used in the food riots of 1766; see Walter James Shelton, *English Hunger and Industrial Disorders* (London, 1973), 130–5.

[82] PRO, 30/8/53, fos. 99–100, cited by Western, *English Militia*, 150.

where rioters swore 'they would knock every country gentleman on the Head, for that they would not be dragged away from their families and sent abroad', and at Chesterfield, in Derbyshire, where protesters declared 'they had rather be hanged in England than scalped in America'. They had 'no confidence in Government', they continued, 'since the [cavalry] men are sent abroad, which are inlisted for 3 years, and on conditions to the contrary'.[83]

Equally disturbing was the absence of any provision for pay and its social implications. In 1745, the volunteer regiments had been financed by the nobility and gentry. The militia regiments, in contrast, were to be financed out of general taxes in which the labouring classes would bear a proportionately heavier burden. This was considered manifestly unfair. Protesters at York declared 'that the Militia Act was a great Hardship upon the Country, by compelling the poorer Sort of the People to contribute equally with the Rich'.[84] Particularly galling to the populace was the prospect of having to join the militia without pay; or, as was widely rumoured, at the common soldier's rate of 6*d*. a day. 'If you would have men raised', ran one anonymous letter to two Lincolnshire gentlemen, 'you may raise them by the assistance of your long green purses and be damn'd if you will.' The author (probably a small farmer) went on to ask 'if a Ticket be drawn and to fall to a poor man's lot to go that has a large family, which of you Buntin ass'd coated fellows will maintain his family till its capable of taking care of itself?' The writer maintained that the militia would raise the poor rates 'and they are as high as need be, so they swear they will not fight for your estates. They will fight for their own lives first and so begin at home.'[85] Similar sentiments were expressed to the Dean of Lincoln. 'We will not fight for what does not concern us, and only belongs to our landlords: let the worst happen, we can but be tenants and labourers as we are at present.' When a local clergyman attempted to counter this disaffection by preaching a sermon 'on the obedience due to civil governors', his hearers retorted: 'aye, he fetches that doctrine out of a book, which our governors do not believe in, and why should we?'[86]

The Dean of Lincoln was disturbed by the utter contempt of authority that anti-militia protesters revealed in the autumn of 1757, especially the fact that the farmers and labourers 'insulted the justices, the gentlemen and even their landlords to their faces'.[87] He was by no means alone in

[83] BL., Add. MS 32873, fo. 311; Add. MS 32874, fo. 159.
[84] *Derby Mercury*, 23–30 Sept. 1757.   [85] BL., Add. MS 32874, fos. 161–2.
[86] BL., Birch MS 4164, Letters and State Papers, no. 18, cited by Sir Francis Hill, *Georgian Lincoln* (Cambridge, 1966), 107.
[87] Hill, *Georgian Lincoln*, 107.

this view. Lord Dupplin remarked to Newcastle that 'there seems to be such an impatience of government, and such a spirit of anarchy raised in the minds of the people, as if not allayed, threatens General Confusion'.[88]

Confusion there certainly was. Gabriel Hanger reported from the neighbourhood of Cirencester that 'the whole Country round me for eight to ten Miles was in the utmost confusion . . . with the sounding of horns, & hallowing, the signals for calling the rioters together'.[89] Protesters responded to the militia by assembling at the inns where the justices and constables had gathered to administer the Act and demanding the lists of those eligible for recruitment. Frequently they physically intimidated the justices and threatened to pull down their houses if the lists were not turned over to them. A few houses were actually levelled, most notably near York. In other places they were badly damaged, especially where crowds were refused beer and money.[90] Quite a few gentlemen were insulted and roughed up during the militia riots, including Sir George Savile, who a year previously had ordered his tenants to sell corn to the poor at 4*s.* a bushel.[91] Some country gentlemen fled for their lives; and in the end few were prepared to defy the crowds' request for the lists without troops or a formidable posse of armed citizens behind them. As Sir Richard Wynn remarked to the Duke of Newcastle, gentlemen who resided far from market towns wilted in the face of mobs of 200 or 300 people when they had only a few servants to defend them. 'I find that Gentlemen are unwilling to do anything', he confided, 'till they are justified how far the Government will support them, and we are as yet unwilling to have it known that troops are coming into the county as we have no certainty when they will be here.'[92]

The militia riots delayed the implementation of the Act for at least a year if not longer. The Act's central promoter, George Townshend, had hoped to see the militia in training by September 1757. Yet no arms were issued to any regiment until August 1758, and the great majority of English counties did not have operative militias until late 1759 or 1760. By that time, some of the popular grievances expressed during the riots had been addressed. Provision for pay was forthcoming, as was sick leave, and county divisions were allowed to raise their men by offering volunteers rather than ballot.[93]

[88] BL, Add. MS 32874, fos. 264–8.   [89] PRO, SP 36/138/117–18.

[90] BL, Egerton MS 4346, fos. 137, 145, 157; *Boddely's Bath Journal*, 5 Sept. 1757; *Derby Mercury*, 9–16, 23–30 Sept. 1757; *Ipswich Journal*, 1 Oct. 1757.

[91] *Berrow's Worcester Journal*, 9 Sept. 1756; *Ipswich Journal*, 17 Sept. 1757.

[92] BL, Add. MS 32874, fos. 425–6.

[93] Western, *English Militia*, 141–2, appendix A.

Quite apart from compromising the Act and forcing the political élite to be more attentive to popular wishes, the militia riots revealed a class hostility that shook the equanimity of many eastern counties gentlemen, few of whom had been confronted with angry food rioters in the previous year. Militia protesters damned gentlemen for their unwillingness to shoulder their fair share of the wartime burden, for their abrogation of paternalist responsibilities towards their tenants and labourers. Gentlemen were castigated for throwing militia families on the backs of farmers; for only keeping the labouring poor alive so they could fight for them; for exploiting a patriotic project in their own self-interest. As the militia riots gathered momentum, other local rural grievances surfaced as well: hostility to the game laws and to game law associations; to enclosures; to further taxes; to systems of marketing that put profit and agrarian improvement above popular claims for a decent subsistence.[94] At Sibsey, 200 people assembled at the West Fen 'by beat of drum & with Colors flying' and protested against recent enclosures by pulling down several dams. They also forced the surveyor-general of the area, Joseph Robertson, to flee his house for Boston.[95] In some counties, anti-militia protests merged with others about grain speculation. In Nottinghamshire, the 'great mobs' who confiscated the lists at Tuxford, Worksop, and Blyth declared that the harvest was nearly all in and plentiful, 'yet the Hoarders keep up the price of wheat'.[96] In Yorkshire such sentiments prompted attacks upon dressing mills and market interventions to fix the price of grain. Sir Richard Wynn reported from Whitby that a militia riot was followed by another against the millers and farmers who had withheld corn from the market. The rioters claimed that they had nearly starved last winter and now felt 4s. a bushel was 'a good price' for what had been 'a plentiful harvest'.[97]

Throughout the areas affected by militia riots, visits to country houses to extort money and victuals were common. But in the East Riding of Yorkshire, in particular, the murmurings against the rich took a levelling turn, with complaints that the gentry had been in possession of their estates long enough. Lord Rockingham was not alone in recognizing this. The mayor of York noted that the 'necessitous, who are much the majority, are endeavouring to promote a levelling principle (which is constantly made use of in their meetings)' and 'wch would prove fatal to the peace & happiness

[94] The linking of local with militia protest was recognized by Lord Dupplin. See BL, Add. MS 32874, fos. 264–8.

[95] PRO, SP 36/138/100–1; Hill, *Georgian Lincoln*, 107.

[96] *Derby Mercury*, 9–16 Sept. 1757.

[97] BL, Add. MS. 32874, fos. 425–6, 444–6; Western, *English Militia*, 300.

of our constitution'.[98] When rioters gutted the house of a local gentleman at Bootham Bar, he organized a huge posse of 500 gentlemen and 'substantial Citizens' to guard the city against further destruction.[99] This incident was considered sufficiently serious to warrant a special commission of oyer and terminer to try those arrested in the disturbances; the first, in fact, in two riotous years. Two ringleaders were sentenced to death by this court and one was hanged as a judicial example to those who would destroy gentlemen's property.[100]

The crisis of 1756–7 was the product of dearth and war. The dearth was only partially attributable to natural causes. Although the wet summer of 1756 pushed up food prices, the continuing shortages of grain in the following year, when the harvest was better and when regulatory controls to ensure adequate supplies were in place, suggest that the speculation in grain was a formidable factor in creating local food shortages. Wartime conditions only aggravated the problem. Some domestic grain was used to feed the troops at home and abroad, and some commentators were very concerned that contractors would starve the countryside in their search for fresh supplies. Dislocations in foreign trade, particularly in the woollen industry, also created formidable unemployment that made the lot of the labouring classes that much harder to bear.

The labouring poor reacted to the crisis by invoking the moral economy, by demanding that corn be brought to the open market so that everyone could have access to the 'staff of life', by insisting that food be available on affordable terms. Although it was alleged in parliament and in the press that the retributory actions of the crowd deterred some dealers from bringing their grain to market, food riots did dramatically expose the speculation in corn and prompted remedial responses from the authorities, such as the implementation of the laws against forestalling and engrossing and public subscriptions to provide grain and flour at below the market rate. In the case of blockages, which constituted about 20 per cent of crowd actions, local supplies bound for export or other parts of the countryside were successfully withheld. Where public subscriptions and emergency measures proved ineffectual in alleviating local dearth, rioters took the law into their own hands by confiscating and fixing the price of grain in local markets. *Taxation populaire*, or forcible price-fixing, was not quite as visible a strategy in 1756–7 as it was to become in the next round of food riots. It constituted 20 per cent of all crowd actions as opposed to 22 per cent

---

[98] PRO, SP 36/138/44; BL, Add. MS 32874, fo. 271.
[99] *Derby Mercury*, 23–30 Sept. 1757.   [100] Western, *English Militia*, 296.

in 1766.[101] But it was increasingly resorted to at the end of 1757 when riot-ers complained bitterly that grain was being withheld from market in spite of regulatory controls and a better harvest.

The crisis of 1756–7 was also noteworthy for the extent to which the moral economy was espoused by groups beyond the crowd. Although E. P. Thompson, in his seminal article on food riots, recognized that a few country gentlemen were strongly critical of grain dealers for speculating on scarcity, he tended to marginalize these voices in favour of a model which emphasized the dialogue between gentry and crowd over the distribution of grain, with the gentry in a real sense being prisoners of the people and their own paternalist rhetoric.[102] Yet it is difficult to accommodate these dissonant voices within a patrician–plebeian polarity, not simply because some of them emanated from the middling sort rather than the gentry, but more generally because ideological conflict and war complicated the politics of grain supply. In 1756 and again in 1757, several towns on the receiving end of food riots instructed their MPs or petitioned parliament for stricter controls upon food supply, recommending measures that would have curbed the market economy in grain in favour of greater consumer protection. These demands were not simply self-serving. They also drew on a patriotic or Country rhetoric that saw grain dealers as part of a wider problem of political venality and self-interest that blighted the body politic and promoted admirals like Byng. Grain dealers were no better than stockjobbers or opportunistic politicians in promoting their own interests above those of society. They were part of the cancer that hindered the effect-ive mobilization of the nation's resources against the French.[103]

In the end, a gentry-dominated parliament did nothing to alter the corn bounty and marketing structure that in the previous decades had served landlords and farmers so well. In effect, it preferred temporary emergency measures and the implementation of old laws against hoarding to see out the crisis rather than accede to stricter controls over the free marketing of grain. In other spheres as well, parliament and the judiciary endorsed

---

[101] Dale Edward Williams, 'Midland Hunger Riots in 1766', *Midland History*, 3 (1975–6), 284. The 1756–7 figures are derived from Caple, 'Popular Protest', appendix A, with a few revisions.

[102] E. P. Thompson, 'The Moral Economy of the English Crowd in the Eighteenth Century', *Past and Present*, 50 (Feb. 1971), 76–136, reprinted in *Customs in Common* (London, 1991), ch. 4.

[103] For a different view of the role of the middling sort in mid-18th-cent. food riots, see Simon Renton, 'The Moral Economy of the English Middling Sort in the Eighteenth Century: The Case of Norwich in 1766 and 1767', in Adrian Randall and Andrew Charlesworth (eds.), *Markets, Market Culture and Popular Protest in Eighteenth-Century Britain and Ireland* (Liver-pool, 1996), 115–36.

policies that favoured market imperatives over the customary expectations of the people. In 1757 parliament repealed the regulatory machinery that gave West Country weavers some bargaining power with their employers, despite protests from the weavers that they would then be subjected to the 'arbitrary will and power' of the clothiers.[104] In the following year, in the wake of a strike by the Lancashire check weavers over the regulation of apprentices and conditions of work and pay, Lord Mansfield sided with the employers in demanding that the weavers disband their combination and recommended the prosecution of all who had contributed to or had managed their charity box; in effect, their strike fund. In March 1759, when the indicted weavers finally appeared in court to hear their sentences, Sir Michael Foster condemned the 'Confederacies' that had 'occasioned the greatest Confusion betwixt the lower Class of People and their Superiors' and dismissed the notion that the Statute of Apprentices (1563) was of any relevance or benefit to the trade. In his view, such regulatory machinery was an unwarranted impediment to the labour market and to the necessary subordination of servants to their masters if industry was to flourish.[105] The stage was set for further attacks upon custom in the interests of freer markets, open competition, and large-scale production.

Ruling-class relations with the common people were severely strained in the opening years of the Seven Years War. One sees little evidence that the traditional codes of patrician rule were sufficient to placate lower-class rancour. Paternalist responses to dearth were undercut by continuing shortages. Whatever publicity and credibility was gained by those gestures was further undermined by the gentry's self-interested attitude towards the militia, whose burden fell disproportionately upon the poor and the farming community in general. Ruling-class equanimity faltered in the face of huge crowds, and if such crowds could not be bought off by money and food or promises of further remedial action, then a show of force was necessary. Over 16,000 troops were available for riot duty in 1757, including eight cavalry regiments,[106] but these were so severely stretched that local authorities sometimes had to raise their own posses to deal with large crowds, particularly in the dense industrial areas of the country. The government was fortunate that no disturbances broke out in the major towns, particularly

[104] *JHC* 27 (1754–7), 741.
[105] Wadsworth and Mann, *Cotton Trade*, 361–9. For similar language about the need for the 'due subordination' of labour, this time in the West Country woollen industry, see [J. Dallaway], *A State of the Case . . . Relating to the Late Commotions and the Rising of Weavers* (London, 1757), pp. iv, 14.
[106] Hayter, *Army and the Crowd*, 94–5, 113.

London, where it kept a sharp eye on food supplies and moved quickly to provide imports of raw materials for the economically fragile Spitalfields silk industry.[107]

One of the mitigating factors to popular insurrection was the local character of crowd actions. Riots did tend to spread rapidly through the countryside in areas where roving bands of colliers were active. But generally they were confined to local markets, or, in the case of the militia riots, to local hundreds. Their targets were specific and usually bounded by local knowledge about dealers, millers, or people in authority. Moreover, the riots of 1756–7 seldom set up a chain of equivalences by which the government or the ruling class became the central target of contention. Riots certainly intersected in interesting ways. High prices and food protests reinforced labour disputes and intensified struggles over impressment; militia riots brought other rural grievances in their train including further protests over the price of grain. Yet despite the fact that virtually every English county experienced some kind of disorder in 1756 and 1757, no popular movement of insurrectionary dimensions occurred. Indeed, at the height of some of the food and militia disturbances, rioters sometimes showed a remarkable reverence for parliamentary authority even if they were prepared to vilify local MPs or JPs. When Colonel Hervey confronted riotous colliers outside Nottingham who were bent upon rescuing their comrades from the town gaol, he asked them why they had not approached the justices: they replied, 'those shod not be their Lords'. But when Hervey asked them why they had not approached parliament, they simply responded, 'it was too late for that'.[108] Similarly, when Lawrence Monck met with militia protesters near his seat in Lincolnshire, he told them, in response to their complaints about Digbying, 'that an Act of Parliament never had deceived them, nor was likely ever to do so'. 'They agreed that if Parliament was not to be trusted, there wou'd be an end of all things,' Monck reported to the Duke of Ancaster, and requested he 'would turn back and give them some ale, and promised to do him no mischief'.[109] The protesters did not exactly fulfil their promise, for some of them rattled the shutters of his windows with clubs and demanded a guinea a list from the constables. Even so, conceding this demand was a small price to pay for social order. Where the demands were more threatening, as they were among the Yorkshire 'levellers', social order could only be restored by a special commission of oyer and terminer and another gallows matinée.

[107] Alfred Plummer, *The London Weavers' Company 1600–1970* (London, 1972), 317–18.
[108] PRO, SP 36/135/305.   [109] BL, Add. MS 32874, fos. 159–60.

3

Liberty Road: The Opposition to Impressment during the Mid-Georgian Era

A poor fellow just turned into the hold, looking up to the iron grates over him, passionately broke out in these terms: 'I am in a dungeon! What have I done to be dragged from my wife and children in this manner? Why was I shut in here? I that am born to be free, are not I and the greatest duke in England equally free born? If I have done nothing, who has power to confine me? Where is the liberty of an Englishman? Or why is not my Lord Mayor here as well as I?'

(James Edward Oglethorpe, *The Sailors Advocate* (London, 1728))

Cheerily, lads, cheerily! there's a ganger hard to wind'ard
Cheerily, lads, cheerily! there's a ganger hard a-lee;
Cheerily, lads, cheerily! else 'tis farewell home and kindred,
And the bosun's mate a-raisin' hell in the King's navee.
Cheerily, lads, cheerily ho! the warrant's out, the hanger's drawn;
Cheerily, lads, so cheerilee! we'll leave 'em an R[un] in pawn!

(An eighteenth-century sea shanty)

Naval impressment was a smouldering and sometimes explosive grievance in eighteenth-century Britain, drawing the persistent ire of portside populations. Ballads and prints highlighted its iniquities; pamphlets its inequities. 'Poor Sailors', reflected Captain Thomas Pasley in 1780, 'you are the only class of beings in our famed Country of Liberty really *Slaves*, devoted and hardly [harshly] used, tho' the very being of the Country depends upon you.'[1] Pasley was but one of many who recognized that the very men assigned to preserve British liberty from foreign threat were denied

---

[1] R. M. S. Pasley (ed.), *Private Sea Journals, 1778–1782* (London, 1931), 61, cited by Daniel A. Baugh, *British Naval Administration in the Age of Walpole* (Princeton, 1965), 147.

the dignity of free-born Englishmen. From the sixteenth century seamen, and, indeed, from 1740 anyone between the ages of 18 and 55 who 'used the sea', were liable to be forcibly recruited into his majesty's navy.[2] Although the state had attempted to regularize the manning of the navy in 1696 by creating a register of voluntary recruits, the experiment proved a failure and eighteenth-century parliaments refused to resurrect it. Henceforth, for over a century, the Admiralty continued the ancient practice of impressing seamen and 'disorderly' people to supplement its manpower in time of war. Despite Britain's maritime resources, despite the Admiralty's bounties for volunteers and its unwillingness to release existing crews, impressed men proved essential to the manning of the fleet, especially as war took its toll of casualties and desertions.

Numerically the number of men pressed into naval service is very difficult to gauge with any accuracy. The few official figures prepared by the Navy Board pertained only to those pressed ashore rather than afloat; and usually in the opening years of a war when the proportion of volunteers was high.[3] Even when the numbers put aboard tenders were known, little account was taken of those who escaped. As one administrator commented in 1781, 'the men who are raised by the regulating Officers & noted in their accounts . . . do not all get on board ships of war, for many desert'.[4] To complicate matters further, many of the men taken up by the press gangs declared themselves volunteers upon capture, or were allowed to do so by the recruiting captains. Others were stragglers and deserters already accounted for.[5] Calculating the number of impressed men is thus a hazardous exercise, but historians have speculated that perhaps a third, even half, of those recruited in the mid-century wars were in reality pressed into service.[6]

---

[2] The age qualification of 18–55 years was introduced in 1740 under 13 Geo. II c. 17. The impressment of seamen was, of course, an older practice. See G. V. Scammell, 'The Sinews of War: Manning and Provisioning English Fighting Ships c.1550–1650', *Mariner's Mirror*, 73 (Nov. 1987), 357–9.

[3] For a discussion of the figures for 1755–7, see N. A. M. Rodger, *The Wooden World: An Anatomy of the Georgian Navy* (London, 1986), 145–7; Larry Neal, 'The Cost of Impressment during the Seven Years War', *Mariner's Mirror*, 66 (Feb. 1978), 48–52.

[4] William L. Clements Lib., University of Michigan, Ann Arbor, Shelburne papers, cxxxiv, no. 61.

[5] PRO, Adm. 1/905 (Cavendish), 2 May 1741, cited by Baugh, *British Naval Administration*, 169; N. A. M. Rodger, 'Stragglers and Deserters from the Royal Navy during the Seven Years' War', *Bulletin of the Institute of Historical Research*, 67 (1984), 56–79.

[6] Roland Usher, 'Royal Navy Impressment during the American Revolution', *Mississippi Valley Historical Review*, 37 (1951), 677–9; Stephen F. Gradish, *The Manning of the British Navy during the Seven Years' War* (London, 1980), 69–70; Christopher Lloyd, *The British Seaman 1200–1860: A Social Survey* (London, 1968), 179. N. A. M. Rodger tends to play

As my opening quote demonstrates, naval impressment during the eighteenth century was denounced as a flagrant violation of the Englishman's birthright. A form of conscript labour for seafarers, impressment was considered a violation of the Bill of Rights and Magna Carta; so constitutionally irregular, in fact, that justices were sometimes cited as condoning resistance to it.[7] Unlike army recruitment, moreover, impressment was not subject to any formal civilian supervision and constituted a potentially vexatious and arbitrary power vested in the hands of the state.[8] As David Hume observed, it was a 'continued violence' vested in the crown 'amidst the greatest jealousy and watchfulness in the people'.[9]

Quite apart from the anxiety this induced in the minds of Britons, especially those with a semblance of sea experience, impressment bore hard on the sailor's lot. It compromised his ability to bargain for his labour; it prevented him from taking advantage of high wartime wages in the merchant marine; it undercut his chances of taking up a trade ashore without discovery and molestation, turning what was sometimes a youthful venture at sea into a potential bondage to the state.[10] Impressment also deprived seamen of the opportunity of replenishing their strength and renewing their social contacts after a long voyage.[11] It exposed them to the hazards of disease that regularly ravaged wartime fleets and sometimes threw families on the parish. Letitia Coleman testified before a London magistrate in June 1757 that 'about three months since her sd Husband was press'd into his Majesty's service and sent on board the Torbay Man of War', with the result that 'she had been forced to beg in the streets'.[12] In ports such as Hull, poor rates rose significantly in wartime as households struggled to survive in the absence of male breadwinners. Small wonder seamen evaded the gangs for fear of being torn from their friends and families.

down the dimensions of impressment, but his figures for Hull, 1759–60, which include men pressed both afloat and ashore, amount to 63% of all recruits. This figure would include stragglers and deserters. See Rodger, *Wooden World*, 153.

[7] *Mist's Weekly Journal*, 18 May 1728. L. C. J. Holt is said to have declared that if a man killed a ganger while resisting impressment he could only be found guilty of manslaughter.

[8] See John Brewer, *The Sinews of Power: War, Money and the English State 1688–1783* (New York, 1989), 49–51.

[9] David Hume, *Essays Moral, Political and Literary*, ed. Eugene F. Miller (Indianapolis, 1987), 375.

[10] On high wartime wages, see Ralph Davis, *The Rise of the English Shipping Industry in the Seventeenth and Eighteenth Centuries* (Newton Abbot, 1962), 135–7.

[11] This was stressed in John Lockman, *The Vast Importance of the Herring Industry . . . to these Kingdoms* (London, 1750), 27.

[12] GLRO, MJ/SPV/1757. See also Westminster Public Library, parish examinations, St Martin-in-the-Fields, 1776–7, F. 5063/377–8, 457.

Impressment thus threatened a seaman's health and welfare as well as compromising his birthright as a free-born Englishman. It was socially discriminatory, reserving personal service to the state to the poorest class of society, to the wage-earners of the Main, and to those whose recalcitrance, irregular ways of life, or dependence upon public charity led the state to make a claim on their labour. Such coercion was sometimes defended as a means of disciplining the workshy and indolent. It was a reasonable charge upon 'the lower ranks of life' to whom the 'offensive and disagreeable public duties' reasonably and inevitably fell.[13] Impressment saved seamen from idleness and intemperance, it was asserted; it made sturdy beggars useful to their country, if only as cannon fodder. It freed the nation, claimed 'Philonauta' 'of idle and reprobate Vermin by converting them into a Body of the most industrious People, and even, becoming the very nerves of our State'.[14] Yet however advantageous to industry and social order, impressment was principally justified as a state necessity, grounded in 'immemorial usage'. It was a residual prerogative power for the defence of the realm. Britain required her wooden walls to repel foreign invaders and to secure her continued wealth, power, and well-being. In the absence of a registered pool of seamen, impressment seemed the only alternative. Although politicians were sometimes reluctant to pronounce on its constitutionality,[15] it was defended as the inevitable price to be paid for national security in the land of liberty.

Opposition to impressment was vocal in the eighteenth century; just how commonplace it was is historically moot. N. A. M. Rodger, in a widely acclaimed monograph on the Georgian navy, has claimed that the hostility to impressment has been exaggerated.[16] In his opinion pressed men frequently reconciled themselves to the rigours of naval service with remarkable rapidity, especially when they sailed with men from their own vicinity. Despite the hostility to impressment, the majority of riots against forcible recruitment emanated mainly from deserters, not from the community at large. This line of argument has been buttressed by the view that the impress service, as it came to be known, became a more responsible institution as time progressed. Under closer Admiralty supervision, regulating officers

---

[13] Charles Butler, *An Essay on the Legality of Impressing Seamen* (London, 2nd edn., 1778), 6.

[14] Philonauta, *The Sailor's Happiness* (London, 1751), 19–20; Butler, *An Essay*, 54; *Gentleman's Magazine*, 32 (1762), 53.

[15] In the debate on the Registry Bill of 1740, for example, Sir Robert Walpole openly doubted whether impressment was legal. *Parliamentary History*, 7 (1739–40), 428.

[16] Rodger, *Wooden World*, 164–82.

were wary of alienating portside populations and increasingly intolerant of lawless, ruffianly gangs sweeping up innocents from the streets.[17] Consequently potential conflicts over impressment were marginalized and the problems of manning the fleet brought within acceptable political and social limits. Impressment may have been an intrinsically troublesome form of recruitment, but it was not a formidable site of protest.

This revisionist interpretation is certainly correct in recognizing the increasing efficiency and accountability of the impress service, but the inference that the administrative reorganization of recruitment tempered protest is suspect. The escalating demand for men during the Williamite wars produced a raw, inexperienced service that was not particularly discriminate about whom it picked up.[18] Pepys noted an upsurge of violence by the gangs in 1692; Defoe condemned the tyranny of 'dragging landmen into the Service' a decade later; and the abuses of the gangs quickly became 'the subject matter of discourse' in the coffee houses and newspapers.[19] The Admiralty subsequently appointed regulating captains to co-ordinate recruitment at the local level. It ordered them to examine the physical condition of the men brought in; to adjudicate exemptions from impressment; to determine the eligibility of substitutes, and so on. In other words, to bring some order to the hitherto indiscriminate operations of the press gangs ashore, many of which had been basically private ventures under the direction of retired naval officers.[20]

Without doubt many regulating officers exercised a constraining influence upon their gangs, if only because there was no iron-clad guarantee that the Admiralty would back up their actions. Yet the hallmark of the mid-century service was not so much its probity—for accusations of violence and extortion by the gangs continued[21]—as its increasing intrusion into the lives of the citizenry. In large part this was due to the changing dimensions of naval warfare and to the deepening search for experienced seamen. In the early years of the century impressment had largely been a southern problem. Its centre of operations was London, the Downs, and the southerly ports of Portsmouth and Plymouth. As late as 1740 the Admiralty's activities remained concentrated in this region, although press

---

[17] Gradish, *Manning*, 58–61.

[18] See John Ehrman, *The Navy in the War of William III 1689–1697* (Cambridge, 1953), 117–19.

[19] J. S. Bromley (ed.), *The Manning of the Royal Navy* (London, 1979), pp. xxvii–xxix.

[20] Ehrman, *Navy in the War of William III*, 117.

[21] In 1757 a regulating officer was court-martialled at Plymouth for impressing the sons of farmers and releasing them for money, by which he was said to have collected £700. *Schofield's Middlewich Journal*, 22–9 Mar. 1757. See also the *Middlesex Journal*, 3–5 Jan. 1771.

warrants were also sent to the civil authorities in other major ports including Bristol, Liverpool, Newcastle, Hull, and Yarmouth.[22] During the Seven Years War, however, the impress service expanded dramatically to meet the government's quotas for seamen, drawing roughly a quarter of its men from the northern ports.[23] Regulating captains, hitherto confined to London, were posted in many provincial ports as well as a few inland towns.[24] This initiative was prompted by the desire to co-ordinate the recruiting drives of the navy in a more systematic fashion: to tap a broader section of the merchant marine; to enlist more landsmen; to take up sailors who had moved inland to evade the press gangs; to recapture stragglers and deserters; to recruit not only regular seafarers, but those who 'used the sea'.

The civil authorities were encouraged to collaborate in this enterprise so that local labour demands could be more satisfactorily co-ordinated with the imperatives of national defence and imperialist expansion. Press warrants were sent to over sixty English towns during the opening mobilization of the Seven Years War and to over seventy during the American.[25] The bait for such participation was an extension of protections in order to reconcile the needs of commerce with those of the state. Statutory exemptions from impressment had been given to sea apprentices and Greenland harpooners in the early years of the century, and a quota system had been arranged for the Thames watermen and the coal trade of Tyne and Wear.[26] These exemptions were reaffirmed in 1740 and more liberal concessions were allowed the whaling industry.[27] More importantly, the Admiralty and other government departments issued protections to a broader range of seafaring and portside men: to crews of ships bound abroad; to coasters and fishing vessels; to watermen, lightermen, bargemen, pilots, and many harbour workers.[28] Between 1740 and 1757 the number of protections rose threefold or more, from 14,800 to approximately 50,000, taking in a sizeable proportion of the merchant marine as well as many riverside trades.[29]

[22] Baugh, *British Naval Administration*, 159.

[23] William L. Clements Lib., University of Michigan, Ann Arbor, Shelburne papers, cxxxix, nos. 62, 64. The figures given here were 28% for 1759–60 and 23% for 1780–1.

[24] See Gradish, *Manning*, 57.

[25] Ibid. 58–9; William L. Clements Lib., Shelburne papers, cxxxix, no. 62.

[26] Greenland harpooners and foreigners were exempt under 1 Anne c. 16. Sea apprentices under 18 years of age were exempt under 2 & 3 Anne c. 6 and those who voluntarily bound themselves were not to be impressed for three years. The colliers were allowed one able seaman for every 100 tons, to a maximum of three. The Thames watermen had to provide 200 men whenever required. See Lloyd, *British Seaman*, 146–7.

[27] See 13 Geo. II c. 3, 17, and 29. [28] See Baugh, *British Naval Administration*, 172.

[29] Rodger, *Wooden World*, 178.

From the seafarers' point of view, this reorganization of British naval power was an unwelcome development. During the wars of William III and Queen Anne, naval administrators had assumed that the merchant marine would normally satisfy the demand for naval manpower without major dislocations to either service. Consequently sailors were recruited for relatively short periods and seasonally demobilized. This symbiotic relationship between maritime commerce and naval power became increasingly problematic as Britain's naval commitment increased, so that by the 1740s seamen were recruited for the duration of war and regularly turned over when their ships arrived back in port. The consequence was that naval service in the Georgian era was riskier than many forms of maritime employment, exposing seamen to the hazards of scurvy, dysentery, and typhus. It was also very disruptive, depriving seamen of the contacts and by-employments that formed part of the seasonal cycles of coastal communities and ports. The Admiralty attempted to make naval service more attractive by increasing bounties to volunteers, regularizing pay, and offering crews the prospect of prize money at least comparable to that of privateers.[30] But none of these financial inducements could compensate for the higher wage that merchant seamen received after 1750, the promptness with which it was paid, and the opportunity to spend it how and when one wished.

The hazards and burden of naval service thus increased over time and only aggravated the opposition to impressment. Nor did the policy of exemptions prevent it from remaining a vexatious issue. Protections may have partially reconciled employers to impressment, but they did little to offset the vulnerability of many riverside workers, let alone seamen. Because the distribution of protections was potentially open to abuse, regulating officers were often suspicious of their authenticity. Any irregularity served as a pretext for a young man's swift removal to the fleet. Furthermore, departmental as opposed to statutory protections were revocable at the Admiralty's discretion. Whenever the demand for men became desperate, the Admiralty would discreetly order a 'press from protections', or a 'hot press' as it was popularly called, leaving every riverside worker vulnerable to forcible recruitment. These raids prompted well-organized employers to bargain with the Admiralty to prevent a serious depletion of their workforce; normally 10–20 per cent of their men were conceded to the fleet. Such negotiations took time and did little to help those already

[30] Whether privateering or naval crews had a better chance of prize money has been a subject of dispute. See Gradish, *Manning*, 75; Rodger, *Wooden World*, 128–30.

taken up. Understandably a hot press often led to violent resistance and invariably to the tramp. In October 1770, a correspondent in the *Middlesex Journal* noted hundreds of workmen passing through St Albans on their way to the north and west to evade the warm press of the gangs.[31]

The imperatives of war thus imperilled the welfare of many workers. But just how many were likely to be caught in the naval net? Historians have sometimes tended to minimize the importance of impressment on the assumption that only mariners were involved. Yet, as we have seen, the statutory definition of those eligible for naval service was quite liberal, encompassing not only merchant seamen but those who 'used the sea' as well as those subject to the vagrancy laws. During the Seven Years War, for example, the manning requirements of the British navy increased by 70 per cent, with a total of over 180,000 men enlisted; allowing for crude natural increase, approximately one in eleven of the adult male workers aged 18–55.[32] In some ports, Newcastle, Liverpool, and Leith, for instance, the percentage of men taken up could be considerably higher. Such a quota could only be met by dredging the gaols and impressing those who worked in 'vessels and boats upon rivers'; a policy which brought the press gang into conflict with bargemen and fishermen whose work on the rivers or coasts was often a seasonal by-employment. One master mariner complained that 'all the laboring Men in Norfolk' were liable to impressment as a result of this policy, 'for as soon as the harvest is over they go to Yarmouth and enter into the herring Fishing Boats for the Season'.[33] Similarly, boroughs like Bere Alston in Cornwall, where many inhabitants eked out a living carrying limestone up and down the river Tamar, suddenly found themselves the object of press-gang raids. Here the lightermen were 'dragged out of their craft like dogs', one newspaper reported, 'leaving their families in great distress'.[34] The same was potentially true of Boston bargemen, the Medway dredgermen, the tackmen of the river Tay, and the Tyneside wherrymen; even of carters like James Bowie, who hauled coals from the keels and confessed that 'he had never been to sea although he had laboured on the river'.[35] On that pretext the Admiralty decided to keep him, as it did John Rose,

[31] *Middlesex Journal*, 18–20 Oct. 1770.

[32] The average number of men recruited in the years 1756–63 was 74,749 per annum; in the previous war it was 43,870 per annum. The figures are taken from Lloyd, *British Seaman*, 262. For the total enlisted during the Seven Years War, see Gradish, *Manning*, 70, 216.

[33] PRO, Adm. 1/3681/370.

[34] *Sussex Weekly Advertiser*, 26 Nov. 1776; see also J. R. Hutchinson, *The Press Gang Afloat and Ashore* (London, 1913), 181–3.

[35] PRO, Adm. 1/1611/159–62 (Cunninghame); 1/3681/241; 1/1497 (Bover), 21 Jan. 1771, 21 Feb. 1778; 1/2220 (Napier), 28 Jan. 1770.

a quarryman employed in gathering coals at the wharfside for a Tyneside limeworks.[36]

Mid-eighteenth-century impressment, then, was increasingly intrusive, socially disruptive, and hazardous to health. What little protection was given to enumerated trades could be whittled away by the imperatives of war. Small wonder that the press gangs were evaded and resisted, not only by the traditional forms of crowd intervention, but also in the courts. Indeed, as we shall see, when radicals rang the tocsin of liberty once again on behalf of the impressed during the unpopular American war and Britain faced the prospect of naval battles on several fronts, the government faced a manning crisis of unprecedented proportions.

Press warrants were issued as early as February 1755 in the run-up to the Seven Years War. Almost immediately the recruiting officers encountered resistance. Some of this came from a predictable quarter, from local officials whose reputation and standing was likely to be compromised by the intrusive and unpopular presence of the press gangs. In London and Newcastle constables dragged their feet over impressment. One even attempted to foil a midshipman's search for sailors by arresting him for profanity.[37] At Yarmouth, the constables were similarly 'rather backward' in helping the press; 'especially in forcing doors', Captain Hollwall reported, 'being greatly afraid of a Justice of the Peace here', who 'proclaimed himself a defender of Liberty a few days past, and threaten'd to Commit any officer that should be guilty of an Act of Violence'.[38] Hollwall confronted the justice about his lack of co-operation and secured from him a promise to retire to his country seat. Yet he recognized that there were 'not many magistrates harty in our Interest'. The same was true of King's Lynn. Here the mayor proved so obstructive that the lords of the Admiralty had to threaten him with a general press of the town before he relented.[39] Even then the regulating officer complained of 'the evasions' which the magistrates used to 'screen and protect' seamen and of the merchants who droned that he had been sent there 'only to distress them'.[40]

Elsewhere the local mayors and magistrates assisted the Admiralty's quest for men, although some were not above forewarning local seamen of an

[36] PRO, Adm. 1/1498 (Bover), 16 Mar. 1778.   [37] PRO, Adm. 1/3677/20, 24.
[38] PRO, Adm. 1/1890 (Hollwall), 21 Feb. 1755.
[39] PRO, Adm. 1/1486 (Baird), letters of 1 and 4 Mar. 1755, Adm. 1/3677/32; Adm. 1/1890 (Hollwall), 21 Feb. 1755.
[40] PRO, Adm. 1/1486 (Baird), 30 Mar., 26 Apr. 1755.

impending press and transforming their ports into an evacuation zone.[41] Not that official tip-offs were always necessary. Seafaring communities were perennially on the alert for the press gangs and the slightest whiff of a warrant or sight of a tender would send men scurrying from the quays. The seamen of Bo'ness had little trouble evading the press tender that ran aground in the mud at low tide, and they subsequently organized a lookout to ensure that they had good notice of the gang's next arrival.[42] In other ports, too, sailors were quickly apprised of the discreet signs of an impending impressment. Captain Ellis Brand reported disconsolately from Ipswich that 'the town had been full of seamen', but 'immediately after the arrival of the post' disclosing that 'press warrants was come down . . . the town was soon clear'd . . . I have not seen the face of a seaman since . . . the fellows are fled into the neighbouring villages.'[43] Captain O'Bryen encountered the same problem in North Shields. 'Such is the Intercourse and Connection between this place and the Coal Crimps in London', he reported to the Admiralty, 'that whatever Transpires there is that instant communicated here.' Upon receiving his warrants, he continued,

I acted with the greatest caution, & went myself over to the Justice in this neighbourhood for his order to all constables &c to assist me; & I did not even tell the said constables my business, neither did they know I wanted to employ them 'till Dark last night, when I went myself with a strong party Thro the whole town of N. Shields, and was not able to procure one Man fitt for his Majestys Service, for letters coming to Newcastle by Sunday Nights Post to Merchts and Coal Fitters, they learn what is talked of in London and so let others know itt.[44]

O'Bryen's experience of the elusive sailor was not uncommon on Tyneside. Further up the river in Newcastle Captain Wheeler met with the same problem. Unable to raise a suitable press gang to take on the Geordie sailors, he sought the assistance of the corporation. To his dismay he found that, once pressing had begun, many seamen had ventured to Sunderland, where a sympathetic justice and formidable mob gave them a safer haven. Wheeler became quite agitated by his inability to impress them without suitable reinforcements, especially when one of his scouts recalled seeing 'at least five hundred fine fellows in Blue Jackets and Trowsers' swaggering through the town.[45] By the time he had assembled a recruiting party and tenders to launch a raid, the seamen were already

[41] PRO, Adm. 1/1783 (Fergusson), 6 Mar. 1755.
[42] PRO, Adm. 1/1783 (Fergusson), 1 Mar., 20 Apr. 1755.
[43] PRO, Adm. 1/1486 (Brand), 26 Feb. 1755.
[44] PRO, Adm. 1/2245 (O'Bryen), 27 Jan. 1755.
[45] PRO, Adm. 1/2660 (Wheeler), 21 Mar. 1755.

departing. Lieutenant Bottrell reported that he had 'the mortification to see droves of seamen leaving this place with their pillowcases and bundles of clothes'. Even so, he believed the service could still bring in a good haul of men. If 'we surprize the place', Bottrell advised, 'I believe we may meet with 24 hours' good amusem't.'[46] And so it transpired, although it was the common people, not the gang, who had the last laugh. When the recruiting party finally stole into Sunderland, it discovered that the seamen had already flown, having been tipped off by the masters of the tenders. As Wheeler dolefully reported, the gang 'rummaged the Town from one End to the Other and got but two men'.[47]

The Tyne and Wear tars made a fool out of the inexperienced Wheeler, who was relieved of his post after another unsuccessful raid in Sunderland and a quarrel with the Navy Board over pay and perquisites. But eluding the gangs in this manner was not uncommon in the ports and fishing villages, especially where sailors were able to avail themselves of good networks, safe hiding-places, and a sympathetic public. Sailors seldom strayed far from port, largely because they hoped to take advantage of the scarcity of maritime labour in time of war and because casual work beyond the quayside was not always easy to come by. Their ability to evade the gangs for long periods often depended upon their relations with crimps and landlords to whom they became indebted, and upon the self-interest of merchants and shipmasters who hoped to recruit them. Captain Fergusson reported that the shipmasters of Greenock had sent their sailors several miles up country 'where they are to keep them till their Lordships sent down Protections which have been wrote for'.[48] Similar complaints were lodged against some Bristolian crimps, who were prepared to hide seamen in the countryside until the outbound merchant fleets were ready to sail, at which time they would turn the sailors over for a premium.[49] It was through an intimate knowledge of these ties, and of the alehouses where seamen were likely to congregate, that regulating captains stood the best chance of finding the experienced mariners that the navy so desired.

Retreating into the countryside was the seaman's most typical response to impressment, but it was by no means the only one. Whenever seamen sensed their physical superiority over the gangs and felt confident of their collective strength, they were quite prepared to confront them. Greenland whalers, in particular, had a fearsome reputation for resisting the gangs, and the statutory protection that they enjoyed served only to enhance their sense of invincibility. Lieutenant Uxedale reported from London in March 1755 that as his men passed Greenland dock with three whalers in custody, 'they were violently assaulted by some hundreds of Men . . . who not only rescued the Men the Gang had Procured, but almost killed three of the press gang by Cutts and Bruises in their Heads and some broken Ribbs'. He admitted that he was absent from the venture because 'he was Apprehensive that if any of the Greenland Men met him, they would have abused him and used him ill, having heard that they had threatened and were determined to demolish him'.[50] A few months later Lieutenant Thane was beaten up when he attempted to impress five Greenlandmen from a boat arriving in Sunderland. According to his testimony, the master steered towards the quayside rather than the pier, where keelmen and boatmen were able to rescue the impressed men while the master and crew drubbed the gang.[51]

Thane regarded the whalers as 'the most resolute seamen of the North Country';[52] Captain Fergusson believed they were the bane of the Scottish coast. Surly, insolent, prone to smuggling in the off-season, they showed 'their Contempt' of a tender off Bo'ness by beating drums and by parading 'Brooms on their Topmaster heads', threatening to 'sweep' the gangs out of the Firth of Forth. On another occasion they had the impudence to rescue pressed men from the tenders.[53] Few seafaring trades were as intrepid as the whalers, and any gangsman who ventured aboard their boats stood to lose his fingers to flensing knives or even have his head shattered by a harpoon.[54] Yet other groups were quite prepared to take on the gangs, especially if they enjoyed community support. When Captain Gordon's gang beat up for volunteers in Bristol in January 1759, he reported, 'three hundred Seamen gathered in a riotous manner, almost killed a person whom they thought belonged to us, wounded the drummer & destroyed the drum threatning Death and Destruction of the officers, searching for them everywhere'.[55] Three months later armed sailors were still openly defying the gangs and the magistrates, forcing Gordon's men further afield in their desperate search for men. On this occasion one of Gordon's most trusted midshipmen, Cornelius Harris, a former seaman

---

[50] PRO, Adm. 1/3677/26–7.   [51] PRO, Adm. 1/2660 (Wheeler), 9 Apr. 1755.
[52] PRO, Adm. 1/2660 (Wheeler), 3 June 1755.
[53] PRO, Adm. 1/1783 (Fergusson), 3 May 1755; Adm. 1/1784 (Fergusson), 3 Feb., 29 Apr. 1756.
[54] *Northampton Mercury*, 11 Nov. 1776. See also *London Ev. Post*, 28–31 July 1759.
[55] PRO, Adm. 1/1834 (Gordon), 1 Feb. 1759.

whose local knowledge of the city had enabled him to ferret out many fugitive sailors, was brutally murdered by thirty armed privateers.[56] By the summer, after further confrontations with the seamen and affrays with the Kingswood colliers and soldiers quartered in Bristol, Gordon reported that every member of his gangs had been wounded and urgently requested more officers. Otherwise, he confessed, 'the Duty cannot be carryed on in this large and Populous City where we have everything to contend with'.[57]

The impressment riots in Bristol were unusually prolonged and violent but by no means uncommon. During the Seven Years War I have discovered similar incidents in twenty-two other British ports and an exhaustive search would doubtless reveal more. These encounters were not always led or instigated by deserters from the navy, as N. A. M. Rodger has suggested.[58] At least three disturbances were protests against the initial introduction of the press, the most dramatic occurring at Deal, where twenty-seven men, 'armed and Disguised, some having their Faces blacked, some with Caps, and others with Handkerchiefs over their heads', attacked the gang and wrecked the rendezvous.[59] Here, as elsewhere, the rioters enjoyed community support, for the Admiralty agent called upon to investigate the riot reported that it was 'very remarkable That almost every Inhabitant in the town of Deal saw the Rioters and yet they all pretend they can't name or with any Degree of certainty describe' them.[60] Indeed, it was only because a few names were revealed in an anonymous letter that the agent was able to prosecute them.

Civilian support for press-gang resisters, however, was not simply passive. Women regularly remonstrated with the gangs and were often more militant than their tearful entreaties in contemporary plays suggested. As one print acknowledged, women might bodily obstruct the gangs, attacking them with mops or whatever came to hand.[61] In London, the *Middlesex Journal* reported in October 1770 that 'a strong posse of ladies' rescued 'a genteel-looking young fellow, intoxicated with liquor' from the clutches of the press gang.[62] At Bristol two wives helped their husbands escape from the tender; elsewhere women were wounded protesting

[56] PRO, Adm. 1/1834 (Gordon), 10, 21 May 1759; *London Ev. Post*, 12–15 May 1759.

[57] PRO, Adm. 1/1834 (Gordon), 17 June 1759.

[58] Rodger, *Wooden World*, 175.   [59] PRO, Adm. 1/3677/28.

[60] PRO, Adm. 1/3677/36–7.

[61] See James Gilray, 'The Liberty of the Subject', BMC 5609, published 15 Oct. 1779. For more passive entreaties by women, see 'The Press-Gang, or English Liberty Displayed', in Hutchinson, *Press Gang*, 307. For further evidence of women opposing press gangs, see Kenneth J. Logue, *Popular Disturbances in Scotland 1780–1815* (Edinburgh, 1979), 121.

[62] *Middlesex Journal*, 4–6 Oct. 1770.

FIG. 1 The Liberty of the Subject

against impressment.[63] Less dramatically, as Captain Wheeler recognized at Newcastle, women could be exceedingly clamorous about the hardships their families would endure if their men were forced into the navy.[64]

Men with a strong sense of collective solidarity were also likely to intervene, particularly keelmen and colliers.[65] At Greenock, the coopers, riggers, carpenters, and caulkers, all of whom were powerfully placed in the burgh, openly defied the gangs, warning local magistrates that 'if they countenanced the press, they must abide by the consequences'.[66] In November 1760, 'a very great Mobb' confronted a gang that had come ashore to impress Greenock dockworkers, forcing the men 'to Fly to their Boat, and then return to the Tender for Shelter'. Later that day, when the lieutenant returned with reinforcements, the mob besieged the gang in the 'Guard House' and compelled it to release a man impressed earlier. To reassert its opposition to impressment, the crowd also destroyed one of the gang's boats, parading it 'in a Triumphant manner through the several Streets of the Town'.[67] Indeed, it was only through the intervention of the military and some of the town's principal inhabitants that a semblance of order was restored.

Even without the support of such visible groups, resistance to impressment could be general and formidable. In London, crowds regularly confronted the gangs, particularly on those festive occasions when the populace congregated in large numbers. In 1761, for example, pressmen recruiting at Southwark fair were 'so severely handled by the Populace that with Difficulty they escaped with their Lives'.[68] Even in smaller ports, mass protests could break out against the provocative actions of the press gangs. At Hightown, near Liverpool, where impressed men had mutinied aboard a tender, a mob rescued one of the mutineers from the press gang and broke open the watchhouse to free another, taking the man 'off in triumph'.[69] At Whitehaven crowds demanded retributive justice of a naval captain who had ordered his man-of-war to fire on a home-coming merchantman that had refused to heave to, wounding several members of the crew as well

---

[63] *London Ev. Post*, 28–31 July 1759; Hutchinson, *Press Gang*, 272–3. See also the account of fishwives attacking the lodgings of an unpopular press captain in Waterford, 1780, ibid. 59.

[64] PRO, Adm. 1/2660 (Wheeler), 28 Mar. 1755.

[65] See Captain Fergusson's efforts to neutralize the potential support that the Duke of Hamilton's colliers and salters might give to the seamen of Bo'ness. PRO, Adm. 1/1783 (Fergusson), 3 May 1755.

[66] Hutchinson, *Press Gang*, 213–14.   [67] PRO, Adm. 1/3678/98–9.

[68] *Whitehall Ev. Post*, 22–4 Sept. 1761; *Public Ledger*, 23 Sept. 1761. On coronation day it required 100 men to take up 30 recruits at the fair. For an example of press gangs recruiting at Horn fair, see *London Ev. Post*, 18–21 Oct. 1746.

[69] *Boddely's Bath Journal*, 25 Oct. 1756.

as some sympathizers on shore. When the captain refused to hand over the master of the ship whom he had taken into custody, 'the mob' grew very 'mutinous' and could hardly 'be restrain'd from committing Outrages and Acts of Violence'.[70] In Edinburgh, where Captain Fergusson had tricked many sailors into believing that the city was somehow immune from the press, only to sweep them up at an opportune moment, a mob besieged his lodgings and threatened to hang him at the town gate. It then 'patrolled the streets' in search of gangsmen, 'attacked their sick quarters', and 'knocked & intirely destroyed the Furniture of a Poor Old Woman because she had privately carried off a seaman who had been confined in her house with a broken leg'.[71] Only the presence of the military prevented further violence.

In both London and the provinces, then, crowd action against the gangs was not uncommon. Regulating officers naturally hoped to avoid such confrontations, well aware that the wear and tear of impressment could diminish naval morale and encourage desertions from the gangs. At the same time, they had no wish to allow their ports to become havens for fugitive seamen. During the Seven Years War Captain Fergusson was very anxious to stamp his authority on the Scottish ports for this reason, even to the point of invoking the aid of the military to do so at Dundee, Leith, and Perth.[72] South of the border, however, where military assistance was requested more sparingly, havens did spring up, especially in those towns where fishermen cherished their informal exemption from impressment as a customary right. Such was the case at Brighton, Poole, and at Parkgate in Cheshire.[73] These small towns, with their tightly integrated seafaring communities, became virtual 'no-go areas' where only the most intrepid gangsman would enter. The same was later to be true of Cork. Here, one captain noted in 1782, the sailors travelled armed in bodies, 'bid defiance to the press gangs . . . and laugh at both civil and military power'.[74]

Opposition to the press gangs did not only take militant or fugitive forms during the mid-century wars. In one important respect the terrain of conflict expanded. The efforts of the Admiralty to win the support of the civil authorities and employers in the process of impressment had the contradictory effect of making impressment a more litigious issue. Magistrates sometimes refused to back press warrants. Employers sometimes sued the

[70] *London Ev. Post*, 15–17 Apr. 1755.
[71] PRO, Adm. 1/1784 (Fergusson), 30 Mar. 1756.
[72] PRO, Adm. 1/1784 (Fergusson), 24 May, 5, 19 July 1756.
[73] Hutchinson, *Press Gang*, 163–4, 181–3, 193–4, 291.
[74] PRO, Adm. 1/1502 (Bennett), 12, 16 Apr. 1782, cited by Hutchinson, *Press Gang*, 164.

Admiralty for loss of trade or cargo, claiming that impressments had disrupted their sailing schedules or endangered the safety of their ships.[75] Workers plied a trade in protections to keep the gangs at arm's length. As early as 1734 Admiral Norris was told that 'there was not three seamen in Deal but what were protected, and that as soon as a man can but get three half-crowns or ten shillings to give to any freeman of Sandwich, he gets . . . a protection'.[76] By the 1740s the trade in all protections had grown to such proportions that the Admiralty ordered that each one should contain a description of its holder together with his abode. Every seaman not carrying his papers should be impressed, the Board advised, but protected men should not be 'as it brings a great trouble and Clamour upon them and they must at last be discharged'.[77]

Rather than evade or confront the press, then, seamen sometimes sought to exploit the ways in which impressment was enmeshed in the law. Such an escalation of legal action clearly troubled the government as the opposition to the Habeas Corpus Bill of 1758 made clear.[78] That bill sought to extend the provision of habeas corpus to impressed men. Had it passed, it would have forced the navy partially to demobilize its forces in wartime. If protections were seen as rights rather than official indulgences, if regulating officers were forced to defend their actions rather than require seamen to show why they remained at large, then the navy's manning operations would have been seriously compromised. These issues were to continue to haunt the Admiralty during the American war.

The opposition to impressment entered a new phase in the 1770s. Two factors transformed the dimensions of the conflict, namely Wilkite radicalism and the growing collective strength of the seamen themselves. The first invigorated the belief that imprisonment was unconstitutional and emboldened civic leaders to take a more aggressive stance against the gangs, especially in ports where pro-Americanism was rife. The second served to stiffen worker resistance to impressment, not simply by direct action, but also by legal challenges and evasion. Together they gave greater cohesion and impetus to the opposition to the press gang.

[75] PRO, Adm. 1/3677/270–1, 3678/259.

[76] Daniel A. Baugh (ed.), *Naval Administration 1715–1750*, Navy Records Society 120 (London, 1977), 112.

[77] Baugh, *British Naval Administration*, 174.

[78] *Parliamentary History*, 15 (1758), 871–97. See also Rodger, *Wooden World*, 187. The bill passed the Commons but was defeated in the Lords. The issue of habeas corpus was raised in Scotland in conjunction with the raid on Perth in May 1756. See PRO, Adm. 1/1784 (Fergusson), 5 July 1756.

In the first half of the century merchant seamen, the principal source of recruits for the fleet, protested against harsh conditions and hard usage by desertion, embezzlement, work stoppages, and even by mutiny and piracy. To a system of authority that was often violent, personal, and arbitrary, seamen employed their own forms of counter-aggression, culminating in acts of personal vengeance.[79] Such recriminative actions informed social relations within the fleet as well, for in 1749 we find demobilized sailors pummelling an unpopular midshipman whom they happened to meet in the street, leaving him with 'hardly any Signs of Life'.[80]

During the 1760s, however, merchant seamen increasingly resorted to the port strike to voice their grievances. Liverpool seamen successfully struck for a minimum wage of 40s. per month in 1762. Six years later, amid soaring food prices, a coal dispute, and a depression in overseas trade, strikes broke out on the Tyne and Wear, Clydeside, and the Pool of London. In response to wage cuts, seamen petitioned magistrates, intimidated employers, and attacked butchers, bakers, and middlemen in the corn trade.[81] In London, parties of sailors boarded ships to demand wages of 40s. a month, and where such commitments were not forthcoming, unrigged the sails. At the same time they began to organize a petition to the King and parliament for redress, warning their mediators of further direct action if their demands were not met. 'Most of us has ventured our lives in defence of His Majesty's Person, Crown and Dignity and for our native country and on all occasions have attacked the Enemy with courage & Resolution & have been Victorious', they complained in a handbill outlining their case,[82]

But since the conclusion of the War We Seamen have been slighted and our Wages reduced so low & Provisions so dear that we have been rendered uncapable of procuring the common necessaries of Life for Ourselves & Familys, and to be plain with you if our Grievances is not speedily redressed there is Ships & Great Guns enough at deptford and Woolwich we will kick up such a Dust in the Pool as the Londoners never see before, so when we have given the Merchants a Coup de Grease [*sic*] we will steer for France where we are well assured we shall meet with a hearty welcome.

---

[79] Marcus Rediker, *Between the Devil and the Deep Blue Sea* (Cambridge, 1987), 226, and chs. 2 and 5.

[80] *Whitehall Ev. Post*, 23–5 Feb. 1749.

[81] See George Rudé, *Wilkes and Liberty* (Oxford, 1962), ch. 6; Walter G. Shelton, *English Hunger and Industrial Disorders* (London, 1973), 184–92; John Stevenson, *Popular Disturbances in England 1700–1870* (London, 1979), 67–72, 123–4; Peter Linebaugh, review of Walter G. Shelton, *English Hunger*, in *Bulletin of the Society for the Study of Labour History*, 28 (1974), 61.

[82] William L. Clements Lib., Shelburne papers, cxxxiii, fo. 367.

Such a threat was taken seriously by the authorities, who ordered a blockade of the river. Confronted with the prospect of a sympathy strike from militant trades in the metropolis, they dealt circumspectly with the sailors, refraining from military intervention and allowing their mass demonstrations in Stepney Fields and to Palace Yard to take their course. This show of solidarity and seeming complaisance on the part of the government strengthened the seamen's hand in their dealings with the shipowners. The result was that most of their demands were met, at least by the Hudson's Bay Company and those with perishable cargoes.[83] This success emboldened seamen to strike for higher wages and greater control over their labour in the next decade, not only in London but at Gravesend, Greenock, Liverpool, and Tyneside.[84] In four of these centres opposition to impressment during the American war was sustained and significant.

During the 1768 strike, London seamen appropriated the cause of John Wilkes for their own, adding a timbre of libertarian, even anti-establishment, rhetoric to their industrial action. Although this appropriation formed part of their theatrical contest with the authorities,[85] the conjunction of Wilkite radicalism with seafaring grievances proved more than fortuitous. As is well known, Wilkes challenged the legality of general warrants when he was arrested for a seditious libel in the *North Briton* no. 45. As the Wilkite campaign gathered momentum in the late 1760s, the demands for due process under the law and appropriate respect for Englishmen's birthrights were applied to a variety of issues, among them impressment.[86] When the government began to mobilize for a potential war with Spain over the Falkland Islands in 1770, radical journalists were quick to query the legality of press warrants. Were not such warrants, radicals asked, really general warrants? Could an act of royal authority, grounded in 'long continued usage', be strictly legal if it ran contrary to the spirit of a constitution enshrined in Magna Carta and the Bill of Rights? Should sailors not be accorded their birthright? And was it not dangerous for '*Englishmen* to admit of any difference between the privileges of *Englishmen* in common'?[87]

---

[83] Ibid., fos. 369, 374.

[84] See C. R. Dobson, *Masters and Journeymen* (London, 1980), 154–70; Henry Clay Randall, 'Public Disorder in England and Wales 1765–1775', Ph.D. thesis (University of North Carolina, Chapel Hill, 1963), 439–43.

[85] On this issue, see E. P. Thompson, 'Eighteenth-Century English Society', *Social History*, 3 (1978), 160–1.

[86] See John Brewer, 'The Wilkites and the Law, 1763–74', in John Brewer and John Styles (eds.), *An Ungovernable People: The English and their Law in the Seventeenth and Eighteenth Centuries* (London, 1980), 128–71.

[87] See 'Constitutional Queries', in the *London Ev. Post*, 27–9 Nov. 1770; see also *Middlesex Journal*, 27–30 Oct. 1770.

Why should 'poor Labourers and honest Mechanics' be torn from their 'peaceful occupations', asked one West Country correspondent, when 'that idle Body called Country Squires, many of whom are born only for the Destruction of Game and the Disturbance of their Neighbours' escaped scot free?[88] In this manner radicals questioned not only the inhumanity and social inequities of impressment but its very constitutionality.

Middle-class radicals were well placed to give some of these arguments political effect, for they were firmly entrenched in the government of the City of London by 1770. As soon as the Admiralty issued press warrants they began a campaign of legal prevarication. In September the Lord Mayor, Barlow Trecothick, an American merchant and Wilkite sympathizer, delayed signing the press warrants on the grounds that they had not emanated from the Privy Council. In the mean time he harried the regulating officers to show why they had begun pressing men within the City's precincts. A month later he wrote to the Admiralty to ask why it had permitted tradesmen to apply for protections when such certificates were unnecessary.[89] Although prodded by Wilkes, he none the less declined to confront the Admiralty over the legality of impressment and ultimately agreed to sign the warrants, with the proviso that the constables would monitor the activities of the gangs and ensure that impressed men were examined by the City magistrates before they were handed over to the regulating officers.[90] In this way at least, he hoped to curb the irregularities of the gangs that had been eagerly reported in the radical press.

This strategy did not satisfy all of his colleagues. Some Wilkite aldermen refused to commit men to the tenders on the grounds that impressment was illegal in the City, a stance that was applauded in Common Council.[91] The incoming mayor, Brass Crosby, still hoped that the City's legal counsel would find some cause to contest the legality of warrants within its jurisdiction so that the City might become an 'asylum to all seafaring men', particularly to those who had 'left that way of life and devoted themselves to other occupations'.[92] But the judgement of the City's advisers, including Wilkes's own lawyer, Serjeant John Glynn, was disappointing in this regard. It upheld the legality of impressment when the safety of the realm was at risk, and advised his lordship to respect the warrants even though they were 'liable to many objections'. The best tactic, the

---

[88] *Berrow's Worcester Journal*, 1 Nov. 1770.   [89] *Middlesex Journal*, 27–30 Oct. 1770.
[90] Ibid. 13–16, 27–30 Oct. 1770.
[91] Notably John Sawbridge and Richard Oliver, see ibid. 30 Oct.–1 Nov., 1–3 Nov. 1770.
[92] Ibid. 15–27 Nov. 1770.

lawyers believed, was to focus upon the abuses of impressment not the principle itself.[93]

To this position the City stuck. Although there were some who wished the City had adopted a more confrontationalist stance, the radicals were divided over the legality of impressment and were reluctant to push their legal arguments too far.[94] During the American war, however, the radicals again sought to contest the legality of impressment, an issue now fuelled by their strident opposition to the war.[95] In October 1776 Lord Mayor Sawbridge refused to back the Admiralty's press warrants and ordered the City marshal to arrest any officer operating within its jurisdiction. While some of the loyalist aldermen defied this order and openly backed press warrants, four officers were arrested in Lime Street ward for attempting to impress two men and committed for assault by three radical, pro-American aldermen. Their intention, the aldermen declared, was to gain 'a legal determination of the grand question respecting press warrants'. But in neither this instance, nor others, was their design successful. All that the City could gain from its well-publicized actions was the discharge of its own constables and watermen; not legal immunity for its own officers and freemen, let alone an acknowledgement of the illegality of impressment. In seeking a writ of habeas corpus for John Tubbs, a City waterman impressed at Gravesend, the City lawyers even argued from the narrow ground of chartered rights confirmed by the crown and offered no fundamental challenge to the crown's right to impress in times of emergency despite the wish of some City politicians to do so.[96] Nor was the general principle of pressing challenged in the suit of John Millachip, a lighterman and freemen of the Needlemakers' Company pressed in March 1777. In fact, when the case came before Lord Mansfield at King's Bench, the City lawyers appeared as reluctant as the crown to push the general issue. 'They are always hanging on the privilege of exemption of Lord Mayor's watermen &c.,' quipped one observer, 'which, in fact, is nothing at all to the public at large.'[97]

[93] Ibid. 22–4 Nov. 1770.

[94] Junius, among others, upheld impressment. See his letters LIX, LXII, and LXIV, printed in the *Public Advertiser*, 5, 18 Oct. and 2 Nov. 1771, and reproduced in *The Letters of Junius*, ed. John Cannon (Oxford, 1978), 291–9, 307–8, 310–13.

[95] See John A. Woods, 'The City of London and Impressment 1776–1777', *Proceedings of the Leeds Philosophical and Literary Society*, 8 (1956–9), 111–27, and John Sainsbury, *Disaffected Patriots: London Supporters of Revolutionary America 1769–1782* (Kingston, 1987), 134–9.

[96] *English Reports*, 98, King's Bench Division, 27, 2 Cowper 516; on the city committee assigned to the case, see Sainsbury, *Disaffected Patriots*, 137.

[97] *Sussex Weekly Advertiser*, 23 June 1777.

The limited victories of the City frustrated many radicals. Lord Mansfield's judgment in *Rex* v. *Tubbs* once more acknowledged the legality of impressment as 'founded in immemorial usage', reinforcing an earlier decision by Justice Foster in *Rex* v. *Broadfoot* in 1743.[98] None the less radical rhetoric fuelled resentments towards impressment. 'What liberty have the poor sailors,' one asked, 'when they are dragged from their habitations, wives and children by infernal press-gangs; and without any regard to their sentiments, forced on board ships of war, to be slaughtered by the sword, or to perish by disease, famine or the climate? Have these wretched men *no right* to their lives and families, *no right* to resist their cruel and inexorable oppressors?'[99]

Such open exhortations to resist an illegal, oppressive practice inevitably encouraged violent opposition to the press gangs. Stiff fights between gangs and sailors were legion, but the American war brought an increase in the number of affrays, particularly with the population at large. At Greenock pitched battles between the press and the mob resumed. At Dover, impressed men were rescued 'by a great Number of tradesmen and others, residents of that Town'.[100] At Bristol, a midshipman taking a pressed man to the rendezvous was stopped by a local woollen draper 'who raised a Mob and took the man from him in the course of which he, the Petty Officer, was very much beat'.[101] In the East End of London, inhabitants rallied to the defence of local draymen taken up by the gang. 'The People assembled,' one newspaper reported, 'followed the sailors, drubbed them and brought back their Companions in triumph.'[102] Further to the west, in the City, a crowd prevented a gang from taking James Blake, a grocer's apprentice suspected of seafaring in the Indies before his indentures. When he was taken out of the shop on Ludgate Hill, one gangsman testified, 'he then made great resistance and called out Murder which brought a great Mob about them; that when they got to St. Paul's Churchyard the mob separated them from Blake so that they saw him no more'.[103] So great was popular opposition to impressment in the capital that recruiting parties increasingly had to resort to swift, hot presses to fill their tenders. Even then, the proportion of pressed men was significantly lower than it was in

---

[98] For a brief review of these cases, see Lloyd, *British Seaman*, 143.

[99] *London Ev. Post*, 2–5 Aug. 1777. The constitutionality of impressment was openly debated at Coachmakers' Hall in December 1777. See Donna Andrew (comp.), *London Debating Societies, 1776–1799*, London Record Society 30 (London, 1994), nos. 146, 149.

[100] PRO, Adm. 1/3681/195; M. K. Barritt, 'The Navy and the Clyde in the American War, 1777–1783', *Mariner's Mirror*, 55 (Feb. 1969), 36.

[101] PRO, Adm. 1/1903 (Hamilton), 12 July 1777.   [102] *Public Advertiser*, 23 Apr. 1778.

[103] PRO, Adm. 1/3680/350.

the provinces, amounting to only 17 per cent of those enlisted ashore by the summer of 1778.[104]

Collective protest of this kind was probably no more violent than it had been during the Seven Years War. But it was increasingly accompanied by less ostentatious forms of resistance. Workers evaded impressment by exploiting its statutory exemptions. Sailors occasionally impersonated foreigners; others pretended, often with their employer's connivance, that they were first mates or masters of ships.[105] Captain John Bover of Newcastle believed that 'many of the Masters' would swear a man was a mate to keep him out of the navy, 'tho' in reality he was not before; and by way of a *Salvo* to their Conscience, have let him act as such for 3 or 4 days, and then turn him before the Mast again'.[106] Sailors also bought protections from publicans or riverside employers. Captain Worth thought that the forty obtained by one Liverpool rigger 'quite sufficient for this port'. More, he opined, 'would only serve to strengthen riots and impede the raising Men for his Majesty's fleet'.

In more open constituencies sailors might trade their muscle or votes for a civic freedom, a privilege that did not guarantee them total immunity from the press, but one which probably enhanced their bargaining power with the regulating officers. In Newcastle seafaring men even enlisted in the militia to evade naval service.[107] Perhaps the most unusual attempt to avoid the press was that of James Meek of Dalkeith, who married the widow of a tuning-fork maker, and under the sanction of her trade indentured a few apprentices, thereby establishing his credentials as a master artisan. Captain Napier, the regulating officer in Edinburgh, thought this a cheap trick and resolutely refused to release him from the tender despite a law suit on his behalf. 'If I was to allow of such a practice', he informed the Admiralty, 'it would be easy for the Seamen to screen themselves in this country.'[108]

Such were the variety of ways in which seamen sought to exploit the statutory and customary exemptions from the press. Once taken, they might

[104] PRO, Adm. 1/5117/9/434. The corresponding figure for provincial towns was 25% (Edinburgh), 68% (Liverpool), and 66% (Newcastle). See PRO, Adm. 1/1498 (Bover), 15 May 1778, 1/2673 (Worth), 29 May 1778, 1/2221 (Napier), 21 May 1778. For an example of London coalheavers organizing themselves into gangs to resist impressment, see *Public Advertiser*, 5 Jan. 1776.

[105] PRO, Adm. 1/2673 (Worth), 8 May, 18 Sept. 1778.

[106] PRO, Adm. 1/1503 (Bover), 20 Jan. 1782.

[107] PRO, Adm. 1/1497 (Bover), 23 Dec. 1776. For an example of protections being offered to sailors who were legitimate voters, see *Newcastle Chronicle*, 9 Sept. 1780.

[108] PRO, Adm. 1/2220 (Napier), 25 Sept. 1777.

attempt to secure their release under the debtor laws. No one could order the arrest of a seaman in his majesty's service for small debts, but under a 1758 statute[109] a civil suit was possible if the debt was £20 or more. The concession was sufficient to cause trouble to the navy. When Jonathan Kelly, a seafarer and publican in Liverpool, was impressed in August 1778 upon his return from a voyage, a local wholesale brewer sued him for a debt of £20 5s. and threatened the press officer with a suit if he was not released.[110] In this case the action was probably genuine, but in others it probably was not. James Dowell, a mate impressed in Newcastle while off duty, was immediately served with a debt of £20, but 'upon particular inquiries' the regulating officer discovered 'this had been done by the advice of some attorney or another, at the suit of his own Mother; & merely to screen him from the King's service'.[111] At Dover, one attorney reported, writs for fictitious debts abounded, and when a notorious smuggler from Eyemouth was sued for debt upon his impressment, the regulating officer in the Firth of Forth feared the custom would soon spread further north of the border. 'If such a precedent were once allowed,' Captain Napier wrote to the Admiralty, 'every Man who is impressed would cause his friends [to] rear up debts against him and procure the judges warrant for taking him ashore.'[112] Napier was not alone in fearing that a flood of debt actions would undermine impressment. The Lord Advocate, Henry Dundas, expressed similar thoughts, while the Admiralty Solicitor, confronted with reports that several arrests had been made alongside and aboard ships in the Nore, wondered whether the Admiralty could claim that the Nore was 'upon the High sea' and therefore beyond civil jurisdiction. Was it not 'a Question of so much Importance to His Majesties Service', he submitted to their lordships, 'as to merit a judicial Determination; and if so, whether it may not be proper . . . to cause Directions . . . to be given to the Commanders . . . at or near the Nore, not to suffer any Bailiffs, in future, to take away any person or Persons belonging to His Majesty's Service'.[113]

Seamen and riverside workers, then, showed plenty of legal ingenuity in evading the press, to a point that the Admiralty contemplated bringing in a bill in 1780 to close the loopholes they so readily exploited.[114] Their

---

[109] 31 Geo. II c. 10, § 27.   [110] PRO, Adm. 1/3680/408, 420.

[111] PRO, Adm. 1/1498 (Bover), 22 Mar. 1778.

[112] PRO, Adm. 1/2220 (Napier), 22 Apr. 1777; for Dover, see Adm. 1/3681/82.

[113] PRO, Adm. 1/3680/256; Adm. 1/2220 (Napier), memo to Napier, 20 June 1777.

[114] *London Courant*, 1 Mar. 1780. Under this proposed bill no seaman could shield himself from the navy by serving in the militia. Nor could he be arrested for debt on board a man-of-war unless the writ had been issued before he embarked. It was also suggested that no debts contracted by seamen ashore could be recovered by law.

success, none the less, depended upon the strength of their local networks, among employers, friends, and relatives. Seamen were less likely to indict the gangs for false imprisonment, for such a course of action required time and money that was usually beyond their means. That strategy was re- served for the middling sort, who, well acquainted with the legal struggles of the City of London, were quite prepared to take regulating officers to court. Captain Cunninghame reported in late 1778 that at a fair near Faversham his recruiting officer was 'obstructed in his duty by the insuf- ferable behaviour of William Sutton belonging to the Kings Mills at that place, who not only raised a Mob & thereby prevented Lieut. Jarvis from entering several Volunteers that he was in treaty with, but at length pro- ceeded to such insolence and abuse to that Officer that he was induced to bring Sutton before me'. Cunninghame promptly dispatched Sutton to HMS *Conquistador*, but Sutton retaliated by obtaining a writ of habeas corpus for his discharge and hired a lawyer to sue Cunninghame for false imprison- ment. The captain informed the Admiralty that he had only been defend- ing one of his most energetic and loyal officers, a man who had the navy's interest 'strongly at heart' and was commended by the local magistrates 'for the quiet manner of conducting the service'.[115] But the Admiralty refused to defend the suit with the result that Cunninghame eventually had to pay Sutton £38 12s. 9d. for his costs and damages.

Individuals with money and influence were quite prepared to take regu- lating officers to court for irregular impressments. Master mariners were quick to demand the recovery of impressed apprentices, and prevarications on the part of captains sometimes led to suits for damages. George Hurry, a Yarmouth merchant, sued Captain Thompson of the *Conquistador* for refusing to release two of his apprentices. He might not have, he confessed, had the Admiralty acted promptly to rectify the abuse, for 'in the general confusion of an impress officers may be excused for taking an apprentice as they cannot have time to examine and see whether he is protectable or not'. But Hurry said he had been forced to apply to the King's Bench for a writ of habeas corpus, and his son had to track down the apprentices as they travelled to the Nore, a tedious business which delayed his ship eighteen days. In the end Hurry brought in an action for damages which included travelling expenses and the cost of funding three men for the voy- age. He would have liked to have claimed more than the £35 12s. 4d. he filed, he said, for he had 'Eight Apprentices on Board in Idleness' while his ship was detained, and 'also a great deal of Trouble and Loss of Time

---

[115] PRO, Adm. 1/1612/129 (Cunninghame).

myself'. His apprentices, he continued, 'were for a long time illegally confined without even a bed to lay upon and I have no doubt but were separate Actions brought for it, a Jury would give considerable Damages to each'.[116] In this instance the Admiralty escaped lightly. George Hurry was not a man to be trifled with. He was a leading member of the Presbyterian congregation at Yarmouth and an outspoken opponent of the American war; a man whose family was very litigious, as his subsequent feud with the registrar of the Admiralty Court at Great Yarmouth revealed.[117] No doubt Hurry's reputation disposed the Admiralty Solicitor to settle his suit out of court.[118]

Shipowners were not the only people to sue naval officers for false impressment. In July 1778 Captain Graham impressed one Richard Wilson, a traveller accompanied by two 'Women of the Town', whom he met at the Black Inn at Stockton-on-Tees. Wilson had apparently criticized the press gangs in the 'most abusive and scurrilous terms . . . they were a vile set of People, and Scoundrels and Rascals as well as those who employ'd them, . . . none but the lowest persons, the very Dregs of the people, would be employed in such a service'. Graham and his fellow officer were incensed by these remarks, and they took Wilson in, believing, so they claimed, that he had 'every Appearance both in Manners and person of being a Seaman, particularly his hands, [which] seem'd as if they had been much accustomed to handling Ropes'.[119] But it transpired that Wilson was a clerk to a London merchant travelling north to settle his affairs in Westmorland. Certainly he was respectable enough to get a Stockton gentleman to stand him bail. And he repaid Captain Graham for his discourtesy by suing him for £60 damages for illegal impressment. He did not get it. The jury only offered him £25. Yet even that amount troubled Benjamin Root, the local barrister assigned to the case, who protested that Wilson's 'scurrility and ill Behavior certainly intitled him to be sent on Board of the Tender'.[120] 'As Things go now,' he reflected in July 1779, 'a Man who wishes to do the best must sometimes act improperly.'

Root's remarks point to some of the difficulties gangs faced during the American war, when anti-ministerial ferment and war-weariness fortified

---

[116] PRO, Adm. 1/3681/27–8.

[117] On this case, see Douglas Hay, 'Prosecution and Power: Malicious Prosecution in the English Courts, 1750–1850', in Douglas Hay and Francis Snyder (eds.), *Policing and Prosecution in Britain 1750–1850* (Oxford, 1989), 365–6. On the Hurry family, see James E. Bradley, *Religion, Revolution and English Radicalism: Nonconformity in Eighteenth-Century Politics and Society* (Cambridge, 1990), 239–40, 311, 404, 411.

[118] PRO, Adm. 1/3681/64.   [119] PRO, Adm. 1/3681/134–6.

[120] PRO, Adm. 1/3681/137.

the opposition to impressment. As James Bradley has emphasized, Britain was deeply divided over the conflict in America in the opening years of the war, with perhaps one in three of the political nation demanding a conciliatory policy towards America and deploring the government's pursuit of what was seen as an impolitic, civil war.[121] Even with the entry of France into the struggle, anti-ministerial feeling ran high, as the demonstrations surrounding Admiral Keppel's controversial court martial made clear.[122] To a significant minority of Englishmen, the resistance to impressment simply underscored Opposition arguments about the disastrous consequences of the American engagement to trade, empire, and liberty, and strengthened reservations about the government's blinkered and incompetent handling of the war itself. As the 1777 parliamentary debate on naval reform revealed, the unpopularity of impressment was very much part of the armoury of the anti-war movement and remained so as the crisis over America intensified.[123]

The Admiralty was well aware of this and sought to keep controversial incidents surrounding impressment out of the limelight. This was particularly the case with murder trials. On a number of occasions gangsmen were charged with the murder of civilians at a coroner's inquest, and in each instance the Admiralty attempted to handle the situation delicately so that local passions would not be fuelled against its recruiting drives. Despite the hesitations of some naval officers, the defendants were handed over to the civil power. Wherever possible, cases were removed from the assizes to King's Bench to await special verdicts, thereby insulating them from popular judgement. Such happened to fifteen gangsmen prosecuted for the murder of an Ipswich publican killed in a search of his house for the crew of a store-ship, and to Rowland Phillips, a midshipman who had attempted to bring in a fishing smack off the Devonshire coast and had fired at its owner out of frustration. In both instances the judges upheld the Admiralty's defence that the men acted in the course of duty.[124] In the one case where a gangsman was successfully prosecuted for murder,

---

[121] James E. Bradley, *Popular Politics and the American Revolution in England* (Macon, Ga., 1986), 207–16. See also his *Religion, Revolution and English Radicalism*, 319–30.

[122] See next chapter.

[123] *Parliamentary History*, 19 (1777), 81–103. Luttrell's bill was introduced into the Commons on 11 Mar. 1777. It was defeated by 106 votes to 52. For an example of an inland town where opposition to impressment converged with opposition to the American war, see the comments on Leicester in the *Public Advertiser*, 7 Jan. 1777.

[124] *Gentleman's Magazine*, 49 (1779) 323, 50 (1780), 72–4; PRO, Adm. 1/3680/317–22, 369. In the first Justice Willes dismissed the case on the grounds that it was impossible to determine who had killed the landlord. In the second the charge was reduced to manslaughter.

significantly at a county assize, the Admiralty Solicitor moved quickly to obtain a respite of the sentence until his majesty's pleasure was known.[125] No gangsman was about to be strung up on the gallows; that would have been disastrous for publicity as well as naval morale. But the jurisdiction of the civil courts had to be respected.

At the local level regulating captains did all they could to temper passions during a disastrous affray. When a recruiting tender fired on several seamen scuttling ashore at the Avon estuary, killing one and injuring two others, the regulating captain moved quickly to defuse the incident. 'As I was apprehensive of a tumult & some disturbance in case the body had been brought up to Bristol,' reported Captain Hamilton, 'I prevailed with the Coroners to take the inquest on board the Rose Tender where the body was, and promised to pay the charges that might accrue from their being obliged to go there.' 'I also ordered the body to be carryed ashore & buryed at St Georges, near Kingroad, in a decent and proper manner,' he continued, and saw to it that the wounded sailors had their wounds dressed by a surgeon.[126] Such steps, it was hoped, would keep the opposition to impressment within manageable limits.

Yet no amount of tact could prevent recruitment from being a time-consuming and vexatious business. No press officer could operate an efficient service without the co-operation of the civil authorities and an unfortunate impressment or miscalculation could easily sour relations between them. When Lieutenant Lowe drew his sword on several Wapping headboroughs and runners of Justice Sherwood, refusing to be detained by such a 'scurvy crew', he soon found himself embroiled in the law.[127] The same was true of Captain Pascal, the regulating officer at King's Lynn. He attempted to impress one of the sea apprentices of the current mayor and refused to release him until his master personally produced his indenture. Convicted of the assault and illegal imprisonment of the apprentice at the Norwich assizes, Pascal was ordered to pay costs and damages when the case was moved to King's Bench.[128] Even where regulating officers went out of their way to cultivate good relations with the magistrates, there was often a price to be paid. Captain Hamilton had to return freemen promptly to the Bristol mayor, and concur with his request to protect the Severn trowmen who brought provisions to the city. When his gangs were foolhardy enough to impress several pilots from Pill, the whole traffic on the river Avon ground

[125] PRO, Adm. 1/3681/270.   [126] PRO, Adm. 1/1903 (Hamilton), 17 Aug. 1777.

[127] PRO, Adm. 1/3680/390–5.   [128] PRO, Adm. 1/3681/109–10, 162.

to a halt, and he had quickly to discharge them lest he antagonize an already politically divided corporation and Society of Merchant Venturers.[129]

Captain Worth of Liverpool did not have to negotiate the political divisions of civic politics in quite the same way, for the corporation of the Mersey port was staunchly loyalist. Yet he had to tread warily lest he annoy the Chamber of Commerce and anger a militant marine that had struck twice in 1775 over wages and layoffs in the slave trade, terrorizing the town for a week.[130] He was persistently plagued by the Liverpudlian passion for privateering, which not only kept many daring seamen at arm's length from the press, but prompted some raids on his own rendezvous. Privateering gangs had been formed, he reported to the Admiralty in August 1778, 'not only to invite but absolutely [to] press men'.

This morning my lodgings was surrounded by a large Body who came to demand a man belonging to their party, impress'd in the course of the Night by our Gang. My answer was no threats should prevail [but] with a man equal in goodness being brought me. That was soon comply'd with by their pressing one. I beg to assure their lordships nothing should have obliged me to listen to any terms from a Mob, had it not been to prevent the house I was in . . . being destroyed, besides having the press Gang insulted and abused by a lawless crew that were at no loss to find hiding places.[131]

Liverpool was a rapidly expanding, raw port, whose unruly salts were more than a match for the press gang. Even when taken, there was no guarantee they would reach the fleet, for mutinies on the Mersey tenders were commonplace, with men forcing the hatches and threatening crews with handspikes and staffs.[132] The situation was only marginally better on Tyneside. Here Captain Bover found plenty of potential material for impressment, for there was a wide range of men who made their livings on the river and not a few who had spent some youthful days at sea. But Newcastle was a radical town in the 1770s over which the loyalist magistracy exercised an increasingly fragile control. When John Wesley's proministerial tract against the American rebels was distributed gratis by the magistrates in 1775, the popular response was to burn the Methodist leader

[129] PRO, Adm. 1/1905 (Hamilton), 25 June 1779.

[130] Randall, 'Public Disorder in England and Wales 1765–1775', 440–3; PRO, Adm. 1/2672 (Worth), 15 Apr. 1777.

[131] PRO, Adm. 1/2673 (Worth), 26 Aug. 1778. On the rough culture of the privateers, see Gomer Williams, *History of the Liverpool Privateers* (London, 1897), 4–6, 26–9, 184–9.

[132] PRO, Adm. 1/2675 (Worth), 11 Sept. 1780; see also 1/2672 (Worth), 25 June 1777, 1/2673 (Worth), 6 Mar. 1778, 1/2674 (Worth), 6 May 1779, 18 Aug. 1779.

in effigy.[133] Three and a half years later, during the Keppel demonstrations, Lords North, Sandwich, and Germain were burnt as the 'abettors of the American war'.[134] Such was the solidarity of Tyneside, Captain Bover reported, 'where the common people know one another almost to a man, and can give a good guess at each others affairs', that informers against seamen were sometimes 'unmercifully beat or rather nearly murthered'.[135] The expectation of a good yield of impressed men from the bustling Tyne thus proved a little elusive, and it required all of Bover's experience, tact, and the raw muscle of his gangs to bring in a good roll of recruits. In the summer of 1777 he found himself intervening on behalf of a midshipman who had been prosecuted 'for using a Man rather severely' and writing to the Admiralty on behalf of one Henry Williams, 'who was unluckily hurt by one of our people whereby he is in a great measure disabled from following his trade'.[136] By the spring of 1778 he was advising the Admiralty to abandon their hot press, because on the Tyne the word went around so quickly that the seamen had 'gone off a good way into the Country'.[137]

During the American war there were many constraints, legal, political, logistical, curbing the activities of the press gangs, and the wonder is that the service operated at all. Yet the evidence suggests that, however cumbersome, expensive, and vexatious impressment happened to be, it did bring men in; and in the three ports for which I have regular figures, namely Liverpool, Leith, and Newcastle, it brought them in on a fairly consistent basis. Why was this so?

Part of the reason was that there were always men desperate or adventurous enough to volunteer. Although the American war saw no harvest failures of any magnitude, unemployment and wage cuts in some of the major ports, brought on by the dislocation of trade with America and the diversion of capital into other areas, buoyed up the initial flood of naval recruits.[138] Furthermore, however unpopular impressment happened to

---

[133] *Newcastle Journal*, 28 Oct. 1775. On Newcastle's radical politics, see Kathleen Wilson, *The Sense of the People: Politics, Culture and Imperialism in England, 1715–1785* (Cambridge, 1995), ch. 7, and Thomas Knox, 'Popular Politics and Provincial Radicalism: Newcastle-upon-Tyne, 1769–85', *Albion*, 11 (1976), 224–41.

[134] *London Ev. Post*, 20–3 Feb. 1779.   [135] PRO, Adm. 1/1497 (Bover), 20 Sept. 1777.

[136] PRO, Adm. 1/1497 (Bover), 22, 28 June 1777.

[137] PRO, Adm. 1/1498 (Bover), 27 Mar. 1778.

[138] Ramsay Muir, *History of Liverpool* (London, 1907), 218–20; Peter Marshall, *Bristol and the American War of Independence*, Local History Association (Bristol, 1977), 13–14. Foreign ships clearing Newcastle dropped from 403 in 1777 to 285 in 1778, to 230 in 1779. See *Annual Register* (1779), 239.

be among seafolk and the poor in general, it was a useful way of ridding the community of undesirables. Magistrates, radical or not, had little compunction about discharging the idle and disorderly aboard Admiralty tenders. 'That government may *compel* the assistance of dissolute and idle people, who have no visible means of getting their living . . . is a point which will not now be controverted,' wrote one correspondent to the radical *General Advertiser*.[139] Such an argument did not go uncontested. 'To force a Man into the Service against his Consent, merely because he has solicited Charity,' reflected one writer, was 'a Species of Tyranny' that could not be 'too severely reprobated'.[140] Yet the energetic recruitment of vagrants and other 'undesirables' remained one answer to the iniquities of the press as well as to the maintenance of law and order.[141] It also offered unscrupulous justices an opportunity for windfall profits, for the freedom of those deemed 'idle and disorderly' could be bought, at a price.[142]

Local communities were sometimes quite happy to use impressment to rid their neighbourhoods of troublesome men. Young men who refused to marry their pregnant girlfriends could find themselves before the regulating officer at the 'rondy'.[143] So, too, could estranged husbands.[144] The parishioners of Sittingbourne in Kent were pleased that Edward Wood, a master of a small fishing smack, was taken up by the press gang. They told Lieutenant Appleby they 'would rather keep his family than such a Riotous fellow should be in the parish'.[145] Similarly, Captain Worth impressed a 'stout fellow' named George Wood 'at the request of the neighbourhood where he lived, being a common disturber of the peace'. The same was true of Captain Bover with respect to an unscrupulous hawker who was said to be the 'terror' of Sunderland and Shields, both 'from his bodily strength and quarrelsome disposition'.[146]

---

[139] *General Advertiser*, 13 May 1779. My emphasis. The printer of this paper was William Parker of Fleet, prosecuted for seditious libel for attacking the government during the Keppel demonstrations earlier in the year.

[140] *Public Advertiser*, 6 Jan. 1776.

[141] For an example of poachers being impressed, see *Derby Mercury*, 19–26 Feb. 1779. For an attempt by JPs to impress two men charged but acquitted of highway robbery, see *Bath Chronicle*, 18 Mar. 1779.

[142] According to 'Marinero', some London trading justices were charging 'vagrants' 1*s*. a head for an informal discharge from the press. See *Public Advertiser*, 17 June 1777.

[143] *Sussex Weekly Advertiser*, 17 Mar. 1777.

[144] *Middlesex Journal*, 27–30 Oct. 1770. In this instance, where a wife informed the press gang of the recent arrival of her husband from the East Indies, the husband retaliated by pawning every item in the house before going aboard the tender.

[145] PRO, Adm. 1/1611/186 (Cunninghame).

[146] PRO, Adm. 1/1498 (Bover), 4 Oct. 1778; Adm. 1/2676 (Worth), 23 July 1781.

Impressment could also be used to reinforce the fabric of authority and labour discipline. Although merchants, mariners, and riverside employers frequently experienced a serious depletion of men in time of war, impressment did afford them an opportunity of weaning the troublesome from their workforce and resisting demands for better pay.[147] In 1771, for example, the seamen at Shields opposed a reduction of wages by striking the sails of all the ships in the harbour, only to have their protest thwarted by the appearance of the *Alderney* man-of-war. Six years later, when the sailors rioted for a raise in wages, the shipmasters set the press gang upon them.[148] Such a tactic had also been used at the southern ports, decades before, for a correspondent reported to the *London Evening Post* that when 'some sturdy Fellows belonging to a Ship near Southampton . . . refus'd to go the Voyage without a Rise of Wages', the master of the vessel 'gave Scent of them to a Press Gang' and had them sent on board a man-of-war.[149]

Master mariners also used the gang to rid themselves of unruly apprentices, and very occasionally to recover those that ran away.[150] Likewise shipbuilders and other riverside employers distributed their protections to reward the loyal and reprimand the recalcitrant. Because employers were such important intermediaries in cases of contested impressments, they were able to use their advantage to exact deference and respect from the vulnerable. This was potentially true of all employers, not simply those in dockland or the merchant marine, for there were cases where tramping artisans or travelling apprentices were taken up by the civil authorities on the grounds that they were not gainfully employed, and it frequently required the personal intervention of their masters, or perhaps a character reference, to have them released.[151]

In a similar fashion political or religious patrons were entreated to secure the discharge of supporters taken up by the navy. During the Seven Years War, Lady Huntingdon was asked to secure the release of several Methodists who had been impressed at Hastings at the instigation or encouragement of a local clergyman.[152] Likewise Lord Townshend, the leading

---

[147] One correspondent recommended that master tailors in London inform on their striking journeymen. See *Public Advertiser*, 13 May 1777.

[148] *York Courant*, 19, 26 Mar. 1771; *London Ev. Post*, 27 Feb.–1 Mar. 1777.

[149] *London Ev. Post*, 3–6 Nov. 1739.

[150] PRO, Adm. 1/1498 (Bover), 6 Jan. 1778; Adm. 1/1904 (Hamilton), 18 Apr. 1778.

[151] See, for example, PRO, Adm. 1/3681/112.

[152] BL, Add. MS 32907, fos. 427–8; 32916, fo. 43; 33053, fos. 282–3. See also Cheshunt College Archives, Cambridge, F1/25 1161. I am indebted to Dr Jeff Chamberlain of the College of St Francis, Joliet, Illinois, and to Susan Foote for these references.

patron of Yarmouth, was solicited to intercede on behalf of a local free-man and master of a small brigantine. He had been impressed off the coast of Ireland and was languishing in Portsmouth hospital with a bad 'rhu-matick paine'. Townshend's influence was also requested to secure the release of a ship's carpenter who was 'sickly & has a Wife & 4 or 5 Children in poor State', and to obtain protections for several local coopers.[153] Impressment, in other words, operated like other aspects of the law in the eighteenth century; it allowed for the discretionary favours of the rich and powerful. For these reasons it was the preferred option of many employers and patrons to the problem of manning the fleet.

In some respects the merchants and shipowners wanted the best of all worlds. When they solicited favours from the government they frequently claimed that the merchant marine was the nursery of the navy; yet they complained vocally about the loss of their men to the press gangs. While they lobbied vigorously for Admiralty convoys during wartime, they were reluctant to release mariners who might have manned them. The contra-dictory postures of the merchants, and the general unwillingness of the propertied classes to pay for an efficient navy, made the question of man-ning an intractable one. It only required popular resistance to impressment and an extended theatre of war to bring it to a crisis.

The difficulties of manning the fleet were already apparent in 1777, when desertion was already beginning to deplete the existing pool of seamen, running at roughly double the rate of the Seven Years War.[154] But these difficulties intensified in the next two years when the active ships in port were short of 5,000–7,000 men. In 1778 Admiral Keppel had complained of the delays in manning the Channel fleet.[155] By the summer of the fol-lowing year, when the prospect of a combined Franco-Spanish force against Britain loomed large, disease and desertion had begun to swamp the sys-tem of recruitment, with the press gangs having to find at least three men for every two in active service, and perhaps even two for one.[156] The situ-ation became so urgent that the government decided to take unprecedented steps to expand the home fleet and to thwart an invasion. It issued orders to impress all seamen, even those with protections guaranteed by statute.

[153] William L. Clements Lib., Townshend papers, 297/3/2, 21, 23.

[154] In the Seven Years War the desertion rate was around 7% of those annually listed for pay. In the American war it was around 13–14%. See Rodger, *Wooden World*, 203 and Usher, 'Royal Navy Impressment', 685.

[155] *The Private Papers of John, Earl of Sandwich, First Lord of the Admiralty 1771–1782*, ed. G. R. Barnes and J. H. Owen, 4 vols. (London, 1932–8), ii. 46–7, 54–6.

[156] Usher, 'Royal Navy Impressment', 682–5; Piers Mackesy, *The War for America 1775–1783* (London, 1964), 116–17.

To secure the gangs from legal recrimination, it suspended habeas corpus in cases of impressment. It did so before seeking parliamentary approval for its actions, a matter which was sought retrospectively.[157] To speed up manning, the government openly broke the law.

Opposition to this unprecedented measure was fully anticipated in some coastal towns and the military was ordered to stand by in case of trouble.[158] At Yarmouth the gates of the town were closed and the bridge drawn up when the mackerel boats 'were stripped of all their men'.[159] On Tyneside the keelmen and colliers were hauled onto tenders, bringing the coal trade to a standstill. 'The Violence of these proceedings must naturally operate to the Misery of Many families,' one correspondent reflected, 'but our Ministry have made this Calamity necessary for the general Protection of the State.'[160] Not everyone viewed the raids with such equanimity. In Newcastle the pitmen 'assembled in a large body . . . armed themselves with cutlasses and bludgeons, and swore vengeance against the gangs that should attempt to press them'. At Shields the resistance of a Greenlander crew gave rise to an acrimonious coroner's inquiry in which one seaman was judged to have been 'feloniously killed by persons unknown'.[161] In Cornwall hundreds of tinners assembled and 'rescued several of their Fellow Workmen' in a bloody and deadly affray. 'Not a press-gang dare venture in any Part of Cornwall to impress any others,' one paper concluded.[162] At Leith, where Captain Napier scoured the shipyards for men, applications were made by employers to delay their transfer to the fleet until the law was clarified. But Napier 'judged it would be folly to obey any interdict' and promptly shipped the men off to the Nore, requesting at the same time that the Solicitor-General inform the judges of the Court of Session of the nature of his instructions.[163]

By and large, the magistrates and merchants of the major ports co-operated with the Admiralty in its hour of crisis. In Liverpool, Captain Worth went out of his way to win the support of the mayor and leading citizens, who promised not only their assistance but a large bounty to encourage volunteers to join up. In Bristol, however, the grand press did nothing to ameliorate the festering tensions between Opposition Whigs and

---

[157] *Parliamentary History*, 20 (1779), 962–9. The pertinent statute was 19 Geo. III c. 75.

[158] *The Correspondence of King George the Third from 1760 to December 1783*, ed. Sir John Fortescue, 6 vols (London, 1928), iv. 362, no. 2666.

[159] *Norfolk Chronicle*, 3 July 1779.

[160] *Public Advertiser*, 7 July 1779; *General Advertiser*, 2 July 1779. Unfortunately Captain Bover's in-letters to the Admiralty during this crucial period are missing.

[161] *Bath Journal*, 19 July 1779; *Newcastle Journal*, 7 Aug. 1779.

[162] *Public Advertiser*, 6 July 1779.   [163] PRO, Adm. 1/2221 (Napier), 28 June 1779.

ministerialists, despite Captain Hamilton's willingness to discharge a free-man taken in the round-up lest it provoke a political row in the corporation.[164] Within the Council, Lord North's supporters failed to muster sufficient support for a loyalist address to the throne; at Merchants' Hall they only narrowly survived an Opposition Whig challenge.[165] In this factious atmosphere the impressment of James Caton, a former sea captain and merchant of known American sympathies, served only to heighten the political feud.[166] Although Caton was quickly released through the legal intervention of John Dunning and Edmund Burke, the episode underscored the recriminative climate in which impressment was conducted in this leading Atlantic port. What was true of Bristol applied *a fortiori* to London. Here the radical-dominated corporation resolutely refused to support the government's recruiting drive, seeing the crisis as yet another example of the government's blinkered, incompetent, and illiberal tendencies. As a result, the government had to use troops to cordon off the Thames during the hot press, bringing trade on the river to a standstill.[167] Even so, London recruited proportionately fewer men for the navy than the provincial ports, where bounties of £18 or more sweetened the search for men and took some of the violence out of recruitment.[168]

The opposition to impressment lost some of its political momentum after 1779, although popular hostility to the gangs continued. In the opening years of the American war the two were inextricably intertwined. The radical preoccupation with individual rights and due process before the law, combined with sympathy for the American cause, fuelled the struggle against impressment and broadened the terrain on which it might be challenged. The result was that impressment became an increasingly litigious issue as well as a target of more customary modes of protest, constraining its application in the ports and forcing the government to sidestep its statutory limitations, if only for a short period of time.

[164] PRO Adm. 1/1905 (Hamilton), 17 June 1779.

[165] *Bath Journal*, 5, 12 July 1779; John Latimer, *The Annals of Bristol in the Eighteenth Century* (Bristol, 1893; reprint Bath, 1970), 439–40.

[166] On the Caton affair, see *London Ev. Post*, 13–15, 17–20 July 1779; *Bath Journal*, 19 July 1779; PRO, Adm. 1/1906 (Hamilton), 5 Feb. 1780, which reveals that Caton attempted to sue Captain Hamilton and Lieutenant Lane for illegal impressment. See also Marshall, *Bristol and the American War*, 15–17.

[167] *Ipswich Journal*, 3 July 1779.

[168] According to the *Public Advertiser*, 3 July 1779, 6,579 men were recruited in the first grand sweep of the press, with 517 from London, 376 from Newcastle, 420 from Hull, 382 from Whitehaven, 370 from Yarmouth, 442 from Liverpool, and no less than 640 from Bristol. For details about bounties, which were derived from various sources, see *London Ev. Post*, 3–6 July 1779 and *Adam's Weekly Courant*, 10 Aug. 1779.

Yet ultimately the radicals came no nearer to resolving the issue than their opponents. Advocates of a minimalist state, they were sceptical of alternative systems of compulsion. Appalled by the inhumanities and arbitrary nature of the press, they were diffident about registration schemes that might enhance government influence. Few middle- or upper-class radicals were able to reconcile their belief in intrinsic liberties of the subject with the requirements of national and local security. Political virtue required some form of social regulation and discipline, as did the imperatives of state defence. 'In general,' argued Junius, 'it is *not* unjust that, when the rich man contributes his wealth, the *poor* man should serve the state in person; otherwise the latter contributes nothing to the defence of that law and constitution from which he demands safety and protection.'[169] Most radicals were more equivocal about impressment than Junius, and certainly less candid about its social ramifications. Yet relatively few were prepared to abandon it outright. Temple Luttrell's bill, which was the closest the radicals came to defining an alternative to the prevailing system of manning the navy, actually retained impressment as a last resort for those who refused to register.[170] Even Granville Sharp, who was one of the driving forces behind the City of London's opposition to impressment, seems to have had little compunction about the forcible recruitment of 'idle wretches' into the navy, emphasizing rather the rights of 'honest' seamen or 'industrious' fishermen to protection from the press gangs.[171] For the recalcitrant and uncooperative, for vagrants and ne'er-do-wells, impressment remained a useful disciplinary instrument.

The disciplinary possibilities of impressment were not lost on the merchants, either, despite the demands that it made on their resources. Indeed, because the manning problem was in the last analysis a local one, merchants powerfully placed in local government could always barter with the Admiralty's representatives about reconciling the needs of the state with those of commerce, and at the same time, through the distribution of protections and the channels of legal redress, reinforce their own position in the community. Certainly impressment was inconvenient, vexatious, and by no means inexpensive, for the fees for Admiralty protections alone were estimated at £24,000 per annum during the American war.[172] Not surprisingly merchants and port employers could be downright obstructive when impressment seriously impaired their economic interests. But it was

---

[169] *Letters of Junius*, 311.
[170] For a brief summary, see Lloyd, *British Seaman*, 173–4.
[171] See Woods, 'The City of London and Impressment', 112, 123–4.
[172] This was the figure cited by 'Marinero' in the *Public Advertiser*, 17 June 1777.

the price to be paid for a state whose capacity to wage war had brought long-term wealth and prosperity to the mercantile middle class. More bureaucratic systems of recruitment would have given merchants and man-ufacturers less bargaining power, both with the central government and with their employees.

To the sailors themselves, and to the craftsmen and labourers who worked the rivers, impressment was the most striking example of the intrusive and discriminatory policies of the wartime state whose imperatives so shaped their lives. Historians have sometimes questioned whether conscription would have been less unjust or chaotic given the continuing shortage of seamen.[173] Perhaps not, but the fact remains that seafarers were the one class for whom compulsory service to the state in wartime remained a real-ity. During the American war, when the rhetoric of liberty vindicated the rights of the 'meanest man in Britain', to use Junius's phrase, the sailors felt this deprivation keenly. When the Edinburgh authorities offered as much as £27 to entice volunteers to enter the fleet during the invasion scare of 1779, very few entered, one newspaper reported, 'so little Effect has Money upon the Mind of the Sailor, when his Liberty, as he calls it, is to be the Purchase'.[174]

---

[173] Rodger, *Wooden World*, 153.
[174] *Adam's Weekly Courant*, 10 Aug. 1779.

4

The Trial of Admiral Keppel

Come listen every honest tar,
Who loves Old England's glory,
Whilst I relate a dreadful spar,
Which chanc'd 'twixt Whig and Tory.

Bold Keppel he a signal gave,
Which brought Sir Hugh to action;
At which Sir Hugh looked very grave,
And now asks satisfaction.
(A favourite ballad sung at Portsmouth,
Morning Chronicle, 29 Jan. 1779)

THINE enemies are cover'd with disgrace
Sir Hugh looks down, asham'd to shew his face
Thy honour thou hast clear'd, part all denial,
It's more a triumph, Keppel, than a trial.
(*Norwich Mercury*, 13 Feb. 1779)

Most admirals in the eighteenth century achieved popularity by spectacular victories. Admiral Augustus Keppel achieved it by a spectacular trial. Court-martialled for his inconclusive engagement with the French off Ushant at the request of his subordinate officer Sir Hugh Palliser, his honourable acquittal in February 1779 was jubilantly celebrated throughout England. According to reports in the London and provincial press over 160 demonstrations were staged in his favour, coupled in most instances with the burning or hanging of Palliser in effigy. Comparable in scale to the Wilkite demonstrations, the Keppel affair rivalled the radical in popular engagement. It was one of the *causes célèbres* of the decade.

The Keppel affair has been conventionally portrayed as little more than an interesting sideline to the American Revolution, an example of the rancorous politics that debilitated the British war effort against the combined powers of America, France, and ultimately Spain. Yet the episode poses the important question of how one might explain and contextualize the country-wide jubilations in favour of Keppel, whose aristocratic airs and mediocre abilities might easily have generated indifference, if not scorn, rather than acclaim. Put bluntly, the Keppelian fervour fits uneasily into a tradition of social history 'from below' that focuses exclusively upon the self-activity of the subaltern classes in sharp juxtaposition to those 'above'. It also contraverts the contrary and now largely discredited view of client populations in the thrall of élitist ideology or deep-rooted conservative mentalities. Rather the episode calls for an examination of the ways in which Keppel's predicament and patriotism was discursively constructed in the public domain and negotiated by a national audience. As such it offers an unusually rich conduit into the popular passions generated by the American war and their complex resolutions.

If the Keppel controversy is explored in this manner, then it necessarily demands some attention to the political culture of the mid-Georgian era; in particular to the development of what Jurgen Habermas termed the 'public sphere', that realm of social life 'in which something approaching public opinion can be formed'.[1] For the trial occurred at a moment when the English press had begun to emancipate itself from aristocratic patronage and rigorous governmental surveillance and prosecution. It was a time when the political horizons of middling Englishmen, whether in London or the provinces, were converging, and when the density of social networks was such that new forms of political association, only tenuously associated with aristocratic factions, had emerged. Within this context, the Keppel trial became more than a battleground of high political manœuvre. It was a political spectacle that mobilized the public sphere in enterprising ways, drawing upon the resources of a more open, accessible politics that featured not only the traditional forms of crowd action, but also the commercial and predominantly bourgeois forms of political expression. It is from the perspective of this new politics of persuasion that the Keppelian fervour of 1779 can best be understood.

When Admiral Keppel assumed command of the Channel fleet in 1776 he had forty years of naval experience behind him. A protégé of Lord Anson, he rose rapidly in the navy, becoming a captain before the age of 20 and leading several expeditions against the French during the Seven Years War.

---

[1] Jurgen Habermas, 'The Public Sphere', *New German Critique*, 1 (Feb. 1974), 49. See also Geoff Ely, 'Re-thinking the Political: Social History and Political Culture in 18th and 19th Century Britain', *Archiv für Sozialgeschichte*, 21 (1981), 427–57.

Yet it was as a political as much as a naval figure that he caught the public eye. A Whig of impeccable pedigree whose grandfather had sailed with William of Orange in 1688, he was a member of the aristocratic cousinage that formed part of Lord Rockingham's inner circle. When hostilities began against America, Keppel opposed the ministry's belligerent policy in the Commons and refused to serve against the colonists. He did, however, agree to serve elsewhere and in November 1776, as British hopes of an early victory in America ebbed and French intervention seemed increasingly likely, he was asked to head the home fleet in the event of a European war.

Politically Keppel was not in a position to refuse. The main thrust of the Opposition's attack upon the government's policy was to highlight the calamitous consequences of civil war in America and the very grave dangers of French intervention at a time when Britain was heavily committed in American waters.[2] In the circumstances Keppel could not have prevaricated without appearing hypocritical and unpatriotic. None the less he had serious misgivings about serving under his political rivals and these were reinforced by his cousin, the Duke of Richmond, who warned him to beware of being ensnared by Lord Sandwich, the first Lord of the Admiralty and one of his major opponents. 'If he has but a bad fleet to send out,' Richmond reflected, ''tis doing Lord Sandwich no injustice to suppose he would be glad to put it under the command of a man whom he does not love, and yet whose name will justify the choice of the nation . . . if blame is to be borne, he will endeavour by every art he is but too much master of, to throw it on your shoulders.'[3]

Sandwich's willingness to deflect criticism of his naval policy by trumpeting Keppel's appointment in the Lords did little to allay this aura of mistrust. Nor did the fact that two of the officers assigned to the home fleet, Sir Hugh Palliser and Lord Mulgrave, were both members of the Admiralty Board and political associates of Sandwich. In addition to these political differences, Keppel's relations with Palliser were strained by a squabble over a sinecure, the lieutenant-generalship of marines, to which Sandwich had appointed Palliser over Keppel's objections in 1775.[4] These difficulties were aggravating enough, and undoubtedly strengthened

---

[2] The Rockinghamites were advocates of conciliation with America in 1776 but were divided over independence. Rockingham did not formally support it until April 1778, openly breaking with the Chathamites over the issue. See Frank O'Gorman, *The Rise of Party in England: The Rockingham Whigs 1760–82* (London, 1975), 337–76.

[3] Revd Thomas Keppel, *The Life of Augustus Viscount Keppel*, 2 vols. (London, 1842), ii. 3–4.

[4] *The Private Papers of John, Earl of Sandwich, First Lord of the Admiralty 1771–1782*, ed. G. R. Barnes and J. H. Owen, 4 vols. (London, 1932–8), ii. 191, 202–4.

Keppel's suspicion that he was being set up by the ministry. But they were compounded by the poor state of the fleet. Although Sandwich had claimed that the home fleet was ready to engage the French 'at a moment's warning',[5] many members of the Opposition, Keppel included, doubted that this was the case. Such scepticism was not altogether misplaced, for Sandwich's efforts to augment the navy had been fraught with problems: over supplies, naval contracts, manning, and the conflicting priorities of his cabinet colleagues.[6] Consequently Keppel attempted to guard his reputation by insisting that his own estimation of the fleet's readiness be written into his instructions.[7] Upon his arrival at Portsmouth he complained 'of having so many raw ships' and was clearly perturbed at the prospect of engaging the French with an inferior force and a politically divided command.[8]

When Keppel finally put to sea on 13 June to cruise between Ushant and the Scilly Isles, he sailed with only twenty ships of the line and a gathering political storm about the ill-prepared state of the navy.[9] His early encounter with two French frigates convinced him that the Brest fleet was vastly superior to his own and so he fell back to St Helen's to await reinforcements. This decision was criticized in both governmental and mercantile circles, especially since it exposed the home-coming West Indian fleets to enemy action.[10] Yet in Opposition eyes, at least, Keppel's action was regarded as prudent rather than craven. It underscored the parlous state of the British navy and the disastrous consequences of an impolitic war which now left Britain vulnerable to her most inveterate enemy, the French. Like Generals Howe and Burgoyne, the *London Evening Post* asserted, Admiral Keppel had been sent out with an inadequate force to 'damn [his] fame and to blast [his] laurels'. In its view Britain's independence, commerce, and European stature perilously rested upon a man whom the ministry seemed impelled to frustrate and vilify.[11]

As it was, the arrival of merchant fleets from the West Indies and the Mediterranean enabled the Admiralty to supply Keppel with a new supply of experienced seamen and further reinforcements. The day before

---

[5] William Cobbett, *Parliamentary History*, 19 (1777), 376; See also Piers Mackesy, *The War for America 1775–1783* (London, 1964), 175; Keppel, *Life of Keppel*, ii. 11.

[6] Mackesy, *War for America*, 165–70.

[7] *Sandwich Papers*, ii. 18–19.   [8] Ibid. ii. 46, 57–8.

[9] Two parliamentary debates, one led by Keppel's cousin, the Duke of Richmond, criticized the government's failure to prevent the Comte d'Estaing from sailing from Toulon in late April 1778. See Cobbett, *Parliamentary History*, 19 (1777), 1145–160.

[10] *HMC Various*, vi. 144, cited by Mackesy, *War for America*, 207–8; cf. Sir George Otto Trevelyan, *George the Third and Charles Fox*, 2 vols. (London, 1929), i. 130. Trevelyan cites a letter from Lieutenant Edward Smith who claimed that the 'voice of the nation' was with Keppel.

[11] *London Ev. Post*, 30 June–2 July 1778; see also 27–30 June, 9–11 July 1778.

he sailed, on 10 July, the Comte d'Orvilliers departed from Brest with thirty-two ships. On the afternoon of 23 July the two fleets sighted one another off Ushant, and what transpired had all the makings of a Braudelian satire. For four days, amid Channel squalls, the two fleets bobbed up and down off the Brittany coast, unable to engage one another on opposite tacks.[12] Keppel's fleet was marginally superior in terms of both ships and firing power. But the rheumatic admiral had not fought a major battle in almost two decades and when he finally confronted d'Orvilliers he proved unable to press home the advantage, largely because the French had immobilized many British ships by firing high into their masts and rigging. The rear division under Vice-Admiral Palliser was particularly damaged and his flagship, the *Formidable*, was put out of action. Consequently he was unable to follow Keppel's signal to re-form the line. This occasioned delays and misunderstandings, and prevented Keppel from resuming the battle that evening. When the mists rose the following morning, the sly old Count had slipped away.

Both Britain and France claimed victory for this encounter, but the outcome satisfied no one; least of all Keppel, whose cruising off Finisterre had brought him prize money, but not fame.[13] Privately the admiral blamed Palliser for the indecisive engagement; publicly he avoided contention.[14] His account of the battle was diplomatically worded and the matter might have been allowed to blow over. But an anonymous letter in the *General Advertiser*, written by Lieutenant Berkeley, one of Keppel's supporters aboard his own flagship, blamed Palliser for the inconclusive outcome.[15] Palliser was indignant. Hailing from a modest Yorkshire landowning family whose fortunes had been squandered by a reckless heir, he had worked his way through the ranks, establishing in thirty years' service a distinguished reputation as a professional seaman. In the circumstances he could not tolerate this stain on his honour. He therefore insisted that Keppel sign a public statement which not only vindicated his own conduct at Ushant but affirmed that Keppel had called him into line on 27 July for the purpose of resuming the battle with d'Orvilliers the following morning. Keppel

---

[12] The most detailed account of the battle is to be found in William Laird Clowes, *The Royal Navy: A History from the Earliest Times to the Present*, 5 vols. (London, 1898), iii. 412–26.

[13] According to the *Norwich Mercury*, 20 Feb. 1779, Keppel's operations off Ushant had brought him £20,000 in prize money, his share of the *Modeste*, a French East Indiaman.

[14] John A. Tilley, *The British Navy and the American Revolution* (Columbia, SC, 1987), 129–30; Clowes, *Royal Navy*, iii. 425; Trevelyan, *George the Third*, i. 137–8.

[15] *General Advertiser*, 15 Oct. 1778; the authorship of the letter was publicly disclosed in the *Public Advertiser*, 5 Jan. 1779. Whether Keppel was cognizant of Berkeley's intention to write the letter has never been determined.

refused, recognizing that such a statement would only incriminate himself. When Palliser ran 'very high upon his own merits', Keppel recounted to Jervis, 'and threw out that in justifying himself he must lay the blame where it belonged', the admiral lost his temper and virtually challenged his subordinate to make his insinuations public.[16] Palliser promptly did so, publishing his own version of the events in the *Morning Post*.[17] His statement quickly precipitated a public row on the conduct of the two admirals, very much along party lines, with the ministerialists supporting Palliser, and the Opposition, Keppel.[18] The vituperative atmosphere that had accompanied Keppel's first expedition resumed.

At the opening of the parliamentary session there were renewed demands for a public inquiry. Lord Sandwich declared this was unnecessary, but in the following week Palliser challenged Keppel to clarify his complaints against him on the floor of the House. Keppel promptly accused him of disobeying orders and an altercation ensued in which Opposition members brayed for Palliser's court martial. Sir Hugh pre-empted them by filing charges against Keppel. As he informed the Commons on 11 December, a trial was the only means left to repair his injured honour. Keppel, he said, had 'endeavoured to load him with the public odium of the miscarriage of that day, and compel him to submit to bear the blame of his own mistakes and incapacity'.[19] In reply, Keppel played the injured innocent and reminded the House that for the sake of naval morale and national unity he had pressed no charges against the vice-admiral, although he might have, given Palliser's rancorous comments in the press. This performance proved the more convincing; at least the Commons felt it just that Palliser be similarly court-martialled and passed a resolution accordingly. As Fitzpatrick wrote to Ossory, 'The House was violently disposed to Keppel, who spoke like a man inspired, and no tool was bold enough to venture one word in favour of Palliser.'[20]

To some this feud was basically a matter of honour that might have been resolved at ten paces as the mists rose over St James's Park. To others it

[16] Keppel, *Life of Keppel*, ii. 81–2.

[17] *Morning Post*, 5 Nov. 1778; Keppel, *Life of Keppel*, ii. 75–8. It has been argued that Palliser's public statement differed from the one he presented to Keppel. This is not strictly true, although the public letter emphasized that Keppel clearly ought to have recognized the disabled condition of the *Formidable*. Cf. Sir Lewis Namier and John Brooke (eds.), *The History of Parliament: The House of Commons 1754–1790* (3 vols.; London, 1964), iii. 246.

[18] The *Morning Post*, a pro-North paper, none the less did criticize the ministry for agreeing to a 'mixed appointment' in the Channel fleet. See *Morning Post*, 7 Nov. 1788.

[19] Cobbett, *Parliamentary History*, 20 (1779), 54–5.

[20] Charles James Fox, *Memorials and Correspondence*, ed. Lord John Russell, 4 vols. (London, 1853–7), i. 204, cited by Loren Reid, *Charles James Fox* (London, 1969), 93.

was indicative of the pitiful divisions that had compromised the British war effort and destroyed its empire. As one commentator remarked, the public had been 'well crammed with bickerings between slicing and sham-victory admirals, between old cashiered generals and new captive ones, between hungry patriots impatient to come in and pampered placemen unwilling to turn out'.[21] To Opposition supporters, however, more was at stake. Many suspected that the court martial was an underhand attempt by the ministry to destroy Keppel. Few believed that Palliser had initiated the court martial without consulting his mentor, Lord Sandwich. One writer speculated that his lordship had been up half the night drafting the articles.[22] Both Palliser and Sandwich, of course, publicly denied any collusion and there was little the Opposition could do short of calling them liars. So Opposition members dwelt upon the Admiralty's decision to proceed with the trial. Burke, Dunning, and Fox all pointed out that the Board had the discretionary power to refuse a court martial. Sir William Meredith even cited chapter and book.[23] Why, then, had the Admiralty not considered the context of Palliser's complaint, especially the fact that he had refrained from indicting his superior for five months? To the Opposition the whole affair smacked of a ministerial conspiracy. 'It seems that the gallant Admiral has been sacrificed to the low artifices of the *selfish* junto,' wrote the *General Advertiser*, 'as have many others, and as every other officer *will*, who engages under their *baneful* influence.'[24] At the very least the affair was indicative of the way in which the ministry had regularly traduced its commanders and undermined morale during the American war, bringing the nation to the brink of ruin.

The opening debates on the Keppel affair sapped the confidence of the ministry and ultimately forced it to commit one cardinal error. This was to agree to hold the court martial ashore in deference to Keppel's poor state of health. The concession transformed the court martial into a public event that arguably rivalled the impeachment of Dr Sacheverell some seventy years earlier. For five weeks in early 1779 the whole attention of the country was focused upon the Governor's chamber at Portsmouth where the court martial was held. MPs flocked there in droves, with the Whig lords providing Keppel with moral support and the Whig lawyers, Dunning,

[21] *Public Advertiser*, 12 Dec. 1778.

[22] Ibid. 22 Dec. 1778. Sandwich's actual role is a mystery. See N. A. M. Rodger, *The Insatiable Earl: A Life of John Montagu, 4th Earl of Sandwich* (New York, 1994), 247.

[23] *Parliamentary History*, 20 (1779), 67. Meredith cited the case of Captain Clements, accused by an officer on board his ship of embezzling stores. The complaint was judged to have been prompted by malice and was dismissed.

[24] *General Advertiser*, 4 Dec. 1778; see also *London Ev. Post*, 10–12 Dec. 1778.

Erskine, and Lee, legal expertise. Lord Shelburne, with pardonable exaggeration, calculated that parliament might have reconvened at the southern port.[25] And for those unable to witness the scandal of the season themselves, there were copious reports in the London and provincial press.

The role of the press proved crucial in transforming the trial into an amphitheatre in which national reputations were played out. During the 1760s and 1770s the press had grown in scope and confidence. In 1775 12.6 million stamps had been issued to the London and provincial newspapers, roughly 34,700 a day, and assuming each issue was read by at least twenty people, then roughly one in six adults perused the press on a regular basis, not to mention those who may have listened.[26] Since the 1750s newspapers had increased the scope of their political reportage, including by 1771 parliamentary debates, and it was hardly surprising that they should seize the opportunity to recount the Portsmouth trial. The London radical newspapers set the pace, with William Parker's *General Advertiser* proudly promoting a 'regular, circumstantial and daily Account of the TRIAL'[27] that arrived in the capital only seven hours later. In Parker's paper the court martial frequently filled two full pages of each issue. But Parker also supplemented his account with poems, ballads, and political commentaries attacking the 'knavish' Palliser and casting the trial as an epic battle between the injured Keppel and a malevolent ministry, between the forces of liberty and despotism. Few papers could match this coverage for speed, wit, or partisanship, but even the provincial press was swept up in the Portsmouth spectacle. The *Bath Chronicle* also prided itself on its 'express account' of the court martial and devoted more than a third of its space to it as it moved towards its finale. Other papers were scarcely less assiduous in keeping their readers in touch with the trial of the decade. Even the *Cumberland Pacquet*, a late starter in purveying the news from Portsmouth, quickly rectified its tardiness with detailed accounts of the courthouse proceedings. As the trial moved towards its verdict, the Whitehaven paper devoted half of its space to it.[28] Without doubt, Keppel's court

---

[25] George Thomas, Earl of Albemarle, *Memoirs of the Marquis of Rockingham and his Contemporaries*, 2 vols. (London, 1852), ii. 369; Lord Edmond Fitzmaurice, *Life of William, Earl of Shelburne*, 3 vols. (London, 1875–6), iii. 41.

[26] See John Brewer, *Party Ideology and Popular Politics at the Accession of George III* (Cambridge, 1976), ch. 8, and J. A. Chartres, 'City and Towns, Farmers and Economic Change in the 18th Century', *Historical Research*, 64 (June 1991), 149.

[27] *General Advertiser*, 7, 12 Jan. 1779. One gentleman at Portsmouth warned readers that their daily reports were sometimes hastily and politically contrived. See *Adam's Weekly Courant* (Chester), 26 Jan. 1779.

[28] The *Pacquet* did not mention the trial until 19 Jan. 1779.

martial was the most thoroughly reported trial eighteenth-century readers had hitherto known. It greatly surpassed that of Admiral Byng, whose trial had merited a column or two in the most inquisitive of papers. It was a political drama of the first magnitude.

Before the trial had even begun the tide of public favour was running against Palliser. Burke reported that the trial had excited more indignation than anything he could remember.[29] This was particularly the case within the navy itself. The ever-popular Lord Hawke refused to preside at the court martial. 'He would sooner cut off his hand', he is said to have remarked, 'than be accessory to such a trial.'[30] Along with eleven other admirals he signed an address to his majesty criticizing the expeditious and rash decision to court-martial Keppel and the blot it would necessarily leave on his reputation and naval morale.[31] This well-publicized support boded well for Keppel, for the professional judgement of naval peers would be likely to carry considerable weight with the members of the court martial.

As indeed it transpired. From the beginning Vice-Admiral Montague, a rough-hewn sailor for whom naval loyalties meant a great deal more than legal technicalities, treated the court martial as a court of honour. At the end of every testimony he asked the witness whether Keppel's conduct had been unbecoming a flag officer. Palliser objected to this solicitation of opinion rather than fact, but he was overruled by the court, with the result that the issues of courage and reputation assumed as much importance as the strategic niceties of Keppel's command.[32] Well might the *Morning Post* complain that the court martial was being 'hurried away by prejudices' and was pandering to naval morale.[33] Not that Palliser's evidence was especially watertight. On the second day of the trial it was disclosed that the logbook of the *Robust*, one of the ships in Palliser's division, had been altered on the orders of Captain Hood subsequent to the news of the court martial. Later it was revealed that the logbook of one of his other witnesses, Captain Digby of the *Ramillies*, had two pertinent pages missing. Although the evidentiary status of logbooks was in dispute and although additions and revisions were not uncommon, these revelations inevitably discredited Palliser's case. So, too, did the news that the logbook of his own flagship was without three critical pages. When Captain Bazeley explained

[29] *Correspondence of Edmund Burke*, iv: *1778–1782*, ed. John A. Woods (Cambridge, 1963), 34.

[30] Trevelyan, *George the Third*, i. 144.

[31] *London Ev. Post*, 31 Dec. 1778–2 Jan. 1779. See also Horace Walpole, *Correspondence*, ed. W. S. Lewis (41 vols.; New Haven, 1971), xxiv. 432.

[32] Keppel, *Life of Keppel*, ii. 111–12; *Sandwich Papers*, ii. 216–17. For criticism of Montague's interventions in the ministerial press, see *Morning Post*, 15 Jan., 6 Feb. 1779.

[33] *Morning Post*, 21 Jan. 1779.

that it had been kicked 'about the orlop, which is generally the case in a man-of-war', Palliser's prosecution began to dissolve into high farce.[34] The trial of Admiral Keppel was becoming Palliser's humiliation.

Within less than a week Palliser's prosecution was badly faltering. 'The first villany about Captain Hood's logbook', wrote Lady Sarah Lennox, 'has silenced all the roguery that was fabricating against the Admiral.'[35] Burke noted that 'when any thing appears very honourable to Keppel out of mere professional Jargon and which borders on Sentiment, the audience cannot be restrained from shewing their Sympathy by clapping'.[36] Outside the courtroom, too, public sentiment ran strongly for Keppel. His levee was warmly attended; that of his opponent was ignored. 'The Populace in Portsmouth, to a man, are in favour of Admiral Keppel,' the *Public Advertiser* reported, 'in as much that ballads are sung in the streets against Sir Hugh Palliser; and whenever Mr. Keppel goes to the court he is huzza'd and applauded.'[37] By the end of the month Palliser must have known that the game was up. 'The business here goes on very heavily and disagreeably,' he wrote to Sandwich.[38] Certainly the gamblers would have agreed, for on 22 January the City coffee houses closed the book on Keppel's trial.[39] The odds were too short; the outcome too predictable. All that one could speculate upon were the consequences.

George III believed that the court martial would create irreparable faction in the fleet. Horace Walpole went further. He predicted that 'Palliser and his accomplices' would 'probably rue the tempest they have brewed'.[40] Undoubtedly there were members of the Opposition who hoped this would be the case. Before the trial was over celebrations in honour of Keppel's acquittal were being organized. Lord Rockingham gave orders for a celebratory fête at his seat at Wentworth Woodhouse as early as 8 February, three days before the verdict. At Whitby on the east coast, local gentlemen organized a subscription 'in full expectation' of an acquittal a day prior to the news.[41] At Dartmouth, 10,000 yards of blue ribbon had been purchased for the cockades and garlands of Keppel's supporters, while in Bath the painter Charles Davis designed several transparencies for the illuminations in the Crescent, one 'a beautiful Figure of Britannia, bearing on

[34] Keppel, *Life of Keppel*, ii. 119.
[35] *The Life and Letters of Lady Sarah Lennox*, ed. Countess of Ilchester and Lord Stavordale, 2 vols. (London, 1901), i. 288.
[36] *Burke Correspondence*, iv. 37.   [37] *Public Advertiser* 16 Jan. 1779.
[38] *Sandwich Papers*, ii. 219.   [39] *Public Advertiser*, 22 Jan. 1779.
[40] *Walpole Correspondence*, xxxiii. 435; *HMC Dartmouth MSS*, i. 441.
[41] *London Ev. Post*, 25–7 Feb. 1779; *Burke Correspondence*, iv. 42.

her Lap the gallant Admiral'.[42] In London, predictably, local politicians busied themselves for the anticipated triumph. In the City 'many respectable gentlemen' applied to the Lord Mayor to illuminate the Monument, and his lordship gave orders to prepare the Mansion House for the forthcoming festivities. At the same time Richard Oliver, the former alderman and member of the radical Constitutional Society, placed 300 candles in his windows in readiness for the rejoicings.[43]

The great publicity given to Keppel's trial and the predictability of the outcome meant that many towns and villages were ready to celebrate his acquittal with the appropriate pomp and ceremony. The news of the verdict reached London on the evening of the 11th, within hours of its declaration, and would have reached Oxford, Cambridge, and most parts of the south-east by the evening of the 12th or the morning of the 13th, taking a further day to reach Lancashire and Yorkshire. Reading and Reigate received the news on the 12th and welcomed it with bells, bonfires, and illuminations. So, too, did Bath, which hired a special courier to bring the verdict as quickly as possible to people who would have known Keppel, a frequent *habitué* of this aristocratic spa. Within hours, the fashionable streets were festooned with pro-Keppelian transparencies that had been painted by local artists weeks before. York heard of the verdict on the 15th, and quickly staged a colourful parade, featuring banners to 'Fame Restored' and 'Innocence Triumphant', and an effigy of Palliser which was hoisted from the yard-arm of a ship at King's Strith and later burnt in a tar barrel. Wrexham heard of the acquittal a day later, and that evening put on a triumphant progress of Keppel that was followed by an 'innumerable mobility' carrying an effigy of Palliser on a 'very conspicuous pole'.[44]

Not all of the celebrations were synchronized to the communications network in a straightforward manner. While most towns appear to have celebrated Keppel's acquittal on or soon after the arrival of the news, some clearly did not. This was true of Chichester, Chelmsford, Deal, and Watford, to name a few. Why this is so is unclear. Political differences within town élites may have affected the timing of the celebrations. At Bristol, where there was a noticeable lag between the news of Keppel's acquittal and its celebration, one suspects that this was the case. But sometimes organizers delayed their celebrations to achieve maximum publicity for their endeavours.

---

[42] *St James's Chronicle*, 13–16 Feb. 1779; *Newcastle Chronicle*, 13 Feb. 1779; *London Ev. Post*, 4–6, 23–5 Feb. 1779.

[43] *Newcastle Chronicle*, 13 Feb. 1779; *Morning Chronicle*, 12 Feb. 1779.

[44] *General Ev. Post*, 22–7 Feb. 1779; *York Courant*, 22 Feb. 1779; *St James's Chronicle*, 13–16 Feb. 1779.

At Plymouth, for example, the news of Keppel's acquittal was celebrated in a fairly spontaneous manner the day after the news was received. But the principal festival in this south-westerly port, which had taken a keen interest in Keppel's leadership of the Channel fleet, was reserved for the 19th. Organized by the commissioners of the dockyard on the other side of Plymouth Sound, it featured a parade of 2,000 shipwrights and rope-makers in the regalia of their trades. Carrying a model of Britannia and Keppel's flagship, they marched with the blue and gold colours of their 'conquering hero' around Plymouth Dock to the applause of some 10,000 spectators.[45]

Few jubilations were as carefully choreographed as those at Plymouth Dock, least of all in the metropolis, whose size and political diversity always added an element of unpredictability to any popular demonstration. In the City the first celebrations of Keppel's triumph were initiated by William Parker, the printer of the *General Advertiser*, who, upon hearing the news from his own express, immediately lit the lamps of his house near St Dunstan's Church, Fleet Street. Very soon a crowd gathered and obliged all neighbours to follow his example, so that by 10 p.m. almost all the streets in the City were lit up. A few disorders took place, largely because some inhabitants were either lethargic or refused to illuminate their windows. An effigy of Sir Hugh was also burnt on Tower Hill. There were a few arrests. One revolved around a 'young gentleman of fortune' who refused to huzza for Keppel in Fleet Street and drew his sword upon losing his hat.[46] But basically the demonstrations in the City were uproarious and exuberant, with the mob firing sky-rockets, squibs, and crackers until daylight.[47]

The same was not true of Westminster. Here a large crowd gathered at York Buildings to watch and applaud another effigy-burning of Palliser. It then moved westwards along the Strand towards Charing Cross, demand-ing lights and smashing all windows that were not illuminated. From here the crowd veered in the direction of Pall Mall in search of Sir Hugh Palliser's residence. The authorities had anticipated trouble; the Admiralty had even taken the precaution of removing much of Sir Hugh's furniture. Yet the peace officers who had been stationed in the vicinity proved powerless to deal with the huge crowd which assembled in St James's Square.[48] They therefore called for two companies of guards, but upon their appearance

---

[45] *London Ev. Post*, 27 Feb.–2 Mar. 1779.   [46] *Gazetteer*, 16 Feb. 1779.

[47] *Morning Chronicle*, 12 Feb. 1779; *Sussex Weekly Advertiser*, 15 Feb. 1779.

[48] PRO, TS 11/976/3529. The depositions suggest the crowd was in excess of 500. The *Sussex Weekly Advertiser*, 15 Feb. 1779, suggested that it reached 10,000, other papers 3,000.

the crowd became 'more outrageous', pelting them and demolishing the windows and shutters of Palliser's house. Consequently the guards secured Pall Mall and the square, 'galloping and striking about, making their way through and over all ranks'.[49] From this position of strength Justice Gilbert then parleyed with the crowd, who agreed to disperse provided his worship dismissed the troops. This Gilbert did, but several rioters ripped out the iron railings at the back of Palliser's house and broke in, destroying the chimney pieces, floorboards, and stone stairs. Four rioters were subsequently arrested, examined at Bow Street, and sent to Newgate. Three were charged with capital felony under the Riot Act.[50]

From ransacking Palliser's house the mob moved on to mete rough justice on Keppel's enemies. Lord George Germain's house in Pall Mall had its windows demolished; so, too, did those of Lord Mulgrave and Captain Hood, both prime witnesses for Palliser. The Admiralty was also attacked, forcing Sandwich and his mistress to abandon their private apartments. What is more, crowds rampaged down Downing Street and attempted to break into the house of Lord North, the first minister of the crown. Sixteen were secured by soldiers under the direction of Justice Addington.[51]

Illuminations were called for the following night and the streets were once again filled with raucous revelry. Palliser's effigy was paraded through the City on a donkey and burnt before the Royal Exchange. There were also roastings of Sir Hugh in Southwark and its neighbourhood.[52] Trouble was again expected in Westminster, but the presence of 500 troops in the vicinity of Whitehall inhibited further attacks upon the ministry and Palliser's supporters.[53] The violence of the 11th, none the less, was used by the government to discredit the Opposition. Ministerial writers insinuated that the mob had been 'worked up to do a great deal of damage in different parts of the town'.[54] They emphasized that the mob was not entirely 'of the lower class', that it had been plied with liquor and directed to its targets. How accurate these accusations were, it is difficult to say. Certainly

[49] *Sussex Weekly Advertiser*, 15 Feb. 1779.

[50] PRO, TS 11/976/3529, TS 11/976/3531; *Morning Chronicle*, 20 Feb. 1779. The four rioters were Edward Groom, a shoemaker, William Smith, a servant to the Earl of Murray, Robert Rickwood, a hairdresser, and John McKay, an apprentice to an oilman.

[51] *St James's Chronicle*, 11–13 Feb. 1779. For an indictment against one rioter at the Middlesex quarter sessions, see GLRO, MJ/SR 3366, indt. 31.

[52] *Morning Chronicle*, 15 Feb. 1779; *Gazetteer and New Daily Advertiser*, 15 Feb. 1779.

[53] *Morning Chronicle*, 13 Feb. 1779. According to Horace Walpole, Lords Weymouth and Sandwich brought out the troops and fearing an 'insurrection' advised the King to retire to Kew. See *The Last Journals of Horace Walpole*, ed. A. F. Steuart, 2 vols. (London, 1910), ii. 249–50.

[54] *General Ev. Post*, 11–13 Feb. 1779.

patriots in the City had helped to orchestrate the demonstrations and to protest at the intervention of the troops. William Parker of the *General Advertiser* had some of his devils distribute handbills deploring military excesses, for which he was prosecuted by the crown at King's Bench.[55] Some members of the Opposition visibly egged on the crowd. John Dalby testified that, at the attack upon Lord George Germain's house, he saw 'Lord George Bentinck encouraging the said mob by pulling off his Hat and Huzzaing & saying that is well done my Lads'. He also swore that Charles James Fox was similarly supportive, both in Pall Mall and at the Admiralty.[56] But in these instances it is likely that the young bucks simply joined the throng after a hard night's drinking at Almack's.[57]

Whatever the role of the Opposition, the riots in London clearly troubled Keppel's closest associates, who had no wish to see the admiral's victory sullied by mob violence. They would have agreed with the *Gazetteer* that 'a popular riot' was 'but a poor triumphal arch to any hero'.[58] On the other hand, the radicals in the metropolis were clearly more tolerant of disorder if it sustained the momentum of protest against the ministry. The *General Advertiser* believed even the ladies of quality would forgive 'the honest emotions of the mob, who in the full flow of their joy . . . confined not their rage within the strict bounds of law, but levelled some marks of resentment against those whom they considered as the foul conspirators'.[59] One writer in the radical *London Evening Post* argued that the demonstrations in favour of Keppel revealed that 'the multitude of this nation only want *leaders* to do themselves *justice*'. The 'spirit of the people without doors', he continued, would 'do more towards rectifying the measures of the Ministry and restoring the constitution of the kingdom than all the opposition within'.[60] This statement did not explicitly endorse disorder. The author stressed that he did not encourage the people 'to exert a spirit contrary to the laws of this country'. At the same time he certainly envisaged a more vigorous role for the populace than that countenanced by the Rockinghamites.

The conflicting priorities of the Opposition certainly complicated the task of restoring some decorum to future public rejoicings in order to project the legitimacy of popular joy. Keppel himself studiously refused to don the mantle of Wilkes. When he returned to town on 16 February he did so as discreetly as possible in order to avoid a triumphal entry to town.[61]

---

[55] PRO, TS 11/976/3531.   [56] PRO, TS 11/976/3531.
[57] Fox, *Memorials*, i. 224.   [58] *Gazetteer and New Daily Advertiser*, 23 Feb. 1779.
[59] *General Advertiser*, 19 Feb. 1779.   [60] *London Ev. Post*, 16–18 Feb. 1779.
[61] Ibid.; *Hampshire Chronicle*, 22 Feb. 1779.

This plan was only partially successful, for Keppel's arrival at Fulham bridge was greeted with illuminations and cannonades, and a 'great concourse of people' congregated outside his house in Audley Square. Keppel courteously acknowledged their presence with three short bows at his drawing-room window. But he refused to play to the popular gallery and pre-empted any major demonstration by quickly leaving to dine at Rockingham's. He must have been relieved that the celebrations which followed were largely confined to illuminations. The only violence that was reported occurred in the upper liberties of the City, where a mob accidentally wounded a few people while parading Palliser in effigy.[62]

Yet Keppel could not avoid the limelight altogether, nor the exultations of the jostling crowd. On 20 February, when Keppel was formally given the freedom of the City for 'his Glorious and Gallant Efforts' at Ushant, the radicals masterminded a victory celebration at the London tavern. The well-publicized procession from Keppel's residence in Audley Square to Bishopsgate resembled a civic parade. Amidst the swirling blue banners embossed with gold anchors, and the blue favours devoted to 'Keppel and Freedom, Virtue Triumphant', the City marshalmen led a cavalcade of coaches filled with naval officers, City aldermen, and councillors. It was joined at the Strand by the Marine Society, a gesture designed to emphasize the non-partisan, patriotic temper of Keppel's naval achievements. At Cockspur Street, however, where 'the multitude' pressed hard against the admiral's coach, some jack tars could not resist unharnessing the horses and drawing it themselves, nor drawing it back again at the end of the evening and chairing the hero of the hour to his house. General Keppel, the admiral's brother, instructed the crowd to depart peaceably, but his words were ignored. Instead, crowds traversed the squares and principal streets of the West End demanding lights and creating 'considerable mischief'.[63] Efforts to restrain popular exuberance had failed, to a point that the moderate *Morning Chronicle* urged the admiral to avoid any more public appearances. 'Such conduct would do him more credit', the paper said, 'than making a public parade into the city, and shaking hands with every greasy blackguard that thrusts forward to his carriage windows.'[64] These words were heeded, for a few days later Keppel cancelled a dinner with the Society of West India Planters and Merchants and issued handbills

---

[62] *Morning Post*, 17 Feb. 1779; *Morning Chronicle*, 18 Feb. 1779. According to the *Ipswich Journal*, 20 Feb. 1779, Lord Hereford narrowly escaped being shot.

[63] *Gazetteer and New Daily Advertiser*, 22 Feb. 1779.

[64] *Morning Chronicle*, 23 Feb. 1779.

requesting that the illuminations cease. 'I cannot but be proud of the demonstrations of joy so generally expressed, and especially in this Metropolis,' he wrote to the chairman, 'yet I feel myself much reprehensible if I afforded a pretense to any one to say that I encouraged any excesses . . . which tend to alarm and disturb the Quiet of the Town, and the more so, as those excesses have been attended with real prejudice to the health & property of many persons.'[65] Like other Opposition Whigs, and more generally many property owners, Keppel was troubled by the rough humour and licence that frequently accompanied popular jubilations.

The London demonstrations revealed the complex cross-currents of metropolitan politics and the difficulties of restraining huge, spontaneous crowds within the limits of constitutional and social propriety. The provincial demonstrations, by contrast, were more structured events that tended to keep popular exuberance within tolerable limits. Many followed, in fact, a familiar festive format. As soon as the news of Keppel's acquittal was known, bells were rung, salvoes fired, and houses illuminated with candles. In the evening, the principal inhabitants would repair to a local tavern to toast the hero of the hour while the common people were regaled with victuals and beer. In a few instances local gentlemen and naval officers organized a ball to celebrate the gallant admiral's acquittal.[66] The central event of most festivities, none the less, was a mock procession and execution of Sir Hugh Palliser in effigy, usually with some reference to the logbooks which had so compromised his testimony. At Bury St Edmunds, for example, the procession featured an effigy of Sir Hugh in a naval uniform with the *Robust*'s logbook under one arm and the five accusations under the other. On the dummy's back was marked 'Judas, Rear Admiral of the Blue'. At York, Palliser's effigy held the logbook of the *Formidable* in his left hand with a halter about his neck, supported by six men with blackened faces. Surrounded by sailors, the float was taken through the principal streets to the tune of the 'Rogues March'.[67] In some instances Palliser was accompanied by effigies of his leading witnesses or reputed ministerial accomplices. At Great Missenden in Buckinghamshire, for example, a devil led Palliser and Captains Hood and Bazeley to the ceremonial bonfire.[68] Further to the north, at Newcastle upon Tyne, Palliser was burnt

[65] Suffolk Record Office, Ipswich, Albemarle papers, HA 67, 461/252; *General Advertiser*, 23, 25 Feb. 1779.
[66] See the celebrations at Deal and Witham in *London Ev. Post*, 18–20 Feb. 1779.
[67] *Leeds Mercury*, 23 Feb. 1779; *York Courant*, 23 Feb. 1779; *London Ev. Post*, 16–18 Feb. 1779.
[68] *London Ev. Post*, 23–5 Feb. 1779.

in effigy along with Lord Mulgrave and Captain Hood, his 'chief mourners', the latter incurring special contempt on account of his political apostacy.[69] In addition, 'three well finished paintings' of Lords North, Sandwich, and Germain, brought from another quarter of the town, were thrown on the bonfire. By contrast, the celebrations at Lewes and Loughborough culminated with a chairing of the 'conquering hero'. At Loughborough an ex-sea captain acted the part of the injured admiral, taking his libations so freely, one correspondent remarked, that he was 'in great danger of being *becalmed* on a *Lee-Shore*'.[70] At Lewes, Palliser was 'dragged through the town in effigy, and after being terribly beaten and mangled by the indignant multitude, he was shot and burnt'. Subsequently, the *Sussex Weekly Advertiser* reported, 'a person representing Admiral Keppel, with his sword drawn, seated in an arm chair properly elevated, was carried triumphantly through the town'.[71]

The celebrations thus drew on a variety of processional forms, electoral, judicial, and civic. Very occasionally they resembled a charivari, for in Windsor and Eton Palliser's effigy was carried around 'with horns and other rough musick'.[72] Few effigy-burning ceremonies, however, appear to have been generated from below, as was often the case in London.[73] Rather they structured popular jubilations, allowing the plebs its brief moment of execration—at Wrexham the effigy was given up 'to the power of the mob'—before Palliser and his crew were consigned to the ceremonial bonfire.[74] Many of them clearly required careful preparation and sponsorship and from the newspapers we can glean some idea of the parties who were involved. Sometimes the demonstrations had civic endorsement. This appears to have been the case at Bungay, Bury St Edmunds, Cambridge, Dartmouth, Doncaster, Gloucester, High Wycombe, Worcester, and Reigate, where the recorder, Richard Barnes, ordered a triple discharge of the castle cannons to celebrate the gallant Keppel's acquittal.[75] In a few others local societies were actively involved. Thus at Wrexham the Investigating Society staged a procession emulating Keppel's own triumphal

[69] As Constantine Phipps, Mulgrave had stood as a radical candidate in the 1774 general election. Although he was not elected for Newcastle, he subsequently sided with the North administration. See Kathleen Wilson, *The Sense of the People* (Cambridge, 1995), 347–8, 351–2, 361.

[70] *Leicester and Nottingham Journal*, 20 Feb. 1779.

[71] *Sussex Weekly Advertiser*, 22 Feb. 1779; *London Ev. Post*, 20–3 Feb. 1779.

[72] *London Ev. Post*, 16–18 Feb. 1779.

[73] Among the exceptions were the effigy-burnings at Rotherham and Bristol. See *London Ev. Post*, 20–3 Feb. 1779; *Morning Post*, 22 Feb. 1779.

[74] For Wrexham, see *General Ev. Post*, 25–7 Feb. 1779.

[75] *London Ev. Post*, 13–16 Feb. 1779; *Norwich Mercury*, 20 Feb. 1779.

parade at Portsmouth.[76] In the smaller boroughs and villages, however, local patrons were the principal sponsors. At Bewdley, in Worcestershire, for instance, the Winnington family had a major hand in the rejoicings. At Ledbury, Squire Skipp laid on a hogshead of cider for the sheep-roasting at High Cross, while in Fowey William Treffry, Esquire, treated the town to a fireworks display and 'a great quantity of wine and punch'. At Woodstock, where effigies of Sandwich, Palliser, and Hood were swung from a huge gallows before the town hall, the demonstration clearly had the blessing of the Duke of Marlborough, for after the mock execution he regaled the inhabitants at Blenheim Park.[77] Elsewhere we discover that the demonstrations were led by local clergymen, militia, army, and naval officers, merchants, gentlemen-farmers, or, more impressionistically, by the 'principal inhabitants' or 'the gentlemen of the town'; in other words, by men of substance or status within their own localities.[78]

At the same time these demonstrations were popular events. At Wentworth Woodhouse, the celebrations exceeded the bounds set by the Rockinghams.[79] At Bath, Leeds, and Liverpool, they took place despite official disapproval. Very frequently they engaged large sections of the population. At Plymouth Dock, the shipwrights used their cherished perquisite of 'chips' for the celebratory bonfire in Liberty Fields.[80] At Tunbridge Wells and Weedon-Beck in Northamptonshire, the demonstrators called on every house as they passed to summon support for Keppel. In Banbury, Rotherham, and Yarmouth, thousands were present at the effigy-burnings, while at Wrexham the festivities were said to have been celebrated by all ranks, 'from the man of fortune to the lowest mechanic'.[81] Even officially sponsored demonstrations prompted unsolicited responses from the inhabitants at large. Thus at Doncaster, where the mayor decorated the Mansion House with bunting and threw an entertainment for the principal inhabitants, windows were illuminated by 'the lowest people in the most obscure alleys'.[82]

[76] *General Ev. Post*, 25–7 Feb. 1779.

[77] *London Ev. Post*, 13–16, 23–5 Feb. 1779; *Gloucester Journal*, 22 Feb. 1779; *Berrow's Worcester Journal*, 25 Feb. 1779; *Sussex Weekly Advertiser*, 22 Feb. 1779.

[78] *London Ev. Post*, 16–18, 20–3 Feb. 1779; *St James's Chronicle*, 20–3 Feb. 1779; *Gloucester Journal*, 22 Feb. 1779; *Leeds Mercury*, 23 Feb. 1779; *Ipswich Journal*, 27 Feb. 1779; *Adam's Weekly Courant*, 23 Feb. 1779.

[79] *Burke Correspondence*, iv. 43.

[80] *London Ev. Post*, 27 Feb–2 Mar. 1779; Henry Francis Whitfield, *Plymouth and Devonport in Times of War and Peace* (Devonport, 1981), 191.

[81] *Jackson's Oxford Journal*, 6 Feb. 1779 (Banbury); *General Ev. Post*, 18–20 Feb. 1779 (Tunbridge Wells), 25–7 Feb. 1779 (Wrexham), 27 Feb.–2 Mar. 1779 (Weedon-Beck); *Ipswich Journal*, 20 Feb. 1779 (Yarmouth); *Leeds Mercury*, 23 Feb. 1779 (Rotherham).

[82] *London Ev. Post*, 20–3 Feb. 1779.

The demonstrations in favour of Keppel clearly transcended client populations and we should not infer from their organization that they were superficially popular. As Lady Sarah Lennox averred, 'nothing is more true than the general & wild joy that has annimated [*sic*] all ranks of people'.[83] Not only did all classes celebrate Keppel's acquittal, they did so throughout the country. A perusal of eight London and eighteen provincial newspapers reveals that no less than 168 towns and villages participated in the rejoicings. Of those reported, thirty-eight were ports, testimony to Keppel's strong following among merchants, seamen, and shipworkers. Forty-nine were significant towns, ranging from Plymouth, Dartmouth, Bristol, and Exeter in the south-west, to Chatham, Canterbury, and Reading in the southeast, to the principal towns of East Anglia, to Leicester, Birmingham, Nottingham, Manchester, and the towns of the West Riding, and the Tyne and Wear. No demonstrations were reported in the staunchly Tory town of Oxford, and those at Manchester may have been partial, for the *Newcastle Chronicle* reported that the 'loyal lads' refused to light up their windows.[84] Against this, Keppel's acquittal was vigorously celebrated in the greater Manchester area: at Salford, Dukinfield, Urmston, Eccles, Oldham, and Stockport.[85]

The *General Evening Post* was thus not exaggerating when it said that Keppel's acquittal had been celebrated 'in most of the great towns in this kingdom'. It was also celebrated in many smaller towns as well. Although no jubilations were reported at Stockton-on-Tees, where inhabitants had earlier burnt several prominent pro-Americans in effigy,[86] no less than eighty minor towns applauded Keppel's acquittal, along with twenty-six villages. This list is far from comprehensive, for newspaper editors frequently alluded to county-wide jubilations in favour of Keppel.[87] In fact, the *St James's Chronicle* believed that the verdict was approved by 'nine-tenths of the People'.[88]

Exaggerations aside, there is no doubt that the rejoicings were nationwide. Although support for Keppel was more modest in the south-west than it was in other parts of the country, it was none the less very impressive.

---

[83] *Letters of Lady Sarah Lennox*, i. 294.

[84] *Newcastle Chronicle*, 27 Feb. 1779. For a musical interlude celebrating Keppel's acquittal at the end of a performance of *Henry V*, see *Prescott's Manchester Journal*, 22 Feb. 1779.

[85] *Manchester Mercury*, 17, 24, 31 Mar. 1779.

[86] Thomas Richmond, *The Local Records of Stockton and Neighbourhood* (Stockton, 1868; reprint 1972), 79.

[87] *St James's Chronicle*, 20–3 Feb. 1779; *General Ev. Post*, 27 Feb.–2 Mar. 1779; *York Courant*, 23 Feb. 1779; *Newcastle Courant*, 27 Feb. 1779.

[88] *St James's Chronicle*, 16–18 Feb. 1779.

It compared very favourably with the support for John Wilkes in the years 1768–71, especially in the south-east and Midlands.[89]

Predictably there were some boroughs in the pocket of Opposition peers and patrons that celebrated Keppel's acquittal. This was true of Calne, which was firmly under the control of Lord Shelburne and returned two strong Keppelians, John Dunning and Isaac Barré, to parliament. It was also true of Chichester, where the Duke of Richmond's influence predominated and for which Keppel and his brother had been MPs. And of Thirsk, whose patrons, the Franklands, supported Fox's motion to investigate Sandwich's management of the navy in March 1779.[90] Finally there was Malton, a burgage borough where the Wentworth Woodhouse family had a strong foothold. Given Keppel's Rockinghamite connections, it could be counted on to commemorate his acquittal.

Alongside these manageable boroughs there were the more populous constituencies where the Opposition was a formidable political force. Radical-Whig centres such as Newcastle, Norwich, Yarmouth, and Worcester celebrated Keppel's victory, as did Bristol, despite its tardy response to a verdict that enraptured its MP, Edmund Burke. Yet what is particularly interesting about the political geography of the 1779 demonstrations is the extent to which they occurred in ministerial-dominated towns. Keppel's acquittal was celebrated in at least nine towns that had sent loyalist addresses to the crown in 1775 supporting its coercive policy in America, although in five of these public opinion was certainly divided over the war.[91] Rejoicings were also reported in boroughs where the government was electorally pre-eminent. Of the sixty-three boroughs which commemorated the admiral's acquittal, nine had returned two or more Opposition members in 1774, twenty-seven had returned one, and another

[89] John Brewer lists seventy-six demonstrations for Wilkes in the years 1768–71. Brewer, *Party Ideology and Popular Politics*, 175. In addition to those who celebrated Keppel's acquittal, there were towns which formally offered him their congratulations: namely, London, Newcastle, Norwich, York, Cambridge, Thetford, Great Yarmouth, Nottingham, Dublin, and Londonderry. Keppel also received letters of congratulation from the Drapers' Company, the Society of West Indian Planters and Merchants, the Grand and Laudable Society of Antigallicans, Trinity House, Newcastle, and the Associated Body of Liverpool Merchants. See Suffolk Record Office, HA 67 461/252, and the *London Ev. Post*, 20–3 Feb. 1777.

[90] For the division list, see *London Ev. Post*, 23–5 Mar. 1779. Where an MP's affiliations are not clear-cut, I have used this division list as a litmus test for political partisanship 1778–9.

[91] These figures exclude those towns that also sent conciliatory addresses. The loyalist addresses hailed from Arundel, Chester, Exeter, Gloucester, Leicester, Liverpool, Sudbury, Windsor, and York. Opposition to the addresses was voiced in Exeter, Gloucester, Leicester, Liverpool, and York, although it was never substantial enough to produce a counter-petition, See James E. Bradley, *Popular Politics and the American Revolution in England* (Macon, Ga., 1986), 78–84.

twenty-seven had elected a full slate of government supporters. In some of these boroughs the ministry was powerfully placed. This was particularly true of the Admiralty boroughs and the Cinque Ports. Here the government proved unable to discourage demonstrations in favour of the Opposition admiral and implicitly critical of the Admiralty. Some of the leading members of the ministry, Lord North, Lord George Germain, Lord Mulgrave, and the electoral manager, John Robinson, also had the humiliation of witnessing Keppel demonstrations in their own constituencies. As did Palliser, who also had to tolerate his own effigy burnt but a few miles from his country seat at Chalfont St Giles.[92]

How, then, should one interpret these joyous celebrations? What do they reveal about popular attitudes towards the navy, the ministry, and the war? At one level the rejoicings were simply a vindication of Keppel's honour. The logbook evidence, upon which the press and the celebrations themselves placed so much weight, underscored the malevolence of the prosecution and Palliser's perfidy. As the label on the Hexham effigy emphasized, Palliser was 'a living monument of FRAUD, TREACHERY and CUNNING' whose 'DUPLICITY and TREACHERY' deserved public reprobation.[93] To a public alarmed by the prospect of a French invasion and disconsolately aware of military factionalism, moreover, the celebrations registered public indignation at unnecessary dissensions within the fleet at such a critical moment in the war. It was an argument that could transcend party considerations and may explain the bipartisan flavour of Keppelian festival in places like Bath and Kendal.[94]

Yet from the beginning the Keppel affair was never divorced from politics and its treatment in the press inevitably disposed the public to take sides. Keppel could be seen simply as the victim of Palliser's malice; but he could also been seen as the victim of ministerial intrigue, if not malfeasance. As the *St James's Chronicle* urged its readers, it was 'well known how busy the Ministry was before the Tryal in promoting everything unfavourable to Keppel, and encouraging Sir Hugh Palliser to his intended prosecution'.[95] One writer in the *London Evening Post* went even further. In his eyes the trial exemplified the 'execrable behaviour' of the ministry and the degree to which 'ministerial craft and Scotch subtlety' had captured the ear of the King.[96] The same argument was made in a handbill entitled

---

[92] *London Ev. Post*, 18–20 Feb. 1779. The demonstration took place at Chesham, in Buckinghamshire.
[93] *General Advertiser*, 24 Feb. 1779.
[94] *St James's Chronicle*, 13–16 Feb. 1779; *General Ev. Post*, 18–20 Feb. 1779.
[95] *St James's Chronicle*, 16–18 Feb. 1779.   [96] *London Ev. Post*, 2–4 Feb. 1779.

'Liberty, Law and Keppel' which contrasted Keppel's impeccable Whig pedigree with the Scottish villains, Bute and Mansfield, who sought vengeance upon this true son of Liberty.[97] How credible this pitch was depended upon one's assessment of the government's involvement and culpability. Even those who were prepared to give the government the benefit of the doubt must have been troubled by the Admiralty's precipitous decision to court-martial Keppel rather than open Ushant to public inquiry. In the light of the trial it appeared vindictive, if not conspiratorial. As one fictional report from 'Hell' stressed, such villainy was of the highest order.[98]

> Of a Seafaring Board,
> Such Tales were encor'd
> That set the whole Band in a Roar:
> For such *Charges* 'tis clear
> Were exhibited there,
> As the World never equall'd before.

There is no doubt that the trial discredited the ministry and undermined its credibility. Although the government's supporters managed to inhibit demonstrations in a few towns, they had to weather a rising tide of anti-ministerialism and defections from their ranks. At Whitby, for example, it was reported that ministerial support had withered away during the trial.[99] This shift in popular opinion was partly attributable to war-weariness. After Saratoga, Britons were confronted with a protracted war against America and subsequently against the Bourbon powers, a predicament which inevitably strained British resources to the limit. By 1778 British trade was seriously affected by American privateering and rising insurance rates, a situation which sapped commercial confidence and increased bankruptcies. The larger ports and merchant marine were also plagued with heavy impressment, which was bloodily resisted and legally challenged in the courts.[100] At the same time the government experienced serious problems in recruiting for the army, to a point that troops had to be quartered in many towns to assist enlistment drives.[101] These issues increased disillusionment with the war and induced the public to heed Opposition

---

[97] Suffolk Record Office, HA 67, 461/255.
[98] The *Diaboliad*, printed in the *Shrewsbury Chronicle*, 6 Mar. 1779.
[99] *London Ev. Post*, 25–7 Feb. 1779.   [100] See Ch. 3.
[101] *Leicester and Nottingham Journal*, 20 Feb. 1779. Troops had to be quartered in Northampton, Kettering, Market Harborough, Loughborough, Nottingham, and Derby to assist in enforcing the new Impress Act.

arguments about the disastrous consequences of the American engagement and the ministry's blinkered and incompetent handling of the war itself.

The Keppel affair provided an important focus for these resentments, calling into question the ministry's capacity to govern. According to 'Agrippa', the trial had made 'the wisdom as well as the honour of the nation ambiguous'. Britain was overtaxed and overextended, yet the Admiralty had persisted in attacking one of the few men who offered any kind of solace.[102] To many Keppel was a scapegoat for the ministry's own incompetence, as the Howes and Barrington had been before him. Some must have followed Isaac Barré in believing that the government had conspired to hide 'the ruinous state and condition of the navy' under Keppel's 'fame and reputation as a seaman and his popularity as an honest independent man'.[103] Once this ruse failed they were intent on destroying him. Others of a more radical bent went further, seeing the only solution to the recriminatory politics of the ministry in the structural reform of parliament. Very occasionally, Palliser was burnt in effigy with Venality and Corruption in the celebrations of 1779, while in London the City radicals advocated 'a Free and Independent Parliament' and toasted the 'free and independent' electors of Great Britain and Ireland.[104]

Predictably pro-American sentiments surfaced in the rejoicings. At Newcastle, where a mass petition had been launched in February 1778 demanding a 'swift and honourable' reconciliation with America and the dismissal of the King's chief ministers, Lords North, Sandwich, and George Germain were burnt as the 'abettors of the American war'. At Liverpool the Captain's society gave a toast to 'a happy and speedy reconciliation with the Americans' and a 'severe drubbing to France'.[105] Similarly at Fowey, celebrants cherished the hope that 'the community of England and America' would be 'firmly united against the common enemy'.[106] In London, too, the city radicals used the Keppel affair to propound pro-American sentiments, urging a 'National Reconcilement with America' at the dinner held in the admiral's honour at the London Tavern.[107]

Pro-American resolutions were none the less couched in fairly general terms. They appealed to anti-war sentiment and shied away from an explicit

---

[102] *Public Advertiser*, 8 Jan. 1779.   [103] Cobbett, *Parliamentary History*, 20 (1779), 400.
[104] CLRO, Journals of Common Council, 67, fo. 211; *London Ev. Post*, 20–3 Feb. 1779.
[105] *London Ev. Post*, 20–3 Feb. 1779; for the 1778 petition in Newcastle, see Wilson, *Sense of the People*, 362–3.
[106] *London Ev. Post*, 25–7 Feb. 1779.
[107] CLRO, Journals of Common Council, 67, fos. 210–11.

endorsement of American independence. Despite the fact that the Rocking-hamites had officially reconciled themselves to an independent America, the Opposition recognized that this was still a very divisive issue and not one that would command unanimous support even within its own ranks. In fact at Bungay, near Norwich, where toasts to the Whig lords, William Beckford, and John Wilkes resounded through the Assembly Rooms, cele-brants expressed the hope of a return of American 'friendship, trade and confidence' and that the colonists might 'obtain everything they can by treaty short of independence'.[108]

Indeed, one may arguably exaggerate the salience of pro-American feel-ing in the Keppel demonstrations of 1779.[109] It constituted an important but minority strain in the celebrations, one most visible in radical centres such as London, Newcastle, and Norwich.[110] In seeking to garner mod-erate support the Opposition chose rather to focus upon the disastrous war policy of the administration and Keppel's victimization at the hands of a corrupt ministry. Keppel himself was rarely portrayed as the pro-American admiral,[111] rather as Injured Innocence, or Virtue Triumphant, or as one of Britain's admirals battling the French foe. At Bath, for ex-ample, illuminations portrayed Britannia crowning the triumphant admiral, while in nearby Bathwick the celebrations of the city chamberlain featured a 12-foot statue of Hercules proclaiming 'BRAVE, HONEST KEPPEL' to bedaz-zled spectators.[112] In William Hayley's *Epistle* Keppel was placed in a pan-theon of naval heroes that included Drake, Hawkins, Blake, Howard, and Anson. In other congratulatory odes his naval exploits against the French and Spanish during the Seven Years War were emphasized. 'True son of Albion, in thyself compleat,' ran one poem from a 'Grateful Briton' in Wigan,[113]

---

[108] *Ipswich Journal*, 20 Feb. 1779.

[109] See Kathleen Wilson, 'The Rejection of Deference: Urban Political Culture in England, 1715–1785', Ph.D. thesis (Yale, 1985), 161–6. This argument is tempered in *Sense of the People*, 253–9.

[110] For pro-Americanism in Norwich, see Wilson, *Sense of the People*, 419–21. In Norwich an anti-war petition in February 1778 was signed by 5,400 citizens. The Norwich Council also voted the freedom of the city to Keppel over the objections of the aldermen. For an account of the celebrations in Norwich, with demands for the ministry's resignation, see *London Ev. Post*, 16–18 Feb. 1779.

[111] For one reference, see *Westminster Magazine*, 7 (Feb. 1779), 64.

[112] *Bath Journal*, 15 Feb. 1779; *Bath Chronicle*, 18 Feb. 1779.

[113] *London Ev. Post*, 30 Jan.–2 Feb. 1779; [W. Hayley], *Epistle to Admiral Keppel* (London, 1779); Anon., *A Congratulatory Ode to Admiral Keppel* (London, 1779); Anon., *Keppeliad: or Injur'd Virtue Triumphant* (London, 1779). See also the poems in the *General Advertiser*, 19 Jan., 4 Feb., 2 Mar. 1779.

Who dares attack thee, meets a sure defeat!
France feels thy pow'r, and Britain's merchants know,
How oft thy arm has crush'd th'insulting foe!
Affrighted Gaul still trembles at thy name,
The boast of freemen, and the pride of Fame:

Keppel's popularizers, in other words, sought to inscribe his exploits within a familiar idiom of anti-Catholicism or anti-Gallicanism.[114] In so doing they evoked the memory of the Seven Years War, years of imperial harmony, victory, and national unanimity, and threw into sharp relief the current political and military crisis. Within this context, Keppel's own fortunes were analogous to those of the nation. Just as the admiral's talents had been abused by the ministry, so Britain's commerce, empire, and naval superiority had been similarly imperilled.

Keppel's predicament was thus cast as a commentary on the parlous state of the nation. It was a patriotic pitch which was inclusive enough to accommodate pro-American and anti-Gallican sentiment, radical calls for reform, and John Bullish rage at Britain's vulnerability to the French. It explains why letters of congratulation flowed not only from radical or Opposition-dominated corporations such as London, Norwich, Newcastle, and York, but from merchants in Yarmouth and Liverpool, the London Drapers, the West India planters and merchants, and the Grand and Laudable Society of Antigallicans.[115] It also explains why huzzas to Keppel were accompanied by toasts to the Whig lords, Chatham, Wilkes, Wolfe, to peace with America, imperial unity, and even to King and Country. Just as the promoters of the American war were vilified in Newcastle, so at Calne Palliser's effigy was burnt in the former clothes of John the Painter, the pro-American arsonist who had attempted to set fire to the naval dockyards at Portsmouth and Plymouth. Equal ignominy, it was argued, should go to 'the v[illain] who attempted to disgrace the navy of England' as to he 'who attempted to destroy it'.[116] Keppel's acquittal could draw quite conservative plaudits as well as radical.

Before the trial was over there were calls in the press for the dismissal of the ministry, especially Lord Sandwich. In London the issue was publicly

---

[114] At Windsor, one of the emblematical devices of the fireworks display included Neptune presiding over the sea, 'with a Scroll in his Hand, on which was transcribed Hawke and Keppel'. *Northampton Mercury*, 22 Feb. 1779.

[115] Suffolk Record Office, HA 67, 461/252. Keppel also received congratulations from the towns of Dublin and Londonderry, from Thetford and Nottingham, and from Trinity House, Newcastle upon Tyne.

[116] For Calne, see *London Ev. Post*, 18–20 Feb. 1779.

debated at Coachmakers' Hall on two occasions in March 1779.[117] The radical Dissenter and pro-American Dr Richard Price even told his Hackney congregation that he hoped the trial would precipitate a crisis similar to the one that followed the loss of Minorca in 1756.[118] But this proved not to be. The government moved quickly to defuse the crisis, forcing Palliser to resign his seat in the Commons and his crown appointments. In the face of protests from Dunning and Fox, it also declined to prosecute the three London rioters committed to Newgate for capital felony. In the Commons it weathered the storm. Although the ministry's majority sank to a little over thirty on Fox's motion on 3 March censuring the Admiralty for sending Keppel out with an inadequate force, some energetic prodding by George III soon restored it to a comfortable margin. Two weeks later, when the Commons debated Dunning's motion on the Admiralty's handling of the court martial, the government majority reached nearly 100. By the time the Opposition moved to demand the dismissal of Lord Sandwich, the government was firmly in control. It was aided by the news of the capture of St Lucia and by Keppel's unwillingness to serve under the present administration, a decision which somewhat tarnished his reputation as an honest patriot. To some independent members, the threat of a combined French–Spanish invasion demanded that naval officers should shelve their political differences.[119]

If the Keppel episode ended inconclusively, the crisis itself represented more than a party and personal feud. It served as a focus for deep-rooted divisions within the country over the American war, divisions that were far from settled by the American Declaration of Independence. As the celebrations in favour of Keppel revealed, pro-American sentiment extended beyond London and radical circles, merging imperceptibly with war-weariness and a deepening disillusionment over Britain's political and economic predicament. To be sure, Britons, even within the Opposition camp, could not agree how to resolve the American crisis. Their views were not well informed about the dynamics of American resistance. Frequently their pro-Americanism expressed a nostalgia for the *status quo ante bellum* rather than a recognition of American independence. Deploring an impolitic, civil war, many could not reconcile themselves to the loss of empire.

---

[117] *Gazetteer and Daily Advertiser*, 16, 23 Mar. 1779. In the previous month there had been a debate as to whether 'so malicious and illfounded' an accusation against Keppel did not demand a strict inquiry into the affair. See ibid. 16, 23 Feb. 1779. I am indebted to Donna Andrew for these references.

[118] *London Ev. Post*, 13–16 Feb. 1779; *Public Advertiser*, 7 Jan. 1779.

[119] O'Gorman, *Rise of Party*, 386. At Coachmakers' Hall there was a public debate as to whether Keppel was justified in striking his flag. See *Gazetteer and Daily Advertiser*, 6 Apr. 1779.

By 1779, of course, attitudes towards America were compounded by the entry of France into the war. Logically this should have proved a fillip to the administration, but the Keppel affair undoubtedly frustrated such an association. While some ministerialists clearly believed that Keppel's own partisanship undermined Britain's security from a French invasion, many people were convinced that the popular admiral, one of the gallant commanders at Quiberon Bay, was a scapegoat for the ministry's own culpability. Keppel's honourable acquittal enabled the Opposition to mobilize anti-Gallican sentiment in its favour and to trumpet the virtues of patriotism at the expense of the ministry. By highlighting Keppel's patriotic fortitude and ministerial malevolence, the Opposition deepened the suspicion of government and the sinews of power which sustained it. By providing a personal focus for governmental malice, corruption, and ineptitude in the context of a protracted and increasingly unpopular war, the trial prepared the ground for reform.

The association of Keppel with reform emerged quite clearly in the general election of 1780. The admiral had hoped to be re-elected for Windsor, which he had represented since 1761. But the court mobilized the servants of the crown against him, even to the point of enfranchising some of the royal retainers overnight. 'Every nerve was strained by government' against Keppel, the *London Courant* reported; 'gentlemen of family and fortune' were prevailed upon 'to make themselves voters for the purpose'.[120] Thus, with a good deal of arm-twisting, the court defeated the admiral by sixteen votes. The Opposition was outraged by this flagrant exertion of royal influence. Erskine saw it as nothing more than government spite. 'The influence, splendour, and advantages of the royal residence', he declared, 'were prostituted to dazzle and to seduce [Keppel's] humble, and, until then, grateful constituents.' Lady Sarah Lennox believed that the King had 'hurt himself a great deal more than he has hurt the Admiral in using his influence & authority to make him lose Windsor'.[121]

The upshot was that Keppel was invited to stand for Surrey by the committee of the county association for parliamentary reform. This decision was endorsed by the Southwark associators under the chairmanship of the radical alderman John Sawbridge.[122] The reform caucus proposed that Keppel be paired with the local radical brewer, Sir Joseph Mawbey, but

---

[120] *London Courant*, 11 Sept. 1780. Among those the court enfranchised were Colonels Egerton and Conway, who both had apartments in Windsor Castle, and the royal musicians.

[121] *Letters of Lady Sarah Lennox*, i. 316–17; Keppel, *Life of Keppel*, ii. 285.

[122] *General Ev. Post*, 19–21 Sept. 1780.

Mawbey was averse to doing this, on the grounds that their joint candidature had not been presented at the general meeting of the freeholders a week earlier. Mawbey's decision caused some embarrassment, for it opened the caucus to accusations that it had flouted electoral proprieties and had foisted a man 'without an acre of land in the county' upon the unsuspecting freeholders.[123] But these objections ultimately carried little weight with the electors. Although 10 per cent of the voters paired Mawbey with his Surrey opponent Thomas Onslow, the vast majority (56 per cent) paired him with the popular Whig admiral as the reform caucus had recommended.[124] The result was a convincing victory for the reform platform. Despite the combined influence of the court, Lambeth Palace, and the powerful Onslow family, Mawbey and Keppel swept the poll, securing impressive majorities in eleven of the fifteen electoral districts. This was done at some expense. Keppel's short, spirited canvass was said to have cost him £9,000.[125] None the less, his public reputation accorded well with an electorate dissatisfied with the conduct of Lord North's war ministry and anxious for change.

What, finally, does the Keppel affair tell us about the nature of popular political culture during the American war? In the first place it illustrates the tremendous importance of the press in shaping the controversy, exploring its ramifications, and relaying them to a national audience. Its running commentary on the trial, in particular, heightened the drama of the event and whetted the appetite of a politically informed and inquisitive public. Certainly the public court martial was tailor-made theatre. But only through the press did the Governor's House at Portsmouth become a national stage where personal reputations and political fortunes were played out. The press, in other words, imparted to the trial a topicality and immediacy that in the eighteenth-century context was probably unprecedented. If the Opposition newspapers had failed the public over the 1775 petitions, as James Bradley has recently suggested,[126] they certainly did not do so over Keppel. The resolute William Parker, imprisoned for publishing a handbill denouncing military violence during the Westminster riots, even managed to keep his readers informed of pro-Keppelian jubilations from his cell in Newgate.[127]

---

[123] Ibid. 21–3 Sept. 1780.

[124] These calculations are based on the *Copy of the Poll for Knights of the Shire for the County of Surrey . . . 27th and 28th Days of September* (Guildford, 1780).

[125] *Gentleman's Magazine*, 64 (1788), 1053.

[126] Bradley, *Popular Politics and the American Revolution*, ch. 4.

[127] For Parker, see Solomon Ludnick, *The American Revolution and the British Press 1775–1783* (Columbia, Mo. 1967), 33–4.

The tremendous publicity of the trial inevitably encouraged its commercialization. Shorthand writers, printers, and publishers competed for the best account, overshadowing the official transcript of the trial. This had happened at Byng's court martial in 1757, with cheap editions, sometimes issued in instalments, snatching sales from the official account. But in 1779 the coverage of the trial was faster and more competitive. Thomas Blandemor's *Genuine Trial*, formally authenticated by the mayor of Portsmouth and endorsed by Keppel's friends, sold out within four days of its publication, despite the cut-throat competition it received from William Blanchard, who publicly disparaged its reliability.[128] Not to be outdone, Richard Cruttwell produced his version in seven sixpenny instalments as the trial was actually running, trading accuracy for accessibility through a distribution network that included booksellers in no less than fifteen West Country towns. Eventually he offered the public a more complete version of the trial, along with Keppel's correspondence to the Admiralty and a dictionary of nautical terms, at 3 shillings for a half-bound demy octavo.[129]

In this heady atmosphere, other entertainers and entrepreneurs cashed in. In the immediate aftermath of the trial London theatre-goers were treated to a comedy called *The Illumination* which included a 'burlesque performance' by Jemmy Twitcher (Lord Sandwich), a hornpipe by Captain Hood 'with alterations from the Manager's Log-book', and a 'new Catch, called *Sir Hugh!* set to a very melancholy and moving tune'.[130] Weeks later they could savour jokes about the trial in a new farce called *The Liverpool Prize*, which ran no less than forty times in the following three months.[131] Alternatively, audiences could gawk at burlesques of popular jubilations in the *British Admiral, or the City in an Uproar*.[132] At the same time the more serious-minded could gather at the Haymarket to listen to a musical ode honouring Keppel,[133] while for the more self-consciously partisan there were prints, busts, and medallions of the valiant hero, not to mention opera caps *à la* Keppel and the ubiquitous blue cockade. The demand for such artefacts was brisk, and the Wedgwoods had little difficulty in selling thousands of busts, cameos, and seals depicting Keppel's ample and hearty features.[134]

---

[128] *Bath Chronicle*, 18 Mar. 1779.   [129] Ibid. 4, 11 Feb., 18 Mar. 1779.

[130] *Morning Chronicle*, 12 Feb. 1779.

[131] Charles Beecher Hogan (ed.), *The London Stage 1660–1800*, part v: *1776–1800* (Carbondale, Ill., 1968), 237–8; *Morning Chronicle*, 4 May 1779.

[132] *Morning Chronicle*, 5, 23 Mar. 1779.

[133] *Morning Post*, 4 May 1779; Hogan (ed.), *The London Stage 1776–1880*, 241.

[134] Trevelyan, *George the Third*, 155; *London Ev. Post*, 23–5, 28–30 Feb. 1779; *Morning Chronicle*, 22 Feb. 1779; *Bonner and Middleton's Bristol Journal*, 6 Mar. 1779.

Some of these artefacts, like Sir Joshua Reynolds's spoons and table cloth inscribed with 'Keppel and Virtue',[135] recalled the jubilant slogans of February 1779, but in terms that idealized the conflict and glossed over its complexity. In a similar fashion Burke would later recall the Keppel affair with nostalgia, remembering how he 'partook of the general flow of national joy that attended the justice that was done to his virtue'.[136] Writing during the French terror, isolated from a Whig party which now appeared dangerously Francophile, the Keppelian jubilations seemed in retrospect to epitomize rightful indignation, the voice of the people tempered and channelled by aristocratic leadership; what Burke would elsewhere describe as a 'grand chorus of national harmony'.[137] This was, of course, a roseate picture. The demonstrations in London had disturbed the aristocratic Whigs. They formed part of a tradition of independent street politics that hardly squared with Whig trusteeship, and they threw up demands for parliamentary reform that the Rockinghamites opposed. Moreover, they revealed, in the destruction of sedan chairs outside the Admiralty and in the jostling and bantering of genteel spectators who would not 'holloa Keppel for ever', a disrespect for rank that Burke and company would have deplored.[138] At the same time, the concordance of patrician and popular anti-ministerialism in the provinces created the illusion that crowd politics could be domesticated and directed towards appropriate ends. Indeed, the Keppelian jubilations may have restored patrician confidence in handling crowds after the unnerving episode of Wilkes. In Scotland, however, the celebrations of Keppel's acquittal were overshadowed by popular resistance to the Catholic Relief Act. The same forces would soon haunt England, with devastating effect.

[135] Keppel, *Life of Keppel*, ii. 193.
[136] Edmund Burke, *Works*, 6 vols. (Oxford, World Classics, 1907), vi. 76.
[137] Burke used the term in *An Appeal from the New to the Old Whigs* (1791). See *Works*, v. 102.
[138] *Morning Chronicle*, 15 Feb. 1779.

5

The Gordon Riots

No Popery   Down with it
George the 3d is a Roman Catholick
(1780 handbill)[1]

'A time of terrour' was how Dr Johnson described the Gordon riots.[2] Many contemporaries would have agreed. The disturbances that gripped London in June 1780 were the most tumultuous and destructive of the century. In the wake of the Commons' refusal to repeal the Catholic Relief Bill of 1778, hundreds of buildings were ransacked, Lambeth Palace, Downing Street, and the Bank of England were threatened with destruction, and the forces of law and order were paralysed, prompting finally military intervention of an unprecedented nature. In the carnage that followed over 200 people were shot dead in the street; as many died in hospital or were treated for wounds. 'Figure to yourself every man, woman and child in the streets, panic-struck,' wrote one military volunteer, 'the atmosphere red as blood with the ascending fires, muskets firing in every part, and consequently women and children lying sprawling in the streets; all the lower order of people stark mad with liquor, huzzaing and parading with flags.'[3] It was an unforgettable sight, which, as contemporary comment testifies, left an indelible imprint on the popular consciousness.

What are we to make of this extraordinary riot? What does it reveal about popular belief at a time of burgeoning radicalism, religious revivalism, and a divisive war? The first scholarly work on the Gordon riots, published at the time of the General Strike of 1926, focused principally on the problem of order. Like some contemporaries, it detected a distinct change in

[1] PRO, WO 34/103/368.   [2] James Boswell, *Life of Johnson* (Oxford, 1980), 1054.
[3] BL, MS 27828, fo. 127, cited by J. Paul de Castro, *The Gordon Riots* (London, 1926), 145.

the nature of the riot after the destruction of Newgate and other gaols. What began as an anti-Catholic protest became a frenzied bacchanalia of outcast London, a spontaneous uprising of the rabble against authority and the institutions which shaped their lives.[4] This theme of degeneration has remained a salient one among those who have wished to sensationalize the riots, or to propound the virtues of a policed society.[5] Nor is it absent from those who, linking the anti-Catholic agitations of the Protestant Association to the excesses that followed, have sought to emphasize the immaturity, volatility, and dangers of early mass movements. Writing in 1949, for example, Sir Herbert Butterfield compared the charismatic hero, Lord George Gordon, to Hitler, and lamented that so enlightened a measure as the Catholic Relief Bill should have offended 'not only rational prejudice, but deep dark passions, strange as Nazi hatreds, and as baffling as anti-semiticism'.[6]

The first major challenge to these interpretations came from George Rudé. Fresh from his study of the crowd during the French Revolution, Rudé embarked upon a detailed examination of the Gordon rioters and their victims. From this research Rudé concluded that the 1780 disturbances were not the product of mass hysteria, whipped by religious fanatics and sectarian fury; nor did they degenerate into looting and arson. Throughout the unrest rioters seldom deviated from their original objectives. Drawing upon a long-standing tradition of anti-Catholicism which had become embodied in notions of the Englishman's birthright, they directed their fury upon leading Catholics, their chapels, and their sympathizers. This did not mean that the rioters were simple surrogates of the Protestant Association and their radical allies in the City. Lord George Gordon and his City supporters doubtless orchestrated the riot and, initially at least, gave it moral support. But the disturbances, Rudé argued, were essentially local and spontaneous, drawing principally upon small employers, journeymen, and apprentices from the neighbourhood.[7] In fact the respectability of the rioters, 'sober workmen' was how Rudé ultimately characterized

---

[4] De Castro, *Gordon Riots*, esp. 235–6.

[5] Christopher Hibbert, *King Mob* (London, 1956); Leon Radzinowicz, *A History of the English Criminal Law and its Administration from 1750*, 4 vols. (London, 1956), iii, ch. 4.

[6] Herbert Butterfield, *George III, Lord North and the People* (London, 1949), 374–9; for a similar emphasis, without the Nazism, see Eugene Black, *The Association: British Extra-parliamentary Political Organization, 1769–1793* (Cambridge, Mass., 1969), ch. 4.

[7] The central argument is set out in George Rudé, 'The Gordon Riots: A Study of the Rioters and their Victims', *Trans. Royal Historical Society*, 5th ser. 6 (1956), 93–114, reprinted in *Paris and London in the Eighteenth Century* (London, 1970), 268–92. See also id., *Hanoverian London 1714–1808* (London, 1971), 178–80, 220–7 and id., *The Crowd in History* (New York, 1964), chs. 3, 13–15.

them,[8] vitiated the notion that the riots were the product of some urban malaise or criminality. This conviction was reinforced by the argument that the rioters expressed both a rudimentary political consciousness and a class bias. Rudé noted that the riots were not directed at the Catholic population as a whole, but at the wealthier ones in the City and the north-west parishes around Holborn. 'Behind the slogan of "No Popery" ', Rudé stressed, 'there lay a deeper social purpose: a groping desire to settle accounts with the rich, if only for a day, and to achieve some kind of social justice.'[9] Indeed, his subsequent work led him to situate the Gordon riots on a libertarian-radical vector which anticipated the labour movements of the nineteenth century. 'For all the illiberal forms they assumed', Rudé concluded in *Ideology and Popular Protest*, the Gordon riots were 'cast in a radical mould, drew on a long radical-Protestant tradition and were inspired (if not promoted) by the most radical elements of the city'.[10] In saying this he reasserted his differences with Edward Thompson, who had earlier argued that popular agitation of 1780 revealed 'something of a mixture of manipulated mob and revolutionary crowd'. Libertarian in inspiration, but swayed by demagogic and inexperienced leaders, the Protestant Association precipitated 'a spontaneous process of riot' that deviated from the original objectives and ultimately degenerated into looting and arson.[11]

We might begin to explore these issues by examining the ideological aspects of the riot, for they have some bearing upon the fanaticism and hysteria which is said to have informed it and also upon its radical affiliations. Popular hostility towards Catholics was, of course, legion. English men and women were reared on Catholic atrocities; state services and popular holidays like 5 November celebrated the nation's deliverance from popery and arbitrary rule. In London the Monument still commemorated the papists' purported responsibility for the Great Fire. This deep-rooted antipathy towards Catholics, and particularly towards perceived Catholic forms of rule, formed a basic stratum of belief and prejudice upon which the riots would emerge. During the crisis the *Remembrancer* emphasized that anti-Catholicism was deeply inculcated from infancy 'by reading the Book of Martyrs and other legends'.[12] And, indeed, the protesters left no doubt that this was the case. One magistrate recalled that when he remonstrated with the crowd before Palace Yard on 6 June 'they quoted scripture

---

[8] *Paris and London*, 283.   [9] Ibid. 289.

[10] George Rudé, *Ideology and Popular Protest* (New York, 1980), 139.

[11] E. P. Thompson, *The Making of the English Working Class* (Harmondsworth, 1968), 77–8.

[12] *Remembrancer*, 10 (1980), 64. See also the *London Courant*, 12 June 1780.

and talked of the cruelty of papists and the persecution their forefathers had undergone for them.'[13]

Yet if popular anti-Catholicism was a necessary cause of the disturbances, it was hardly a sufficient one. Since the seventeenth century, and certainly since 1745, the popular fear of Catholics had been declining, although it was periodically invoked during invasion scares. Within London itself, the Irish Catholic population of approximately 25,000 lived on reasonably amicable terms with their neighbours.[14] Aside from the odd sectarian scuffle, the last major anti-Irish riot had occurred in 1736. Moreover, the Catholic Relief Act of 1778 was, strictly speaking, a quite modest measure which passed both Houses of Parliament with little debate or dissension.[15] Essentially the Act repealed two Williamite statutes against the growth of popery, thereby granting Catholics freedom of property and commerce and exempting their priests from the threat of life imprisonment if they celebrated mass or educated Catholic children.[16] The only crucial proviso was that Catholics had to take an oath of allegiance to the crown and renounce Jacobitism and the temporal authority of the pope to qualify. As the supporters of the Act emphasized, the Act did not repeal all the penal statutes against Catholics;[17] nor did the Act give Catholics rights to political representation or office-holding. Rather it was a gesture of amity to those loyalist Catholics whose only dissent from the constituted political order was one of religious conscience. It was passed to facilitate the support of Catholics for the American war.

The Act was nevertheless viewed with considerable misgivings outside parliament. Since the 1760s there had been a religious revival in the metropolis, inspired principally by Methodism and often militantly anti-Catholic. 'Field Preachers inveighed with the utmost vehemence against Popery', one commentator recalled, and 'The Flying Book of Martyrs was rummaged

---

[13] PRO, PC 1/3097.

[14] Figures concerning the size of the Catholic population vary a great deal. The 1767 returns listed only 10,000, but Eamon Duffy has claimed there were at least 25,000 in 1746. See Jean Alain Lesourd, *Les Catholiques dans la société anglaise* (Lille, 1978), i, chs. 2–3 and Eamon Duffy, 'Richard Challoner 1691–1781: A Memoir', in Eamon Duffy (ed.), *Challoner and his Church* (London, 1981), 13. For an argument that wishes to stress the continuities of popular anti-Catholicism, see Colin Haydon, *Anti-Catholicism in Eighteenth-Century England, c. 1714–80* (Manchester, 1993), chs. 6, 7.

[15] Cobbett, *Parliamentary History*, 19 (1777–8), 1137–45.

[16] 18 Geo. III c. 60. The statutes repealed were 11 & 12 Wm. III.

[17] One commentator calculated that there were still sixteen penal statutes against Catholics on the books, including those which subjected priests celebrating mass to a stiff fine and one year's imprisonment. See *A Defence of the Act of Parliament Lately Passed for the Relief of Roman Catholics* (London, 1780), 21 n.

from the beginning to the end to find out instances of pretended popish cruelty.'[18] This was in response to the renewed confidence and growth of the Catholic Church, which under Bishop Challoner had developed permanent self-supporting missions, new schools, and a proselytizing ministry that warned servants and tradesmen of the dangers of religious enthusiasm.[19] In the eyes of many Protestant zealots the 1778 Act simply abetted the Catholic cause. Especially galling to Protestant zealots was the elimination of the £100 reward for the successful conviction of practising Catholics, a clause that compromised the campaign against Catholics by people like William Payne, a master carpenter and London constable, soon to become one of the staunchest supporters of the Protestant Association. Deprecating the prosecution of popery by such 'common informers', the Act purposefully reserved the surveillance of Catholicism to the urbane, cosmopolitan social élite who dominated parliament, the bench, and the corridors of power.[20]

The 1778 Catholic Relief Act thus signalled the victory of religious urbanity over religious evangelism. In practical terms it endorsed the aristocracy's right to preside over the future of English Catholicism and denied middling citizens the right to challenge Catholicism in the courts. To Protestants who equated Catholicism with idolatry, persecution, and foreign slavery, this was national treachery.[21] It was especially so because of the political conjuncture in which it took place, that of the American war.

Officially the Protestant Association distanced itself from the bitter disagreements over the war that divided metropolitan opinion during the late 1770s. At the outset it declared it was 'not formed to promote the views

---

[18] James Barnard, *The Life of the Venerable and Right Reverend Richard Challoner* (London, 1784), 162–3.

[19] Duffy, 'Challoner', 9–15; Sheridan Gilley, 'Challoner as Controversialist', in Duffy (ed.), *Challoner and his Church*, 107–8; Barnard, *Challoner*, 194–5. Four new Catholic charity schools were founded between 1764 and 1780: Lincoln's Inn Fields (1764), Hammersmith (1765), Virginia Street, Wapping (1778), and Moorfields (1780). See T. G. Holt, 'Some Early London Catholic Schools', *London Recusant*, 5 (1975), 46–54.

[20] Payne was singled out for criticism by Burke in 1780. There were also allusions to his anti-Catholic activities in the original debates on the 1778 Act. See Cobbett, *Parliamentary History*, 19 (1777–8), 1137, 1145, and 21 (1780–1), 710. Payne's activities and outlook are admirably traced in an unpublished paper by Joanna Innes of Somerville College, Oxford, entitled 'William Payne of Bell Yard, Carpenter, c. 1718–1782: The Life and Times of a London Informing Constable', to appear in her *Inferior Politics* (Oxford, forthcoming). See also Barnard, *Challoner*, 156–93.

[21] Gerald Newman has emphasized the idea of the Protestant Association as 'a popular counterforce against what was felt to be the un-English conduct of the upper classes'. His interpretation differs from mine, however, over the political ramifications and religious context of this polarity. See Gerald Newman, *The Rise of English Nationalism* (New York, 1987), 208–9.

of party, or to embarrass the measures of government at this important crisis'.[22] Unofficially, it played upon popular anxieties. Although the government had endorsed the 1778 Relief Act to cement Catholic loyalty at a time when France had entered the war, the Association took the opposite view. Noting the anti-Gallican and anti-ministerial feeling that had surfaced during Admiral Keppel's trial in February 1779, it questioned the sagacity of this policy, focusing upon the perfidy of both French and Catholics.[23] In this context, repeal was seen as a manifestly loyalist but nonpartisan measure, safeguarding English liberties from the Catholic threat within and without at an important crisis in national and imperial politics. At the same time, the rhetoric of the Protestant Association sometimes sailed close to the radical wind. Various supporters linked the Relief Act with the Quebec Act of 1774 and with ministerial incursions upon British liberty in America. The Reverend Dr Bromley, for example, minister of the Fitzroy Chapel and a Middlesex associator, called the Quebec Bill 'a most wicked and pernicious piece of business, and thought the late act to take off restraints from Papists an arrow shot from the same quiver'.[24] Others agreed. 'The seas of Protestant blood, wantonly shed in this ruinous and calamitous war,' wrote an associator from Newcastle, 'too strongly prove that the subversion of civil and religious liberty is the grand point where all operations center.'[25] The campaign for repeal was thus also projected as part of the larger struggle against ministerial oppression.

Not all radicals saw the issue this way. Wilkes believed the modest concessions granted to Catholics in 1778 to be quite unexceptional. The same was true of the Duke of Richmond, the most radical nobleman in the Westminster Association. He was not prepared to place the Relief Act in the same category as the Quebec Act of 1774, for there was a crucial difference between the conditional toleration of Catholics reared in the British system of liberty and subject to loyalty oaths and registration, and the maintenance of a state-endorsed Catholic establishment. The latter institutionalized Catholicism in a manner that was intrinsically inimical to liberty, whereas the first, as one correspondent in the radical *London Courant* asserted, allowed freedom of conscience to flourish in 'liberty and ease'.[26] This line of argument was pushed further by progressive Dissenters such

[22] *An Appeal from the Protestant Association to the People of Great Britain* (London, 1779), 3.

[23] Ibid. 55–8.

[24] Cited by John Sainsbury, *Disaffected Patriots: London Supporters of Revolutionary America 1769–1782* (Kingston, 1987), 156.

[25] *Protestant Packet or British Monitor* (Newcastle, 1780), 167–8. Thanks to Joanna Innes for this reference.

[26] *London Courant*, 11–13 June 1780.

as Joseph Priestley. As far as he was concerned, English Catholicism had shed its persecutory spirit with the inexorable rise of the Enlightenment and was really a declining force. Consequently the objectives of the Protestant Association could only be counter-productive, stoking the embers of religious discord and bigotry and giving Catholicism a new lease of life. It was far more politic to counter Catholicism through religious toleration and proselytizing than to 'imitate that church in the very thing for which we condemn it'.[27]

Radicals were thus divided on the issue of repeal and this division ran through the ranks, as the debates on London's Common Council reveal.[28] In view of this, it is impossible to regard the Protestant Association, still less repeal, as radical. Rather one should regard it as a protean, populist movement, rooted in the evangelism of the metropolis, which cross-cut orthodox political alignments. Indeed, the Association attracted figures across the political spectrum: from ministerialists such as Alderman Evan Pugh and the philanthropic merchant John Thornton, to moderate Opposition MPs like Charles Barrow of Gloucester, to city radicals like Frederick Bull. It did, however, adopt radical forms to press for repeal, holding monthly general meetings, distributing handbills, advocating instructions to MPs, and embarking upon mass petitioning. Radicals sometimes eyed this strategy with suspicion and deliberately distanced the PA from the Association Movement for parliamentary reform that was gaining ground in the towns and counties of England. In April 1780, for example, associators in Middlesex fought off a proposal to annex repeal to their political agenda.[29] In view of the violent Scottish resistance to the Relief Act, some feared that Lord George Gordon's fanaticism would throw all popular associations into disrepute at a critical moment in the campaign for parliamentary reform. Their fears were not unfounded.

Although Lord George Gordon was ultimately acquitted of high treason for fomenting the riots of 1780, there is little doubt that he intended to

---

[27] Joseph Priestley, *A Free Address to Those who have Petitioned for the Repeal of the Late Act of Parliament in Favour of Roman Catholicks* (London, 1780), in *The Theological and Miscellaneous Works of Joseph Priestley*, ed. J. T. Rutt, 24 vols. (London, 1817–31), xxi. 499–513.

[28] *Morning Chronicle*, 1 June 1780. In the debate on the motion to petition parliament for the repeal of the 1778 Act radicals led the debate. The motion was moved by Josiah Dornford and seconded by James Sharp, common councilman for Lime Street. The two major opponents of the petition appear to have been Charles Lincoln, common councilman for Lime Street, and Alderman John Sawbridge. Sawbridge agreed to present the petition along with Alderman Frederick Bull, but only because he saw himself as a delegate of the City, not out of personal conviction. Sawbridge's actions have sometimes been misrepresented by historians. See John Stevenson, *Popular Disturbances in England 1700–1870* (London, 1779), 88.

[29] *London Ev. Post*, 11–13 Apr. 1780.

apply as much popular pressure as he could to the campaign for repeal. The decision to call a mass meeting on 2 June 1780 was controversial, and it was only under the threat of Lord George's resignation as president of the Association that the motion passed.[30] As a result, some 50,000 members of the Protestant Association mustered in St George's Fields and marched upon parliament to present their monster petition. Approximately 17,000 remained to hear the outcome.

The move to besiege parliament in such a manner was an audacious step. The leading lights of the Protestant Association knew the plan was technically illegal and had advised Gordon that this was so.[31] Earlier petitions had been presented by delegates, not by such overwhelming numbers. The numbers certainly overwhelmed the Westminster justices, who with seventy-six constables were quite unable to control the crowds. Before the Commons several MPs were forced publicly to swear that they would repeal the Act. In the approaches to the upper house, which was sitting to hear the Duke of Richmond's motion on annual parliaments, their lordships were jostled, heckled, and assailed with the cry of 'No Popery'. Generally speaking it was the ministerialists who bore the brunt of the crowd's anger. The Archbishop of Canterbury had his wig pulled off and 'his canonicals torn to pieces'; other bishops were similarly insulted. Lord Mansfield was 'daringly abused' to his face and had the glass of his carriage broken, while the Lord President of the Council, Lord Bathurst, was kicked in the legs.[32] The lobby of the Commons became so tumultuous that Lord George Gordon was invited to placate the crowd and to urge it to disperse. Instead, he reported those members in opposition to the petition and reiterated his belief that only repeal would prevent violence. Faced with an intransigent Commons, the message was clear. It only took a little prompting from the leaders of the populace to generate plans for retribution. As one printer deposed, 'the general cry among them was they would have redress, or else'.[33]

Although Sir George Savile's residence was originally targeted for destruction because he was the author of the Relief Act, the crowd quickly turned its attention to the principal places of Catholic worship. On the first evening the chapel of the Sardinian ambassador in Lincoln's Inn Fields was burnt to the ground; that of the Bavarian ambassador in

---

[30] *A Narrative of the Proceedings of Lord George Gordon* (London, 1780), 2. See also the testimony of James Fisher and Erasmus Middleton in PRO, TS 11/388/1212, 1213, and Gordon's own narrative in BL, Add. MS 42129, fos. 5–6, 11.

[31] PRO, TS 11/388/1212.

[32] *Public Advertiser*, 5 June 1780; *Annual Register*, 23 (1780), 257.

[33] PRO, SP 37/14/189. One of the leaders active in the Commons' lobby was William Payne. See PRO, PC 1/3097.

Warwick Street was ransacked before troops and cavalry arrived to save
the building. The following evening the crowds focused their attention upon
the chapel in Ropemakers' Alley, Moorfields, but the City marshal managed to dissuade them from destroying it.[34] The rioters returned, however, the next day and began sacking the chapel, despite the presence of
a file of soldiers from the Tower under the direction of Lord Mayor Brackley
Kennett. The mayor justified his refusal to read the Riot Act on the grounds
that there were innocent women and children in the crowd. The truth was
that he feared popular retribution.[35] Such action was taken against a number of Westminster magistrates who apprehended or examined rioters in
the following week.

In the first four days the rioting followed a fairly predictable pattern.
The main targets remained the chapels and schools, in Westminster, the
City, and the East End. The houses of prominent Catholics were also threatened, including that of their leader, Lord Petre, and William Mawhood, a
wealthy woollen draper and personal friend of Bishop Challoner. But few
at this stage were harmed, despite the fact that 'the general conversation
at the alehouses' foretold an attack upon 'the Private Houses of Roman
Catholicks'.[36] The only other victims of collective violence, in fact, were
Sir George Savile, whose house in Leicester Fields was partially ransacked
on 5 June; and two Westminster tradesmen, Sampson Rainforth JP and
Stephen Mabberley, who were responsible for the arrest and committal
of the fourteen rioters apprehended outside the Sardinian chapel. In other
words, the crowd scarcely deviated from the original cue of the Protestant Association. To underscore its solidarity with Lord George Gordon,
it sported the blue cockades of the Association and paraded the Catholic
relics of the Moorfields chapel before his house in Welbeck Street, burning
them in the adjacent fields.[37] It awaited the return of the Commons on
6 June when it hoped that the repeal of the Relief Act would once more
be considered.

The Commons, however, once more refused to bow to popular pressure.
It deplored the intimidation of the House; urged the crown to prosecute

[34] Carrington and Payne's Law Report, 5 (1833), 286.

[35] PRO, PC/2/138–41; *Rex* v. *Kennett*, Carrington and Payne's Law Report, 5 (1833),
282–96.

[36] PRO, SP 37/20/41, 47; *The Mawhood Diary*, ed. E. E. Reynolds, Catholic Rec. Soc.
50 (London, 1956), 150–1; James Langdale, 'Thomas Langdale, the Distiller', *London Recusant*,
5 (1975), 42–5.

[37] William Vincent (Thomas Holcroft), *A Plain & Succinct Narrative of the Riots and
Disturbances in the Cities of London and Westminster and the Borough of Southwark* (2nd edn.
London, 1780), 24. Gordon's servant is said to have asked them 'for God's sake to go away
and that his Lordship would not support their cause if they went on so'. PRO, SP
37/20/271.

the rioters; recommended compensation for the Catholics whose property had been destroyed; and promptly adjourned until 8 June. At this point the riots escalated. After a crowd had dragged Lord George Gordon's chariot through the streets in popular triumph, protesters broadened their jurisdiction to include not only Catholics but members of the establishment. Lambeth Palace was threatened; so, too, were the residences of the Archbishops of Canterbury and York. Crowds also directed their anger upon leading members of the government *and* the Opposition who were known to be sympathetic to the Act, a departure from their earlier strategy outside parliament.[38] These included Lord Rockingham, Burke, Dunning, Lord North, and Lord Mansfield, the Lord Chief Justice, who was closely associated with the Scottish 'junto' and who had earlier discouraged the prosecution of Catholics, especially by petit bourgeois zealots like William Payne. In other words, the whole cosmopolitan hierarchy, the powerful men whose tolerant or errant attitudes were undermining 'true Protestantism', came under review.[39] As my opening quotation suggests, this hierarchy also included the King, who was suspected of having converted to Catholicism. 'Damn ye King and ye Pope,' exclaimed one small card picked up by the authorities. 'Dethrone him or else he will Massacre you all,' suggested one handbill. To the 'True Protestant' who wrote it, George III deserved to lose his head for abandoning his coronation oath.[40]

So the anger of the crowd swung dramatically against the political establishment. What is more, in sheer defiance of the Commons' resolution that the Attorney-General prosecute the rioters, the crowd wreaked vengeance upon the law. Magistrates who brought rioters to account or intervened to protect supporters of the Act had their houses pulled down. Only those who publicly recanted were spared. When Justice Charles Triquet found himself the subject of crowd reprisals in Bloomsbury Square, he begged his assailants 'to distinguish between their friends and Enemies, that he was as great an Enemy to Popery as they could be'.[41] By this means and by humouring the crowd with a few shillings, he saved his house.

But the reprisals of the populace did not end there. On the evening of 6 June a crowd assembled before Newgate and demanded the release of

---

[38] *Public Advertiser*, 5 June 1780. The paper reported that the 'patriotic noblemen', including the Dukes of Devonshire and Richmond, Lord Camden, and the Earl of Shelburne, 'had their carriages conducted with great respect and honour to the door of the House' on 2 June 1780.

[39] The notion that the rioters and supporters of the Protestant Association were 'True Protestants' was affirmed in a handbill before parliament on 6 June, entitled 'True Protestants no Turncoats'. See Vincent, *Plain & Succinct Narrative*, appendix G.

[40] PRO, WO 34/103/325, 368. See also BMC 5534, 5669, 5680–1.

[41] PRO, PC 1/3097.

the rioters who had been confined there to await trial. Receiving no satisfaction from the keeper, Richard Akerman, they set fire to his house, broke
in, and released all prisoners. From there the assailants moved on to New
Prison, Clerkenwell, where they again demanded freedom for the anti-
Catholic rioters. The keeper, Samuel Newport, told them there was none
in the gaol, but 'the Mob told him they were determined to take them out,
and to break open all the gaols in London that night'.[42] Forcing open the
gates they released all but one murderer, whom they refused to set at large,
declaring 'they would let no murderers loose on the world'.[43] From there they
moved on to the Clerkenwell bridewell, to the Fleet, and to other prisons
in the metropolis, releasing hundreds of debtors from King's Bench prison.

The 'gaol delivery' of 6 and 7 June was clearly designed to frustrate
the course of justice against 'true Protestants' and to show the government
that the protesters meant business. It also had wider social connotations.
Lower-class Londoners feared Newgate as a typhus-ridden hell, whose
verminous bunks and poor subsistence on the 'Common Side' made life
unbearable without drink. Known as the 'Queen Ken', the 'Nark', the 'Little
Ease', its destruction in 1780 may also be seen as a protest against the
iniquities of the prison system. Certainly the way in which the keys of
Newgate were brandished about and accorded destructive powers would
suggest as much.[44] Perhaps the breaking into and burning of prisons connoted a contempt for the law in general; some unsympathetic observers
thought so. Whatever the reason, the prospect of dangerous malefactors at
large in a city where the forces of law and order appeared powerless struck
fear in the minds of the propertied classes in London. People evacuated
their homes and middle-class sympathy for the rioters, where it existed,
quickly evaporated. Even the leading activists of the Protestant Association began to have misgivings about the riot and distanced themselves
from its activities, although without necessarily renouncing repeal.[45] Lord

---

[42] PRO, PC 1/3097.   [43] *A Narrative of the Proceedings of Lord George Gordon*, 33.
[44] Peter Linebaugh, *The London Hanged* (London, 1991), 335, 345–6; 'Queen Ken' and
'Nark' were also canting terms for prisons or bridewells in general, see *A New Canting
Dictionary* (London, 1725); on Newgate, see W. J. Sheehan, 'Finding Solace In Eighteenth-
Century Newgate', in J. S. Cockburn (ed.), *Crime in England 1500–1800* (Princeton, 1977),
229–45.
[45] The Common Council of London petitioned once more for repeal of the Relief Act on
7–8 June, although the motion encountered more opposition than it had done in May. See
CLRO, Journals of Common Council, 63 (1780), 29, 61, 69, and *London Courant*, 10 June
1780. One radical who flamboyantly continued to support the riot was William Moore, a
printer and writer formerly associated with the *North Briton*. In the *Thunderer*, 8 June 1780,
he congratulated the Protestant Association on their noble cause, declaring it had 'long been
the design of both the court and ministry to establish arbitrary power and the Roman Catholick

George Gordon, who tried to intercede with rioters in the City on 7 June, is said to have told them that he had no objection to their pulling down Roman Catholic chapels, but that they should not have 'touched private property'.[46]

In the newspapers the condemnation of the rioters as a lawless, licentious mob became almost universal, and some began to argue that religion had become a pretence for looting and plunder. As the radical Duke of Richmond later stated: 'Robbers, thieves, felons, and all the rabble which form part of the mob in great and populous cities, took an advantage of the large numbers of people who collected themselves upon that occasion, and under the pretext of religious reformation, committed the most horrid, criminal and daring outrages, not only against private property but against the laws of their country.'[47] It is upon this kind of testimony that the degeneration thesis was built.

It is difficult to determine how anarchic the riot became in its final stages. After 6 June contemporary accounts were quite alarmist, and Protestant associators, in particular, had a vested interest in denouncing the disturbances as a serious deviation from the repeal campaign. Some looting did go on, more than the legal records reveal, for the crown prosecution was more successful in collecting evidence for constructive treason or capital felony under the Riot Act than it was for offences against property.[48] Even so, it was probably not substantial. Contemporaries were closer to the mark, however, in emphasizing the amount of drinking which accompanied the riots. Quite apart from Langdale's distillery in Holborn, which was broken into and set on fire by the mob on 6 June and became the scene of a drunken, sometimes fatal frolic, there was plenty of drink to be had. Pulling down houses was hard work. It took a crowd anything from one to three hours to throw out the furniture, rip out the windows and floorboards, and pull off the tiles from the roof. Not surprisingly, mob captains frequently called for pails or barrels of beer to help the men along.[49] One justice testified

religion in England, and to overturn the laws and constitution of the British Empire'. He then reiterated many of the old themes of Protestant martyrology. He was arrested by Alderman John Wilkes. See PRO, WO 34/103/231–3, and BL, Add. MS 30866, fo. 242.

[46] PRO, SP 37/14/163, 193; see also Gordon's account, BL, Add. MS 42129, fo. 52.

[47] *Gazetteer*, 20 June 1780.

[48] Rudé cites 15 brought to trial for theft at the Old Bailey, of whom 7 were found not guilty. Rudé, *Paris and London*, 282.

[49] *The Proceedings on the King's Commission of the Peace, Oyer and Terminer and Gaol Delivery for the City of London* (Dec. 1779–Oct. 1780), 622 (hereafter *Old Bailey*); *The Proceedings on the King's Special Commission of Oyer and Terminer for the County of Surrey 10 July 1782*, ed. Joseph Gurney (London, 1780), 57 (hereafter *Surrey*).

that at the destruction of a pub in Long Lane, Southwark, he saw Oliver Johnson give 'liquor to the populace' and drink 'some himself, which made him very sick; he drew towards me, there was a pump, he leaned his head against the pump and puked a great deal; it came out of his mouth like water, half a pint, I suppose, or more.'[50] Riots were sometimes carried out in a revelrous mode, and we should not exaggerate, as does Rudé, the sobriety and respectability of the participants. Francis Place recalled 'the lower order of people stark mad with liquor, huzzaing and parading with flags'. One apprentice confessed to his master of the 'fine fun' he had been having pulling down the chapel of the Sardinian ambassador; another rioter told of the good times he had making 'no less than six fires'.[51]

This is not to suggest that the riots lost all direction. Rudé is essentially correct in suggesting that the disturbances seldom deviated from their original course. After the second adjournment of the Commons on 6 June, the crowd turned its attention to Catholic houses. It did so with a strong sense of ritual and legitimization. Crowds sometimes rang bells upon arrival. Following statutory precedent by which magistrates were empowered to search houses for Catholic books, captains called for the 'book', that is, the Book of Common Prayer, or a Protestant Bible, and searched houses for evidence of Catholic allegiance.[52] Some care was taken to ensure that the resident was truthful. Thomas Hornyold, a packer on Coleman Street, had his house searched twice for 'books of Popery' before the mob 'went off swearing' he 'had deceived them and would return'.[53] When Charles Lee heard that the crowd was about to sack his house in Golden Lane, he hung out blue ribbons and revealed his bible, but the crowd remained unsatisfied, and 'made a ring' around him, so he testified, and 'swore me to my religion'.[54] Similarly, crowds were attentive to the possibility of malicious accusations by factious neighbours. Elizabeth Curry of East Bermondsey, for example, whose house was next door to a chapel and who drew suspicion upon herself by removing some of her effects, pacified the crowd by kissing her Book of Common Prayer; but two of her neighbours charged that a crucifix was hidden upstairs. The crowd did not believe them, however, and insisting they had accused Curry out of 'spite', threw them out of the house.[55]

[50] *Surrey*, 69.　　　[51] BL, Add. MS 27828, fo. 127; *Old Bailey*, 542, 591.

[52] PRO, KB 8/79/228, SP 37/20/289; *Old Bailey*, 532, 626. The statutory precedent was 3 Jas. I c. 5. The same point has been made by Haydon, see *Anti-Catholicism*, 228–9.

[53] De Castro, *Gordon Riots*, 123. Hornyold's name is not listed among the claimants for damages, so it is likely that the mob did not return to gut his house. See PRO, Work 6/110, 111.

[54] *Old Bailey*, 622.　　　[55] PRO, KB 8/79/199–201.

In carrying out these rituals, crowds assumed the place of authority. In their own eyes they did what the Anglican establishment should have done, immobilize the Catholic foe in their midst. These extra-legal forms of action were quite discriminatory. As the crown prosecutors themselves admitted, they were directed at Catholics, or those directly involved in upholding the Catholic Relief Act and frustrating popular resistance to it.[56] Very occasionally the rioters threatened the houses of other denominations whom they suspected of Catholicism. This happened to the Moravians in Nevill's Court, who wisely 'let the rioters convince themselves . . . of our not being Roman Catholics'. This did the trick, for when the rioters returned to find the chapel open for inspection, 'not one attempted to come in and they soon dispersed'.[57]

But did the riot have any social overtones beyond these anti-Catholic objectives? In what sense could the disturbance be termed a social as well as politico-religious protest?

Rudé's arguments on this score appear to me to be somewhat misleading. It is true that the geographical incidence of destruction was weighted towards the wealthier areas rather than the parishes and districts in which the majority of Catholic workers lived. At least half of the victims lived in Holborn and the City; a noticeable number in Southwark; and relatively few in the riverside parishes of Whitechapel, Wapping, St George-in-the-East, or the crowded alleys of St Giles-in-the-Fields.[58] Most lived in middling property or better, although they were not necessarily well-off, for over half (58 per cent) lived in houses rated between £10 and £29 per annum and less than a quarter at £40 or over.[59] Even so, there is little doubt that the victims of the riots were richer than the average London Catholic and indisputably more substantial than the rioters themselves.

Yet it would be wrong to infer from this that the rioters systematically embarked upon a form of social levelling, a rough justice against the rich. Social resentments did surface during the disturbances. 'Protestant or not,' the shipwright William Heyter is said to have exclaimed, 'no gentleman need be possessed of more than £1000 a year, that is money enough for every gentleman to live on.' Such comments were unusual, as the justice's comments on this case revealed, and, indeed, there were some very real

---

[56] PRO, TS 11/33/1213.   [57] De Castro, *Gordon Riots*, 139.

[58] My figures, derived from PRO, Work 6/110, 111, suggest the following geographical distribution: Holborn division 44 (including 5 from Bloomsbury); City 31; East End 20; Southwark 17; Clerkenwell 14; Westminster 10; Bermondsey and Rotherhithe 5.

[59] George Rudé, 'Some Financial and Military Aspects of the Gordon Riots', *Guildhall Miscellany*, 6 (Feb. 1956), 31–42. Rudé's analysis in his earlier article on the Gordon riots tended to exaggerate the wealth of the rioters. See *Paris and London*, 287.

doubts about whether Heyter had actually voiced them.[60] Nevertheless, rioters did reap the advantages of their sudden superiority in the streets by asserting their rights to the traditional festive gratuity with a sardonic confidence and momentary contempt for rank. 'O God bless this gentleman', mocked rioters to an apothecary who had been forced to concede half a crown, 'he is always generous.' Others dispensed with such civilities. 'Damn your eyes and limbs,' exclaimed a discharged sailor to a well-to-do cheesemonger in Bishopsgate, 'put a shilling in my hat, or by God I have a party that can destroy your house presently.'[61] Not surprisingly, in the heady atmosphere of the riot, the houses of a few wealthy tradesmen and masters were threatened, whatever their religion. George Peppit, for example, was charged with 'threatening his Master's House saying there was no King, no Government, every Man for himself'. G. McCannon asked for a guard on 8 June to protect 'a very large Estate', perplexed that the 'daring armed licentious rabel' had singled him out.[62]

Yet the murmurings against the rich did not generate anything resembling a *jacquerie*, a ritual pillaging of the privileged. Aside from the magistrates, the vast majority of the gentlemen, merchants, and manufacturers whose houses were actually attacked were Catholic.[63] The pattern of rioting, in fact, followed logically from the militant Protestants' declared objectives and from the war of nerves that had ensued between the crowd and parliament. When the Commons refused to consider the petition for the repeal of the Relief Act, crowds sacked the most obvious symbols of Catholicism, the chapels, threatening at the same time to immobilize the Catholic community. After the second adjournment they tried to do just that. As far as they were able, the rioters focused their attention upon the most visible and influential members of the Catholic community. They attacked the houses of gentlemen and tradesmen who were likely to give financial support to the foundation of new chapels and schools, the principal objection of Protestant associators to the Relief Act.[64] They

[60] *Surrey*, 11. Two deponents, a boatbuilder and a ropemaker, both described as 'substantial tradesmen', denied that he did. PRO, SP 37/21/275–6, 308–10. Baron Eyre refused the jury's plea for mercy, stating to them 'the danger of extending mercy to the Person who had disclosed Principles so destructive to society'. A further attempt to obtain a royal pardon appears to have been successful.

[61] *Morning Chronicle*, 30 June 1780; *Old Bailey*, 452.

[62] PRO, PC 1/3097, WO 34/103/223.

[63] Ralph Thrale, the Southwark brewer, was one exception. His distillery was saved by his manager's foresight in 'amusing the mob with meat and drink and huzzas'. See Hibbert, *King Mob*, 100 n.

[64] William Mawhood, for example, the woollen draper whose house was threatened three times during the riot, had contributed towards Richard Dillon's chapel in Moorfields. The chapel was destroyed by the rioters. See *Mawhood Diary*, 117 n.

destroyed large distilleries such as Thomas Langdale's in Holborn, which was thought to harbour a chapel. Similarly, alehouses were a favourite target of the crowd because these were centres of sociability and also of religion. It was not unusual in the 1780s for alehouses to rent rooms for religious meetings. Indeed, what is instructive about the victims of the rioters is not so much their wealth—as we have seen the majority were no richer than the average middling tradesman—but the crucial role they played in servicing the Catholic community. Over a quarter were involved in the drink trade, principally as publicans. A further quarter were food retailers, dealers, or pawnbrokers.[65] Five of the 124 victims who were compensated for the destruction of their property were schoolmasters. One was a newsman. In other words, it was not the gentility or wealth of the victims that is striking, especially if one eliminates the parliamentary supporters of the Relief Act and the justices, but their intermediary status within the Catholic community, as sources of information, sociability, and credit.

Precisely which houses were pulled down, of course, depended upon a variety of factors. One was clearly the disposition of military forces, whether regulars or, after 6 June, volunteers. St James's, Piccadilly, had a large Catholic population, but it was too close to the Westminster barracks and to the Horse Guards for comfort.[66] In contrast, Holborn and the City of London had more accessible targets because of their jurisdictional complexities and because the forces of law and order were either overextended, defunct (as was the case with the City militia), or sympathetic. Quite apart from Lord Mayor Kennett's supine attitude, some marshalmen simply refused to act. As one told Thomas Gates, the uppermarshal, 'he would not come to protect any such Popish rascals' because he had sworn the oaths of allegiance, abjuration, and supremacy upon taking office.[67]

Southwark was also a riot-prone area until the South Hampshire regiment arrived and the hastily formed volunteer association moved into action.[68] So, too, was the East End, where the chapels in Virginia Lane and Nightingale Street were pulled down, although the Catholic population here was poor and organizationally less important, as well as openly resistant to further destruction. Among other things, the Irish coalheavers

[65] PRO, Work 6/110, 111. Particulars of losses sustained during the Gordon riots. The breakdown of the 124 whose occupational status can be identified is as follows: esquires, gentlemen 14.5%; professions, 'genteel' trades 9.2%; food and small ware retailers 18.5%; drink trade 26.6%; brokers and dealers 7.2%; artisans 16.9%; labourers, lodgers 4.8%.

[66] In this respect it is worth noting that attacks upon property in the vicinity were frequently frustrated by the cavalry or repulsed by gunfire.

[67] CLRO, Repertories of the Court of Aldermen, 184 (1780), 209–10.

[68] See *Surrey*, 44–5.

of Wapping threatened reprisals upon dissenting meeting-houses if further damage ensued.[69]

Apart from the military logistics of the riot, local factors could also come into play. Neighbours sometimes remonstrated with crowds to save popular Catholics. In the case of Thomas Dodd, they blocked the doorway 'begging the mob not to fire the house'.[70] Similarly, Nicholas Hillyer attempted to intercede on behalf of a Catholic neighbour in East Bermondsey, while a fishwoman deplored the sacking of Captain Alexander French's house in Rotherhithe, declaring that he had been charitable to the poor.[71] The local standing of Catholics could thus complicate the political imperatives of the riots, but it could also reinforce them. Catholics who had been officious in bringing neighbours before the law might find themselves in double jeopardy. Such was the case of John Lebarty, an Italian who kept a pub and slop shop in St Katherine's Lane near the Tower. He had incurred unpopularity through his duties as parish watchman, and the attack upon his house was accompanied 'by a sort of rough music', with a cacophony of frying pans, tongs, and bells.[72]

In a number of respects, however, the disturbances did move beyond their original boundaries. In the final phase, the riots began to centre upon crimping and sponging houses and the tolls of Blackfriars bridge. Crimping or recruiting houses had long been unpopular during wartime in riverside parishes and engendered a full-scale riot some fourteen years later.[73] Sponging houses, temporary lock-ups for debtors seeking to raise bail before a suit came to trial, were equally detestable. In the opinion of Richard Holloway, a debtor often found himself 'marred in and surrounded by a set of wretches, whose daily bread depends upon the misfortunes of others'.[74] According to one account no less than twenty were burnt down in the borough on 8 June.[75] As for the tolls raised to pay for Blackfriars bridge, they had originally been scheduled to expire in 1770, and then in 1778; but the City of London ultimately decided to make them permanent in order to finance other projects.[76] To small traders south of the river

---

[69] PRO, SP 37/14/147–8. So, too, did the Irish chairmen in St James's and Covent Garden, with the result that the Swallow Street meeting-house had to be guarded.

[70] *Surrey*, 104.   [71] Ibid. 5–7.

[72] *Old Bailey*, 508–11; PRO, KB 8/79/221. P. B. Clayton and B. R. Leftwich, *The Pageant of Tower Hill* (London, 1932), 229.

[73] *The Autobiography of Francis Place*, ed. Mary Thale (Cambridge, 1972), 34–5; John Stevenson, 'The London "crimp" Riots of 1794', *International Review of Social History*, 16 (1971), 40–58.

[74] Richard Holloway, *A Letter to John Wilkes Esquire* (London, 1771), 28.

[75] *A Narrative of the Proceedings of Lord George Gordon*, 45.

[76] See CLRO, Misc. MS 348.5; *Reasons Humbly Offered for an Immediate Discontinuance of the Tolls on Blackfriars Bridge* (London, n.d.) to be found in Guildhall Library, London.

they remained a smouldering grievance, and the tollhouse was pulled down on the evening of 7 June in a swathe of destruction that included King's Bench prison, the Surrey bridewell, and the Fleet.

The social grievances which emerged during the final phase of the riot, then, were specific and concrete. They addressed the petty exactions and humiliations that might oppress the small traders, artisans, and mariners in their everyday lives, ones which had been given considerable publicity since the 1770s as part of an informal radical agenda. But how are we to interpret some of the other actions of the crowd? The attacks upon the Inns of Court, the Bank of England, the Pay Office, for example? Do these not suggest a more portentous challenge to authority, as some contemporaries suggested?[77]

The raids upon the Inns of Court, in fact, paralleled those upon the gaols. The initial objectives of the crowd were specific. As one contemporary remarked, the popular fury against the Temple and Lincoln's Inn was prompted 'by something more than their levelling idea of destroying every public building'.[78] The populace went there to seek out a number of parliamentary supporters of the Relief Act: principally John Dunning, the master of the Temple, and the Bishop of Lincoln, whom it confused with the Bishop of Peterborough, the most outspoken episcopal supporter of the 1778 bill. The attacks upon public institutions like the Pay and Excise offices and the Bank of England were more symbolic. They were the culmination of the dialogue between crowd and authority, the last outburst of anger against a perfidious establishment. The attack upon the Bank, in particular, was spontaneous rather than planned. The rioters did not cluster in the alleyways surrounding the Bank and attempt to smoke out the troops and volunteers who defended it. They paraded flamboyantly before its gates, led by a man on a drayhorse caparisoned with the fetters of Newgate. In the last analysis this was an act of transgression rather than subversion, redolent of misrule.

What conclusions, then, might we offer about this most complex riot, the most formidable commotion in England since the Western rising of 1685? In the first place I would emphasize the extent to which the rioters adhered to their original political objective, the repeal of the Relief Act. The rioters saw themselves as the shock troops of the Protestant Association, exerting political pressure upon an intransigent parliament and underscoring the

---

[77] The *Remembrancer*, 10 (1780), 13, said the raid on the Bank was 'the most serious circumstance in the whole riot'.

[78] *Fanaticism and Treason, or, a Dispassionate History of the Rise and Progress and Suppression of the Rebellious Insurrections in June 1780* (London, 1780), 74.

unpopularity of a measure which they regarded as detrimental to English liberty and its sense of national identity. Whether that affiliation was acknowledged by the supporters of the Association or not, the crowd shared the same fears about the growth of popery. There was a basic convergence of belief, which, once invoked by Lord George Gordon's audacity, could not be dispelled. In a limited sense this was a 'licensed' demonstration. The Protestant Association orchestrated the riot in its initial stages and the crowd presumed, with some justice, that its huge following would support or connive at its actions, especially in the City where its supporters were politically well placed. But the crowd always retained some autonomy from its political leaders. It did not simply follow their writ. It operated within well-established conventions of popular politics which had allowed it a crucial, though subaltern, role.

Since the mid-century, and certainly since Wilkes, there had been a rough and often fruitful concordance between crowd action and progressive elements in the metropolis. Crowds helped to create the space for libertarian politics; their interventions tipped the political balance of forces in ways which helped to amplify arguments about liberty and parliamentary reform. But, *pace* Rudé, this convergence of forces was contingent rather than inevitable, and in 1780 it came unstuck. The reasons were partly ideological and partly the result of changing political practice. As we have seen, the campaign for the repeal of the Relief Act confounded contemporary political alignments. While there were radical resonances to the repeal campaign, the Relief Act was not viewed by all radicals as yet another ministerial incursion upon liberty. Those influenced by Enlightenment ideas, in particular, regarded the qualified toleration of domestic Catholics to be perfectly reasonable and, indeed, consonant with Britain's libertarian status.

These divisions were compounded by the fear that the conventional modes of crowd action, its festive, raucous street politics, might not be compatible with the new modes of association and political edification generated by the radical movement since Wilkes. John Wilkes himself, of course, had revelled at the prospect of crowds rallying to his standard, and his middling supporters had successfully promoted a radical calendar of public anniversaries around his triumphs that momentarily eclipsed that of officialdom. Yet while radicals recognized the potential role of the crowd as the shock troops of Liberty, they were also concerned that popular excesses might prove counter-productive. In an open letter to the Middlesex freeholders and 'the Common People' in April 1769, for example, the *Middlesex Journal* warned its readers to avoid 'an ill-placed, and extravagant assertion of that LIBERTY which we wear next to our hearts' lest 'it degenerate into licentiousness' and give ministers 'a fresh pretense for nipping' at its roots.[79] Predictably, few radicals supported a substantial extension of the franchise, fearing that the venality and volatility of the crowd might compromise reform. Many would have followed William Beckford in believing 'that it was not the mob, nor two hundred great lords that made us firm: the middling rank of men it was in which our strength consisted'.[80] It was here that the real bulwark of freedom and the animating impulse of the people's will could best be discerned, embodied in addresses, instructions to MPs, and associations.

The Gordon riots ruptured the partnership between the crowd and the radicals. Some radicals were sympathetic to the repeal of the Relief Act, but in the end virtually all were appalled by the collective violence inflicted upon Catholics and the opportunity such violence gave to others. John Reynolds, a prominent Wilkite, initially showed some sympathy for the rioters, his son recalled, but by Wednesday, 7 June, he was prepared to flee the city and the country, if need be, fearing the excesses of mob rule.[81] Radicals were especially angry that the crowd had provided the government with a pretext to take unprecedented military action to control the disturbances, namely the decision to deploy the military without civil direction. They were also very concerned that the excesses of the crowd would be thrown on their shoulders, discrediting extra-parliamentary modes of political action in the process. As one anonymous writer complained to the Secretary of State, the riots 'were the ripe fruit of those seeds of sedition sown long ago by the Pseudo-Patriots of this country'.[82] In this context radicals were especially relieved when Wilkes's apothecary and Middlesex associator Henry Maskall, indicted for his involvement in the riots, was acquitted after a long trial. His acquittal helped to exonerate the radicals from any responsibility for the riots. Even so, radicals feared that the cause of reform would be irreparably damaged by the crowd actions of 1780. In the opinion of 'Marcus', the mob had furnished the ministry with a pretext 'to rivet the chains of perpetual slavery upon us'. He continued: 'Your unprecedented behaviour will necessarily incline many friends of the public cause to court absolute power in order to shelter themselves from your depredations: your licentiousness has undone, in a

---

[79] *Middlesex Journal*, 8–11 Apr. 1769.

[80] Horace Walpole, *Memoirs of the Reign of King George the Third*, ed. Sir Denis Le Marchant, 4 vols. (London, 1845), i. 192–3.

[81] Frederick Reynolds, *The Life and Times of Frederick Reynolds*, 2 vols. (London, 1826), i. 131–2.

[82] PRO, SP 37/20/191.

moment, what the virtue of true patriots has been endeavouring to establish this long time.'[83]

One should not, therefore, overemphasize the radical lineaments of the
Gordon riots. In radical eyes, the riots were a paradigm of plebeian degeneracy: headless, lawless, and politically counter-productive. And while the
repeal campaign drew on radical support and used extra-parliamentary
modes of organization that radicals had themselves espoused to get their
message across, it was a populist and nationalist movement first and foremost. Fundamentally, it was a protest against the religious urbanity of the
cosmopolitan establishment which arrogated to itself the right to determine the future growth of British Catholicism. To the Gordon rioters this
initiative was a major betrayal of Britain's Protestant and libertarian heritage, a sell-out of all they stood for.

Some historians, in reconstructing popular notions of anti-Catholicism,
have emphasized their traditional and reactionary nature. Colin Haydon
has recently argued that the Gordon riots resembled a Catholic *grande peur*.
Their chief characteristics, he claims, 'were old fashioned: the aims; the
symbolism; the xenophobia in wartime; and above all, the old mythology
of Popery'.[84]

This seems to me to be too categorical. It is true, of course, that the
rioters were able to draw upon a deep reservoir of anti-Catholicism. They
invoked the *Book of Martyrs* and paraded the relics of Catholicism in a
manner redolent of a seventeenth-century religious riot. In some instances
their actions touched deep religious anxieties. One Catholic woman in
Spitalfields declared 'she still hoped to see the day when she should
be enabled to wash her hands in the blood of heretics'.[85] By contrast, a
silk dyer declared 'he had the pleasure of seeing a Roman Catholic school
burnt down' because such 'schools did harm in increasing the number of
Catholics'.[86] Yet in a disturbance replete with rumours of an American plot,
a French plot, a ministerial plot, and a patriot plot, there were no verbal
or written expressions of impending Catholic massacres. Nor were there
any effigy-burnings of the Pope or leading Catholics despite the great many
fires that scorched the streets.[87] In fact compared to the anti-Catholic riots

---

[83] *London Courant*, 15 June 1780.   [84] Haydon, *Anti-Catholicism*, 243.

[85] *Gazetteer and New Daily Advertiser*, 7 June 1780.

[86] PRO, WO 34/104/369.

[87] See *The Reminiscences of Henry Angelo*, ed. Joseph Grego, 2 vols. (London, 1904), ii.
111–16. Christopher Hibbert claimed that the Pope and St Patrick were burnt in effigy on
the sites of burnt-out chapels, but I have found no evidence that this was the case. See Hibbert,
King Mob, 70. Haydon cites an example of a dead dog with a crucifix in its paws being hung
up on a wall. Haydon, *Anti-Catholicism*, 234.

in London in 1688, or the backlash against Jacobitism in 1745, the symbolism of the Gordon riots was noticeably less traditional.[88] Admittedly,
some of the old anti-Catholic imagery turned up in the satirical engravings
of the crisis. In one print Father Petre, James II's former confessor and a
man who was regularly burnt in effigy by the London mob in the early
eighteenth century, is seen leading a 'mangy whelp' with a crown (George
III) to Rome. In another, it is the devil-of-a-Bute, fulfilling the same task,
while in a third, a tonsured George is praying before a Catholic altar while
county and Protestant petitions lie scattered on a latrine floor.[89]

Yet on balance there are fewer references to the Scarlet Whore, to
Catholic atrocities, and a more muted emphasis upon Protestant martyrology.[90] The principal referents of 1780 were altogether more secular
and political, framed by the divisive politics of the American war. They
included the court's authoritarian leanings, manifested by its assault upon
Protestantism and liberty at home and abroad; and the King's renuncia-
tion of his coronation oath.[91] It is conceivable, of course, that the crowd
remained immune to these referents, but various incidents suggest not.
Among them would be the popular acclaim given to the pro-American
noblemen on the day that the Protestant Association's petition was presented, and the popular resistance to the arrest of the radical writer William
Moore, noted for his denunciations of the corrupt, pro-Catholic court in
the *Thunderer*.[92] The popular Protestantism of 1780 thus appears more self-
confident and libertarian than its earlier manifestations. Drawing upon a
substratum of traditional hostilities about Catholics, it also addressed the
anxieties which surrounded George III's controversial policies.

In a sense, then, I am arguing for a more political interpretation of the
Gordon riots than has been offered by previous authors. While the riots
did get out of hand, we cannot use the drunkenness and arson to deprec-
ate the political consciousness of the participants. Nor can we characterize
the demonstrators as a 'licensed mob' operating on behalf of external interests. Rioters shared the political passions of the Protestant Association even

[88] See John Miller, 'The Militia and the Army in the Reign of James II', *Historical Journal*,
16 (1973), 659–79; id., *Popery and Politics in England 1660–1688* (Cambridge, 1973);
Nicholas Rogers, 'Popular Disaffection in London during the Forty-Five', *London Journal*,
1 (May 1975), 5–27.

[89] BMC 5680, 5666, 5670.

[90] The *Gospel Magazine* for June 1780 reproduced an engraving of popish atrocities opposite its title-page, but such imagery was less evident than earlier in the century.

[91] For the Scottish connection, particularly with respect to Lord Mansfield, see PRO, WO
34/104/31–2.

[92] BL, Add. MS 30866, fo. 242.

Fig. 2 A Priest at his Private Devotions

if their actions embarrassed its members. On these issues I side with Rudé. Where I disagree with that pioneer historian of the crowd is on his ideological and social interpretation of the riot. The disturbances of 1780 were not directed at the rich; they were directed at the most visible and influential members of the Catholic community, and at the cosmopolitan quality who believed in a qualified toleration for the rejuvenated Catholic Church which had emerged under Bishop Challoner. Beyond this context the social protests of the crowd tended to be concrete and specific, directed at crimps, sponging houses, and tolls; although, as we have seen, the attack upon the gaols, the Bank, the Inns of Court, and the threat to St James's and Downing Street, suggest that, at its most exasperated, the crowd struck out at authority in general. As for the ideological dimensions of the riot, I do not see them following a radical-libertarian vector. On the contrary, the Gordon riots drew upon populist, national sentiments that did not square with conventional political alignments. It remained to be seen how these forces could be accommodated in contemporary political discourse.

6

Crowds, Festival, and Revolution, 1788–1795

The 1790s have been widely regarded as a critical decade in the development of popular politics in Britain. Fired by the twin experiences of the American and French Revolutions, the publication of Paine's *Rights of Man* in 1791 saw a dramatic growth in democratic radicalism among artisans and the labouring poor, and a corresponding loyalist reaction of unparalleled proportions. The social penetration of democratic ideas, and the extent to which British politics became polarized along class lines, has been hotly debated among historians. So, too, has the lineage of radicalism, the question of whether the popular societies of the 1790s drew inspiration from momentous developments across the Channel or from a more indigenous tradition of popular constitutionalism, one shaped by the legacy of Britain's own revolutions and the divisive American war. It is not my intention fully to engage these controversial issues here. But they do form a necessary context for my principal theme, the exploration of festival and political ideology in this troubled era. What particularly interests me is the way in which radicals, reformers, and reactionaries marshalled popular support in the public domain and how the robust traditions of street politics were mobilized, reshaped, and ruptured in the process. It is, in brief, a study of how popular political culture was reconstituted under the imperatives of revolution and war.

THE 1688 JUBILEE

The Gordon riots, as we have already seen, made both conservative Whigs and radicals increasingly sceptical about the virtues of crowd politics. At the same time, political festival was so integral an aspect of contemporary life that it could not be abandoned. To have done so would have vitiated the very foundations of a social order that prided itself upon its political heritage, however defined, and undermined the authority of the gentry and, increasingly, the middling sort, who were its principal interpreters. The issue was raised most dramatically in 1788, the centenary of the Glorious Revolution. A critical touchstone for contemporary politics, it was an anniversary that could hardly be avoided.

Some commentators, fearful that the commemoration would inevitably stoke the embers of political disaffection and unsettle the social order, hoped that the festivities would be cut to a minimum and organized, as in Scotland, as an officially endorsed day of thanksgiving. One writer even suggested that the day could best be spent in 'silent and candid devotion'.[1] Others urged magistrates to curb illuminations and bonfires in the interests of order. 'The memory of what happened from the *patriotic* band in St. George's Fields', *The Times* reminded its readers, 'is yet alive in the minds of the people.'[2] Most none the less recognized that the suppression of popular jubilations would prove counter-productive and, indeed, contrary to the spirit of the very traditions that were to be commemorated. As the *Manchester Mercury* emphasized, 'We owe to the Revolution the Privilege of determining whether we shall hold such a public Assembly or not.'[3] All that could be hoped was that the day would be free from riot and celebrated with suitable decorum.

By and large this was the case. Although *The Times* fully anticipated the anniversary would be commemorated with the usual licence, riot, and inebriety, the festivities were remarkably orderly. To be sure, a few Quakers who failed to illuminate their windows faced popular retribution. Charles James Fox was even burnt in effigy in Westminster, where he had incurred some unpopularity for his opposition to Admiral Hood in the by-election a few months earlier.[4] But by and large the celebrations passed peaceably enough. Despite the fact that the jubilee took place in the wake of the Regency crisis, there was a strong disposition to celebrate the event in as harmonious a fashion as possible, with local organizers facilitating good cheer by laying on barrels of beer and victuals for the poorer inhabitants. Indeed, the civic parades and marketplace convivialities were frequently commended in the press for their 'regularity and decorum', which accorded well with a revolution that was said to have facilitated social progress and civility.

---

[1] *The Times*, 4 Nov. 1788.   [2] Ibid.   [3] *Manchester Mercury*, 21 Oct. 1788.
[4] *The Times*, 6 Nov. 1788; *Morning Chronicle*, 7 Nov. 1788.

Commemorating the revolution was not, of course, new. As we have already seen, the established Church had set up a special service on 5 November to highlight the nation's deliverance from popery in 1605 and William of Orange's historic landing eighty-five years later. Even so, the preparations for 1788 were unusually elaborate and energetic. Town committees were formed to commemorate the jubilee and subscriptions for revolution dinners and balls were launched with gusto. Corporate towns continued to process to church to hear revolution sermons. But on this occasion their activities were supplemented, if not eclipsed, by the activities of local associations, whether Revolution societies, clubs, freemasons, or friendly societies, some of whom chose to commemorate 4 November rather than the conventional 5th to distinguish their festivities from the official Anglican ceremonies. Their celebratory enthusiasms, and the balls and dinners that were held to honour the jubilee, tended to steal the show.

In Bristol, Hereford, Leicester, Newcastle, and Dundee, for example, Revolution societies led the festivities. At York, the Rockingham club organized a dinner for 200 gentlemen at the York tavern, with the local nobility and county MPs very much in evidence.[5] Elsewhere prominent citizens and neighbouring gentry gathered to celebrate the jubilee at local taverns or Assembly Rooms.[6] At Derby, for instance, the rejoicings were said to have been conducted in a 'very capital stile', with ladies in fancy dresses with orange and blue ribbons gracing the celebratory ball.[7] Sometimes local grandees organized their own festival. Without doubt the most extravagant festival of this kind occurred at Holkham, in Norfolk, where Thomas Coke entertained the county élite to a grand feast, a fire-works display, and a representation of William's landing at Torbay on his estate's lake. Twelve hundred guests were said to have been regaled by this county magnate at prodigious expense, while barrels of beer were condescendingly distributed to nearby villagers so they could partake of the joy of a jubilee.[8]

Coke's fête was an exceptional event, designed to restore his flagging political fortunes in the county. Yet the presence of so many dignitaries at the festivities was no less self-serving. The participation of Whig politicians, in particular, was designed to impress upon the public their impeccable revolutionary heritage and their role as trustees of the nation. At

---

[5] *Newcastle Chronicle*, 1, 8 Nov. 1788.

[6] See, for example, the reports of the Birmingham and Derby festivities in *Felix Farley's Bristol Journal*, 15 Nov. 1788, and the *Bath Chronicle*, 13 Nov. 1788.

[7] *Hampshire Chronicle*, 24 Nov. 1788.   [8] *Ipswich Journal*, 15 Nov. 1788.

Whittington, the Duke of Devonshire and other Whig lords dined in the very house where the 1688 coup was hatched. The next day they graced the parade at nearby Chesterfield, riding in their carriages along with 400 gentlemen on horseback, the members of the town corporation, and 1,000 clubmen, whose white wands were topped with blue and orange favours with 'REVOLUTION' inscribed upon them. At York, Henry Duncombe, the county MP and grandson of William III's leading financier, chaired the proceedings.[9] Similarly in London the celebratory dinner of the Whig club gave the old revolutionary families pride of place at the head table and toasted the houses of Russell and Cavendish with the wish that their names would 'always be united in defence of liberty'.[10] To emphasize further their clan's contribution to the progress of liberty, party spokesmen resolved to establish a pillar at Runnymede to enshrine the Glorious Revolution as the culmination of a historic struggle for ancient liberties.

Few gentlemen could offer such a venerable pedigree as a Cavendish or a Russell to cap the jubilee, but this did not deter them from stamping their presence on such an important festival. At Pen Hill, near his seat at Kirkley in Northumberland, the Dean of Winchester erected an obelisk to commemorate William III's landing. Similar projects were launched by the gentlemen of Hertford and the Independent Friends of Edinburgh, one of the principal Whig clubs in the Scottish capital.[11] In a more paternalist fashion, the gentlemen of Hull organized a subscription for the release of local debtors, while at Manchester the stewards prevailed upon the local captain of the dragoons to pardon a deserter.[12]

More typically, local patrons treated their friends, tenants, and poorer inhabitants to traditional largess. At Ashton-under-Lyne and Altrincham, the Earl of Stamford presented the genteel celebrants with a 'fine doe', the ultimate hallmark of aristocratic benevolence. At Chapel-en-le-Frith, the local squire 'was pleased to bestow a fine Sheep which was roasted whole in the Street, and with a handsome Subscription from him, seconded by a great Number of respectable Inhabitants, the same was distributed to the Poor with above two Loads of Flour baked into Loaves'.[13] In Hull, York, Derby, Selby, Ludlow, and Reigate, local dignitaries such as Sir William

---

[9] *Leeds Mercury*, 21 Oct., 11 Nov. 1788; *Derby Mercury*, 6–13 Nov. 1788; *Gentleman's Magazine*, 64 (1788), 1020–1.

[10] *General Ev. Post*, 4–6 Nov. 1788.

[11] *Felix Farley's Bristol Journal*, 15 Nov. 1788; *Newcastle Chronicle*, 8 Nov. 1788; *London Chronicle*, 8–11 Nov. 1788.

[12] *Manchester Mercury*, 11 Nov. 1788; *Leeds Mercury*, 25 Nov. 1788.

[13] *Manchester Mercury*, 11 Nov. 1788 (Ashton); 25 Nov. 1788 (Chapel-en-le-Frith).

Milner and Lord Clive laid on barrels of beer. At Wooler the populace were said to have been 'regaled with as much ale as they could drink'.[14]

These conventional marks of munificence sought to underscore the benefits of gentry rule to the poor, just as the more permanent monuments emphasized the gentry's commitment to limited monarchy and the defence of the people's liberties. As the *Morning Chronicle* declared, in terms that many gentlemen would have admired:[15]

When we remember the privileges that we acquired by that Revolution and reflect whereby every citizen was restored to the rank which he was destined by nature to hold amongst his species, that his person and house, his family and fortune, became sacred from outrage, that he was no longer subject to the capricious cruelties of a despot, nor being made the prey of a servile misrepresentation of the law, that the three estates of the Empire were finally balanced and the rights of the lowest plebian made secure to him as the prerogatives of the sovereign, what must be the exhortations of an Englishman's heart on this proud day, what must be his joy when he thinks that after a century hath passed the great temple of Liberty which King William erected stands unimpaired and that he sits secure under its strong and beautiful dome?

As this statement suggests, the tone of the celebrations was often self-congratulatory. The revolution of 1688 was the 'true date of English freedom'; the time when 'the grand and beautiful system of our constitution was finally settled'.[16] William III had rescued the nation from popery and tyranny and had secured Protestantism, the rule of law, and a balanced polity. From this foundation social progress and economic prosperity had flowed. Britons could pride themselves in having the best constitution in Europe and amid the hoopla there was a strong disposition to put the trauma of the loss of the American colonies behind them. Even those who admired the American republic sometimes cast it as a legacy of Britain's revolutionary past.[17] The jubilee was an opportunity to glory in British achievements, not dwell on past and present failures.

Yet amid the euphoria political differences inevitably insinuated themselves into the festivities. Smarting from the unpopularity of the East India Bill and their defeat at the general election four years earlier, Whig clubs throughout the country used the jubilee to boost their flagging fortunes,

---

[14] *Newcastle Chronicle*, 8 Nov. 1788; *Public Advertiser*, 7 Nov. 1788; *Whitehall Ev. Post*, 11–13 Nov. 1788.

[15] *Morning Chronicle*, 5 Nov. 1788, also reprinted in the *Northampton Mercury*, 8 Nov. 1788.

[16] *Morning Chronicle*, 5 Nov. 1788; *Newcastle Chronicle*, 1 Nov. 1788.

[17] *Public Advertiser*, 1 Nov. 1788.

not only emphasizing the party's crucial contribution to liberty, particularly that of its martyrs, Hampden and Sidney, but sometimes calling for its enlargement. At Norwich, the Blue and White reformers of the Independent club raised their glasses to 'Equal liberty to all mankind and virtue to defend it', a toast that was accompanied by one demanding an end to slavery.[18] In Swansea, the predominantly Dissenting company used the opportunity to campaign for the repeal of the Test and Corporation Acts, raising a toast to 'the cause of civil and religious liberty all over the world'. The same was true of the Whiggish, Dissenting merchants who met at Merchants' Hall, Bristol.[19] In fact, wherever celebrations were leavened by Dissent, calls for religious toleration inevitably intruded upon the proceedings. In his sermon to the Revolution society of London, for example, Dr Andrew Kippis expatiated on the additional liberties that had been granted by George III to Protestants and Catholics and looked forward to the time 'when every man might have the free and full exercise of his religious principles according to the dictates of his conscience'.[20] This line of argument, propagated in many sermons or orations, saw the 1688 revolution as setting precedents for further reform, one consonant with the emphasis upon social and economic progress and judiciously counterposed to the orthodox Anglican position concerning the settlement's finality.

The differing interpretations of 1688 emerged most explicitly in London, where a wide variety of societies commemorated the centenary. At the Crown and Anchor on the Strand, the Foxite Whig club indulged in self-congratulatory acclaim, emphasizing its party's own contribution to the establishment of liberty. In contrast, the Pittite Constitutional club organized a bumper supper at Willis's rooms under the chairmanship of Lord Hood in which it situated the 1688 revolution within a trio of epic deliverances that included the Spanish Armada of 1588 and a 1788 that was noteworthy for the solidity of Pitt's 'mild administration'. In its eyes, the true significance of 1688 was its immutability, and its 1,200 celebrants pledged themselves to maintain that settlement 'in its purity' and to oppose any attempt to 'usurp the prerogatives, rights or privileges of either branch of the Constitution'.[21]

Both the Whig club and its rival espoused an élitist perception of the 1688 revolution, a conviction that its historic principles were best protected by responsible statesmen. This interpretation was not shared by the more radical Revolution society whose members included many of the leading

[18] C. B. Jewson, *The Jacobin City* (Glasgow, 1975), 13; *Norfolk Chronicle*, 8 Nov. 1788.
[19] *Felix Farley's Bristol Journal*, 8 Nov. 1788; *General Ev. Post*, 11–13 Nov. 1788.
[20] Cited in the *Morning Chronicle*, 5 Nov. 1788. [21] *Public Advertiser*, 7 Nov. 1788.

figures of the reform campaigns: Lord Stanhope; MPs Henry Beaufoy and John Sawbridge; the radical preachers Joseph Towers and Richard Price; and veteran associators such as Capel Lofft. Closely linked to the Society for Constitutional Information and radical Dissenting circles, this society endorsed an emphatically contractarian view of the revolution which extolled both the rights of resistance and popular sovereignty, the notion that all civil and political authority was derived from the 'people'.[22] This view had long been part of the Whig canon, but it had been significantly diluted during the course of the eighteenth century to legitimize parliamentary sovereignty and the political stability of a regime whose symmetry made resistance rights academic. The Revolution society revitalized those principles in ways that the Americans would have appreciated, making government far more accountable to popular consent as well as enshrining civil rights as 'sacred and inviolable'. Significantly, its toasts on 4 November began with the 'Majesty of the People' and ran through a gamut of reforms including demands for 'a fair and equal representation in Parliament', before ending with the hope that 'when Kings lose their utility, may the People find their dignity'.[23]

The Revolution society's reading of 1688 was an explicit endorsement of a radical position that had been forged in the vortex of the Wilkite and American controversies. Combining historical with natural rights, it saw the revolution as a vindication of popular sovereignty whose promise was unfulfilled.[24] As such it stood in dramatic contrast to the views of the Foxite and Pittite societies which tended to emphasize the efficacy, if not permanency, of the 1688 settlement as the basis of English liberties. Yet these differences were muted by the prevailing form of the celebrations, which were exclusive rather than expansive. For all its emphasis upon the 'Majesty of the People', the Revolution society eschewed a jubilation that would encompass large sections of the political nation. This decision was at least consistent with the society's notion that 1688 was a bloodless and non-violent revolution, a fiction that marginalized popular resistance to the

---

[22] *An Abstract of the History and Proceedings of the Revolution Society in London* (London, 1789), 14–15.

[23] *Morning Chronicle*, 6 Nov. 1788. The society advocated an end to naval impressment and to the slave trade, a reform of the criminal code, and a militia rather than a standing army.

[24] For a useful summary of this position, see H. T. Dickinson, *Liberty and Property: Political Ideology in Eighteenth-Century Britain* (London, 1977), ch. 6. See also Kathleen Wilson, 'Inventing Revolution: 1688 and Eighteenth Century Popular Politics', *Journal of British Studies*, 29 (1989), 349–86, and id., 'A Dissident Legacy: Eighteenth Century Popular Politics and the Glorious Revolution', in J. R. Jones (ed.), *Liberty Secured? Britain before and after 1688* (Stanford, Calif., 1992), 299–336.

Stuart regime. But even so, the Revolution society declined to incorporate the libertarian artisan and shopkeeper in its emancipatory festival. It did not, for example, organize a mass parade of the London trades in a manner reminiscent of the Philadelphian celebration of American independence on 4 July 1788, one that was widely reported in the British press. Nor did it sponsor a grand gathering of delegates from other Revolution societies to celebrate this central event in British liberty; a strategy that was adopted by the French in their Fête de la Fédération in 1790.[25] Like other Revolution societies, its celebration of the centenary at the London tavern privileged bourgeois space and the eminently respectable character of its participants.[26] This was far removed from the fraternal and egalitarian *élan* of American and ultimately French revolutionary festival. Despite their paean to popular sovereignty in 1788, British radicals continued to betray a deep scepticism of the political capacities of the common people and were not prepared to revise the prevailing modes of commemorative politics in a manner consonant with their ideology. Indeed, judging from newspaper reports, they were less likely to indulge the masses with token bouts of festive *bonhomie*.

If radicals failed to develop a genuinely democratic style of festive politics in 1788, they also strove to neutralize their political differences with other groups. As Andrew Kippis stressed in his sermon to the London Revolution society, the centenary was an occasion of joy in which complaints about the inadequacy of the status quo should not be allowed to 'obscure the sunshine of this day's festivity'.[27] The result was that the three principal societies in the metropolis were able to find some common ground. The Revolution and Constitutional clubs agreed to support the Foxite resolution to erect a pillar at Runnymede. The Revolution society's proposal to promote a new annual holiday on 16 December, the day when the Bill of Rights was passed by parliament, was similarly endorsed.[28] Amity proved the order of the day. Indeed, judging from the omnibus toasts that were proposed in other parts of the country, celebrants were generally not

---

[25] For the federative festivals in France, see Mono Ozouf, *Festivals and the French Revolution*, trans. Alan Sheridan (Cambridge, Mass., 1988), ch. 2. For a full account of the federal procession in Philadelphia, see *Gentleman's Magazine*, 64 (1788), 748, 826–8, 923–4, 1018–19.

[26] The Leicester Revolution society, for example, organized three separate dinners for its 672 members. Like its London counterpart, it did not plan a more participatory festival. The same was true of similar societies at Norwich and Yarmouth, all of whom toasted the 'Majesty of the People'. See *Northampton Mercury*, 8 Nov. 1788; *Norfolk Chronicle*, 8 Nov. 1788.

[27] Cited in the *Derby Mercury*, 19–26 Mar. 1789.

[28] This proposal was moved in the Commons by Henry Beaufoy in Mar. 1789. It passed the first reading but was defeated in the Lords.

prepared to press their differences too far. At Manchester, for example, the thirty-five toasts that were proposed at the Hotel on 5 November were couched in unexceptional terms, and those that were capable of radical constructions engendered no discord.[29] In fact, the goodwill that characterized many festivities led some to hope that political differences would be permanently accommodated. 'May the unanimity of this commemoration', ran one toast from Birmingham, 'seal the extinction of parties.'[30]

The differences which surfaced during the celebrations none the less continued to smoulder. The political visibility of Dissent during the jubilee troubled some Anglicans, and, as the Dissenters themselves geared up for another repeal campaign, political conflict sharpened. Particularly distressing to traditionalists was the Dissenters' emphasis upon natural rights and the inadequacies of the revolution settlement, which, through the high publicity given to the proceedings of the London Revolution society, had been given a good airing in the press. Had these sentiments been suitably counterbalanced by the royal presence at the jubilee, conservative reservations might have been assuaged. But the celebrations took place when the King was suffering from his first bout of porphyria, amid fervid speculations about a possible regency and change of government that would have brought Fox to power. This state of affairs cast a shadow upon Pittite celebrations of 1688, despite the efforts of the traditionally Tory press to keep the public informed of King George's progress and toasts in places like Birmingham for his 'speedy recovery'.[31] The hope that the jubilee would not sanction 'abstracted and unfruitful speculations' but strengthen the country's adherence to 'approved constitutional principles' had not materialized to everyone's satisfaction.[32] What was required was an occasion to reassert the royal contribution to Britain's political and social progress since 1688.

THE KING'S RECOVERY, 1789

The opportunity came in March 1789, upon news of the King's recovery. To the refrain of 'God Save the King' towns and villages throughout the country celebrated the blessings of divine providence in restoring the King to full health. At Lancaster, it was said that 'every age, class, sect and

---

[29] See *Manchester Mercury*, 11 Nov. 1788; John Bohstedt, *Riots and Community Politics in England and Wales 1790–1810* (Cambridge, Mass., 1983), 104.

[30] *Felix Farley's Bristol Journal*, 15 Nov. 1788.

[31] Ibid. Some papers concentrated upon the King's health to the virtual exclusion of the centenary celebrations; for example, *Trewman's Exeter Flying Post*, *Jackson's Oxford Journal*, *Berrow's Worcester Journal*, *Hampshire Chronicle*.

[32] *Felix Farley's Bristol Journal*, 25 Oct. 1788.

denomination amongst men was . . . swallowed up in the universal deluge of gratitude and joy'.[33] In the traditionally Tory areas of the country, in particular, these celebrations were especially exuberant, with local patrons financing the festivities and in some instances regaling their tenants and neighbouring farmers at their country seats. Outside Ludlow, for example, Dr Green assembled a huge bonfire before his hall to entertain the local 'villagers and peasants'.[34] At Halton and Whitchurch, Lady Irwin opened all the public houses at her own expense as well as providing an ox for the populace 'who were assembled in great numbers'. Similarly at Wiston, in Sussex, an ox and 'an immeasurable quantity of liquors' were 'indiscriminately served to all who chose to partake of them' on the orders of the resident squire.[35] Not all patrons, of course, were as carefree in their favours. At Fakenham, in Norfolk, the poor were mustered for a public procession with the Sunday school children (to the strains of 'O the Roast Beef of Old England') before they were treated to a dinner in the marketplace, a strategy that was designed to impart 'regularity and good order' to the festivities. The same was true at Dereham, some 14 miles to the south, where the amount of drink was also strictly regulated to prevent 'all scenes of folly, irregularity, riot and drunkeness, too usual on public occasions'.[36]

These marks of munificence were accompanied by bells and illuminations; in the larger towns by firework displays and transparencies depicting the King's regained health. One at the esplanade at Weymouth depicted Fame proclaiming the King's recovery with Britannia on her left and Neptune on her right, while at her feet Malice, Envy, and Detraction were mangled by the British Lion.[37] The most magnificent were to be found in London, especially those commissioned for the official thanksgiving on 23 April. In Greek Street, Josiah Wedgwood displayed an Etruscan-style transparency of Hygeia restoring the sovereign to Britain. Sir Joseph Banks presented one 'representing His Majesty on his Throne with the genius of Physic recrowning him; in his hands were the globe and sceptre; on one side was the figure of Peace, and on the other side that of Plenty, whilst Britannia was seated at his feet'. The crowning jewel, however, was undoubtedly the transparency at the Bank. Seventeen feet high and suspended some fifteen feet in the air, it depicted Britannia with the cap of liberty, seated in a triumphal chariot, over which were Hygeia and two cherubs symbolizing Peace and Plenty. In the foreground was the personification of the

[33] *Leeds Mercury*, 17 Mar. 1789. [34] *Shrewsbury Chronicle*, 28 Mar. 1789.
[35] *Sussex Weekly Advertiser*, 27 Apr. 1789; *Leeds Mercury*, 17 Mar. 1789.
[36] *Norfolk Chronicle*, 4, 18 Apr. 1789. [37] *Hampshire Chronicle*, 23 Mar. 1789.

City, accompanied by Commerce and Liberty. High up was a profile of the King, encircled by palm and olive branches.[38]

The celebrations commemorating the King's recovery were clearly an orchestrated show. They entailed elaborate preparations, financing, and a choreographed display of ruling-class grandeur and munificence that even small employers sometimes tried to emulate. In some areas subscriptions were launched to help the poor celebrate the day.[39] Even in London paupers, debtors, and workmen were treated to porter and roast beef, while in nearby Turnham Green, Lord Heathfield provided the traditional ox for the celebratory roasting.[40] Efforts were also made to contain popular exuberance within reasonable limits. Despite the 'rude serenade' of marrow bones and cleavers that resounded through the metropolis, it was the quality rather than the plebs who dominated the streets in the first round of festivities. According to *The Times*, 'the train of carriages at one time extended from Oxford Street to the end of Pall Mall, from Charing Cross to St. Paul's, from thence to the Exchange'.[41] This genteel presence was still very formidable at the official thanksgiving for the King's recovery the following month, for even the royal family found itself unable to view the transparencies and illuminations because of the 'immense croud of carriages' at Ludgate Hill.[42]

Yet if the celebration of the King's recovery was judiciously staged, the response it elicited was not entirely orchestrated from above. Certainly the festival was always something of a poor man's holiday; more so than the 1688 jubilee. At Lewes, money was given to every householder to buy beer for the festivities. In the Potteries, where local wakes were vigorously observed, the junketing lasted three days. In the village of Brassington, some 30 miles to the east in Derbyshire, the locals purportedly had 200 gallons of ale at their disposal, a gift that must have kept them in a glorious state of inebriation.[43] Amid this robust conviviality, friendly societies, charity clubs, workmen in specific trades, and even occasionally whole villages were allowed to show their paces by marching in jubilant accord to the royal anthem.[44]

At the same time, popular curiosity about the King's health continued unabated in some parts of the country, with clusters of people awaiting

[38] *The Times*, 25 Apr. 1789; *Shrewsbury Chronicle*, 2 May 1789.

[39] See, for example, the accounts of the celebrations at Skircoat in Halifax, and at Pontefract and Barnsley, in the *Leeds Mercury*, 24 Mar., 28 Apr. 1789.

[40] *The Times*, 12 Mar., 25, 27 Apr. 1789.   [41] Ibid. 11 Mar. 1789.

[42] *Leeds Mercury*, 5 May 1789.

[43] *Derby Mercury*, 26 Mar.–2 Apr. 1789; *Sussex Weekly Advertiser*, 16 Mar. 1789.

[44] *The Times*, 12 Mar. 1789; *London Chronicle*, 21–4 Mar. 1789; *Derby Chronicle*, 23–30 Apr., 30 Apr.–7 May 1789.

the London mail. Even in the metropolis pro-monarchical sentiments were effusive. 'There is no proof of affection and respect which was not shewn the King during the course of his late indisposition and long convalescence,' Henry Meister recalled, 'for several weeks past that his Majesty has been perfectly restored to health, the famous motet of *God Save the King* has been constantly called for in the theatres.'[45] In fact, crowds vied with one another to catch a second glimpse of the monarch during the thanksgiving procession to St Paul's.[46] The preoccupation with the King's health, therefore, was often quite genuine. At Middleton One Row in Teesdale, every cottage within a 2-mile radius was said to have 'blazed with light'. At Winchester, where the populace believed that the transparency at the Dolphin Inn depicted the King in a straitjacket, it promptly smashed the windows and would have probably pulled the house down had not the mayor intervened.[47] It would not brook any frivolous or demeaning aspersions on the King's 'madness'.

How far instances such as these illustrated the resilience of patriarchalism, a notion vigorously defended by J. C. D. Clark, remains a moot point. Monarchicalism was not incompatible with progressive views on the revolution settlement, a point underscored by the willingness of Dissenting congregations to celebrate the King's recovery. In fact the Dissenting ministers of Lancashire and Cheshire coupled their joy at the King's recovery with a determination to press for the repeal of the Test and Corporation Acts.[48] At the same time, some of the jubilation at the King's recovery clearly connoted a distaste for the Foxite alternative in the shape of the dissolute Prince of Wales. Plaudits to Pitt for his 'constitutional endeavours' in fighting off this challenge resounded from many a dinner table and bonfire, and masquerades celebrated the 'Death and Funeral Procession of Mrs Regency'.[49] The festivities, in other words, were always something of a Pittite triumph, a point recognized by the crowds in London and elsewhere who hissed his opponents and sang the 'Death of the Fox'.[50] Even so, the celebrations did underscore the strength of the 'Anglican cultural nexus' in the country and parsons certainly exploited the occasion to trumpet the

---

[45] Henry Meister, *Letters Written during a Residence in England* (London, 1799), 26.

[46] *The Times*, 24 Apr. 1789.

[47] *Hampshire Chronicle*, 16 Mar. 1789; *Newcastle Courant*, 4 Apr. 1789.

[48] *General Ev. Post*, 4–6 Nov. 1789; see also *Shrewsbury Chronicle*, 25 Apr. 1789, and *Hampshire Chronicle*, 16 Mar. 1789.

[49] *The Times*, 1 Apr. 1789; *Shrewsbury Chronicle*, 14, 21 Mar. 1789; *Hampshire Chronicle*, 23 Mar. 1789; *Leeds Mercury*, 24 Mar. 1789.

[50] *The Times*, 11, 14 Mar., 24 Apr. 1789. The politically partisan dimension of the 1789 celebrations is ignored by Linda Colley in her 'The Apotheosis of George III: Loyalty, Royalty and the British Nation 1760–1820', *Past and Present*, 102 (Feb. 1984), 94–129, and *Britons: Forging the Nation 1707–1837* (New Haven, 1992), ch. 5.

values of a stable, divinely ordained order at whose apex stood the King. They also took the opportunity to extol the virtues of limited monarchy as enshrined by law and the judicious balance of royal prerogatives and popular rights that sustained it. At Oswestry, for example, the Reverend Dr Lewis preached a sermon from Ecclesiastes 7: 14, underlining 'the blessings we enjoy under our present beloved Monarch as to religion and liberty'.[51] For many Tories this reassertion of royal authority on the King's recovery served as a fitting counterpoint to the potentially subversive resonances of the jubilee. Radicals deplored this display of royalist exuberance; Richard Price believed it bordered on idolatry. Yet the carefully choreographed ceremonies of 1789, even before captive and often dependent audiences, signalled that popular royalism was still a force to be reckoned with.

THE FRENCH REVOLUTION

During the centenary celebrations the first flickers of an impending crisis in France had led radicals to hope that the most notorious *ancien régime* in Europe might be reformed. 'May the dawn of liberty on the continent', ran one of the toasts of the London Revolution society, 'be soon succeeded by the bright sunshine of personal and mental freedom.'[52] Developments in France soon fulfilled these expectations. The summoning of the Estates General in the spring of 1789 and the dramatic turn of events which followed, culminating in the Declaration of the Rights of Man in August, convinced radicals that the dawn of French freedom had at last broken. The November meeting of the Revolution society was fulsome in its praise of the French Revolution. Dr Price recalled with pleasure that he had lived to see 'nations panting for liberty, which seemed to have lost the idea of it' and moved a resolution that congratulations be sent to the newly formed French National Assembly for their contribution to freedom and the prospect it gave to France and Britain 'of a common participation in the blessings of civil and religious liberty'.[53] Behind this gesture of solidarity with the French lay a commitment to Enlightenment ideals and an optimism that further reforms at home would be quickly forthcoming.

The lead given by the Revolution society was soon taken up by other radical groups. Within a month the Society for Constitutional Information agreed to emulate their brethren's vote of congratulations to the National

Assembly. At a dinner on 16 December at which leading members of the Revolution society were present, the company raised its glasses to the destruction of the Bastille, the abolition of privilege, the new rights of representation, as well as to 'the Glorious Aera in which the Bill of Rights was signed and the Privileges of Britons secured'.[54] Amidst this euphoria, plans were laid for a concerted campaign for parliamentary reform and further encouragement was offered to the Dissenters in their efforts to repeal the Test and Corporation Acts.

By the spring of 1790, however, the prospects for reform looked bleak. In March 1790, the Commons defeated a motion to introduce 100 new county members on a householder franchise and roundly rejected another for repeal. With these defeats, radicals increasingly turned their attention to France. The Revolution society enthusiastically established links with French patriotic societies in an attempt to further Anglo-French amity and the international brotherhood of freedom. Within a year it had corresponded with at least twenty across the Channel and helped sponsor an Anglo-French festival at Nantes to commemorate the English revolution of 1688 and the establishment of that city's first popular assembly.[55] At home it celebrated the fall of the Bastille with gusto, toasting the 'glorious Revolution in France' and 'the triumph of liberty' before a relic of the infamous prison surmounted on a tricoloured cockade.[56] This initiative was taken up by the friends of liberty in other towns, making 14 July a new feature in the radical calendar. In 1791 Benjamin Cooper reported that 'a great number of Cities and principal Towns in England, Scotland and Ireland' held meetings on Bastille day.[57]

These Francophilic enthusiasms did not initially evoke much opposition. The public welcomed the fall of French absolutism and applauded its most flamboyant symbolic act, the storming of the Bastille. Representations of this political drama were performed in London and elsewhere at places like Sadler's Wells, Astley's, and the Royal Circus in a suitably sensationalist mode. 'You may be sure the iron cage and skeleton within

[54] PRO, TS 11/961/3567, fos. 201, 204–6.

[55] *The Correspondence of the Revolution Society with the National Assembly, and with Various Societies of the Friends of Liberty in France and England* (London, 1792), *passim*; Goodwin, *Friends of Liberty*, 127.

[56] *Gazetteer and New Daily Advertiser*, 15 July 1790.

[57] *Correspondence of the Revolution Society*, 224; for celebrations at Yarmouth in 1790, and Birmingham, Edinburgh, Glasgow, Leicester, Liverpool, Norwich, and Manchester in 1791, see Goodwin, *Friends of Liberty*, 156–7, 180–2, *Leeds Mercury*, 19, 26 July 1791, [Joseph Towers], *Thoughts on National Insanity* (London, 1797), 12, and A. Temple Patterson, *Radical Leicester* (Leicester, 1954), 69.

it have not been forgotten,' Meister reported, 'which are dragged out of a dungeon with horrible cries.' But 'to efface the impression made by such melancholy cries,' he continued, 'the representation is closed with a beautiful decoration representing Britannia seated in a triumphal car, holding transparent portraits of the *King and Queen of Britain'*.[58] In its commercial rendering at least, Liberty's victory in France remained derivative of England's long-standing constitutionalist heritage.

Yet the totality of the French revolutionary crisis inevitably gave way to misgivings and, ultimately, alarmism. Burke's early diatribes against the revolution may have been premature, but his *Reflections* certainly shaped conservative fears of French developments. The first signs of unease came in the wake of the French Federation in July 1790. Avidly reported in the British press, this national celebration of solidarity for the new order at the Champ de Mars in Paris was heralded in progressive quarters as an awesome event; 'the grandest spectacle that any nation or people ever exhibited, and which indeed has no parallel in history'.[59] Predictably it was quickly commercialized, with Astley staging a musical sketch of the grand ceremony at the Royal Grove within a matter of weeks. Yet conservatives were troubled by this massive mobilization of the nation under the leadership of Lafayette, 'a pantomime-general', one remarked, 'looking round to catch the attention of an ignorant crowd with as much stage trick as the Merry Andrew at Covent Garden'.[60] Not only did its choreography privilege the people in disturbing ways, it also devastatingly flouted royal dignity. Especially disturbing was Louis Capet's explicit demotion to the status of a mere citizen and the laconic prints which portrayed the unhappy monarch choking down the constitutional oath to the words 'Do you suppose this will go down like a wing of a chicken?'[61] In conservative eyes, the humiliation of the French King signalled a 'solemn mockery of Revolution principles', an ominous departure from Britain's constitution in which royal prerogatives propitiously balanced popular liberties.[62]

Events at home served to sharpen these reservations. As we have seen, radicals had initially applauded the revolution as France's 1688. As late as March 1791 Benjamin Cooper had written to the patriotic society of Montpellier: 'it must be confessed we could not but celebrate *your* glorious

---

[58] Meister, *Letters*, 29–30.   [59] *Gazetteer and New Daily Advertiser*, 19 July 1790.
[60] *Public Advertiser*, 23 July 1790.
[61] See Meister, *Letters*, 30. For conservative prints emphasizing the King's 'degradation', see *Gazetteer and New Daily Advertiser*, 26 July 1790. For comments on the King's demotion, see *Public Advertiser*, 20 July 1790.
[62] *Public Advertiser*, 23 July 1790. See also 20 July 1790.

Revolution as a commemoration of our *own*.'[63] But increasingly radicals began to shape their criticisms of the English constitution in the light of the French experience, to see developments across the Channel as worthy of emulation.[64] The issue of whether the British should take their cue from the French was not absent from the festivities of the first Bastille day, when Horne Tooke attempted to differentiate Britain's emancipatory project from that of her neighbours on the grounds that the British had a libertarian heritage and did not have 'to build a ship from the keel'.[65] It re-emerged four months later, at the annual celebrations of 1688, when Richard Price proposed a toast hoping Britain's parliament would become a 'National Assembly'.[66] Although Price subsequently published an explanation of this toast to avoid misrepresentation, claiming nothing more was meant than a reform of the Commons, his notoriety in conservative circles as an egalitarian and constitution-wrecker remained undispelled. His remarks did little to remove the suspicion that he was a rank Jacobin; nor did they allay the rising anti-aristocrat and anti-clerical temper of radical thought and the belief that France was now the 'instructress of the world'.[67]

Public fears of English Jacobinism were compounded by the growing polarity of provincial politics. In several towns the campaigns to repeal the Test and Corporation Acts had precipitated a loyalist reaction, stoking the embers of religious discord that had informed politics during the American war and two generations earlier. Burke, of course, had done much to link Dissent with Jacobinism, castigating the Dissenters as those 'importunate grasshoppers of the hour' whose speculative politics and French enthusiasms imperilled the state and the social order. And while the style of his diatribe was not designed for a general audience—it was principally directed at the Whig aristocracy in an effort to forestall a radical shift in Opposition politics—his popularizers in the press drove the message home. Burke's pamphlet received its fair share of criticism from both moderate reformers and radicals alike. But it did help to bring conservative fears into

---

[63] *Correspondence of the Revolution Society*, 44.

[64] For one example, see the *Gazetteer and New Daily Advertiser*, 30 Oct. 1790, which commended the French for having placed toleration 'upon the widest foundation' and 'for having placed the *active citizen* in the most honourable station in the community'. The ministerial press, the paper claimed, was most 'anxious to prevent Englishmen from comparing the new Constitution of France with their own, a comparison that is not likely to produce the most pleasing satisfaction'.

[65] Ibid. 15 July 1790.

[66] Ibid. 15 Nov. 1790; for Dr Price's explanation of this toast, see ibid. 23 Nov. 1790.

[67] Goodwin, *Friends of Liberty*, 129.

sharper focus at a time when the fate of the Bourbon monarchy hung in the balance and when Paine was defiantly trumpeting the virtues of the French revolutionary imperative. Certainly it helped to fuel the hostility at home to pro-French sentiment, to a point where some conservatives feared that the 1791 celebrations of the fall of the Bastille would precipitate widespread sedition and disorder. One writer advised Pitt to protect the Bank of England, the royal palaces, and all public buildings on Bastille day. A magistrate in Deal even suppressed a local anniversary meeting.[68] This Francophobia was sufficiently strident to force radical societies to plan their celebrations with some circumspection. In London, the Society for Constitutional Information, hitherto a strong supporter of the French Revolution, advised the friends of liberty to avoid contentious resolutions on Bastille day. Fox and Sheridan thought it more prudent to stay away from the Crown and Anchor dinner which attracted large crowds and 'a party of stout constables'.[69] At Manchester, where the local Constitutional society had enthusiastically welcomed Paine's *Rights of Man*, members were also warned against proposing controversial motions; and against wearing French cockades. Even so, a handbill circulated the town urging 'true Englishmen' to pull down the tavern where the reformers assembled and to break 'the brains of every man who dined there'. Had the leader of the society, Thomas Walker, not been borough reeve, with 200 special constables at his disposal, trouble might well have ensued.[70]

Violence did break out in Birmingham where there had already been a loyalist reaction to the highly visible Unitarian ministry of Joseph Priestley and his outspoken support for the repeal of the Test and Corporation Acts. As at Manchester, efforts were made to deter the reformers from celebrating Bastille day. In the week before the meeting a handbill had circulated the town in which praise for Gallic liberty was coupled with a condemnation of the British parliament, the clergy, and the King. This so enraged loyalists that violence was openly threatened and intimidatory notices were pasted on the walls demanding 'destruction to the Presbyterians' and a reaffirmation of 'Church and King'.[71] The reformers were

[68] PRO, HO 42/19/78, 107. See also the anonymous letter urging Henry Dundas to be prepared for 14 July celebrations in HO 42/19/88.

[69] Goodwin, *Friends of Liberty*, 179, *Leeds Mercury*, 19 July 1791. Little trouble ensued in London, but some plebeians demanded the release of Lord George Gordon from Newgate so that he could attend the Crown and Anchor meeting. On the SCI's endorsement of the French Revolution in March 1791, see PRO, TS 11/961/3567, fo. 221.

[70] Bohstedt, *Riots and Community Politics*, 107; Goodwin, *Friends of Liberty*, 180.

[71] R. B. Rose, 'The Priestley Riots of 1791', *Past and Present*, 18 (Nov. 1960), 72–3; PRO, HO 42/19/138.

somewhat taken aback by this hostility and for a time contemplated abandoning their celebration. But they ultimately decided to proceed with their plans, disowning any responsibility for the handbill and assuring the public of their constitutionalist intentions. This was underscored in their celebratory decorations, the centrepiece of which was a sculpture of George III with an obelisk of Gallic Liberty breaking the bands of Despotism on one side and British Liberty 'in its present enjoyment' on the other.[72] 'Surely', their public response ran concerning the celebration of the French Revolution, 'no *Freeborn Englishman* can refrain from exulting in this addition to the general mass of human happiness.'[73]

Unfortunately the crowd that assembled outside the Hotel on 14 July was not of the same libertarian disposition. With the active encouragement and tacit protection of local Tory JPs,[74] it quickly directed its anger at the Dissenting chapels and houses of the leading reformers once the meeting had dispersed. Priestley's house and laboratory at Fair Hill was completely destroyed. So, too, were the residences of the Dissenting bourgeois élite, including that of William Hutton, the historian, stationer, and reforming enthusiast. Indeed, in three days of almost uninterrupted rioting the homes of twenty-seven reformers and their associates were attacked or threatened, the bulk of the mob's fury falling on the leading Dissenting radicals in the town and its vicinity. By the time troops arrived from Nottingham the mob had ranged as far south as Kingswood, visiting Dissenting chapels and country houses in Ladywood, Edgbaston, King's Heath, and Moseley, where the furniture of the Dowager Countess Carhampton was carefully removed before the hall was burnt down. Even after the troops' arrival there were ripples of discontent at Bromsgrove, Hagley, and Halesowen, forcing the light horse to scour the countryside within a 10-mile radius of Birmingham in search of rioters.[75]

Priestley and some of his friends believed the disturbances were the product of sectarian bigotry. In an open letter to the inhabitants of Birmingham he declared that religious discord had been stoked up 'by the discourses of your teachers, and the exclamations of your superiors in general, drinking confusion and damnation to us'.[76] Later he attributed the riots to the malice of the High Church party, who had deliberately incited the scum

---

[72] PRO, HO 42/19/396–7.   [73] *Leeds Mercury*, 2 Aug. 1791.
[74] For the complicity of the justices of the peace, see PRO, HO 42/19/290–3, 301–5, 309, 311, 313, 317, 319, 321, 325, 327, 348–9.
[75] PRO, HO 42/19/207; Rose, 'Priestley Riots', 75–6.
[76] A copy can be found in PRO, HO 42/19/207.

of the town to disorder.[77] Certainly there was some truth to this. John
Brooke, the under-sheriff of Warwickshire and county coroner, later the
secretary to the local loyalist association, had encouraged the mob to attack
the meeting-houses. His fellow justices, Benjamin Spencer and Joseph
Carles, had winked at disorder. The latter had even told rioters not to leave
'those Presbyterian Dogs a place standing'.[78] Once mobilized, moreover,
the justices found it hard to restrain crowds from looting and exacting
beer and money from potential victims. Carles reputedly remonstrated with
rioters before John Ryland's house that they had transgressed their licence
to 'plunder, break down and destroy'.[79] But his words went unheeded.
While the riots remained centrally directed at reforming Dissenters and
their associates, there were degenerate side effects.

At the same time Priestley's explanation was too summary. It overlooked
the social and political complexities of the riot. What gave particular
poignancy to Birmingham's sectarian antagonisms was not religious differences *per se*, but the particular conjunction of religion and politics in
the period 1785–91. It was the Dissenters' visible advocacy of civil and
political rights, their public enthusiasm for the French Revolution, that
had rekindled old sectarian antagonisms and potentially challenged the local
bases of power. These developments troubled the Tory county hierarchy,
but they were not without some popular purchase in a town where the
penetration of Painite ideas was still skin-deep and where the buckle and
button trade was facing an uncertain future with the growing popularity
of laced shoes and covered buttons. These new-fangled fashions became
associated in the popular mind with France and by extension, with revolutionary events across the Channel, a juxtaposition that reinforced the credibility of Tory paternalism and the notion that the Dissenters were both
political subversives and indifferent to local prosperity.[80] Established
fashion thus became identified with the established order and Dissenters
with neither. Liberal, presumptuous, and socially aloof, hostile to the moral
economy and the customary expectations of the poor, the rich Dissenters
of Birmingham were easy targets for populist rancour. William Hutton's
self-aggrandizing reformist projects, his officious supervision of the local
Court of Requests, and his strictures to the poor about their lack of

---

[77] Joseph Priestley, *An Appeal to the Public on the Riots in Birmingham* (1792), in *The
Theological and Miscellaneous Works of Joseph Priestley*, ed. J. T. Rutt, 24 vols. (London,
1817–31), xix. 407.
[78] PRO, HO 42/19/317.   [79] PRO, HO 42/19/313.
[80] John Money, *Experience and Identity: Birmingham and the West Midlands 1760–1800*
(Montreal, 1977), 261–3.

economy only added fuel to the flame.[81] It did not take much encouragement from Church and King justices, who had their own scores to settle
with the Dissenting élite, to ignite popular loyalism and watch the show.

Although some conservatives were concerned that popular violence would
ultimately prove contagious and counter-productive, others were pleased
that the friends of liberty had received such an exemplary setback. The
commanding officer at Birmingham, Colonel De Lancey, thought 'that the
advantages that will be derived to the publick will very much counter-
balance the sufferings of a few individuals'.[82] With this verdict, *The Times*
agreed. It was entirely predictable, the paper argued, that Britons would
object to anniversaries in commemoration of the French Revolution,
which, while not treasonable, hardly breathed 'the spirit of loyalty'.[83] In
its view the Birmingham riots sprang from 'the LOYALTY of the people and
the utter abhorrence in which the principles of a REPUBLICAN SYSTEM OF
GOVERNMENT are held by the people at large'.[84] Despite the disorder, 'the
real sovereignty of the Constitution' had rightfully 'trampled over the mock
Majesty of the people'.[85] In language that parodied the Lunar society's pro-
gressivism and deliberately drew reformist ire, it suggested that radicals
would have to pay heed to the 'Electrical Patriotism' of the populace; otherwise they would find their houses similarly 'Bastilled'.

RADICALISM AND LOYALISM 1792–1795

The Birmingham riots were a setback for the friends of liberty, but by no
means an irrevocable one. By the summer of 1791 it was clear that the
dissemination of radical ideas was beginning to bear fruit. In the wake of
the disturbances came reports of a very different political disposition in
other centres of provincial manufacture. At Leicester, where the 'murmurs
of most of the manufacturers and Common People' had given cause for
alarm, handbills were found on churches and other public places with the
words 'No Church, No Pitt, Revolution for ever'.[86] At Sheffield, where
labour relations in the cutlery trade had reached breaking point and where
the enclosure of the manor had fuelled resentment against the local oligarchy, rioters attacked the property of the leading beneficiaries and stuck

---

[81] On Hutton, see ibid. 16–22. The lock-up of the Court of Requests was broken into
during the riots and its prisoners were released. See Rose, 'Priestley Riots', 73. I owe this
dimension of the riot to Douglas Hay.
[82] PRO, HO 42/19/192.   [83] *The Times*, 1 Aug. 1791.
[84] Ibid. 19 July 1791. For another view that the celebration of 14 July was offensive to
King and country, see the letter by Edward Inge, town clerk of Coventry, in PRO, HO
42/19/157.
[85] *The Times*, 18 July 1791.   [86] PRO, HO 42/19/246–7.

'treasonable inscriptions' on the walls.[87] In the countryside, too, social grievances were being sharpened by the French experience. Richard Walker reported from Tattenhall, near Chester, that a local cheesemonger declared his opposition to tithes with the hope that the clergy would soon be stripped of their privileges as they were in France, even to the point of toasting that Britain might be similarly 'convulsed in Church and State'.[88] All were evidence of the growing sensitivity to French revolutionary rhetoric, particularly among small masters and artisans.

It was Tom Paine who transformed the parameters of the debate over the French Revolution. His denunciation of the British constitution and audacious support of the French fortified democratic rhetoric and the imperatives of reform. By 1792, his forthright defence of 'the rights of the living' had emboldened artisans of a questioning temper to form their own associations. In about twenty towns throughout England and Scotland, popular democratic societies emerged. In London, Norwich, and Sheffield, they rapidly proliferated, forming 'divisions' or 'tythings' that spread into the countryside. Even in areas where clubs and debating societies had not been woven into the texture of political life, radical activity surfaced. In the Plymouth dockyards, for example, hitherto a bastion of patriotism, the bread-and-butter clubs became forums for political discussion.[89] At Newcastle under Lyme, where Paine's writings found an enthusiastic audience among newly formed societies, it was reported that 'more than two thirds of this populous Neighbourhood' were 'ripe for Revolt, especially the lower class of Inhabitants'.[90] The same was said of the Durham coalfield, where the accessibility of Paine's works had raised the tempo of protest against high taxes, coal duties, and the extravagancies of the court.[91]

Conservatives were predictably alarmed by these developments. The rather sedate Revolution societies had been easily visible; the newcomers were more difficult to locate. Moreover, the phenomenal popularity of Paine's writings, which were distributed in their thousands in cheap editions through the auspices of the SCI and local societies, appeared ominously subversive. Not only was Paine's work unequivocally republican, it was also stridently egalitarian, linking political with economic demands. How far these ideas were immediately assimilated into the outlook of the

[87] PRO, HO 42/19/257, 295–7. For an account of the struggle, see Goodwin, *Friends of Liberty*, 160–6.

[88] BL, Add. MS 16925, fo. 145.   [89] BL, Add. MS 16927, fo. 41.

[90] PRO, HO 42/22/474.

[91] BL, Add. MS 16927, fos. 45–6; see also the comments of the Bishop of Durham in the aftermath of the 1793 strike, PRO, HO 42/23/768.

popular societies remains a moot point, but there can be no doubt their
subversive potential startled the propertied. 'How long will men acquiesce
in laws which condemn them to poverty when they are to be maintained
on no other ground than . . . natural rights?' asked the erstwhile reformer
William Windham.[92] He was not alone in believing that Paine's iconoclastic
rhetoric and critique of privilege would erode the 'habitual respect' for property. 'Payne is a dangerous book for any person who does not share in the
spoil to be left alone with,' echoed one London merchant to Dundas, 'and
it appears that the book is now made as much a standard book in this country, as Robinson Crusoe & the Pilgrims Progress, & that if it has not its
effect today, it will tomorrow.'[93]

By the summer of 1792 the dramatic spread of Painite radicalism had
thoroughly alarmed the propertied classes. The Whig Friends of the People
attempted to hold the line by exhorting radicals to pursue a constitutional
path, but their intervention only emboldened the government to issue a
proclamation against seditious writings and simultaneously to prosecute
Paine's *Rights of Man*. With this tonic to loyalist militancy, many middling
reformers, well remembering the Birmingham riots, kept their heads low.
Bastille day celebrations correspondingly declined. Only the most intrepid
decided to honour the day, and then without advertising their meetings
in advance for fear of another loyalist backlash.[94] Even so, the Aldgate
Friends of the People, Painite not Whig, defiantly praised the National
Assembly and wished its army every success in its impending struggle
against counter-revolutionary forces.[95] This gesture of solidarity was
renewed by several popular societies in subsequent months as Austro-
Prussian armies invaded France and the revolution took a left turn. By
November 1792 both the London Revolutionary society (in what proved
to be its swan song) and the more plebeian associations had endorsed the
French republic and the demise of monarchical 'tyranny'. 'It is a maxim
of mine', wrote one Scottish radical, 'that a king should be sacrificed to
the nation once in a hundred years.'[96] In a new wave of Gallic euphoria,
French freedom was extolled as being 'far superior' to British; toasts were
raised to 'the Virtue of Revolutions'. In London two radical societies burnt
in effigy George III's brother-in-law, the Duke of Brunswick, the commander

[92] *The Windham Papers*, 2 vols. (London, 1913), i. 104.   [93] PRO, HO 42/22/623.
[94] *Leeds Mercury*, 21 July 1792; Goodwin, *Friends of Liberty*, 238; Carl B. Cone, *The English
Jacobins* (New York, 1968), 132–3. For the LCS decision not to celebrate Bastille day, see
Selections from the Papers of the London Corresponding Society 1792–1799, ed. Mary Thale
(London, 1983), 17.
[95] *Gazetteer and New Daily Advertiser*, 16 July 1792.   [96] PRO, HO 42/23/16.

of the Austrian and Prussian armies defeated by the French at Valmy. Elsewhere, plans were launched to plant liberty trees, those symbols of regenerative freedom first popularized by the Americans in their resistance to the Stamp Act and widely revered by the French.[97] Some of these plans were blocked by the authorities, but in Dundee and Perth, where radical societies had been recently formed, liberty poles were conspicuously erected in the centre of town. They even found their way south of the border, cropping up in Alnwick and South Shields.[98] Such demonstrations of radical solidarity were capped by a large-scale festival at Sheffield celebrating the French army's success at Valmy. Here, in the provincial mecca of radicalism, 5,000–6,000 supporters participated in a parade through the streets in which a banner was displayed condemning Burke's contempt for popular radicalism and the government's prosecution of Paine.[99] Tom's 'Truth' had become 'Libel' at the hands of the ministry, the banner declared, and British liberty was now in peril. It was a defiant assertion of popular rights in the face of government censure.

In the same month the government and its supporters began to co-ordinate their resources to stay the onward march of radicalism. In mid-November Justice Ashhurst delivered a charge to the grand jury of Middlesex in which he exhorted his audience to stem the tide of sedition that was undermining the social fabric. On 1 December the government issued a royal proclamation mobilizing the militia to meet the 'radical invasion'. A week earlier John Reeves had announced the formation of a loyalist association to counteract the groundswell of sedition and encouraged like-minded souls to do the same. Within months his call, assisted by the government's press network, was answered by 1,500 local societies, creating a movement of prodigious proportions.[100]

Not all loyalist associations were of the same stamp. To pledge allegiance to King and constitution did not necessarily rule out reform, although it would have clearly drawn the line against the republican, distributive radicalism of Paine.[101] In fact, reformers sometimes attempted to insinuate the

---

[97] PRO, HO 42/23/292, 424–5. On the effigy-burning of the Duke of Brunswick, see *General Ev. Post*, 6–8 Nov. 1792 and *The Times*, 8 Nov. 1792. On a similar attempt in Norwich, see PRO, HO 42/22/520. On the tree of liberty, see BL, Add. MS 16921, fo. 122, 16923, fos. 10–11.

[98] PRO, HO 42/24/171, 574; *Ipswich Journal*, 8 Dec. 1792; Kenneth J. Logue, *Popular Disturbances in Scotland 1790–1815* (Edinburgh, 1979), 148–54.

[99] HO 42/23/436–7; *Star*, 4 Dec. 1792; E. P. Thompson, *The Making of the English Working Class* (Harmondsworth, 1968), 113.

[100] Robert R. Dozier, *For King, Constitution, and Country* (Lexington, Ky., 1983), 55–64.

[101] On the reformist resolutions, see Austin Mitchell, 'The Association Movement of 1792–3', *Historical Journal*, 4 (1961), 62–3 and Donald E. Ginter, 'The Loyalist Association Movement of 1792–3 and British Public Opinion', *Historical Journal*, 9 (1966), 179–90.

prospect of change into their addresses. Where this proved impossible, as at Yarmouth, different resolutions were passed by opposing factions.[102] Even so, loyalist declarations which mentioned reform were in a conspicuous minority. In the propertied front against Painite radicalism, conservative resolutions similar to those framed by Reeves held sway.

Reeves's project was pre-eminently a policing operation. A lawyer, former governor of Newfoundland, and paymaster of the Westminster police magistrates, his natural disposition was to stimulate the surveillance and prosecution of Painite radicalism. This was to be achieved in three ways. In the first instance the loyalist associations sought to enforce public conformity to the campaign against republicanism by mobilizing local authorities and employers against radical sympathizers, sometimes to the point of pressuring all local householders to declare their allegiance. In the Suffolk village of Halesworth, for example, there was a door-to-door canvass for signatures, only seven villagers refusing to sign.[103] Such a tactic worked best in smaller face-to-face communities where the consequences of social ostracism could be severe, but even London parishes policed their neighbourhoods and pressured tradesmen into conformity.[104] This strategy was buttressed by a strict surveillance of taverns and alehouses, whose landlords were threatened with the loss of their licences if they permitted radical groups to meet on their premises. Judging by the number of loyalist declarations by the alehouse keepers themselves, this warning was taken very seriously. Thomas Hardy later recalled that the loyalists 'overawed the publicans so much than none of them would admit us into their houses', forcing the London Corresponding Society to meet privately and continually to shift its rendezvous.[105]

Besides attempting to dislocate the activities of the radical societies by clamping down on public houses, the loyalist associations answered the government's call in May 1792 to sniff out sedition, corresponding with Whitehall on cases which seemed to merit crown intervention, but also prosecuting some themselves. The creation of associations to co-ordinate and finance private prosecutions was not new; similar societies had been formed throughout the eighteenth century, sometimes in response to royal proclamations. But their extension into the political sphere was novel. Predictably it met with some protests on the grounds that it would create a

---

[102] *Ipswich Journal*, 15 Dec. 1792; Mitchell, 'Association Movement', 63.

[103] *Ipswich Journal*, 5 Jan. 1793. At Woodbridge, the local association recommended all employers and traders to 'inform their servants, journeymen, apprentices, neighbours and all persons' of the dangers of courting radical ideas. See *Ipswich Journal*, 26 Jan. 1793.

[104] [Daniel Stuart], *Peace and Reform: Against War and Corruption* (London, 1794), 19.

[105] *Papers of the London Corresponding Society*, 30.

climate of vigilance that was inimical to the values of a free society. The Friends of the Liberty of the Press, for example, claimed that such unauthorized sedition-hunting intruded upon private opinions and intimidated juries to acquiesce to the forces of reaction, thereby undermining any libertarian gains made by the Libel Act of 1792.[106] These fears proved hyperbolic, but they were not altogether unjustified. Although some juries refused to be cowed by the loyalist backlash, the exemplary punishments of sedition and the informal harassment of well-known Jacobins did stay the radical advance, especially in areas where it had gained a fragile foothold. The provincial press, in particular, was severely weakened, with the *Manchester Herald* and other radical newspapers in the Midlands and North succumbing to either prosecution or intimidation.[107]

Broadly speaking, loyalists hoped to close down radical space. Legal prosecutions or their threat were only part of this strategy. Equally important was the active propagation of loyalism, by address, sermon, tract, and festival. All were well-tried aspects of the loyalist arsenal, having been deployed with varying degrees of success during the Forty-Five, the American war, and in the opening years of the French Revolution. Yet the tremendous and seemingly imponderable appeal of Painite ideas, which surfaced even in areas of confirmed loyalism, made conservatives uncertain of their audience. Reeves, for instance, appears to have entertained quite élitist notions of how associations should run. But others felt his proposals were too exclusive. One correspondent from Lincolnshire believed that Reeves's emphasis upon gentlemanly associators would deter the 'middle Class of Society' from joining the movement, 'either by modesty on the one hand, or by a jealousy of the superior distinction on ye other'.[108] Another advised that loyalist societies would prosper more successfully if their advertisements appealed more broadly to 'inhabitants' or 'Englishmen'.[109] Behind these differences lay issues of style and pitch, the extent to which loyalist societies should emphasize social hierarchy and deference or a populism that sailed close to the radical wind.

---

[106] *Morning Chronicle*, 24 Jan. 1793. See also Joseph Towers, *Remarks on the Conduct, Principles and Publications of the Association at the Crown and Anchor in the Strand for Preserving Liberty and Property against Republicans and Levellers* (London, 1793).

[107] On these matters, see Clive Emsley, 'An Aspect of Pitt's "Terror": Prosecutions for Sedition during the 1790s', *Social History*, 6 (May 1981), 155–84, and id., 'Repression, "Terror" and the Rule of Law in England during the Decade of the French Revolution', *English Historical Review*, 100 (Oct. 1985), 801–25. Emsley's study arguably downplays the inhibiting influence of the prosecutions for sedition. His comparison with my own work on the Hanoverian accession is rather forced: (1) because we are often dealing with different courts and different legal evidence and (2) because many of my cases were taken from quarter sessions recognizances and rarely went to trial.

[108] BL, Add. MS 16919, fo. 162.   [109] Add. MS 16922, fo. 24.

Such differences were most marked in relation to the labouring poor. Sarah Trimmer believed the working population would be satiated with a tract and a loaf every Sunday. Regular doles and moral instruction, she declared, would gradually 'put a whole neighbourhood of poor people into good humour with their superiors'.[110] Yet it was frequently argued that such eleemosynary strategies would be quite insufficient to placate a politically articulate populace whose exposure to Painite ideas undermined their allegiance to the current regime.[111] What were required were popular tracts or ballads outlining the palpable benefits of British rule in contrast to the social anarchy of the French Revolution and the follies of radicalism. A few even believed that loyalism could be fortified by drawing upon the revolutionary experience itself, either by insisting upon oaths to King and Country or by emulating the popular *tricolore*.[112]

No consensus was necessary on these issues because the formation of loyalist associations was left to local initiative. But the responses that Reeves received from local chairmen did prompt him to compete more keenly with the Society for Constitutional Information for the popular market. Although the Crown and Anchor initially focused upon weightier tracts such as Paley's *Reasons for Contentment* and Justice Ashhurst's *Charge*, it was soon publishing and distributing cheaper tracts such as *One Pennyworth of Truth* and Hannah More's *Village Politics* as well as prints, songs, and broadsides. The message of these was frequently crude and xenophobic, full of anti-Gallican rhetoric in which an honest, industrious, and ample John Bull is favourably juxtaposed to an undernourished, vagabond Jacobin; or to untrustworthy Painites such as 'Judas MacSerpent' who would ensnare the unwary to believe in the empty promises of equality.[113]

At the same time many tracts did compare Britain's libertarian trajectory with that of France. Britain's long-standing tradition of liberty, so the argument went, had brought palpable gains for everyone: a rule of law, security of property, religious concord, domestic and commercial felicity. By contrast, the French revolutionary experience had engendered scarcity, atheism, unparalleled political violence, and the spectre of mob rule. Although authors did invoke the image of a stable, hierarchical society and the beneficial mutualities of rich and poor, the language of loyalism was often nationalist and libertarian rather than patriarchal. In fact the loyalist

---

[110] Add. MS 16921, fo. 122.

[111] BL, Add. MS 16919, fos. 149–50; 16920, fos. 18–19; 16926, fo. 36.

[112] Add. MS 16919, fos. 67–8, 144–5.

[113] For a useful account of this propaganda, see Robert Hole, 'British Counter-revolutionary Popular Propaganda in the 1790's', in Colin Jones (ed.), *Britain and Revolutionary France: Conflict, Subversion and Propaganda*, Exeter Studies in History 5 (Exeter, 1983), 53–69.

defence of existing inequalities drew less on arguments drawn from natural law and the great chain of being than upon those derived from political economy.[114] Inequality was an inevitable and necessary feature of capitalist society, but for the diligent and enterprising there were opportunities for personal advancement.

The saturation of the market with loyalist tracts and songs was accompanied by a vigorous display of festival. Christmas doles and New Year's day parades revitalized loyalist allegiances. At Halifax, for example, the local benefit societies processed the town 'wearing blue silk sashes round their shoulders and cockades in their hats with the words (in silver) KING AND CONSTITUTION'. Later they heard a sermon in which it was claimed that 'none but True Englishmen enjoy the pleasing fruits of sterling Liberty'.[115] Royal anniversaries, too, saw a new lease of life, even those of the royal family which were not normally celebrated outside court. Thus at Manchester, over 100 gentlemen of the Church and King club celebrated the Queen's birthday to the resounding toasts of the King, the Queen, the royal family, and Britain's mixed constitution.[116] To these one should add the personal appearances of the monarch himself. 'Prodigious crowds of people of all ranks' were said to have assembled in St James's Park and Parliament Street to testify their loyalty to the King as he rode to the Lords in mid-December. Some even offered to draw his carriage themselves. 'What supreme delight must our PATRIOT MONARCH have experienced on this occasion!' wrote one paper at a time when the nation awaited news of Louis Capet's fate, 'a SOVEREIGN who thus reigns triumphant in the Hearts of a FREE, BRAVE, and GENEROUS PEOPLE.'[117]

The most typical and publicized feature of loyalist festival, none the less, was the effigy-burning of Tom Paine. The execration of the radical hero was initially an endorsement of his prosecution by the crown for seditious libel. Two weeks before his trial *in absentia* at the London Guildhall, Paine's effigy was hanged at Croydon before a crowd of 1,000 people. By the time the trial took place, he had been burnt in effigy at several places in the West Country as well as in Ipswich and Lancashire.[118] In Bristol, Paine

---

[114] See Gregory Claeys, 'The French Revolution Debate and British Political Thought', *History of Political Thought*, 11 (Spring 1990), 73–80.

[115] *Leeds Mercury*, 12 Jan. 1793. For other examples, see *Manchester Mercury*, 8 Jan. 1793.

[116] *Manchester Mercury*, 22 Jan. 1793. For loyalist activity on other birthdays, see *The Times*, 5 June 1792, 17 Aug. 1793; *Manchester Mercury*, 11 June 1793; *Sun*, 21 Aug. 1793.

[117] *Felix Farley's Bristol Journal*, 15 Dec. 1792.

[118] *The Times*, 8, 20 Dec. 1792; *Manchester Mercury*, 18 Dec. 1792; *Bristol Gazette and Public Advertiser*, 20 Dec. 1792; *Felix Farley's Bristol Journal*, 22 Dec. 1792; *Ipswich Journal*, 22 Dec. 1792.

was burnt three times in two days: first at Redcliffe Hill in the shadow of the spires of the most imposing Anglican church in town; and subsequently at Brandon Hill and the Old Market. Thereafter Paine's immolation became a fairly regular feature of Church and King junkets, sometimes capping the formation of new loyalist associations. Thus at Didsbury, where the locals had assembled 'to give a public testimony of their loyalty', Paine was formally tried by a mock jury, found guilty, led to the place of execution by a band, probably playing the 'Rogue's March', and there executed 'amidst the acclamations of a great concourse of people from the surrounding country'.[119]

Just how many effigy-burnings of Paine occurred in the winter of 1792–3 it is impossible to say. Newspapers seldom reported all the cases that came within their purview and sometimes admitted that they did not have the space to do so.[120] In the cluster of newspapers I have examined, I have been able to trace some 189 effigy-burnings of Paine. Given the nature of eighteenth-century reporting and the constraints of space that prevented even the most loyalist of printers from publishing all the cases they received, it is quite plausible that Paine was burnt in 300 or so towns and villages in England and Wales.[121] This would make Paine the most burnt-in-effigy personality of the century, Guy Fawkes excepted. Whether these figures can be read as a straightforward barometer of popular loyalism is another matter. We are left with the paradox that the author of one of the century's bestsellers—250,000 copies of the *Rights of Man*, parts I and II, were sold by 1793—was also the most publicly reviled.

Many of the reported effigy-burnings were a ritualized finale to a loyalist meeting dominated by local property holders. Predictably, many were sponsored by such men. At Newton in the Willows, near Wallington, one Captain Legh officiated; at Didsbury, the members of the local hunt. At Prestwich it was the 'respectable inhabitants of the township' who organized the effigy-burning; similarly at Disley, where Squire Legh of Lyme distributed three fat bullocks to the poor.[122] Even where this is less evident it is clear that magistrates and local dignitaries licensed, if not encouraged, anti-Paine parades, rolling out the barrels of beer to lubricate the proceedings. In some instances they connived at the harassment of

---

[119] *Manchester Mercury*, 5 Feb. 1793.

[120] *Shrewsbury Chronicle*, 18 Jan. 1793; *Leicester Journal*, 4 Jan. 1793; *Manchester Mercury*, 8 Jan. 1793.

[121] In due course I plan to write a fuller account of these effigy-burnings.

[122] *Manchester Mercury*, 18 Dec. 1792, 5 Feb., 26 Mar. 1793. See also *Berrow's Worcester Journal*, 24 Jan. 1793 and *Ipswich Journal*, 29 Dec. 1792, 5 Jan. 1793.

Paine's known supporters. At Manchester the local authorities allowed a Church and King mob to besiege the house of Thomas Walker and other reformers while at Thorp, near Royton, the resident magistrate turned a blind eye to the disruption of a reformist meeting even though 'he lived within a few yards of the scene of the riot'.[123]

Burning Tom Paine was a ritual that was principally carried out in small towns and villages. Nearly two-thirds of those reported in the press took place in centres with less than 2,000 inhabitants; 16 per cent occurred in villages or townships with less than 500. In some whole parishes were mustered to hear diatribes against Tom Paine and his works.[124] Against this, anti-Paine parades did not necessarily take place in milieux one usually associates with social deference. Outside the larger towns, many of those reported in the press occurred in townships or villages with industrial or mixed economies, often with populations of 1,000 or more.[125] Effigy-burnings of Tom Paine were fairly well distributed throughout the south of England and Midlands, but they were noticeably clustered in four geographical areas: in the textile districts of the south-west, around Exeter and again in Wiltshire and east Somerset; in the mining district of Somerset around Midsomer Norton, and more conspicuously in the Northumberland-Durham coalfield; and in the cotton district around Manchester. None of these areas were noted for their cordial labour relations. Some, the south-west in particular, had established strong traditions of collective action over the century. And many were situated in or very close to areas that had rioted over provisioning during the mid-century decades. In other words, there is a marked concentration of loyalist festival in areas noted for their industrial bargaining and rebellious spirit. How can this be explained?

It cannot be interpreted, I would argue, as conclusive evidence of the strength of popular loyalism in these areas. Some of the effigy-burnings of Paine were clearly political interventions designed to offset the contagion of radicalism amongst potentially sympathetic workforces. In some of the Wiltshire and Dorset towns, for example, the burnings were sponsored by the military as a morale-boosting exercise. Captain Crawford of the Queen's dragoons reported to the Home Office that he had ordered mock executions of Paine to counteract the disaffection that the troops had encountered in local pubs and markets.[126] This was true of Bridport, which

---

[123] Alan Booth, 'Popular Loyalism and Public Violence in the North-West of England, 1790–1800', *Social History*, 8 (Oct. 1983), 299–301.

[124] *Shrewsbury Chronicle*, 1 Feb. 1793; *Hampshire Chronicle*, 14 Jan. 1793.

[125] These conclusions are based upon occupational information found in the 1801 census, *British Parliamentary Papers*, 6 (1801–2), *passim*.

[126] PRO, HO 42/23/466 b–c.

Crawford described as 'a very disaffected place', and of Trowbridge and Bradford, where 'there are some of the most violent Levellers'. A similar strategy appears to have occurred at Leeds, where Painite ideas had been well received by journeymen cloth-dressers; and at North and South Shields. Here widespread opposition to impressment and a protracted strike for higher pay by both seamen and keelmen had fuelled unrest, giving rise to cries of 'No King, Tom Paine for ever'.[127]

Confronted with this sort of disaffection, loyalist sponsors were often careful about where they staged their Paine-burning rituals. No effigy-burnings were reported in some of the larger disaffected towns such as Norwich, Sheffield, and London, for fear they would badly backfire. In Newcastle, where one commentator reported that the streets were 'crouded with Workmen of all Descriptions unemployed, who all seem to be waiting for some Change',[128] Tom's mock execution was promoted at the nearby Crowley ironworks at Winlaton and Swalwell, where economic self-interest in the shape of profitable naval contracts would probably encourage loyalist exuberance. Even then, sponsors had to face the prospect of political contention, for months earlier the iron workers had been berated for their loyalism by 'a tumultuous assembly of keelmen and their wives, who threw such quantities of stones that it was esteemed little less than a miracle that more of them did not lose their lives'.[129] In other areas of the country too, effigy-burnings seem to have been promoted in politically safe havens adjacent to potentially hostile environments: at Frome, from the seclusion of Mells Park; in the Devon weaving district of Cullompton and Bradninch, at the smaller agricultural villages of Butterleigh and Silverton. In this way loyalists hoped to avoid unwelcome reprisals and parade their popularity.

This did not mean that Paine-burning loyalism was always superficially popular. Anti-Painite activity struck strong roots among those friendly societies and benefit clubs who feared their small stake in British society might be undermined by Paine's distributive radicalism, which had advocated

---

[127] PRO HO 42/24/613–14; Robert Isaac and Samuel Wilberforce, *The Life of William Wilberforce*, 5 vols. (London, 1838), ii. 3–5. On the strikes on the Tyne, see Norman McCord and David E. Brewster, 'Some Labour Troubles of the 1790s in North East England', *International Review of Social History*, 3 (1968), 366–83. McCord and Brewster, however, play down the importance of Painite ideas, which surface not only in the reports of Joseph Bulmer, whose testimony they discount, but in other quarters. See PRO, HO 42/22, Powditch to Pitt, 3 Nov. 1792, cited in Thompson, *The Making*, 112, and HO 42/23/772–4.

[128] PRO, HO 42/23/772.

[129] Cited by M. W. Flinn, *Men of Iron: The Crowleys in the Early Iron Industry* (Edinburgh, 1962), 248.

state pensions for the aged. In towns where sectarian rivalries informed popular politics, loyalist sentiment could also be fuelled by a continuing hostility to Dissent. It was no accident that Paine was sometimes burnt in association with Priestley and that the old Tory slogan of 'Down with the Rump' resonated through the streets.[130] In Cambridge mobs shouting 'King and Constitution' ransacked the houses of prominent Dissenters and demolished the new meeting-house. At Guisborough the Dissenting chapel was set on fire. At Uttoxeter, crowds protested the opening of a new meeting-house by smashing its windows and burning its preacher in effigy; while in Birmingham, the establishment of the 'Loyal True Blues' precipitated attacks upon prominent Dissenting reformers in a style reminiscent of 1791.[131] Here, as in Manchester, traditional antagonisms generated a populist Toryism that gibed at the bourgeois pretensions of progressive Dissent.

If sectarian animosities provided one setting for counter-revolutionary militancy, the religious revival probably provided another. Orthodox Wesleyan communities were always officially loyalist, and this loyalism continued in the immediate aftermath of Wesley's death, as the declaration of the Leeds Conference in 1793 revealed.[132] Certainly loyalist diatribes against Jacobin atheism and the potential destruction of domestic felicity would have found a responsive audience among the God-fearing, sober, Methodist communities of the industrial heartlands. It was not accidental that the Kingswood colliers, weaned from their insubordinate past by intensive proselytizing, were vociferously defensive of the existing order, parading in their hundreds with fellow members of their friendly societies before torching Tom Paine in effigy.[133] Not that Methodism was an automatic indicator of loyalism. At the inception of the counter-revolutionary mobilization, Reeves received a report from Wellingborough of a Methodist preacher who was propagating radical views, and in subsequent years the Kilhamite Connexion would gain a reputation as supporters of Tom Paine.[134] But while the democratic ethos of the Methodist sects could stimulate radical ideas, the prevailing strength of orthodox Wesleyanism in the early 1790s probably worked against them. Reverence to the founder and a revulsion to Jacobin impiety enabled the loyalist associations to mobilize these chapels to King and Country.

[130] For an example of Priestley being burnt in conjunction with Paine, see BL, Add. MS 16924, fo. 62.
[131] *Ipswich Journal*, 8, 22 Dec. 1792, 5 Jan. 1793; *Star*, 5, 25 Dec. 1792.
[132] Thompson, *The Making*, 45.   [133] *Bristol Gazette and Public Advertiser*, 7 Mar. 1793.
[134] BL, Add. MS 16919, fo. 158; Thompson, *The Making*, 49.

More generally, however, it was the conjunction of Painite radicalism with the accelerating crisis in France that shaped the loyalist response. Such a conjunction was visibly exemplified by bedecking Paine's effigy with a *tricolore*, or by styling him 'Monsieur Égalité'.[135] Even the more conventional execution of the notorious 'leveller', the *Rights of Man* in one hand, a pair of stays in the other, connoted the upstart quality of speculative politics whose imperatives had led to the guillotine. The onset of the Terror, the ensuing economic dislocation, the pseudo-trial and execution of the King, all reinforced British prejudices about the political authoritarianism of their traditional enemies and the dubious benefits of 'Liberty and Equality'. The French, declared one loyalist, had traded 'Slavery' for 'licentious Anarchy, overlooking that Golden mean which Liberty, like the Moral Virtues, consists in'.[136] 'Englishmen', declared another, were 'not likely to learn liberty from men who for centuries have submitted to a regular course of slavery'.[137] Such sentiments appealed pre-eminently to the propertied owners who feared that French equality would undermine their stake in British society. But it could evoke a broader patriotism as well as drawing upon the allegiance of the industrious and devout. Even those with nothing to lose were sometimes fearful of revolutionary anarchy, fears that were sedulously fanned by loyalist propaganda. 'I have heard the Common Labourers at their work,' one correspondent wrote to Dundas, 'nay women and children, on repeating the Cruelties of the French to them, vow vengeance and utter imprecations against these Murderers.'[138]

In part, then, the loyalist associations played on the politics of fear. They projected the image of anarchy and violence across the Channel, an image of a regime whose political destination was uncertain but whose political style was sanguinary. What had French liberty gained, asked one poem on Louis XVI, 'but guilt, and shame, | Famine, and blood, and sword'?[139] Against this rhetoric and its accompanying symbols, the cadaverous sansculotte, his Medusan sister, the bloody *bonnet rouge*, the piked head, and the guillotine, it was difficult to advance the virtues of freedom and internationalism upon which the radical cause had been predicated. 'Liberty,' one radical sympathizer later reflected, 'sometimes caricatured with rags

---

[135] A Frenchified effigy of Paine was burnt at Kingswood and at Bath. See *Bristol Gazette and Public Advertiser*, 7 Mar. 1793; *Bath Journal*, 25 Feb. 1793.

[136] *Liberty and Equality, Treated of in a Short Story Addressed from a Poor Man to his Equals* (London, 1792), 35.

[137] W. Savell Esq., to the loyalist meeting of the Pevensey Rape, 17 Dec. 1792. *Sussex Weekly Advertiser*, 24 Dec. 1792.

[138] PRO, HO 42/24/286. [139] *Ballad on Louis XVI* (n.p., 1793?), 14.

and wretchedness, and at others exhibited in horror and blood, has been held up, or rather forced upon the attention of the English, in order to induce them to hug their own chains, and congratulate themselves upon their supposed freedom.'[140]

In fact, loyalist propaganda was neither so penetrating nor so absolute. In London, radical recruitment rose rather than fell in the wake of the loyalist backlash. Elsewhere radicals refused to be cowed by the politics of fear, although their efforts to counter loyalist symbolism were compromised by the conservative appropriation of space, semi-official harassment, and the drift to war. Prior to February 1793 the Sheffield Constitutional society had organized a number of radical demonstrations, reviling Burke rather than Paine, burning the Duke of Brunswick in effigy in October 1792 to celebrate the expulsion of invading armies from France. Other societies in London had followed suit, even to the point of commending General Dumouriez's conquest of the Low Countries.[141] But radical festival began to disintegrate in the wake of the loyalist upsurge, giving way to more individualistic protests. Republican graffiti were chalked up on parsonages and gentlemen's doors. Loyalist handbills, even royal proclamations against sedition, were torn down. In London, radical manifestos were artfully substituted for those of the Crown and Anchor, making it appear, one indignant loyalist reported, that they emanated from Reeves himself![142] This jocose strategy was accompanied by ironic letters to the arch-loyalist fulfilling his worst fears about the march of equality; or commenting on the latest effigy-burning. Thus the 'Hampshire Sedition Hunters' from Winchester reported:

that last Monday their Committee met but having nothing to do—they ordered an effigy for Tom Pain to be made, dressed in Black, the Church giving the Coat, the College the Waistcoat and Breeches, and the Corporation the Hat, Wig, and a Halter—they also caused a Mob to assemble to carry this Effigy about the City— but this Mob was not numerous as the Militia Men, nowhere, refused to join— The Mayor and Alderman—being of the true Jacobite Breed, gave money to the Mob to Halloo—Church and King—and then to burn the Effigy—now as this Mob was not a Republican Riot—but legally set on foot by us Associators for Church and King, we did not suppress it.

---

[140] John Skill (trans.), *The Means of Obtaining Immediate Peace, Addressed to the King and People of Great Britain* (London, 1795). The pamphlet was originally published in French in London in 1794.

[141] Goodwin, *Friends of Liberty*, 248–9. For an effigy-burning of Burke at Sheffield in January 1793, see *Morning Chronicle*, 22 Jan. 1793.

[142] BL, Add. MS 16921, fos. 127–8.

The letter concluded that 'when the Mob got drunk, some few did cry out Tom Pain for ever—Tom Pain for ever'. But the author assured Reeves that they were 'very drunk' and few in number, 'for you may depend on all in our list being of the right sort—having amongst us forty Parsons'.[143]

Radical culture sought to expose the superficial spontaneity of loyalist festival as well as mocking its architects. Its language was sometimes very blasphemous, countering 'God Save the King' with 'God Save Tom Paine', applauding France's new 'Shaving Machine', and daring to imagine a new farce,'LA GUILLOTINE! or GEORGE'S HEAD IN THE BASKET' at the 'Federation Theatre in Equality Square', in the course of which would be sung 'CA IRA and BOB SHAVE GREAT GEORGE OUR *****!'[144] At other times it wittily appropriated conservative constructions for its own. *Hog's Wash* and *Pig's Meat* were the radical answer to Burke's 'swinish multitude'; Adam, the evangelicals' original sinner from which social acquiescence and subordination flowed, was recharged as 'a true SANS CULOTTES, and the first revolutionist'.[145] This subversion of language was often self-consciously Gallic, flying in the face of loyalist litanies.

Prior to the Gagging Acts radicals remained embattled contestants in the war of words. Indeed, their adoption of the French 'right of subsistence' and their continued attack upon what Thelwall called the 'rotten borough system of corruption, peculation and monopoly' infused new meanings into the bread riots of 1794–6 and politicized areas relatively untouched by radical ideology, or at least where radical roots remained fragile.[146] The local magistrates 'gave us plenty of Ale & spirits to urge us on . . . when we were rioting for Church & King', noted one Birmingham reformer, but 'Now we are rioting for a big Loaf we must be shot & cut up like Bacon Pigs'.[147] Of the known towns and villages that burnt Tom Paine in 1792–3, one in six rioted against the high price of provisions in the next three years, revealing the degree to which loyalism was contingent upon the strenuous maintenance of social reciprocities between rich and poor.[148]

---

[143] BL, Add. MS 16928, fo. 5.

[144] Gwyn A. Williams, *Artisans and Sans-Culottes* (New York, 1969), 72.

[145] Charles Pigott, *A Political Dictionary* (London, 1795), 3. At a festival in January 1793, the members of the Sheffield Constitutional society defiantly toasted 'The Swinish Multitude. May they hold in contempt the man who first gave that appellation to Free Britons.' See *Morning Chronicle*, 22 Jan. 1793.

[146] John Thelwall, *Peaceful Discussion and not Tumultuary Violence* (London, 2nd edn. 1795), 4; Roger Wells, *Wretched Faces: Famine in Wartime England 1763–1803* (Stroud, 1988), ch. 9.

[147] Wells, *Wretched Faces*, 136.

[148] According to my calculations, 33 of the 186 places where Paine was burnt rioted over the price or distribution of food in the years 1794–6.

None the less, the radical command of public space remained very precarious. The first general meeting of the London Corresponding society, set up to address the King for 'a Speedy Peace & a Reform in Parliament', had to change its venue because the landlord was threatened with the loss of his licence. The second, a month later, to elect delegates to the convention in Edinburgh, had to be held in the open air at Spitalfields. It inevitably caused a great stir, and indeed some tongue-in-cheek speculations that 'Tom Paine was come to plant the tree of liberty'. It was also heavily policed, to a point where the number of constables and magistrates under the direction of Patrick Colquhoun almost equalled the number of LCS members present.[149] Predictably it led to the arrest of the sympathizer who offered his field for the meeting, one Thomas Briellat, a pump-maker; not for any mishap on the day, but for allegedly propounding the virtues of revolution and republicanism the previous year. Within months Briellat was sentenced to twelve months' imprisonment, a £100 fine, and security for his good behaviour for three years to the tune of £500 for himself and £250 for his sureties. After his release he emigrated to America.[150]

The open meetings of the LCS frequently attracted crowds of 2,000 to 3,000. Hardy reflected that at the first open-air meeting in October 1793 'many who came there to ridicule and abuse, went away converted and afterwards joined the society and became zealous promoters of the cause'.[151] But the LCS was subjected to continued legal harassment. Landlords were intimidated. Spies infiltrated its meetings looking for the slightest treasonable gesture. Thelwall mocked one named Edward Lavender by alluding to 'a perfume employed by Ministers to scatter the Essence of Despotism over Mankind', but urged his audience not to hurt a hair of his head, or that of his fellow-informers, 'as the proceedings of that [day] would make their Masters hairs stand on end'.[152] The purpose of the meeting at Chalk Farm, 14 April 1794, was to present a remonstrance to the throne demanding annual parliaments and universal suffrage. It was also proposed to effect a union between the radical and reformist societies, including the Whig Society of the Friends of the People and the SCI. The 'proceedings' in question were probably the resolution dissolving 'the social compact between the English Nation and their Governors' if the government tolerated further incursions upon liberty similar to the repression of the British Convention and the savage sentences meted out to its delegates. It was a

---

[149] *Papers of the London Corresponding Society*, 81, 89.   [150] Ibid. 89.
[151] BL, Add. MS 27814, fo. 59, cited by Thrale, ibid. 87.   [152] Ibid. 138–9.

defiant gesture of solidarity with Margarot and Gerrald, both sentenced to fourteen years' transportation for their participation in Edinburgh, and a tocsin to popular sovereignty.

Within a month the government had confiscated the papers of the LCS and arrested its leaders. It also bore down on the Constitutional society, whose annual meeting had been filled with Francophilic fervour to the strains of 'Ça ira' and the 'Marseillaise' as well as bitter denunciations of the wartime coalition and the constitution.[153] The treason trials of 1794, of course, brought their momentary triumphs. At the Old Bailey crowds hissed and hooted the judges, drew Hardy and Erskine in triumph, and, but for the vigilance of the Lord Mayor and the Light Horse Volunteers, would have illuminated the town.[154] Radical celebrations were held at the homes of Horne Tooke and Lord Stanhope, and also in Sheffield and Norwich. In February 1795, a public dinner to commemorate the acquittals was staged at the Crown and Anchor in the Strand, attended by 1,300 'respectable Citizens'.[155]

The trials none the less took their toll, depleting the resources of the LCS, destroying the SCI, and weakening the links between the metropolitan and provincial reform societies. Some of these contacts were resumed as the radical movement gathered strength in 1795. At a huge open-air meeting at Copenhagen Fields in October, the LCS drew up a remonstrance to the King demanding reform, a speedy peace, and the dismissal of the government, and took steps to mobilize the hunger-ridden country into 'one grand political Association'. But the government took advantage of the demonstrations outside parliament three days later, at which the King was hissed and his carriage window broken, to push through the Treasonable Practices and Seditious Meetings Acts. The opposition to these two bills, which resonated through centres like Derby, Norwich, and Sheffield as well as precipitating mass meetings in London, constituted the last great constitutional protest of the century. Instructively, petitions against the Gagging Acts, as they were popularly called, drew four times as many signatures as did those in their favour.[156]

After 1795 the radical movement faced insuperable difficulties, both legal and financial, towards forging an open democratic culture. The years 1792–5 had nevertheless seen the first tentative steps towards formulating the

---

[153] Goodwin, *Friends of Liberty*, 329–31.   [154] PRO, HO 42/33/347–8.

[155] Goodwin, *Friends of Liberty*, 362–3, 379–80; Jewson, *Jacobin City*, 50.

[156] John Dinwiddy, 'Interpretations of Anti-Jacobinism', in Mark Philp (ed.), *The French Revolution and British Popular Politics* (Cambridge, 1991), 48.

strategy of the mass platform which re-emerged with vigour after the Napoleonic wars. At the convention in Edinburgh and in centres like Norwich, Sheffield, and London, radicals struggled to create an awesome demonstration of the people's constitutional rights to full citizenship through boisterous meetings, lectures, mass petitions, and anti-parliaments, deriving their strength from the network of popular clubs and societies which sustained the movement through hard times. This platform radicalism broke with the established conventions of popular politics in significant ways. Despite its histrionics, its often biting satire, its language of menace, its talk of constitutional arming, this platform eschewed riot and rabble-mongering. Radical supporters were persistently encouraged to be orderly at their open-air meetings, and rostra were sometimes erected so that they could participate fully in the deliberations. It was only by the 'persevering efforts of *reason*', one radical reminded his readers, that the people could 'hope to defend and preserve that inestimable jewel, LIBERTY'. 'Tumult and disorder', he continued, were 'the detestable engines to which their base and bitter enemies alone can wish them to resort'.[157]

The platform thus advanced claims to legitimacy that went beyond the libertarian exuberances of the eighteenth-century crowd, drawing upon and extending the strategies of the more respectable societies which earlier had extolled the radical promise of 1688 and the French Revolution. Unlike those societies, whose style of address and use of space had been pre-eminently geared to the middling sort, its language of exclusion was unequivocally democratic. The break with the past was nowhere more dramatic than in its convivial conventions. In the refurbished radical litany, the acquittals of Hardy, Thelwall, and Horne Tooke assumed a new significance, the names of Margarot and Gerrald joined the cult of martyrs, and the tricoloured cockade and the liberty cap were hoisted in defiance. Radical festival continued to have some seventeenth-century inflexions; toasts to Hampden, Sidney, and Russell remained quite commonplace. But the historical reference points were less libertarian than democratic, drawing increasingly upon the struggles of the late eighteenth century. Paine and Cartwright were correspondingly commemorated for their open defence of democratic rights, whether derived from natural right or Anglo-Saxon mythology. The 5th of November belonged to Hardy rather than William

---

[157] *Account of the Proceedings of a Meeting of the London Corresponding Society, Held in a Field at Copenhagen House, Monday, Oct. 26, 1795* (London, 1795), 3. Three rostra were erected at this meeting and the general resolutions and remonstrances were read to each and voted upon before being put to the whole.

of Orange.[158] After the centenary of 1688 and the loyalist mobilization of 'Liberty and Property', the constitutional victories of the seventeenth century seemed dubiously radical. At least the inspiration the radicals drew from the seventeenth-century experience, such as the rights of resistance and the right to frame new governments, extolled by Joseph Gerrald at the British convention of 1793, had to be inscribed within a more emphatically democratic discourse.[159]

One of the ironies of the years 1788–95 was that it was the loyalists rather than the radicals who most vigorously deployed the traditional tactics of eighteenth-century popular politics. Reeling from the Wilkite débâcle, loyalists began to mobilize popular passions around royal anniversaries and national victories in a more determined manner, capitalizing upon the commercialization of politics in the process. The loyalist effusions of the American war formed part of this process; but from 1788 onwards one detects a new confidence in loyalist festival, a more reflexive strategy of wooing the crowd. Sometimes, as radicals intimated, this strategy was formulaic, predictable, and hollow. One pamphlet recalled that several men who were hired to burn Tom Paine in effigy waited on the Devon gentleman who employed them to ascertain 'if there was any other *gemman* among his friends who he wished to have burned, as they were ready to do it for the same quantity of beer'.[160]

But, as we have seen, loyalist demonstrations cannot be simply ascribed to rent-a-mob tactics or to the choreographed unanimity of deferential communities. In some areas, large towns like Birmingham and Manchester among them, they did have some popular purchase. Elsewhere, co-ordinated loyalist propaganda, bolstered by local vigilance and legal examples, created a veritable climate of fear. The effigy-burnings of Paine were not a reliable index of popular loyalism, whose transience and volatility was greater than historians have sometimes imagined. But loyalist festival could create an illusion of confidence in government that was sometimes difficult to dispel, especially when radicals lacked a stable public forum for exposing its deficiencies. Loyalist festival certainly inhibited radical activity in

---

[158] On radical festival in the early 19th cent., see James Epstein, 'Radical Dining, Toasting and Symbolic Expression in Early Nineteenth-Century Lancashire: Rituals of Solidarity', *Albion*, 20 (Summer 1988), 271–92, and id., 'Understanding the Cap of Liberty: Symbolic Practice and Social Conflict in Early Nineteenth Century England', *Past and Present*, 122 (1988), 83–91.

[159] *An Account of the Proceedings of the BRITISH CONVENTION held at Edinburgh, the 19th November 1793* (London, 1794), 15.

[160] *Tom Paine's Jests: Being an Entirely New and Select Collection of Patriotic Bon Mots, Repartees &c on Political Subjects* (London, 1794), 35.

areas where it was weak. Understandably, radicals were sometimes caustically critical of the gullible proclivities of the mob, just as they were aware of the attractions of loyalist libation. 'The British have little to celebrate', remarked Charles Pigott,

but they still have their royal festivals when *oxen are roasted entire*; and, as if the people were not already sufficiently stupefied, they are to be further lethargized by dint of BEEF and PORTER, of GLUTTONY and DRUNKENNESS. Then they are taught to shout 'God Save the King' and to believe all human virtue and morality contained in that senseless sound, The only GENIUS which displays itself in these our *English festivals*, is the Genius of Brutality, the Genius of Delusion, or the Genius of Confusion, the whole system of right and wrong confounded.[161]

Pigott looked enthusiastically across the Channel, where Jacques-Louis David had been masterminding real festival with revolutionary panache. In 1795 he despaired of the English crowd and its radical potential. Others were less pessimistic. The year of 'famine' saw an upsurge in radical rhetoric, even in areas that seemed incurably loyalist. The loyalists might command festive space; they did not necessarily command the loyalties of the 'people'.

---

[161] Pigott, *A Political Dictionary*, 43–4.

7

Crowds, Gender, and Public Space in Georgian Politics

In April 1719 Margaret Hicks was indicted at the Old Bailey for speaking 'several Scandalous and Seditious Words' against the King.[1] The prosecuting witness, Paul Miller, testified that he heard Hicks curse the King, 'whereupon he told her she had no business to meddle with *King George*'. Hicks replied, 'G—d D—n King George and you too.' Miller retorted that 'he suppos'd she was Drunk'; Hicks denied the allegation, and the very clear imputation that her actions were impulsively transgressive. To drive her point home, she told Miller to 'come the next Morning' to hear her 'do the same'. Miller did just this, and Hicks repeated the imprecation despite warnings from Miller that 'she might be hanged for it'. Hicks defiantly answered, 'she would rather be hanged for that than anything else; if she could have his Heart's blood, she'd stab him with the knife she had in her hand. That the first time King George came by [her] Door she would stick him.' This violent denunciation of the new King was confirmed by other witnesses, and as Hicks had 'nothing to say for herself' beyond a blunt denial, the jury found her guilty. She was sentenced to six months' imprisonment and a 40s. fine, a fairly stiff sentence for seditious words, and one that was likely to keep her in gaol beyond the expiry of her term.

The case of Margaret Hicks raises some interesting questions about the role of women in Hanoverian politics, ones that historians have seldom addressed. Although women dot the historical landscape of popular protest in the eighteenth century, there has been little effort to gauge their overall contribution. Work on female activism in popular demonstrations

---

[1] *Old Bailey Proceedings* (8–11 Apr. 1719), 4. I thank Andrea McKenzie of the University of Toronto for this reference.

has tended to focus on conflicts such as bread riots rather than more overt forms of political contention. And the result has been that historians have tended to stress the novelty of women's entry into politics in the aftermath of the Napoleonic wars and their relative lack of confidence in so doing. I am going to argue for greater continuities between the eighteenth and nineteenth centuries, and to suggest further that women's participation stemmed fundamentally from their position at the centre of neighbourhood life, as informal commentators upon community relations and as workers and consumers in street stalls and markets. I shall also suggest that women's role in popular politics was at times singularly advantageous to their neighbourhoods, despite, or because of, their presumed political incapacity; and that their local knowledge was critical in influencing the pattern of community politics. I do so with an eye not only to the actual participation of women in street or marketplace politics, but also to the ways in which women were discursively inserted in public representations of that space. The two cannot be easily dissociated, for the salience of women in popular politics was often intimately associated with particular perceptions of the political order and the legitimacy or illegitimacy of popular political activism.

Women's exclusion from the realm of formal politics in the eighteenth century is well known. Although there was no legal bar to women's voting in parliamentary elections until 1832, social convention and prejudice prevented them from doing so. The only place where women routinely voted was at the mock-elections of Garrat, those parodies of the political process at which the politically excluded burlesqued their betters.[2] Beyond this topsy-turvy world, women's exclusion from the realm of electoral politics was unequivocal, reinforced by theories of gender difference. James Fordyce stated the orthodox view in his *Sermons to Young Women* in 1771, reminding his female readers that

Nature appears to have formed the faculties of your sex for the most part with less vigour than those of ours: observing the same distinction here as in the more delicate frame of your bodies . . . You yourselves, I think, will allow that war, commerce, politics, exercises of strength and dexterity, abstract philosophy and all the abstruse sciences are most properly the province of men.[3]

Such statements of gender difference inhibited women from playing anything more than a secondary role in politics. Under a 1739 legal decision

---

[2] *London Ev. Post*, 21–3 May 1754; John Brewer, 'Theater and Counter-theater in Georgian Politics: The Mock Elections at Garrat', *Radical History Review*, 22 (1980), 7–40.

[3] James Fordyce, *Sermons to Young Women*, 2 vols. (London, 1771), i. 271–2.

women were allowed to vote in vestry elections and very occasionally exercised that choice. Élite women could also use their social and economic influence in parliamentary elections. Countess Spenser reported to her daughter of her efforts to canvass for her family's candidates in the Northampton election of 1774, recalling how the mob drew her cabriolet through the streets to the cry of 'Spenser for ever—Tollemache and Robinson—no Langham'.[4] Yet such interventions were normally only tolerated within a limited patronal sphere. Ten years later, Countess Spenser's daughter, the Duchess of Devonshire, and her circle encountered considerable opposition and a good deal of ribald comment for their energetic canvass on behalf of Charles James Fox at the Westminster election. Such ladies, remarked the *Post*, were 'perhaps too ignorant to know that they meddle with what does not concern them, but they ought at least to know that it is usual, even in these days of degeneracy, to expect *common decency* in a married woman, and something of *dignity* in a woman of quality'.[5] Pro-government prints maliciously depicted the Duchess offering sexual services to West End butchers and generally using her feminine wiles to infatuate 'gaping tradesmen' into voting for the disreputable Fox. They saw her actions as a scandal upon her family name and a dereliction of her family responsibilities, a clear example of the perils of petticoat politics.[6] This last image underscored the transgressive nature of female interventions in public political space and the nefarious mix of sexual intrigue and political influence in high places. It was redolent of the parading of the boot and petticoat by London crowds in 1768 in opposition to the Earl of Bute, who was thought to have advanced his standing at court through an affair with the Dowager Queen.[7]

The Duchess of Devonshire's participation in the Westminster election of 1784 was flamboyant and exceptional, but we should not infer from the dismissive criticism that she encountered that women were excluded from such occasions. In the many prints that have survived for this election, women are quite visible: as the opponents of a proposed tax on female

---

[4] *Georgiana: Extracts from the Correspondence of Georgiana, Duchess of Devonshire*, ed. Earl of Bessborough (London, 1955), 15.

[5] *Morning Post and Daily Advertiser*, 8 Apr. 1784. For an illuminating account of Devonshire's debut in Westminster politics, see Anne Stott, ' "Female Patriotism": Georgiana, Duchess of Devonshire, and the Westminster Election of 1784', *Eighteenth-Century Life*, 17 (Nov. 1993), 60–84.

[6] The phrase 'gaping tradesmen' was used by the *Whitehall Ev. Post*, 1–3 Apr. 1784, in its criticism of Devonshire's canvass.

[7] For an example of a London crowd parading a boot and petticoat, see *Westminster Journal*, 14 May 1768.

FIG. 3 The Two Patriotic Duchesses on their Canvass

servants; as street and stall sellers involved in the campaign treating; as wives alarmed by the electoral blandishments that were offered to their husbands; as the spectators of electoral parades; as the partisans of electoral affrays. Certainly the activism of the Devonshire coterie and the tax on female servants served to highlight the discursive visibility of specific women in this particular election. But that visibility also served to reveal the commonplace: the very real presence of plebeian women in the hurly-burly of electoral politics.

We should not find this especially surprising. Plebeian women were an important part of the urban service sector in the eighteenth century and predictably played a quite conspicuous role in its electoral junkets. As tavern servants they provided hungry voters with wine, beer, and victuals; as street sellers they had cockades and ribbons at hand for the partisan parties that thronged the hustings; and they were doubtless the predominant distributors of the handbills and ballads that caricatured the candidates and the broader political issues they sought to represent.

Yet beyond these menial tasks women were also part of the wider unenfranchised public that believed it their right to watch, to comment, and to be amused by an event that was imbued with as much ceremony as many annual anniversaries. Certainly women rarely participated in the huge electoral parades and entries that were a regular feature of eighteenth-century elections, at least before the end of the century.[8] Nor did they attend the electoral dinners of the clubs and parish associations that sometimes served as an informal base for electoral campaigns. These remained very much a male terrain. But women were sometimes present at the electoral treating that accompanied eighteenth-century elections. At the Cumberland election of 1768, for example, Sir James Lowther opened up twenty alehouses at Cockermouth for the entertainment of 'Men, Women and Children, of all Ranks, Friends or Enemies'.[9] Women were also present at the large open-air nomination meetings of the candidates and participated vicariously in the theatre of street politics that accompanied every election. At the Norwich mayoral contest of 1728, women strewed flowers before the Tory alderman, Thomas Harwood, in his victory parade to his residence.[10] In the Middlesex election of 1802, the 'male and female' partisans of Sir Francis Burdett lined the streets of London in their dark-blue cockades to greet

---

[8] Frank O'Gorman, 'Campaign Rituals and Ceremonies: The Social Meaning of Elections in England 1780–1860', *Past and Present*, 135 (May 1992), 84. O'Gorman notes the presence of élite women in the Nottingham canvass of 1803. I have not found any examples of women's participation in electoral parades before 1780.

[9] *Westminster Journal*, 23 Apr. 1768.   [10] *Mist's Weekly Journal*, 15 June 1728.

their candidate, shouting 'no Bastille, no Governor Aris' at his opponents' supporters to remind them of the scandalous death of Mary Rich in the Cold-Bath-Fields prison.[11] At the Bristol election in the same year, where the idiosyncratic Tory-radical David Lewis was decisively defeated, he paid his final respects to the public by declaring at the hustings that he did not care 'three pence for the whole of them, and that in coming forward he only intended to *restore* the *rights of mankind*'. Upon which 'a fishwoman' hugged him and gave him 'a hearty smack', so *The Times* reported, and 'put an end to his oration, to the no small amusement of the spectators'.[12]

Women, then, joined in the electoral theatre of the Hanoverian era. They also participated in the community rituals that were a consistent feature of the eighteenth-century political calendar. In the opening decades of the century, in particular, women were accorded a special role in the official ceremonies. In the coronation-day festivities at Bristol in 1702, for example, and in the Queen's royal entry to Bath a few months later, 'young maidens' dressed in white and 'richly attired' virgins, 'many of them like Amazons with Bows and Arrows', were deliberately foregrounded to reinforce Anne's identity as the new Elizabeth, evoking the two symbols of the Tudor Queen as *divina virago* and Diana, the chaste goddess of hunting.[13] At the celebrations of the Peace of Utrecht eleven years later, young women were again central, wearing royal garlands, parading in white dresses with the symbols of peace, imparting to the proceedings a strong hope of party reconciliation and social regeneration.[14] And if women's visibility on such occasions waned with the demise of the Queen, it was not altogether extinguished. Young women were formally represented in a few of the coronation-day parades of the first two Hanoverian monarchs. In 1761 the town of Northampton invited the inhabitants of its neighbouring villages to parade through the streets with their 'Kings' and 'Queens'.[15] Indeed, whenever the health of the body politic or the royal body was a central motif of a celebration, the purity and reproductive power of young women was brought into focus. Predictably, in the jubilations that accompanied the recovery

---

[11] *The Times*, 14 July 1802. See also the account of the following day, where it was reported that 'all the old women, children and rabble of Brentford' cheered Burdett, whose carriage was drawn by the mob through the town, to shouts of 'Burdett for ever—and no Bastille'.

[12] *The Times*, 8 July 1802.

[13] *London Gazette*, 27–31 Aug. 1702; John Latimer, *The Annals of Bristol in the Eighteenth Century* (Bristol, 1893; reprint Bath, 1970), 45–6. I thank Benjamin Klein of Brown University for these references and for allowing me to see chapter 5 of his forthcoming doctoral dissertation.

[14] *Post Boy*, 10–14, 14–16, 19–21 May, 2–4, 14–16, 21–3 June 1713.

[15] *Northampton Mercury*, 28 Sept. 1761; *Political State of Great Britain*, 34 (Oct. 1727), 354; *Flying Post*, 13–16, 20–3 Nov. 1714.

of George III from his first bout of porphyria in 1789, the symbolic significance of the female body was once again marshalled, not only in the image of Hygeia, the female goddess of Health, but in the actual physical presence of young women. In the King's first tour after his recovery, for example, hundreds of 'young ladies, decorated with white ribbons' met the royal couple at the Honiton turnpike, while at Mount Edgcumbe, sixteen girls in white strewed the royal path with roses, carnations, jasmine, and myrtle.[16]

The female body served as the symbol of the nation's health and, indeed, in the figures of Britannia and Liberty, as the symbols of national unity, patriotism, and independence. Yet women themselves were active celebrants of royal-cum-national anniversaries or victory jubilations. In the early years of the Hanoverian accession, women sported gilded oak sprigs on Restoration day, and more intrepidly white roses on 10 June, the Pretender's birthday. In 1716, several women of Kingston upon Thames threatened to tear out the eyes of the mayor for attempting to ban a celebration of Queen Anne's accession.[17] Four years later, three London women pointedly dressed in mourning on the King's birthday to display their Jacobite sympathies. By contrast, women celebrated the coronation of George II so energetically in the villages around Stony Stratford and Towcester, collecting timber from the royal forests for their maypoles and garlands, that the authorities feared the damage would run into thousands of pounds. Women also actively applauded Cumberland's victory over the Jacobite rebels at Culloden in 1746 by sporting the Duke's colours of green and red in their ribbons and breast-knots.[18] Such a public parading of colours frequently culminated in toasts around the bonfire—in the eighteenth century rarely an exclusive male space for raucous jollity—and, if local patrons were benevolent enough, a sheep or ox roast.[19] As late as 1821, at the coronation celebrations at Brighton, where forty oxen were roasted for a crowd of over 30,000 people, 'many scores of lovely women' were said

[16] *A Diary of the Royal Tour* (London, 1789), 63, 81. For transparencies of Hygeia, see *Shrewsbury Chronicle*, 2 May 1789; *The Times*, 14 May 1789.

[17] *Robin's Last Shift*, 31 Mar. 1716; *Norwich Gazette*, 25 May–2 June 1717; Paul Kléber Monod, *Jacobitism and the English People, 1688–1788* (Cambridge, 1989), 211.

[18] *London Ev. Post*, 1–3 May 1746; *Farley's Bristol Newspaper*, 8 July 1727; *Weekly Journal, or Saturday's Post*, 4 June 1720. For an example of women sporting emblematical mottoes on the recovery of King George in 1789, see *Derby Mercury*, 26 Mar.–2 Apr. 1789.

[19] For women present at bonfire toasts, see SP 44/798/156–60, where a woman testified that she heard seditious toasts at one of the Hereford bonfires on 10 June 1718. In 1761 the *Northampton Mercury* reported that a female seller of black puddings who had 'drank pretty freely of the Liquor given to the Populace' at the coronation-day festivities in Hereford subsequently set herself on fire with her night candle. *Northampton Mercury*, 12 Oct. 1761.

to have 'submitted to the squeezings of the multitude' to obtain their share of the feast. At Manchester, where 401 barrels of ale, 20 oxen, and 60 sheep were distributed to the populace, women certainly received their fair share of the festive offerings, for Absalom Watkin was appalled to see some of them lying 'dead drunk in the streets'.[20]

There is enough fragmentary evidence to suggest that plebeian, even middling, women had few reservations about entering public political space in the long eighteenth century. To what degree they were engrossed by the political controversies of the day is perhaps a more disputable point, for it could be argued that their participation was predominantly social rather than political, a simple reflex of their families' own loyalties; and perhaps an index of the limited sphere within which they moved. Certainly historians have sometimes implied as much, noting that female activism was more conspicuous over 'bread and butter' issues than it was over straightforward 'political' ones.[21] This distinction, I shall argue, is misleading in two respects: it underestimates female involvement in political protest; it also implies a narrow definition of politics that excludes very real struggles over family livelihoods from its ambit.

When one addresses the question of gender in popular politics of the late Stuart and Hanoverian era, one interesting incongruity emerges. Women are strikingly marginal, if not invisible, in the major riots of the period; yet they appear rather more conspicuously in cases involving seditious words or political defamation. Tim Harris has found no evidence of women in the demonstrations of the Exclusion crisis, but he does note their involvement in roughly 10 per cent of all cases involving seditious words.[22] My own research on the early Hanoverian era would tend to confirm this picture. No women are known to have been arrested in the coronation-day riots of 1714, and only one, perhaps two, in the metropolitan disturbances of 1714–16. Even in the meeting-house riots of 1715, for which hundreds were arrested, only thirteen women were indicted, seven for Halesowen alone.[23] On the other hand, women were prominent in cases

---

[20] *The Diaries of Absalom Watkin: A Manchester Man 1787–1861*, ed. Magdalen Goffin (Dover, NH, 1983), 51. *Sussex Weekly Advertiser*, 28 July 1821.

[21] Robert Shoemaker, 'The London "Mob" in the Early Eighteenth Century', *Journal of British Studies*, 26 (July 1987), 285; Jane Rendall, *The Origins of Modern Feminism: Women in Britain, France and the United States, 1780–1860* (London, 1985), 201. For a somewhat different explanation of women's activism, but one that is also restrictive in that it implies that women's political action was confined to issues, principally economic, that immediately concerned them, see Anne Lawrence, *Women in England 1500–1760* (London, 1994), 247.

[22] Tim Harris, *London Crowds in the Reign of Charles II* (Cambridge, 1987), 193.

[23] PRO, Assi. 4/18/167, 241–2, 247, 321–2.

involving seditious words in Berkshire and Buckinghamshire. In London, where we have some 238 prosecutions for the period 1714–16, women featured in 15 per cent of them.[24] In these cases we find women cursing the King in the street and marketplace, sometimes in the language of popular profanity. Thus Mary Jones was committed to gaol for swearing 'the Prince of Wales is a bastard, his mother's a Whore, and King George a Rogue', alluding to the familiar narrative of the King's cuckoldry at the hands of Count Königsmarck.[25] We also find women accused of drinking Jacobite or anti-government toasts, of participating in political brawls in the alehouse, of inciting a crowd to attack a Whig mughouse, of protesting against the harsh prosecution of Jacobite rebels in 1715, and even attempting to inveigle the guards into releasing one from Newgate prison.[26] In 1718, the London crowd that raised money for Robert Harrison, pilloried for seditious words, featured 'a vile lewd woman commonly known by the name of Catherine Priest', witnesses testified. She 'was very active amongst the said Mob', they deposed, and damned 'the Court & the jury who condemned the said Harrison'. Other women, it was reported, cried, 'God bless the hands that give him money, and the devil rot those that pelt him.'[27]

We thus find plenty of evidence of female political contention, even if women's visible participation in political riots usually appears to have been marginal. How can this paradox be resolved?

It can be resolved by first considering the complexities of crowd description in the eighteenth century. Newspaper accounts tended to describe rioters in collective, gender-neutral terms, such as the 'mob', the 'rabble', the 'populace', the 'common people', and very occasionally the '*canaille*'. In so far as they attributed any gender specificity to these interventions, they generally assumed that the rioters were male, a discursive convention that harked back to the seventeenth century when mobs were usually associated with young male apprentices. Thus, in the Wilkite demonstrations outside King's Bench prison in May 1768, newspapers rhetorically remonstrated with 'countrymen' for their revelrous antics when it was

[24] The figure for 1745–6 is comparable. Seventeen of the 93 (18%) cases of disaffection in London, mainly for seditious words, involved women.

[25] GLRO, WJ/SR 2265, gaol calendar, April sessions 1716. For women in Berkshire and Buckinghamshire, Monod, *Jacobitism and the English People*, 250.

[26] For an example of a woman insulting another 'before her husband's door and raising a Mob . . . in the Street and using Scandalous words reflecting on the King', see GLRO, WJ/SR 2388, rec. 83, 12 June 1722.

[27] PRO, SP 35/12/225; *Norwich Gazette*, 12–19 July 1718; *Berrow's Worcester Post-Man*, 25 July–1 Aug. 1718.

also known that women were present and, indeed, injured when troops opened fire.[28] Women were sometimes described as a 'female mob' in contexts where their participation was predicted, such as in food riots. But where they were singled out in specifically 'political' disturbances, and this was not very often, it was usually in conjunction with 'boys' or 'children'.[29] In other words, it came with the insinuation that the disturbance was politically trivial and inconsequential. The most illuminating example of this comes from Horace Walpole, who, terrified by the disorders of the Gordon riots and their potentially insurrectionary impulse, was relieved to discover that the rioters proved in the end (or so he thought) to be 'two-thirds apprentices and women'; that is, within his frame of reference, people without politics. On reflection, however, he was vexed at the thought of 'these Catalines, without plan, connection or object' throwing a 'million' inhabitants into consternation, and of the government retaining two camps of soldiers outside the metropolis 'lest a Negro miss and her regiment of street walkers should overturn the state'. 'I am so ashamed', he confessed, 'of this *denouement* of a tragedy.'[30]

Walpole's disparaging attitude to female political activism was perhaps more vocal than others, but it was not untypical of his age. It was reinforced by legal practice. Magistrates and peace officers often confronted crowds with only rudimentary policing capabilities. Their disposition was to single out those rioters whom they believed to be the most culpable: especially those 'captains' who led the mob; or those who carried seditious standards or effigies; or those actively engaged in pulling down houses. In most cases these were men, confirming cultural preconceptions about the gendered nature of politics.

Moreover, women sometimes fed these prejudices by dissembling political ignorance in their own self-defence. In 1769 two female fruit sellers were brought before the Lord Mayor for illuminating their baskets on Wilkes's birthday and crying out 'Wilkes and Liberty'. They played humble pie and were dismissed.[31] Fifty years earlier, Ellen Vickers and her daughter were taken up for distributing a ballad called 'No fence for Rogues, or turn in, turn out, turn up, turn down, turn which way you will you can't save your bacon'.[32] It was a satire on the Whig propensity for political

---

[28] *St James's Chronicle*, 10–12, 12–14 May 1768.
[29] For examples of the use of the term 'female mob', see *Manchester Mercury*, 3–10 May, 7–14 June 1757.
[30] Horace Walpole, *Correspondence*, ed. W. S. Lewis (41 vols.; New Haven, 1971), xxv. 60, 66. The 'Negro miss' to whom Walpole refers was Charlotte Gardiner, hanged for pulling down the house of John Lebarty on Tower Hill on 8 June 1780.
[31] *Daily Advertiser*, 1 Nov. 1769.   [32] PRO, SP 35/11/33.

revenge in the wake of the Hanoverian succession. The women pleaded that they cried the paper 'purely for Want of bread' and insisted that they were ignorant of the contents. Vickers, however, admitted that she had hawked ballads 'ever since ye time of Dr. Sacheverell's Tryal' and that she had worked regularly for Andrew Hinde and Francis Clifton, both well-known Jacobite printers.[33] Given her experience and her links to the Jacobite press, it is dubious that she was as politically naïve as she professed. The magistrate certainly did not think so, for he committed her to the house of correction for one month's hard labour.[34]

It seems likely, therefore, that women's political activism was more substantial than the historical record would have us believe. Men were certainly the most visible or vocal participants in political disturbance, but riots were often forms of community action in which women could and did play a role. Take, for example, the case of the Salisbury Court riots, the most significant disturbance in early Hanoverian London in which Tory crowds attempted to suppress a Whig mughouse that had been set up within their territory with a view to curbing political disaffection. At first glance the riot appears as the culmination of male faction-fighting between the Jacks and the 'Mugites', a ritualized form of violence that had punctuated political anniversaries since the accession. This was undoubtedly the case, and five male rioters paid for it with their necks as the first London casualties of the Riot Act. Yet such a narrative does not disclose the contribution of women to the confrontation. Women incited the crowd to attack Read's Whig mughouse, and one of them (who had damned the company as 'Presbyterians') had to be rescued from the clutches of the mughouse partisans.[35] In fact, many women gave evidence on behalf of the Tory rioters at their trial. Afterwards, at the funeral of Thomas Bean, one of those executed for his part in the riot, an estimated 200 women planned a demonstration of sympathy which included 'a turn around all the mughouses' in the vicinity.[36] A month later, a female servant at Read's prosecuted Phyllis Bevan for assaulting her 'in the street, whereby she lost out of her bosome a Tortoiseshell Snuff Box . . . calling her Mugghouse Bitch & raising a Mobb upon her to the hazard of her life or Limbs'.[37]

The Salisbury Court riots revealed the intensity of party strife at the Hanoverian succession and the degree to which women were caught up in a community protest by a cluster of Tory parishes against Whig intrusions.

---

[33] On these printers, see Monod, *Jacobitism and the English People*, 47–8.
[34] PRO, SP 44/79A/121. [35] *Political State of Great Britain*, 11 (1716), 227.
[36] See *Old Bailey Proceedings* and Guildhall, MS 17875, the diary of Carleton Smith.
[37] CLRO, London sessions, Dec. 1716, rec. 4.

The same could be said for the Bridgwater riot of 1721. Bridgwater was a West Country Tory town under Whig military occupation in 1721, and the tense national situation, together with the general hostility to billeting, generated a war of nerves between the town and the dragoons. When the company commander pressured the town council to ban celebrations on the Pretender's birthday, his patrols were confronted with a sea of white roses, and a garland of 'Roses, Hornes & Turnipps' was anonymously placed over the officers' quarters.[38] Prominent in defying the troops were the women of Eastover, who brazenly wore their roses in their bosoms. When a dragoon named John Read attempted to confiscate one of them from a washerwoman, 'a great many women fell upon the said John Read, pulled him by the hair, and with their nailes much scratched his face'. As he and his company bid a hasty retreat, 'A great Mobb followed them, throwing dirt and stones . . . calling them many opprobrious names', declaring 'they would wear White Roses in spite of King George and all his Rogues'.[39] Such 'acts of Violence & Sedition', as John Oldmixon described them, continued all day, with women raising the tocsin every time the dragoons marched through Eastgate to drag off demonstrators. During one confrontation, when a butcher was cudgelled to the ground for attempting to defend his sister's right to wear the rose, a pregnant woman interceded on his behalf and prevented further violence by declaring, 'you won't offer to strike a woman big with child for you may kill her'.[40]

The Bridgwater women used their female 'vulnerability' to disarm the troops in 1721, just as the mayor used their presumed political 'incapacity' to exculpate himself from any responsibility for the riots, claiming that he had taken care 'that none but some few ignorant women and Children . . . wore any White Rose'.[41] Yet in fact the riot disclosed just how integral women could be in defending the politics of a particular community.

We can get a better sense of just how important that role could be by examining the participation of women in the Gordon riots, the most tumultuous riot of the century and the one in which women were accorded considerable publicity. Eighty women were prosecuted in these disturbances, of which twenty-four were convicted of felony, seven being hanged. Although women were rarely at the forefront of these riots, they were very visible on the streets, aiding and abetting the men who pulled down Catholic houses, extorting money from property owners as part of the mob's rough

---

[38] SP 35/27/54.   [39] SP 35/27/38.
[40] SP 35/27/228.   [41] PRO, SP 35/27/255.

justice, stealing clothes from the burning edifices, including two petticoats from Lady Mansfield, whose husband had incurred popular wrath not only for his cosmopolitan tolerance of Catholics, but because he was closely identified with the 'Scottish junto' at the apex of power. No women are known to have been active in the delivery of Newgate, but one helped burn the bakehouse at King's Bench in the company of her common-law husband.

What is especially interesting about the role of women in the riots is the part they played south of the river. As the riots spread southwards away from the squares where the most prominent pro-Catholic politicians lived and where some of the most prestigious Catholic chapels were located, anti-Catholic rioters ventured into areas where they could not act without local knowledge. Women here acted as critical intermediaries, directing wrecking parties to known Catholic houses and seeing that 'mob justice' was done. Sarah and Elizabeth Hanwell, for example, incited the crowd to pull down Elizabeth Curry's house in East Lane, Bermondsey, insisting that Curry was a practising Catholic and not a Protestant, as she had pretended by kissing the Book of Common Prayer. Suzannah Nutt confirmed the religious affiliation of a publican in Golden Lane, claiming there had been an Irish wake in the house.[42] Not all women were happy about the rough justice meted out to Catholics, especially if they had been neighbourly or charitable to the poor. Over twenty women, most of them illiterate, gave evidence against informers or rioters who placed the political imperatives of riot above local solidarities. On the other hand, a few women used the opportunity of the riot to settle old scores. On Tower Hill, Mary Roberts had fallen out with John Lebarty, an Italian publican who, in his capacity as constable, had removed her from the parish for 'audacious behaviour'. For several nights she 'swore she would have his house down', calling him an 'old Portuguese [*sic*] bouger' who deserved his fate. Eventually she sought out a mob in the Minories to do the job, leading the way with a 'sort of rough music'.[43]

The three episodes I have investigated reveal the active role that women played in the informal community politics of the Hanoverian era. Although women never played as conspicuous a role as men in the political riots of the period, they were an important part of the infrastructure of community action, disseminating ballads and broadsides, emboldening men to collective protest, rallying neighbourhoods in their defence,

---

[42] *Old Bailey Proceedings* (Dec. 1779–Oct. 1780), 533; PRO, KB 8/79/199–201.
[43] *Old Bailey Proceedings* (Dec. 1779–Oct. 1780), 509–11.

flamboyantly parading the symbols of sedition, and, as the Gordon riots revealed, using their knowledge of local networks and reputations to influence the course of action.

If this is so, then we should not draw too hard a line between women's role in popular politics and other forms of collective protest. All these instances suggest that women's activism stemmed principally from their role as the informal mediators of neighbourhood relations; a role that is strikingly evident in the importance that women attached to local reputations, particularly in defamation cases, where women become increasingly visible over time as prosecutors and defendants.[44] In London especially, women were very active in intervening in street quarrels and conflicts. In the late Stuart and early Hanoverian era they were more likely to be bound over for riots against the person or 'about the house' than their male counterparts. The same was true among those bound over to the quarter sessions as disturbers of the peace or defamers.[45]

In the 'informal community politics of riot', to use a phrase of John Bohstedt, women could be strikingly interventionist. At Billinghurst in Sussex a group of women staged a rough music against a man who had abused his wife, carrying him in a blanket to the local pond where he was 'severely duck'd several times' before 200–300 spectators and only released upon promising to 'never misuse' his wife again. At Bath, women remonstrated against the shameful treatment inflicted upon a private in the Bedfordshire militia for failing to pass the morning muster, catcalling the officers, and generally raising a rumpus at the evening roll-call.[46] Women were also vociferously energetic in protesting the strict rules that governed the public access to paupers in workhouses and in joining mobs that opposed the building of large-scale institutions of this kind. In August 1765, for example, 'a mob of four or five hundred men and women' assembled in Wickham Market in Suffolk, and broke into the room where the local gentry were deliberating upon the erection of a new workhouse for the hundreds of Loes and Wilford, forcing the gentlemen to sign a paper 'promising not to meet any more on that business, on pain of having their

[44] Robert Shoemaker, *Prosecution and Punishment* (Cambridge, 1991), 20, 58, 66; Tim Meldrum, 'A Women's Court in London: Defamation at the Bishop of London's Consistory Court, 1700–1745', *London Journal*, 19 (1994), 1–20; Laura Gowing, 'Gender and the Language of Insult in Early Modern London', *History Workshop Journal*, 35 (Spring 1993), 1–21; J. A. Sharpe, *Defamation and Sexual Slander in Early Modern England*, Borthwick Papers 58 (York, 1980).

[45] Shoemaker,'London "Mob"', table 2, 283.

[46] *Bath Chronicle*, 30 July 1778; *London Ev. Post*, 4–6 Feb. 1748.

brains instantly beat out'.[47] Later they were part of the crowd that demolished the Bilchamp workhouse and threatened another at Nacton.

Where women's livelihoods were imperilled by higher taxes, vexatious tolls, or the imminent loss of male wage-earners, they were noticeably active. This was true of the Glasgow malt-tax riots of 1725 and of the Bristol bridge riots of 1793, where eight women whose ages ranged from 13 to 55 were either killed or wounded protesting the continued imposition of tolls by the corporation.[48] It was also true of the London anti-crimp riots of 1794. Women were part of the 'mixed multitude' that assembled to pull down a crimping-house in Shoe Lane. One woman with five children and 'far advanced in pregnancy' with a sixth even mustered a crowd around a recruiting office in Whitecombe Street where she believed her husband was imprisoned.[49] And it is especially so of many anti-impressment confrontations. In the North-East, for example, in 1793 and again after the Peace of Amiens, women besieged local rendezvous and threw stones and brickbats at the press gangs. At Whitby, where the rendezvous was destroyed, one woman was prosecuted for her participation at the York assizes. At Newcastle, two other women were also prosecuted for rescuing men from the gang and obstructing the lieutenant in his duty, while at South Shields his counterpart was 'attacked by a Multitude of Pilots and Women'.[50] Female resistance to impressment, already visible in the mid-century decades, continued on vigorously during the French wars.

Nowhere, of course, was female participation more significant than in the bread riots, the foremost struggles for subsistence of the eighteenth and early nineteenth centuries. Precisely how frequently women joined in or initiated market interventions is very difficult to determine given the conventions of crowd description that I have already mentioned. The figures

---

[47] *Lloyds Evening Post*, 20–3 Sept. 1765; see also ibid. 2–4 Sept. 1765.

[48] *Morning Chronicle*, 23 Oct. 1793; on the Bristol bridge riot, see Philip D. Jones, 'The Bristol Bridge Riot and its Antecedents: Eighteenth-Century Perceptions of the Crowd', *Journal of British Studies*, 19 (1980), 74–92, and Mark Harrison, ' "To Raise and Dare Resentment": The Bristol Bridge Riot of 1793 Re-examined', *Historical Journal*, 26 (1983), 557–85, and his *Crowds and History: Mass Phenomena in English Towns, 1790–1835* (Cambridge, 1988), 271–88.

[49] *Whitehall Ev. Post*, 19 Aug. 1794; *Sussex Weekly Advertiser*, 1 Sept. 1794; PRO, HO 42/33/222–3. On the anti-crimp riots, see John Stevenson, 'The London "Crimp" Riots of 1794', *International Review of Social History*, 16 (1971), 40–58 and his *Popular Disturbances in England 1700–1870* (London, 1979), 166–9.

[50] On the North-East confrontations, see Norman McCord, 'The Impress Service in North-East England in the Napoleonic War', *Mariner's Mirror*, 54 (1968), 165–6 and Elizabeth Gaskell, *Sylvia's Lovers*, ed. A. W. Ward (London, 1906), pp. xxiv–xxvi.

we currently have are basically inconclusive. John Bohstedt found that women were involved in 77 (32 per cent) of the 240 food riots he has sampled for the period 1790–1810 and dominant in 35 of them (15 per cent). Roger Wells, on the other hand, in a more extensive survey of food riots for the years 1794–1801, concluded that women were the principal actors as opposed to general participants in only 34 of 391 riots (9 per cent).[51] My own researches into the 1756–7 and 1766 riots reveal that women are mentioned as participants in 14 per cent and 12 per cent of the reports respectively. On the basis of this evidence it would be hazardous to come to any firm conclusions about the gendered nature of the English food riot.[52] We know that women participated; we do not really know how often. It seems likely that informants or correspondents were more likely to mention female activists in food riots as time went on, but this, as I shall explain in a moment, had more to do with the discursive visibility of women in popular movements than with any significant surge in their grass-roots activism.

None the less, we might hazard a few generalizations about the nature of female involvement in bread riots. Women were rarely conspicuous in the roving bands of protesters who scoured the countryside in search of grain, or who entered towns to commandeer supplies or to attack mills or barges. These tasks generally fell to well-organized groups such as male colliers or tinners, although one can find examples, such as in Wiltshire in 1795, where a throng of men and women, reputedly numbering 'more than 2000 persons', roamed the countryside demanding that farmers sell their corn locally at 26s. a sack.[53] Where mobile combinations of men muscled in on food supplies in a fairly dramatic manner, women were certainly present. Women might be used as human shields to deter troops from potential repression. When in 1783 the militia came to disperse a crowd

[51] Roger Wells, *Wretched Faces: Famine in Wartime England 1763–1803* (Stroud, 1988), tables 1–12; John Bohstedt, 'Gender, Household and Community Politics: Women in English Riots 1790–1810', *Past and Present*, 120 (1988), table 1. See also John Bohstedt, 'The Myth of the Feminine Food Riot: Women as Proto-citizens in English Community Politics, 1790–1810', in Harriet B. Applewaite and Darlene G. Levy (eds.), *Women and Politics in the Age of the Democratic Revolution* (Ann Arbor, 1993), 21–60.

[52] On this issue I side with E. P. Thompson, who was sceptical that one could quantify women's involvement in food riots. See E. P. Thompson, *Customs in Common* (London, 1991), 307–10.

[53] *London Chronicle*, 23–5 July 1795. See also the account of men and women attacking mills in Dorset in the *Derby Mercury*, 13–20 May 1757. How far afield this group went is difficult to determine. Cynthia Bouton has stressed the limited geographical range of women's activism in French food riots. See Cynthia Bouton, *The Flour War* (University Park, Pa., 1993), 154–8.

at Etruria that was unloading corn, flour, and cheese from two boats and selling it at two-thirds of the market price, the rioters 'drew up in opposite lines, placing their wives and children in front, daring the soldiers to fire, and threatening to pull down Keel-Hall [the seat of Major Sneyd, the commanding officer] and to burn Newcastle if a gun was fired'.[54] Women also gave moral support to the roving bands of protesters, sometimes pointing out mills or dealers whom they felt were deserving targets, or urging militants to press on with their objectives. In 1756, for example, when the Bedworth colliers entered Coventry to confront the magistrates about the lack of local supplies and to threaten to fix the price of corn themselves if nothing was done about it, it was reported that 'many of the Coventry People of the lower class (both Men and Women), patted the Colliers on the back, & urged them to go thro with what they had begun'.[55] Occasionally women would assist the militants in their design. Thus in December 1756, 'several women' joined the tinners' march on Padstow to break open the warehouses and to stop a vessel bound for the Guinea coast, whose cargo was thought to include grain.[56] In carrying out these confrontational missions, women would even adopt male aliases. The 'women ringleaders' of the Stockton mob in 1740 were called Admiral Vernon and Admiral Haddock respectively, both naval commanders known for their courage and militancy.[57]

Women were more likely to be active in food riots within their own local neighbourhoods. These interventions could take quite militant forms, not because women necessarily had any gendered immunity from arrest and prosecution, but because women's protests were often viewed, by the authorities and participants, as sensitive markers of communal disapproval. In 1753, in protest against the movement of grain to other areas of the country, women demolished a 'French' weir at Taunton while 'the men stood looking on, giving the women many huzzas . . . for the dexterity of their work'. Some five weeks later, they led 'some hundreds of weavers and woolcombers' through the town to 'the beating of a frying pan', vowing to drown all those who attempted to repair it.[58]

---

[54] *Gentleman's Magazine*, 53 (Feb. 1783), 262. Interestingly, the report in *Aris's Birmingham Gazette*, 17 Mar. 1783, concerning this incident made no mention of the women, illustrating how difficult it is accurately to quantify women's participation in food conflicts.
[55] PRO, SP 36/135/283-8.   [56] *Derby Mercury*, 24-31 Dec. 1756.
[57] PRO, SP 36/91. Sir W. Williamson to the Bishop of Durham, Monkwearmouth, 24 May 1740.
[58] *Gentleman's Magazine*, 23 (1753), 343, 390, cited by Robert F. Wearmouth, *Methodism and the Common People of the Eighteenth Century* (London, 1945), 21-2.

Direct action by women was seldom as flamboyant as this incident, but it was often decisive in withholding local supplies of grain. Women stopped wagons or barges of corn bound for other markets. In 1757 a group of 'Welsh Women' seized a wagon load of corn at Hereford market and 'after a smart Skirmish, in which their Opponents were worsted, they tied Cords to the Waggon, and fastening them to their Bodies . . . triumphantly carried off their Prize'.[59] Women also remonstrated with dealers about their high prices. In 1800 an old woman at Bath quarrelled with a 'seller of potatoes' about his 'exorbitant price' and 'in her passion overturned a large basket of potatoes, which were quickly gathered up and carried off by the surrounding women and children'.[60] These sorts of marketplace confrontations could escalate to physical attacks upon hawkers, badgers, or bakers, the destruction of their property, and the confiscation of their produce for all to share.[61] They could also lead to price-fixing. At Taunton in 1757, a group of tradesmen's wives, 'induced by the example of the Females in the next County', assembled at the marketplace and 'by means of their united Vociferations and repeated Clamours, constrained the farmers to bring down the price to 6s. 6d. [from 8s. 6d. a bushel] which the good Women were willing to pay'.[62] At Bewdley, a group of women entered the market, ripped open the sacks of corn, and insisted upon their being sold at 7s. a strike. At Exeter, the women of St Sidwell's, egged on by their husbands, demanded their corn at 6s. a bushel, and, when the farmers prevaricated, warned them that if they did not comply 'they would come and take it by force out of their Ricks'.[63] Such 'Amazonian' actions, as the press called them, probably became more frequent as the century progressed. In mid-July 1795, it was reported that women had 'assembled in considerable bodies' in the market towns of Suffolk and Norfolk and had waylaid shipments of corn bound for other parts of the country. A few months earlier women had been conspicuously active in fixing the price of food in the West Country; in the next round of scarcity in 1800, in the North and Midlands as well.[64] By this time women had added new props to their repertoire of protest: exhibiting adulterated food about the town; hoisting loaves of bread or beef steaks

[59] *Derby Mercury*, 21–8 Jan. 1757; *Manchester Mercury*, 7–14 June 1757; *London Chronicle*, 28–30 July 1795.

[60] *Shrewsbury Chronicle*, 16 May 1800.

[61] *Derby Mercury*, 13–20 May 1757; *Manchester Mercury*, 3–10 May, 31 May–7 June, 7–14 June 1757; *London Chronicle*, 7–9 Apr., 21–3 July, 4–6 Aug. 1795; *Shrewsbury Chronicle*, 26 Sept. 1800.

[62] *Oxford Gazette and Reading Mercury*, 16 May 1757.

[63] *Manchester Mercury*, 16–26 Apr. 1757; *Boddely's Bath Journal*, 23 May 1757.

[64] Wells, *Wretched Faces*, 110 and tables 1–9.

on sticks and periodically lowering them to signify demands for a fall in price; and sometimes parading a mourning loaf draped in black crepe. Within a decade such loaves would be streaked with ochre symbolizing 'bleeding famine decked in sack cloth.'[65]

Not all price-fixing was carried out by women. Nor were struggles over the supply of food the special province of 'housewives'.[66] The term has a somewhat anachronistic air about it, connoting a well-defined, gendered division of labour within households that did not become commonplace until the middle of the nineteenth century with the triumph of domestic ideology. In fact, men as well as women could mediate with dealers and the authorities about familial subsistence, as did one deputation of men from Diss in Norfolk, who in 1795 told the local magistrate that 'their wages were so small, and the price of bread so high, that they were unable to support their families'.[67] Yet women's role in food riots did not stem from their position as productive partners within the household economy, as John Bohstedt has recently argued, but from their emblematic status as familial and, by extension, community caregivers and from their intimate knowledge of market practices.[68] Housewives or not, women were more involved in face-to-face marketing than men, more attuned to neighbour-hood gossip, and more adept at detecting frauds and adulterations. In this context, it is noteworthy that, during the food shortages of 1756–7, women's role in food rioting increased at precisely the point at which the accusations about artificial scarcities became most intense. In these situations, women's local knowledge about short-weight provisions, inferior flour, and hoarding became critical.

Women were more active in food disturbances than in any other kind of eighteenth-century protest. They are certainly less visible in labour disputes than men, largely because they were unorganized. Yet in situations where women's employment was compromised by technological change or trade policies, they could be important players. In 1720, for example, women from the textile district of Spitalfields joined men in protesting

---

[65] Malcom I. Thomis and Jennifer Grimmett, *Women in Protest 1800–1850* (London, 1982), 38–9; Bohstedt, 'Myth of the Feminine Food Riot', 39; *London Chronicle*, 21–3 Apr. 1795. See also A. J. Peacock, *Bread or Blood* (London, 1965), 79.

[66] The Hammonds described 1795 as 'the year of . . . the revolt of the housewives'. See J. L. and Barbara Hammond, *The Village Labourer* (London, 1927; repr. 1966), 116.

[67] *London Chronicle*, 22–4 Oct. 1795.

[68] John Bohstedt, 'Gender, Household and Community Politics', *Past and Present*, 120 (1988), 88–122, and id., 'Myth of the Feminine Food Riot', 21–60. Cf. E. P. Thompson, 'The Moral Economy of the English Crowd in the Eighteenth Century', *Past and Present*, 50 (Feb. 1971), 115–16, and id., *Customs in Common*, 233–5, 306–36.

against the continued importation of Indian calicoes. At least three were convicted 'for cutting and wounding Women in the streets, wearing Callicoes [*sic*]', two of whom received sentences of three months' imprisonment. Seventeen years later, the women of Macclesfield, the mainstay of the silk industry in the town, 'rose in a mob and burnt some [ribbon] looms, and when their leaders were arrested, released them from prison'.[69] Lancashire and West Country women also protested against the introduction of the spinning jenny used in factories, which reduced the opportunities for spinning at home. Indeed, one magistrate called in to save two factories from 'the Depredations of a lawless Banditti of colliers and their wives' believed the women to be a good deal 'more clamorous' than the men.[70] In the early nineteenth century women were also active in some of the early struggles for collective bargaining in rural industry and in factory settings. In 1811, women employed in the lace-running industry of Nottingham organized themselves into a combination to raise wages, sending 'emissaries . . . into all the neighbouring Towns and Villages to unite and collect Money for their Purpose'.[71] Three years earlier, in the first large-scale strike of the cotton spinners in Lancashire, the women were said to be 'more turbulent and mischievous than the men. Their insolence to the soldiers and special constables is intolerable, and they seem to be confident of deriving immunity from their sex.'[72] As we shall see, women's employment in the factory, in particular, had an important bearing on their participation in the radical platform of the early nineteenth century.

Before we address that theme, we must now consider how women fared in the denser political space of the early nineteenth century. I say denser because the decades after 1790 saw a rapid expansion of the popular press, a deep penetration of political ideologies, both radical and loyalist, the advent of the first popular political societies, and a growing visibility of women as the objects of social and political discourse. From one point of view the period was one of unprecedented advance for women. In the efflorescence of popular radicalism after 1815, women entered the public political stage in new ways. In the re-emergence of the mass political platform after the

---

[69] Alfred P. Wadsworth and Julia De Lacy Mann, *The Cotton Trade and Industrial Lancashire 1600–1780* (Manchester, 1965), 301, cited by Maxine Berg, *The Age of Manufactures 1700–1820* (London, 1985), 145; *Worcester Post Man*, 29 Apr.–6 May 1720.

[70] Berg, *Age of Manufactures*, 143; Adrian Randall, *Before the Luddites* (Cambridge, 1991), 102.

[71] PRO, HO 42/118, Revd R. Hardy to Richard Ryder, Longborough, 19 Dec. 1811.

[72] *The Times*, 25 June 1808.

Napoleonic wars, women voted at meetings, presented addresses, and formed their own political associations. By the end of 1819 at least twenty-five female reform societies had been formed in the manufacturing districts of Lancashire and Scotland, spreading to Yorkshire, Nottinghamshire, the North-East, and the west of England.[73] In the following year, more than twenty-five female addresses were sent in support of Queen Caroline. They solicited over 70,000 signatures and, while half of them came from the industrial heartlands or London, they spanned a wider geographical area, emanating from as far afield as Cornwall, Devon, Huntingdonshire, and Edinburgh.

The new forms of female activism none the less emerged in a context that was hardly conducive to their expansion or wholehearted acceptance. During the war loyalists had attempted to mobilize the domestic capabilities of women in the service of the nation, exhorting them, in Linda Colley's words, 'to act as angels of the state rather than as British citizens on a par with their menfolk'.[74] Accompanying this thrust was a concerted attempt to engender public festival in new directions. Partly as a product of the urban renaissance, partly in reaction to the almost Rabelaisian atmosphere that informed popular revels, local magistrates and big-wigs re-choreographed urban festival to inhibit mob activity and to instil in it greater decorum and civility. Bonfires and crackers were discouraged in favour of firework spectacles that circumscribed roving rascality and immobilized the crowd. Ox roasts were more studiously supervised and sometimes replaced by huge public dinners in market squares and open fields to which workmen and their families were invited. At the Cliffe celebrations of the peace in 1814, for example, 600 members of the parish partook of a meal of roast beef, veal, ham, and plum pudding, and the distribution of John Barley-corn was carefully regulated by gender, with the men receiving a quart of strong beer and the women a pint.[75] Often these dinners were followed by a tea for the women and children of the town, organized by the local young ladies. Occasionally they were followed by street parades and rural sports. Overall there was an attempt to domesticate popular festival, to repres-ent the festivity as a family affair, in which women, in particular, could

[73] The first was established at Blackburn in June 1819. By the end of 1819, female reform societies had been formed in Ashton, Blackburn, Halifax, Huddersfield, Hull, Leeds, Leigh, Macclesfield, Manchester, Middleton, Nottingham, Oldham, Rochdale, Royton, Stockport, Winlaton, Wolverhampton, Yeadon, and the west of England. There also appear to have been societies in the Glasgow area: at Elderslie, Galston, Kilbarcham, Johnstone, Millerston, and Paisley and Rutherglen.

[74] Linda Colley, *Britons: Forging the Nation 1707–1837* (New Haven, 1992), 280.

[75] *Sussex Weekly Advertiser*, 13 June 1814.

participate without fear of molestation as the demure wives and daughters of a familial body politic.

Women, then, were invited to occupy public space on ceremonial occasions, but in terms that emphasized their role as the representatives of the private, domestic sphere. A firm line was drawn between these decorous entries and other forms of public activism, and the spectacle of female rebellion during the French Revolution was brought into service to deter women from more concerted forms of political participation. From 1789 onwards the London and provincial papers closely followed the tempestuous events in Paris, in particular the role of women in the march to Versailles and in the attack on the Tuileries three years later. The old image of the woman as fury, whose unruliness and unbridled sexuality could not be contained in the political vacuum opened up by the revolution, became part of the common discourse of the day. Readers were horrified to learn of *poissardes* (fishwomen) taunting the King to shout 'Vive La Nation' and harassing a male English visitor to parade a piked head or join their procession.[76] They were aghast when they learned that at the execution of Marie Antoinette, whose character was greatly sentimentalized in the British press, three women had ventured to the guillotine to dip their handkerchiefs in her blood. 'How can we wonder at any actions committed by a horde of wretches', reflected the *General Evening Post*, 'who surpass in wickedness everything which the history of tyrants has taught us, or that the most fanciful imagination could picture.'[77]

The image of the radical termagant was very resonant at the birth of the female radical societies. George Cruickshank's grotesque portrait of the first Blackburn meeting drew on well-established anti-Jacobin tropes of radical anarchy, with women donning caps of liberty, daggers in their hands, and predictably wearing breeches. One newspaper saw them as the real successors of the women of the French Revolution, 'the *Poissardes* of Paris, those furies in the shape of women, who committed so many murders, and were foremost in so many scenes of horror'.[78] This sort of misogyny inevitably extended to sex. In one print, a radical woman held a phallic-like liberty pole and cap between her knees while another gestured to her sisters that she felt 'great pleasure in holding this thing'um-bob in my hand'. The message was clear: women had only entered the liberty stakes to be sexually serviced. 'The public scarcely need be informed', remarked

---

[76] *General Ev. Post*, 10–13, 15–17 Oct. 1789.   [77] Ibid. 22–4 Oct. 1793.
[78] *New Times*, 13 July 1819, cited by James Epstein, *Radical Expression: Political Language, Ritual and Symbol in England, 1790–1850* (New York, 1994), 88–9.

FIG. 4 "Much Wanted. A Reform among Females!" A sexual satire of the female reformers at Blackburn, 1819

The Times, 'that the females are well known to be of the most abandoned of their sex.'[79]

The emergence of the female reform societies in the summer of 1819 was part of the rapid politicization of the North and the growing class-consciousness of its industrial workers. Women did not play a key role in the outbreaks of machine-breaking known as Luddism that deluged the textile districts in 1811–12 and again in the aftermath of the war. Nor were they active in the armed risings that grew out of these mobilizations. One weaver active in the abortive Grange Moor rising of 1820 was specifically told by his fellow union men not to tell his wife 'for fear it might alarm her'.[80] This did not mean that women were simply passive observers of these movements. They clearly joined in the conspiracy of silence that surrounded them, and in more spontaneous ways proffered their support. In April 1812, women were conspicuously present in the attack upon Burton's power-loom mill in Middleton. Five were charged with riot and breaking windows, and were heard to curse 'the souls of those that worked in the Factory'.[81] In the same month women joined in the descent upon provisioning shops at Gee Cross near Hyde that was led by a man styling himself 'General Ludd'. A few months later, stockingers' wives in Nottingham hoisted a halfpenny loaf streaked with red ochre and tied with a 'shred of black crepe'. Under the leadership of a woman named 'Lady Ludd', who was chaired by disaffected members of the West Kent militia, they protested around the streets against spiralling bread prices.[82]

Women played a peripheral, but critically supportive, role in Luddism. In subsequent agitations, their presence became essential to sustaining the momentum of working-class radicalism. At the Manchester march of the Blanketeers in 1817 the 'women of the lower class' were noteworthy for their militancy, raising 'a very general and undisguised cry' that 'the gentry

[79] *The Times*, 13 July 1819. The same phrase appears in the *Manchester Exchange Herald*, 13 July 1819, see Epstein, *Radical Expression*, 89. See also the debates on the Seditious Meetings Prevention Bill of 1819, in which Lord Castlereagh deplored the participation of women in mass meetings and reminded them that 'when the French republicans were carrying on their bloody orgies, they could find no female to join them except by ransacking the bagnios and public brothels'. He hoped women would desist from political activism and resume 'the innate decorum and innate sense of modesty which the women of this country possessed'. *Parliamentary Debates*, 41 (23 Nov. 1819–28 Feb. 1820), 391.

[80] PRO, HO 48/25, evidence of Joseph Tyas of Raistrick, weaver. See also the evidence of William Sedden, of Dodsworth, warehouseman, whose mother attempted to prevent him from going.

[81] Thomis and Grimmett, *Women in Protest*, 47.

[82] Ibid. 38–9; Robert Glen, *Urban Workers in the Early Industrial Revolution* (London, 1984), 182. See also *Leeds Mercury*, 25 Apr., 2 May 1812.

had had the upper hand long enough and that their turn was now come'.[83] In the following year, they were drawn into the strike wave that swept across the cotton district, not only as factory workers who were prepared to turn out in protest against wage cuts, but as members of an industrial community who denounced the harsh exploitation of wage-earners by 'overgrown capitalists' and their refusal to countenance a further statutory regulation of factory hours and conditions. Several women whose male kin were imprisoned or injured during this strike wrote a pamphlet detailing their privations, and enjoined those who wanted 'a just remuneration for their Labour' to join a union society to defeat the duplicity and greed of the employers.[84] More generally, women joined the strike parades in conspicuous numbers, mobilized credit for those out of work, and heckled scabs before the factory gates. One Manchester magistrate reported to London that 'The women (who are infinitely the worst) & children are always put in front of the mobs the men keeping aloof—they make as you may suppose a considerable tumult in shouting &c & the mob always takes care to get off before or the moment the military appear—this makes the thing altogether extremely harassing, but no good can in any instance now be done without the constant aid of the military.'[85]

The 1818 strikes linked industrial grievances with parliamentary reform and inevitably raised the issue of what role working-class women might play in the broader radical movement. Hitherto women had not joined the hundreds of Hampden clubs and union societies that had sprouted up across the industrial heartland of England and Scotland, although there is evidence that they wished to do so. For example, women had been active on the fringes of the Stockport Union from its very beginning, although they had never been formal members of a weekly class.[86] Many radicals were probably happy with this state of affairs, and preferred to have women play an informal auxiliary role in radical mobilization. One Middleton leader even enjoined women to use their sexual charms to embolden men to radical action, suggesting they should 'teaze their Husbands till they promised to do their endeavours to reform their grievances' and advising them 'not to stretch [their] legs in bed with them till they espouse this great cause'.[87]

---

[83] Glen, *Urban Workers*, 206.

[84] PRO, HO 42/181, *To All Persons Friendly to, and Desirous of Establishing an Union on Legal Principles* (Manchester, 1818). I thank Fred Donnelly of the University of New Brunswick for this reference.

[85] PRO, HO 42/179/214–16. See also the fine account of this summer of strikes in Robert G. Hall, 'Tyranny, Work and Politics: The 1818 Strike Wave in the English Cotton District', *International Review of Social History*, 34 (1989), 433–70.

[86] Glen, *Urban Workers*, 231.   [87] PRO, HO 42/178/440.

But after the 1818 strikes and the decision to allow women to vote in the open-air meetings of the platform, female participation in political unions inevitably became part of the agenda.

Leading radicals defended the formation of the female political societies that blossomed throughout the textile districts in the second half of 1819, if only because they recognized that such a venture might stimulate a movement that had to regroup after the failure of the 1818 strikes. They were more divided in what this might mean in terms of women's rights. Cobbett, for one, opposed a women's franchise. So, too, did a writer in the *Gorgon*, who said it was too divisive an issue to be supported.[88] Masculinist definitions of democracy were firmly rooted in radical ideology. Women's rights were not easily accommodated within appeals to England's constitutional past, even though Samuel Waddington raked historical precedent in an attempt to find some.[89] Nor were they unproblematically grounded in natural rights theory, where women had been conventionally excluded on account of the invented distinction between the political sphere of civil society and the natural sphere of the family. In the 1820s this exclusion would be challenged on a number of fronts. But in 1819, at a critical stage in the development of the mass platform when radicals were struggling for political space in an extremely hostile legal climate, few were prepared to make votes for women part of the radical programme.[90] This proscription even extended to ultra-radicals like John Bagguley who had been imprisoned for his role in the 1818 strike. In an open letter to the 'Female Reformers of Stockport', he declared that 'the female part of the nation' had 'too long been kept in a kind of slavish inferiority' and looked forward to the day when there would be 'female Newtons, Lockes and Hampdens' who would advance women's rights and undo 'the inequality of the sexes'.[91] Yet while he denied that women were 'formed of different materials' from men, and disparaged the notion that political or philosophical pursuits 'would destroy their maternal softness', Bagguley shied away from asserting their rights to full citizenship. Women could contribute to the radical movement by acting as 'rational companions to their Husbands', heightening their joys, alleviating their sorrows, and giving them 'good council'. Female enfranchisement was too contentious an issue to be endorsed.

---

[88] *Gorgon*, 25 July 1818, cited in PRO, HO 42/178/426–9.

[89] *Republican*, 10 Sept. 1819.

[90] One who did was George Phillips MP. Instructively and with condescension, the *Manchester Observer* believed this signified that the 'age of chivalry' was not dead. See *Manchester Observer*, 9 Oct. 1819.

[91] PRO, HO 42/188/138.

Votes for women had, however, been debated in London as early as 1780. Mary Wollstonecraft had advanced the claim in her initial response to Burke over the French Revolution, even though she subsequently gave some ground to her opponents by suggesting that politically conscious women should strive to become 'more and more masculine' in the assertion of their rights.[92] It would have been surprising if this issue had not been mooted by radical women in 1819, in the flurry of activity that surrounded the formation of their own reform societies. Indeed, there is evidence that women did harbour such thoughts. At the second Stockport reform meeting in mid-July 1819, a Mrs Hallworth requested the male audience to withdraw for fear that their inexperience in political debate should be subject to ridicule. Once the men were out of the way she pledged herself to work for reform 'until we fully possess those constitutional liberties and privileges which are the birthright of every English man and woman'; a vow that, potentially at least, opened the door to female suffrage.[93]

Even so, female reformers never pushed this demand as part of their platform. Their aim was rather to co-operate with the 'different classes of workmen' in seeking the redress of their industrial grievances through political means, most notably through annual parliaments, universal (male) suffrage, and a secret ballot. Since those grievances were thought to stem principally from Old Corruption, they also pledged themselves to educate their sons and daughters to a knowledge of their 'natural and inalienable rights' so that they could form 'just and correct notions of those legalized banditti of plunderers who now rob their parents of more than half the produce of their labour'.[94] As James Epstein has emphasized, this was a programme of moral support for popular radicalism that drew its 'legitimacy from traditional claims for motherhood, not citizenship'.[95] As the female reformers of Ashton-under-Lyne remarked:

why should not we (if nature formed us for helpmates) follow up to nature's plea and exert the talents we possess in aiding the men in their laudable endeavours for redress of the grievances of which we complain? . . . if the reformers have both *women* and *truth* on their side, they cannot fail of proving victorious . . . Let us

[92] Mary Wollstonecraft, *Vindication of the Rights of Woman*, ed. M. B. Kramnick (Harmondsworth, 1975), 80; Donna Andrew, ' "The Passion for Public Speaking": Women's Debating Societies', in Valerie Frith (ed.), *Women and History: Voices of Early Modern England* (Toronto, 1995), 183.
[93] *Leeds Mercury*, 7 Aug. 1819.
[94] *The Times*, 21 July 1819, quoting the resolutions of the Stockport Female Union society.
[95] Epstein, *Radical Expression*, 88.

prove that we are true-born English women and that we are determined to bear this illegal oppression no longer.[96]

This did not mean that the female reformers' role was inconsequential. Nor can it be simply read as a token acknowledgement by men of female participation in earlier struggles. Women's activism was of vital importance to radical education and reproduction, to the creation and dissemination of a radical political culture. It drew cannily upon evangelical notions about the regenerative power of women as mothers, unsettling the political conservatism that frequently accompanied domestic ideology. Female participation was especially critical to the expansion of radical political space, which had received a series of setbacks through legislative repression and loyalist propaganda. At the time that the female political societies were formed, radicals were attempting to revive the mass platform after a period of prohibition, well aware that the government might re-enact the Seditious Meetings Act of 1817 which had severely restricted open-air meetings by working people.[97] To counter this possibility, radicals encouraged women to march in their parades and carry their political banners in order to underscore the respectability of the platform, its disavowal of mob or insurgent activity. In defending this strategy, radicals even drew an analogy between this sort of involvement and that of the élite women who had presented the colours to the volunteer regiments during the French wars.[98] From this perspective, radical women were represented as the moral force of a different kind of female patriotism.

Yet the banners that women bore to the radical rallies of 1819 also allowed for a more subversive, militant construction. At a time when the government was alarmed by rumours of arms drilling and the manufacture of pikes, the female reformers of Royton carried a red flag with the inscription 'Let us die like men [*sic*] and not be sold as slaves'. Another group paraded a banner representing Britannia with the slogan 'God armeth the Patriot'; while a group of female reformers from Galston near Glasgow unfurled one urging Britons to rise and assert their rights.[99]

---

[96] *Manchester Observer*, 17 July 1819.

[97] The Seditious Meetings Act, 57 Geo. III c. 19, or at least its provisions regarding the calling of public meetings and the regulation of lecture rooms, had expired in July 1818, although the government was prepared to implement it again if necessary. See Castlereagh's speech in the Commons at the introduction of the bill, in *Parliamentary Debates*, 25 (25 Jan.–25 Apr. 1817), 603. There were, in fact, calls among the magistrates and property owners for its revival in 1819. See PRO, HO 42/189/312, 351–4.

[98] William Cobbett, *Weekly Political Register*, 23 Oct. 1819, cols. 268–9.

[99] *Champion*, 22 Aug., 7 Nov. 1819.

At many of these meetings, moreover, the ceremonial highlight of female activism was the presentation of red caps of liberty to the male leaders on the hustings. Phrygian caps, of course, were an essential part of Liberty's accoutrement, symbolizing freedom from slavery. They were commonplace in eighteenth-century political discourse, used by radicals and conservatives alike. At the recovery of the King in 1789, for example, the Bank of England had displayed a giant transparency, 15 feet wide by 17 feet high, portraying a triumphant Britannia bearing the staff and cap of liberty.[100] One could hardly find a more respectable sponsor than that. Women, moreover, had sometimes impersonated Liberty in political parades. In 1768, in the wake of the St George's Fields 'Massacre', 'a little girl, representing *Liberty*, with her spear and cap' and 'covered all over with Black Gauze' was drawn in a miniature carriage around Fleet Street and St Paul's 'amidst a numerous concourse of spectators'.[101] More provocatively, the victory parade of Warren and Birch in the 1802 Nottingham election featured a 'French Goddess of Liberty' (or in some accounts a Goddess of Reason) attended by twenty-four virgins dressed in white, 'followed by the Tree of Liberty and the tri-colour'd Flag' and a band of music playing 'Millions be free'. The goddess was clad in 'salmon or flesh-coloured apparel' and in hostile reports readily believed to be 'in a state of ENTIRE NUDITY'.[102] Female liberty-bearers had a long and colourful history.

In 1819 liberty caps were markers of both libertarian and radical revolution. They had British and Gallican connotations, having been part of the symbolic repertoire of the sansculotte and pro-Jacobin artisan since the 1790s, and heavily publicized as such in James Gillray's satirical cartoons. Their Jacobin pedigree was provocative enough for one Lancashire magistrate to declare in 1819 that 'if the Cap of Liberty has now any symbolical meaning the Revolution has actually commenced'.[103] Radicals used this politically ambiguous symbol to revitalize the platform in the early nineteenth century, one that would draw the constitutionalist and Jacobin wings of the movement together. The willingness of women to parade and present liberty caps in 1819 helped to advance this strategy. Their presence upheld the polyvalence of the sign and allowed radicals to assert both the respectability and resolute militancy of their movement.

[100] *Shrewsbury Chronicle*, 2 May 1789.

[101] *Leeds Mercury*, 4 Apr. 1769; *Northampton Mercury*, 3 Apr. 1769.

[102] *The Times*, 20 July 1802; E. P. Thompson, *The Making of the English Working Class* (Harmondsworth, 1968), 493; id., 'The Making of a Ruling Class', *Dissent* (Summer 1993), 381.

[103] John Lloyd, Stockport, June 1819, in PRO, HO 42/188/27–8.

That strategy ultimately backfired. Thomas Wooler believed that women had a 'talismanic' immunity from military assault that would ensure that radical meetings would not be dispersed by force. '*Soldiers* and *police officers,*' he declared, 'they cannot be arrayed against WOMEN!!! That would be despicable in the extreme.'[104] Yet despite the very conspicuous presence of women at the reform meeting at Manchester on 16 August 1819, many of whom had paraded into town with their flags and caps of liberty as members of female reform societies from neighbouring towns, the yeomanry cavalry cut their way across St Peter's Field to arrest the radicals on the hustings and to confiscate their 'subversive' emblems. One cavalryman ceremoniously hoisted up a cap of liberty 'upside down' as if to celebrate his victory over radical forces.[105]

Yet if the meeting was forcibly disrupted by the yeomanry, the radicals themselves were able to draw moral capital from the episode. Over 100 women were wounded or killed in the mêlée, and the picture of cavalrymen cutting down unarmed women scorched the imagination. One poem talked of the '*English Janizaries* of the *north*' dyeing 'their maiden blades in woman's blood'.[106] At a Wakefield reform meeting soon after Peterloo, a radical speaker declared the yeomanry to be 'unnatural monsters to slaughter women . . . may the sweet smile of female affection never beam upon their countenances'.[107] At Sheffield, where female reformers congregated to mourn their fallen sisters, one of the flags displayed a cavalryman cutting down a woman. Indeed, the representations of Peterloo, unlike those of St George's Fields fifty years earlier, regularly foregrounded women as the innocent victims of military repression, despite the fact that there were proportionately as many women wounded or killed in the 1768 'massacre' as in 1819.[108] In 1768 radicals chose an innocent bystander in the shape of

---

[104] *Black Dwarf*, 14 July 1819, 16 Aug. 1820.

[105] *Leeds Mercury*, 4 Sept. 1819. As late as 1831 a conservative curate could regard the topping of an equestrian statue of William III with a tricoloured cap of liberty as a 'revolutionary act'. See [John Eagles], *The Bristol Riots: Their Causes, Progress, and Consequences* (Bristol, 1832), 96.

[106] *Black Dwarf*, 24 Nov. 1819.

[107] *Leeds Mercury*, 4 Sept. 1819; *The Times*, 29 Oct. 1819. Women were not always represented as victims of political repression. At a meeting at Rutherglen, near Glasgow, one of the flags represented women fighting back in the shape of Liberty pummelling a male Tyranny. See *The Times*, 29 Oct. 1819.

[108] In the St George's Fields 'Massacre', seven people were killed of whom two were women, including one, Margaret Walters of the Mint, who was pregnant. Several women were also injured. Yet the Wilkites made little of this, choosing instead to emphasize the death of 19-year-old William Allen at the hands of two grenadiers. On the 1768 'Massacre', see George Rudé, *Wilkes and Liberty* (Oxford, 1962), 51, 54–5, id., *Paris and London in the Eighteenth Century* (London, 1970), 235 n., *Daily Advertiser*, 11, 17 May 1768, and *Westminster Journal*, 14 May 1768.

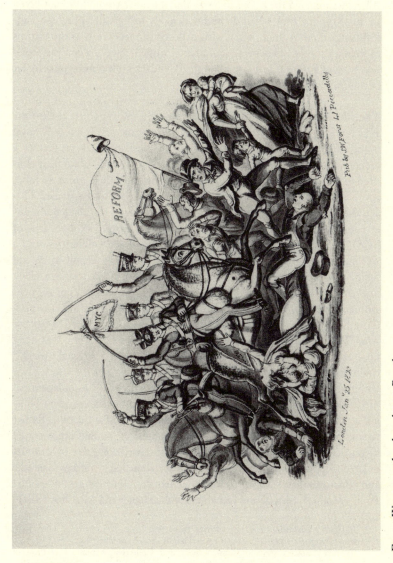

Fɪɢ. 5 Women under the sabre at Peterloo

William Allen, the 19-year-old son of a publican, to highlight military repression, despite the fact that at least one woman, Mary Jeffs, an orange-seller, was shot in the stomach and died at St Thomas's Hospital two hours later.[109] Part of the reason for this, no doubt, was that the coroner's verdict against Allen incriminated the troops in a way that the other verdicts did not. Even so, in 1819, at a time when domestic ideology had greater purchase, radicals singled out women, often with children in their arms, as the victims of military might. This more sentimental trope helped deepen the moral revulsion of Peterloo and expanded the boundaries of public sympathy far beyond the radical constituency.

The advent of female political societies in 1819 was regarded at the time as an 'entirely novel and truly portentous circumstance'.[110] It was only novel in the sense that female radicals developed political organizations that were independent of men and took formal responsibility for educating their children in radical principles and raising money for the radical cause. In other respects it is worth stressing continuities in female political activism. That activism, I have argued, remained rooted in the long-standing traditions of community politics, centring on a desire for customary standards of living, the integrity of family life and neighbourhood solidarities, and a willingness to mobilize a wide repertoire of collective action to defend them. This repertoire changed over the course of the Hanoverian era, albeit unevenly, from an informal politics of riot to a more formal engagement with contemporary politics through petition, address, and the mass platform. Even so, the women of the first political societies continued to espouse what Temma Kaplan has called a 'female consciousness', one that drew upon the conventional division of labour by gender and privileged women's traditional role as the preservers of life.[111] In staking out their new place within the mass platform, women did not stress their role as independent producers within the factory system, nor their right to independent political action as citizens, although this was certainly mooted at the time. Rather they stressed their role as mothers and daughters of families immiserated by burdensome taxes, oppressive laws that outlawed collective bargaining, inflated prices, and a political system that rechannelled resources to an idle and select minority. As the Manchester female reformers reminded 'the Wives, Mothers, Sisters, and Daughters of the Higher and Middling Classes

---

[109] *St James's Chronicle*, 10–12, 14–17 May 1768.
[110] *Annual Register*, 61 (1819), 104, cited in Thomis and Grimmett, *Women in Protest*, 92.
[111] Temma Kaplan, 'Female Consciousness and Collective Action: The Case of Barcelona, 1910–1918', *Signs: Journal of Women in Culture and Society*, 7 (1982), 545–66.

of Society', a 'Male Union' for reform was the only way of battling the 'Borough Tyrants' who had brought them only misery and squalor and would soon degrade 'the middle and useful class of society' as well. 'Dear sister,' the letter continued, 'how could you bear to see the infant at the breast drawing from you the remnant of your last blood, instead of the nourishment which nature requires; the only subsistence for yourselves being a draught of cold water?' It went on to urge their more affluent sisters 'to exert your influence with your fathers, your husbands, your sons, your relatives and your friends' in demanding parliamentary reform and an end to the immiseration they experienced.[112]

Although the female reformers of Manchester were prepared to appeal to the common familial sentiments that potentially united women of all classes, within their own communities they placed burgeoning class priorities over gender claims to political equality. Within two decades, as women's experience of political organization matured, this choice would become tension-fraught and problematic.[113] It was not so in 1819 because women's political activism on the platform was only beginning, and because the political conjuncture of the post-Napoleonic era demanded class solidarity. At a time when political space for reform was such a contentious issue, circumscribed by law and an increasingly visible military presence, female intervention in a traditional idiom was a necessary strategy to reinvigorate radicalism, to disarm critics, and to impress upon the public the community-based nature of popular grievances. How this strategy played itself out in 1820, when Queen Caroline returned to England to reclaim her regal rights, is a subject to which we now turn.

---

[112] *Black Dwarf*, 28 July 1819; also printed in the *Manchester Observer*, 31 July 1819.

[113] See, for example, the letter of Susanna Inge, a member of the Female Charter Association of the City of London, in the *Northern Star* (2 July 1842), 7. The literature on this theme is now extensive. See Dorothy Thompson, 'Women and Nineteenth-Century Radical Politics: A Lost Dimension', in *Outsiders* (London, 1993), 77–102; Jutta Schwartzkopf, *Women in the Chartist Movement* (London, 1991); Anna Clark, *The Struggle for the Breeches* (New York, 1995).

8

Caroline's Crowds

God save Queen Caroline,
Britain's own heroine,
God save the Queen.
Be thou her strength and stay,
In her adversity,
And from dark treachery,
God save the Queen.

(Lines composed by Samuel Bamford,
Manchester Observer, 15 July 1820)

The Queen Caroline affair was the *cause célèbre* of 1820, a political bomb-shell that exploded throughout Britain. From Caroline's sudden return to Britain to reclaim her regal rights until her infamous trial for adultery a few months later, the public was fixated both by the personal battle between the royal dandy, George IV, and his dubiously respectable consort, and by its political and constitutional ramifications. From the beginning the public rallied to the cause of the 'wronged' Queen. Crowds gathered to welcome her and to express sympathy for her ordeal. Countless deputations attended her at Brandenburg House. And the abandonment of the bill which sought to strip her of her royal privileges and pave the way for a royal divorce was greeted with jubilation throughout the country. It was a spectacular popular mobilization, arguably the greatest of the whole Georgian era; one, Hazlitt claimed, that 'struck its roots into the heart of the nation' and 'took possession of every house or cottage in the kingdom'.[1]

Of enormous contemporary interest, the affair was none the less ignored by successive generations of labour historians. G. D. H. Cole made

---

[1] William Hazlitt, *Complete Works*, ed. P. Howe (Toronto, 1934), xx. 136, cited in Thomas W. Laqueur, 'The Queen Caroline Affair: Politics as Art in the Reign of George IV', *Journal of Modern History*, 54 (Sept. 1982), 417.

no mention of it in his short history of the British labour movement. E. P. Thompson glossed over it in *The Making of the English Working Class*.[2] The confrontation between two royal incorrigibles seemed incidental to the main narrative of working-class history which centred upon the post-war depression, the rebirth of the popular political societies, Peterloo, and the working-class struggles of the Reform Bill and beyond. While a few historians of the next generation sought to integrate the episode back into the orthodox framework of labour-radical history,[3] the Queen Caroline affair has largely served to highlight different histories. To Craig Calhoun the event was the last great populist agitation, one that exemplified the traditional and non-class character of British radicalism prior to the 1820s.[4] To Thomas Laqueur the radical critique of monarchy that the affair promised to generate relapsed into melodrama and royalist fantasy, underscoring ultimately the extent to which the political system was deeply grounded in the libertarian conventions of the previous century and stable enough to withstand the blasphemies of political misrule.[5] And if this interpretation imparted to the affair the comic and cathartic qualities of a royal soap opera, feminist historians stressed the degree to which that 'soap' was gendered. To Anna Clark the Caroline agitation was 'the last spectacular eruption of transgressive, unruly plebeian radicalism', one that laid bare the fraught and fractured sexual politics of labouring families.[6] To Davidoff and Hall it prefigured, in the idealization of Caroline as the 'symbol of dependent womanhood' and as a wife to whom connubial felicity had been denied, the more sedate sexual politics of the Victorian middle class.[7] Clearly the Queen Caroline affair has come to mean many things. It has become grist for a postmodern reading; one that reveres difference and 'ex-centricity' and refuses to totalize.

---

[2] 'Into the humbug of the Queen's case we need not inquire. It displayed every vice of the Radical movement . . . on the largest scale.' E. P. Thompson, *The Making of the English Working Class* (Harmondsworth, 1968), 778. Thompson recanted from this view in a subsequent book review. See 'The Very Type of Respectable Artisan', *New Society* (3 May 1979), 176.

[3] Iorwerth Prothero, *Artisans and Politics in Early Nineteenth-Century London* (London, 1979), ch. 7. See also John Stevenson, 'The Queen Caroline Affair', in J. Stevenson (ed.), *London in the Age of Reform* (London, 1977), 117–48, where the affair is seen as the last great London-dominated popular agitation.

[4] Craig Calhoun, *The Question of Class Struggle* (Chicago, 1982), 105–15.

[5] Laqueur, 'The Queen Caroline Affair', 417–66. For a different reading of the political misrule of 1820, see Roger Sales, *English Literature in History: 1780–1830 Pastoral and Politics* (London, 1983), 178–86.

[6] Anna Clark, 'Queen Caroline and the Sexual Politics of Popular Culture in London, 1820', *Representations*, 31 (Summer 1990), 31–68.

[7] Leonore Davidoff and Catherine Hall, *Family Fortunes: Men and Women of the English Middle Class 1780–1850* (London, 1987), 149–55.

I do not propose such a reading here, although I certainly acknowledge that the appeal of Caroline was richly connotative, polysemic, and diverse, conducted in a variety of genres, melodramatic, sentimental, parodic. What interests me about the Queen Caroline affair, and what has not been emphasized, is how the diverse perspectives of Caroline's plight could generate a unified ensemble of meanings that were compelling enough to thwart a royal divorce and to compromise ministerial policy. Critical to the chain of equivalences that polarized the public against the crown and ministry was the double articulation of the Queen as the victim of domestic and political oppression. In the latter case, it was the injustice of a political trial through the unusual precedent of a Bill of Pains and Penalties and the under-hand, secretive manner in which the evidence against the Queen was collected that made Caroline's plight homologous to that of a burgeoning radical movement reeling from the effects of Peterloo and the Six Acts. Both Queen and 'People' could be seen as victims of political iniquity, of a debased oligarchy that had lost its legitimacy to rule. Such a construction had a particular resonance in the industrial North where the airing of economic and political grievances had been thwarted by the legal armoury of the Combination and Gagging Acts and outright repression. Seen in this context, the Caroline affair was not a populist moment without class resonances, nor one where gender identities preponderated over those of class; but one in which class and gender identities were fruitfully, if temporarily, combined. Far from being a diversion from radical working-class politics, the Queen's cause was successfully brought within its ambit, although radical leaders never lost sight of its contingent and delimiting possibilities as a focus for their discontents.

Without doubt the Queen Caroline affair was a woman's question that drew conspicuous support from women on her behalf. Building on the resurgence of female political activism during and after the Napoleonic wars, women of the propertied and working classes rallied to the Queen. Middle-class wives and daughters attended civic and parochial deputations to the Queen. They organized tea parties in her honour and their presence was very conspicuous at the Queen's triumphal procession to St Paul's in November where they were said to have crowded the balconies hours before the formal proceedings began.[8] Lower-class women played their part,

---

[8] *Leeds Mercury*, 2 Dec. 1820. 'As early as eight o'clock crowds of elegantly dressed ladies took their seats in the different houses along the line of procession. Their appearance contradicted . . . the vile slanders of those who have unblushingly asserted that none but the very meanest order of Females commiserated with the sufferings of the Queen. We never, on any occasion, recollect to have seen a brighter or more fascinating assemblage of female loveliness . . . than the windows of Fleet-street and Ludgate-hill presented.'

too. At Sibsey, on the abandonment of the bill, 'men, women and children of both sexes assembled rejoicingly, then paraded the streets . . . accompanied by a band of music'.[9] At Liverpool, the female cordwainers and several female friendly societies, one specifically named after the Queen, joined the jubilant procession in her honour, as indeed they did at Chorley and Chester.[10] So close was the bond that some working-class women felt towards the Queen that they presented her with gifts. The female straw plait weavers of the Midlands offered her a bonnet; the Loughborough lacemakers a dress; five poor women from Sandwich even sent her 'a very fine fat pig'.[11]

A particularly important way of garnering support for the Queen was for women to sign addresses on her behalf that were independent of those of their menfolk. Papers of very different political persuasions such as *The Times* and the *Republican* encouraged women to associate in this manner, on the grounds that it was 'natural that a more exquisite feeling should exist in their bosoms on this subject, than in those of their husbands, fathers, or brothers'.[12] To this call women responded. Although a few middle-class women had qualms about entering the public sphere in this way—the organizer of one address apologetically remarked that she gave up a week 'usually devoted to the more tranquil and not less honourable cares of her family' to rally support for the Queen[13]—many women took to the task with gusto and thousands of signatures were raised in a matter of days. Approximately twenty-seven female addresses were presented to Caroline soliciting well over 70,000 signatures. They not only hailed from established radical centres such as London, Bristol, Nottingham, and from the industrial North, but from St Ives near Huntingdon, Shrewsbury, Truro, and Beverley.[14]

---

[9] *The Times*, 17 Nov. 1820.

[10] *Liverpool Mercury*, 24 Nov., 1 Dec. 1820; *British Press*, 29 Dec. 1820.

[11] *Morning Chronicle*, 20 Nov. 1820; Laqueur, 'The Queen Caroline Affair', 427.

[12] *Republican*, 21 Apr., 21 July 1820; *The Times*, 28 Sept. 1820. Women did also sign town addresses wherever they were allowed to do so. At Framlingham in Suffolk, for example, the address was signed by 1,105 men and 1,084 women. See A. F. J. Brown, *Chartism in Essex and Suffolk* (Chelmsford, 1982), 16.

[13] *Champion*, 19 Aug. 1820. The address stressed how 'unaccustomed' the ladies were to 'public acts'.

[14] Nine female addresses are listed in the *Annual Register* (Sept. 1820), 423–4. From this source, Home Office files, and newspapers I have recovered the following: Ashton-under-Lyne, Bath, Beverley, Blackburn, Bray, Bristol, Clifton and Kingsdown (Bristol suburbs), Edinburgh, Exeter, Halifax, Leeds, Leicester, Lewes, London (Married Ladies), Manchester, Marylebone (Married Ladies), Newcastle under Lyme, Newcastle upon Tyne and Gateshead, Nottingham, St Anne Limehouse, St Ives, St Luke's Islington, Sheffield, Shrewsbury, Southampton, Truro, Warrington, Worcester. The last was disputed by *Berrow's Worcester Journal*, 30 Nov. 1820, although to my knowledge no one challenged the veracity of the others.

In some instances, these addresses were the result of concerted pressure to participate in what was emphatically seen as a 'woman's cause'. At Newcastle, for example, where women were initially excluded from the address sponsored by the town's radicals, they campaigned successfully for their own.[15]

In these ventures women frequently identified with the Queen as the bereaved mother and victimized wife, in terms that often expressed their own anxieties or experience of domestic strife. Caroline's daughter, Princess Charlotte, had been a popular figure, idealized as a romantic heroine who had defied her father and married for love before dying in childbirth in 1817. Her loss had been especially felt by her mother, or so it was projected, because Caroline's access to her daughter had been restricted upon separation from her husband. Among other things, she was neither informed about nor invited to her funeral. Caroline's own ill-treatment by the future George IV, moreover, was notorious. The Prince, whose earlier marriage to the Catholic widow Mrs Fitzherbert had never been officially recognized, had been induced to marry his cousin, Caroline of Brunswick, in the hope that parliament would redeem his debts. It was a marriage of convenience from the beginning, and within a year the royal couple had gone their separate ways. Not content with this estrangement, however, George vigorously probed into Caroline's extra-marital behaviour in the hopes of securing a divorce while he caroused with his mistresses. When female addressers alluded to the 'Delicate Investigation' of 1807,[16] the occasion when the Prince unsuccessfully accused his wife of bearing an illegitimate child, they placed the 1820 ordeal within the same persecutory narrative. Indeed, because that ordeal was carried on before an unreformed parliament rather than a normal court of law, and according to procedures that seemed highly prejudicial to the defence, it was doubly damning. Not only did it shield the King's infidelities from public exposure and reinforce the double standard, but it set dubious precedents for the future. As the Ladies of Edinburgh insisted in their address to the Queen:

the principles and doctrines now advanced by your accusers do not apply to your case alone, but if made part of the law of this land, may hereafter be applied as a precedent by every careless and dissipated husband to rid himself of his wife, however good and innocent she may be, and to render his family, however amiable,

---

[15] *Champion*, 16 July 1820. For the radical origins of the address, see PRO, HO 52/1/351–2.
[16] See the address from the Female Inhabitants of Halifax, printed in the *Champion*, 16 Sept. 1820.

illegitimate; thereby destroying the sacred bond of matrimony, and rendering all domestic felicity uncertain.[17]

Caroline's marital ordeal was thus identified with women's vulnerability within marriage; her legal disabilities with theirs. No female address used the royal scandal to develop a critique of the legal status of women within marriage, still less to campaign for a reform of the divorce laws.[18] Caroline's female supporters chose rather to frame their arguments within the context of conjugal fidelity and obligation. In defending the Queen's honour female addressers were implicitly vindicating their own status as wives and mothers within the companionate family. Yet this rather sentimental and largely middle-class reconstruction of Caroline had to address the thorny question of Caroline's innocence and purity. Caroline, after all, was no paragon of virtue. There were enough rumours circulating about her indiscretions at the time of the Delicate Investigation to question her respectability, let alone the gossip that crossed the Channel concerning her gaddings on the continent. Lady Bury saw her at a Genevan party in 1814 'dressed *en Venus*, or rather not dressed further than the waist'. Others reported her posing for a portrait as the repentant Magdalene, 'her person very much exposed'.[19] More significantly, her association with her Italian courier, Bartolomeo Bergami, appeared to be more than a close working relationship, as loyalist caricatures of the couple mischievously depicted.[20] In fact, Bergami's rapid promotion in the royal household did little to allay these rumours. Caroline's supporters sometimes tried to fob all this off as a matter of manners rather than morals. Her flamboyance and lack of protocol had been misinterpreted. 'A woman of unguarded, and sometimes of even unfeminine manners', remarked the *Examiner*, her only fault was a 'grossness of impulse'.[21] Not everyone, of course, found this very convincing. A Derbyshire man believed there was 'not a bigger whore in Billingsgate' and that her sexual promiscuity had to be 'huddled up' lest it damage her cause.[22] As a symbol of innocence there is no doubt that Caroline was an unstable signifier.

---

[17] *British Press*, 14 Sept. 1820. See also the Queen's reply to the female inhabitants of Bristol, which makes the same point. *British Mercury*, 25 Sept. 1820.

[18] The question of divorce reform was raised in the *Black Dwarf*, 19 July 1820. The paper opposed easier access to divorce on the grounds that it would engender greater marital discord and diminish parental affection and obligation.

[19] Stevenson, 'The Queen Caroline Affair', 119; Alan Palmer, *George IV* (London, 1975), 85.

[20] See *The New Pilgrim's Progress; or, A Journey to Jerusalem* (London, 1820), in *Radical Squibs and Loyal Ripostes*, ed. Edgell Rickword (Bath, 1971), 237–68. See also the *British Monitor*, 27 Aug. 1820, on the 'Adventures of La Dame Caroline'.

[21] *Examiner*, 27 Aug. 1820.   [22] PRO, HO 40/15/343–4.

To some this did not matter. Caroline was a victim of familial mal-evolence, driven from 'the path of virtue' by a drunken, dishonest, and profligate husband.[23] More positively, the Queen was perfectly justified in taking a lover once her husband had denied her consortium; a line of argument that had a particular resonance for plebeian women, for whom common-law marriages (and desertion) were not unusual.[24] In any case, the spectacle of a pot-bellied debauchee taking his wife to court for adultery smacked of sheer hypocrisy, as did the spectacle of known aristocratic liber-tines sitting in judgment upon her. As the *Republican* remarked, 'a brothel never held together such a set of indecent fellows'.[25] In the ribald tradition of plebeian radicalism, the whole affair took on a comic and satirical char-acter.[26] The King had been cuckolded; his masculinity undermined by a defiant female who had paid him in kind for his infidelities. When the people of Kentish Town carried about a 'hideous, bloated effigy' of the King at the abandonment of the Bill of Pains and Penalties, they were no doubt thinking that he had received his come-uppance in more ways than one.[27]

For those who wished to sustain the image of Caroline as the innocent, injured party, there was always the escape route of the trial itself. The King did not prosecute the Queen for divorce, at least not directly. That would have brought his own infidelities on the carpet. Instead, the law officers of the crown introduced a Bill of Pains and Penalties in the Lords in an attempt to degrade the Queen for an 'adulterous intercourse' with Bergami, adding a divorce clause as a corollary. Normally such bills were reserved for near-treasonable offences of public import, not matrimonial causes, but the King was interested in a swift divorce before a court he could trust to do his business. Lord Liverpool protested that, had the Queen respected her bar-gain to stay out of the country on a generous pension, all this would have been unnecessary.[28] To this the Queen's supporters replied that the whole process was unconstitutional and 'unmanly'; especially so, since the King

---

[23] *Republican* (10 Nov. 1820), 364. See also the *Black Dwarf* (14 June 1820), 809. 'If the wife had erred, the first question asked is, *How did her husband treat her?*'

[24] Clark, 'Queen Caroline', 48; John R. Gillis, *For Better, for Worse: British Marriages, 1600 to the Present* (New York, 1985), 111, 190–228; David A. Kent, ' "Gone for a Soldier": Family Breakdown and the Demography of Desertion in a London Parish, 1750–1791', *Local Population Studies*, 45 (1990), 27–42. Kent reveals that over 12% of all parish examinations for St Martin-in-the-Fields, 1750–91, involved desertions.

[25] *Republican* (20 Oct. 1820), 354.

[26] See Iain McCalman, *Radical Underworld* (Cambridge, 1988), 162–77.

[27] *Examiner*, 12 Nov. 1820.

[28] On the failure to negotiate a settlement with the Queen to keep her in exile and the decision to introduce a Bill of Pains and Penalties against her, see J. E. Cookson, *Lord Liverpool's Administration: The Crucial Years 1815–1822* (Hamden, Conn., 1973), 229–49.

was not officially a party to the suit. Wooler declared such bills were 'mere arbitrary inventions . . . unwarrantable expedients to gratify the vengeance of power for destroying persons whose actions had not exposed them to punishment by law'.[29]

The evidence culled to substantiate this 'mockery of justice' was equally damaging. Collected by the Hanoverian envoy to Rome through the auspices of spies and informers and presented to the Lords in a green bag, it reeked of intrigue and conspiracy. The bag quickly became a symbol of all that was rotten in the case, and the Queen's supporters were soon trampling green bags under foot, parading them derisively on a pole, hawking their 'Last Dying Speech and Confession', or kicking them around like a football.[30] To compound matters, the actual testimony used in the trial was far from conclusive. The crown prosecutors mustered evidence of Bergami kissing and plausibly fondling the Queen, of preparing her bath and (as secretaries were wont) having easy access to her bedroom. They speculated on what went on during the sea voyage from Jaffa to Italy, when Caroline and Bergami reclined on the deck of a polacca beneath a closed awning. But ultimately the Attorney-General resorted to the argument that the Queen's 'degrading familiarity' with Bergami was prima-facie evidence of her adultery. When the prime Italian witness, Theodore Majocchi, wilted under cross-examination, the Opposition press had a field day. His frequent response to Brougham's questioning, 'Non mi ricordo', became the butt of ridicule and satire, displayed on placards and converted into verse:

> Sometimes it means 'I do forget,'
> Sometimes it means 'I don't',
> And very often it will stand
> For 'rather not' or 'won't.'
>
> Sometimes with very little help
> It means both No and Yes,
> Or something rather less than more,
> Or rather more than less.[31]

In the circumstances the Queen's innocence seemed clear enough. Would she have returned to England, her supporters asked, if the evidence against her had been incriminating? Under British law and in the face of questionable testimony, was she not entitled to the presumption of innocence?

---

[29] *Black Dwarf*, 30 Aug. 1820.
[30] *Liverpool Mercury*, 25 Aug. 1820; *British Press*, 14, 30 Nov. 1820; *Morning Chronicle*, 26 Nov. 1820; PRO, HO 52/1/358–9.
[31] *Examiner*, 27 Aug. 1820.

Popular sympathy for the Queen could draw on male chivalry and female disgust at her ill-treatment by her husband. But it also drew on clear comparisons between the Queen's predicament and those of the politically excluded. Just as the Queen was the victim of ministerial power, and, by extension, of the 'Borough-mongering System', so, too, was the bulk of the population whose post-war economic grievances had been ignored and whose meetings had been repressed. At the time of the Caroline affair, a good many radical and labour leaders were in gaol or awaiting trial;[32] often, as was the Queen, on the testimony of spies and informers. This was recognized by the radical press and by the Queen's supporters, who saw in the Queen's ordeal an echo of their own oppression. Many addresses linked the Queen's cause with the constitutional rights of the people. Some alluded to other victims of ministerial power such as Henry Hunt, the radical orator arrested for his role at Peterloo, who had urged his supporters to rally to the Queen.[33] Those from Manchester predictably identified the Queen's plight with the assault upon popular liberties at St Peter's Field the previous year, when eleven people were killed and over 400 injured by the sabres of the local yeomanry cavalry. 'The same power which scourged us is now oppressing you', the artisans and mechanics declared; 'it is not less our interest than our duty, therefore, to stand up against your Majesty's enemies, who are also the enemies of the rights and liberties of the whole People.'[34] These sentiments were voiced in both Manchester and Ashton-under-Lyne on the anniversary of Peterloo where the Queen's cause was taken up by the mourners.[35] They were reiterated at the celebrations of Henry Hunt's birthday in industrial Lancashire where toasts to the Queen accompanied those to Hunt, to Cartwright, to the 'cause of liberty all over

[32] Thompson cites seventeen, including Henry Hunt, Thomas Wooler, Richard Carlile, Sir Francis Burdett, and Sir Charles Wolseley. Thompson, *The Making*, 768. To this list one should add the spinners and weavers imprisoned under the Combination Acts. See A. Aspinall, *The Early English Trade Unions* (London, 1949), 314–15; R. G. Kirby and A. E. Musson, *The Voice of the People: John Doherty, 1798–1854* (Manchester, 1975), 22–3. For a fairly detailed list of those arrested or waiting trial, see the returns of prosecutions for political libel and seditious conduct, HO 52/2/378–530.

[33] See, for example, the address from the women of Ashton-under-Lyne, printed in the *Manchester Observer*, 25 Nov. 1820. For Hunt's letter to the 'male and female reformers' of England, Scotland, and Ireland, urging them to support the Queen, see PRO, HO 48/24, dated 25 July 1820.

[34] *Black Dwarf*, 30 Aug. 1820. For similar sentiments, see the address of the females of Ashton-under-Lyne, printed in the *Manchester Observer*, 25 Nov. 1820. The Manchester letter attracted the attention of the law officers of the crown, who thought it 'mischievous', but not libellous enough to merit prosecution. See PRO, HO 48/25, 4 Sept. 1820.

[35] *Manchester Observer*, 19 Aug. 1820. A copy can be found in PRO, HO 40/14/167–70.

the world', and, significantly, to 'Labour, the source of wealth';[36] and again somewhat later, on the release of the leaders of the striking cotton spinners from Lancaster Castle.[37] The association of the Queen's plight with radical grievances was also to be found in Glasgow and in Liverpool, where a radical declared before a meeting of over 1,000 people that 'of all the Conspiracies entered into by the Ministers, this against the Queen was the most base—Even more base than that of Oliver and the Derby conspiracy; or than that by which Brandreth suffered, *whose blood*, with that of others shed upon the scaffold, still *cried out for Vengeance*'.[38]

The remark of the Liverpool radical revealed the insurrectionary impulse that still smouldered in the North and Midlands in the aftermath of the Cato Street conspiracy and the Grange Moor uprising, when 300 or so radicals from the textile villages around Barnsley and Huddersfield assembled with the aim of establishing a 'free Government'.[39] In the wake of those failures, the central problem confronting the popular movement in 1820 was how to re-establish the radical platform in the wake of the Six Acts. Those Acts, as is well known, placed very severe restrictions on popular assembly and the press, reinforcing the government's powers of search, arrest, and imprisonment and closing down public space for the airing of popular grievances, whether political or economic. The Queen's affair provided the radicals with an opportunity to challenge this repressive regime and they took it. As Hunt astutely pointed out, 'no seditious meeting act can apply to her [Caroline], no multitude, however numberous, can be deemed sedition for its numbers'.[40] Early in January 1820 a London spy reported that 'fellows with *Horns* were *proclaiming* the arrival of the Queen and selling papers to that effect'.[41] This mock proclamation

---

[36] *Manchester Observer*, 11, 18, 25 Nov. 1820. The Queen was toasted at radical meetings at Manchester, Oldham, Preston, Ashton-under-Lyne, Royton, Leigh, Bolton, and Stockport. For this radical culture, see James Epstein, 'Radical Dining, Toasting, and Symbolic Expression in Early Nineteenth-Century Lancashire: Rituals of Solidarity', *Albion*, 20/2 (Summer 1988), 271–91.

[37] *Manchester Observer*, 3 Mar. 1821. The toast ran: 'Queen Caroline—may she always remember that she has identified her interests with those of the people.'

[38] PRO, HO 40/15/135. For Glasgow, see HO 40/14/138.

[39] For the Grange Moor rising, see Thompson, *The Making*, 776–7. See also the depositions in HO 48/23. In Sheffield insurgents planned to capture weapons from the local barracks in preparation for a general rising of the North in April 1820. See F. K. Donnelly and J. L. Baxter, 'Sheffield and the English Revolutionary Tradition, 1791–1820', *Int. Review of Social History*, 20 (1974), 419–20.

[40] PRO, HO 48/24, 25 July 1820. The law officers marked this passage in Hunt's open letter to the reformers. They were obviously very troubled by its implications.

[41] PRO, HO 40/15/6.

proved premature, but once the agitation in favour of the Queen gathered momentum upon the arrival of the Queen in England on 5 June, it proved virtually unstoppable. Political caricatures and squibs, hard to prosecute under the Six Acts, rolled off the radical presses. In July John Shergoe reported that 'Men & Boys have been employed by Benbow, Fairburn &c to circulate in the metropolis & for 50 miles round it, vast quantities of Bills, Placards and publications of a seditious and inflammatory nature, with a view to inflame the passions of the Lower orders into acts of Violence agst the Constituted Authorities & . . . to stop the investigation in the House of Lords respecting the Queen.'[42] Within weeks similar handbills were circulating as far afield as Stockton, Yarmouth, Weston-super-Mare, and Penzance. In Somerset one correspondent reported that 'every village is explored by the Hawkers who distribute Papers relative to the Queen, her Trial, her Misfortunes, her injuries &c. These are openly disseminated as not being liable to the charge of sedition, however they may partake of a seditious character.' Written in prose and verse, the author continued, 'they now supply the place of Tales and Ballads' and were remarkably successful in soliciting support for the Queen.[43]

Accompanying this sea of seditious and often ribald literature were the mass meetings and processions to Brandenburg House, some of which were technically illegal under the provisions of the Seditious Meetings Prevention Act of 1819.[44] Early on in the Queen Caroline agitation, magistrates had monitored meetings held to address the Queen to ensure they did not detour from their official agenda.[45] But as the campaign for Caroline gathered momentum, magistrates thought it inadvisable to intervene, and many trades marched to Hammersmith in their thousands, sporting white favours, trade emblems, and sometimes clear referents to the royal controversy. 'Every Wednesday,' wrote Thomas Creevey, referring to the parades through London, 'the scene which caused such alarm at Manchester

[42] PRO, HO 40/15/33. On political satires that circumvented the Six Acts, see J. Ann Hone, *For the Cause of Truth: Radicalism in London 1796–1821* (Oxford, 1982), 345–6.

[43] PRO, HO 40/14/273; for the other areas, see PRO, HO 40/14/43, 84–5, 359–60.

[44] 60 Geo. III and 1 Geo. IV c. 6 banned all unauthorized meetings of fifty or more persons held 'upon any public Grievance, or upon any matter in Church or State, or of considering, proposing or agreeing to any Petition, Complaint, Remonstrance, Declaration, Resolution, or Address upon the Subject thereof'. Notice of such a meeting had to be delivered personally to resident JPs six days ahead of schedule. Meetings of corporate bodies were exempt from this Act, among others, and so the incorporated trades and parishes that addressed the Queen could presumably claim exemption under this provision. In addition, seditious flags or banners, and marching to music or in a military order, were forbidden at all meetings.

[45] Henry Jephson, *The Platform: Its Rise and Progress*, 2 vols. (New York, 1892), i. 435–6.

is repeated under the very nose of Parliament and all the constituted authorities, and in a tenfold degree more alarming.'[46] This may have been hyper-
bole, but the main point was correct. 'All the *six new acts* that were to crush
the radicals', remarked Wooler, 'are only available for *waste paper*.'[47] The
best that the government could do was to ensure the allegiance of the troops
in the 150-odd barracks throughout the country; a goal that seemed dis-
concertingly difficult amid incidents of soldiers fraternizing with radicals
and a near-mutiny in London.[48]

The central fact is that Caroline's supporters successfully reappropri-
ated public space and created the conditions in which the ministry ultimately backed away from prosecuting the Queen. As Cobbett remarked,
the abandonment of the bill was 'THE PEOPLE'S TRIUMPH over those who
had so long triumphed over them'.[49] This was recognized in the victory
celebrations. Alongside the placards and transparencies heralding the
triumph of 'Virtue' and 'Innocence' were those that underscored the
popular contribution to the victory. On the first night of the rejoicings in
London William Hone displayed a blue flag inscribed to 'The People' over
his house on Ludgate Hill. In Holborn, a fellow printer exhibited a transparency of the Queen whose motto ran: 'The glorious effects of public opinion, and its best ally, a *free* press.' On the Strand, another enclosed a printing
press within a triumphal arch over which hung a cap of liberty, the emblem
of popular defiance against repression and of popular rights, both legal and
democratic.[50] In Southwark, where Cobbett believed the illuminations to
have been brightest, a supporter displayed a bust of the Queen encircled
in laurel leaves. Underneath were the very words that Caroline had used
in her response to the artisans' address in August: 'The industrious
classes constitute the chief energy of the nation. In the great fabric of society, they are the strength at the bottom which supports the ornament at

[46] Cited by Cookson, *Lord Liverpool's Administration*, 270. For the parades, see Robert Huish, *Memoirs of Caroline, Queen Consort of England*, 2 vols. (London, 1821), ii. 591–615; J. H. Adolphus, *The Royal Exile, or Memoirs of Caroline*, 2 vols. (London, 1821), ii. 440–2.

[47] *Black Dwarf*, 25 Oct. 1820.

[48] PRO, HO 40/14/152–3, 208, 329–30; 40/15/139–40; Stevenson, 'The Queen Caroline Affair', 123–4; *The Greville Diary*, ed. Philip Whitwell Wilson, 2 vols. (London, 1927), i. 127. Several privates in the Leicestershire militia actually had the courage to address the Queen. The Lord Lieutenant of the county, the Duke of Rutland, demanded to know who they were, but received no satisfaction from Alderman Wood, who informed him instead that he had received an address from 300 more men sympathizing with their action. See *Black Dwarf*, 30 Aug. 1820.

[49] *Cobbett's Weekly Political Register* (18 Nov. 1820), 1211.

[50] *Examiner*, 12 Nov. 1820. On the richly connotative character of the cap of liberty, see James Epstein, 'Understanding the Cap of Liberty: Symbolic Practice and Social Conflict in Early Nineteenth-Century England', *Past and Present*, 122 (Feb. 1989), 75–188.

the top.'[51] Outside London, too, the people's contribution to the victory was emphasized: at Chorley with a banner applauding 'The Power of Public Opinion'; at Dewsbury, with the motto 'Public Opinion triumphant'; at Linlithgow, with a representation of 'Britannia in triumph, holding a Cap of Liberty, and a British Tar holding a flag with the inscription "Britons never shall be slaves".'[52]

This aspect of the 1820 demonstrations has been played down in accounts of the Queen Caroline affair, which have concentrated instead on the more traditional, transgressive character of collective action; at least outside London. Craig Calhoun, for instance, saw the jubilations surrounding the bill as spontaneous rather than organized, as more prominent in the rural areas of the South than in the radical North, as more carnivalesque than radical. The agitation, he claimed, represented a 'jarring shift away from that which led to Peterloo'.[53] Similarly, Tom Laqueur, while recognizing that the celebrations constituted a 'massive, unprecedented political mobilization against an incumbent government', viewed them as 'highly personalized', xenophobic, and 'still expressed through the rituals of the old regime'. [54] Indeed, both invoked, albeit in somewhat different contexts, Max Gluckman's notion of the 'rituals of rebellion' to suggest that the demonstrations, and the discourses in which they were embedded, were parodying power rather than subverting it.[55]

It is certainly true that the jubilations resonated with the rituals of inversion. William Hone's transparency, exhibited on three occasions in November 1820, depicted a triumphant and incandescent Britannia displaying a cap of liberty in one hand and a wreath of the injured Queen in the other, while ministerial vermin scattered in all directions.[56] As for the King himself, he was submerged in the filth of his own accusations, his boots and crotch in the air, his crown soiled by a slop pail in which floated a tricolour. It was an image that appropriated patriot virtue for the Queen, lampooned loyalist alarmism, specifically the accusation that Caroline's supporters were Jacobin subversives, and proudly proclaimed the power of the press. It also literally turned the King upside down.

---

[51] *Examiner*, 12 Nov. 1820; *Cobbett's Weekly Political Register* (18 Nov. 1820), 1214. For the Queen's reply to the artisans and mechanics' address, see the *Champion* (19 Aug. 1820), 531.

[52] *British Press*, 25 Nov. 1820; *Leeds Mercury*, 25 Nov. 1820; *Liverpool Mercury*, 1 Dec. 1820.

[53] Calhoun, *Class Struggle*, 108–15.

[54] Laqueur, 'The Queen Caroline Affair', 456–7, 464–5.

[55] Calhoun, *Class Struggle*, 114 n.; Laqueur, 'The Queen Caroline Affair', 465 n.

[56] For an exposition of the vermin, see *The Political Showman: At Home!* in *Radical Squibs*, 276–92.

FIG. 6 The Transparency of William Hone

Such symbolism was familiarly carnivalesque, as were many of the street jubilations. They featured bells, bands, fireworks, and illuminations. They involved attacks upon aristocratic supporters of the bill, and jeers against known adulterers, especially the King himself, who was reviled in the familiar idiom of cuckoldry or proclaimed, ironically, as one who had not been cuckolded by his 'innocent' Queen.[57] The jubilations often culminated in effigy-burnings of the principal Italian witnesses; not out of sheer xenophobia, but as a demonstration of revulsion against the perjured lackeys of a corrupt ministry.[58] Hence their *autos-da-fé* in conjunction with green bags. At Tiverton, for example, where the procession of the friendly societies featured 'an elegantly-dressed female on horseback carrying the cap of liberty' and 'Britannia on horseback, supported on each side by young men with drawn swords', effigies of Majocchi, Sacchi, and Demont, the principal witnesses against the Queen, were drawn in a cart accompanied by an executioner and 1,200 persons. Later that evening, the effigies were committed to the bonfire along with a combustible green bag full of serpents.[59]

The celebrations for Caroline also featured dinners for the better sort and tokens of largess for the crowd: ale and ox roastings. In the larger centres such victuals were often raised by subscriptions from the Queen's supporters and were dispensed to the poor. At Horbury, for instance, four fat sheep were purchased by public subscription and roasted at the public houses for 420 poor men, who were each given a pint of ale. (Their female counterparts had to make do with tea.[60]) In smaller centres the local gentry would do their paternal duty in a similar fashion, and in some of the new industrial districts factory masters assumed the same role. At Heckmondwike, for example, it was reported that 'the principal manufacturers regaled their workmen in the most liberal manner with roast beef, ale &c.' The same was true at Congleton, Knutsford, and Nottingham, while at Merthyr Tydfil the ironmaster William Crawshay inaugurated the proceedings with an impressive cannonade.[61]

---

[57] See the demonstrations at Manchester and Ormskirk, reported in the *Liverpool Mercury*, 1 Dec. 1820, where celebrants mischievously paraded flags on the abandonment of the bill with the words, 'Heaven be praised! the king is not a cuckold!'

[58] To underscore this point it is noteworthy that the Queen's own Italian witnesses were welcomed with a street parade when they arrived at Dover. See *Champion*, 7 Oct. 1820, *Bristol Mercury*, 9 Oct. 1820.

[59] *British Press*, 14 Dec. 1820.   [60] *Leeds Mercury*, 9 Dec. 1820.

[61] *Leeds Mercury*, 18 Nov. 1820; Laqueur, 'The Queen Caroline Affair', 456; *Bristol Mercury*, 20 Nov. 1820.

Yet to describe these demonstrations as simply carnivalesque, steeped in the paternalistic rituals of the old regime, would be to understate their complexity and significance. To begin with, many celebrations were not spontaneous expressions of joy at the abandonment of the bill. Although bells were rung and candles set out on the news of its withdrawal, many communities organized a 'general illumination' days, even weeks, later. These were choreographed events, with parades, processions, public meetings, dinners, and allegorical transparencies; that is, magic lantern-type representations of the victory. Like the dinner toasts and the style and content of the processions, they expressed different and sometimes competing narratives of the event. Some saw the 'defeat' of the bill as an opportunity, however implausible, for a royal reconciliation, presumably on the fiction that the King had been ill-advised. Thus a transparency at Colchester portrayed 'Fame, with a wreath; a Dove with an olive branch; two Crowns, with "G.R." and "C.R." '[62] The ladies of Tenterden, to take a different example, focused on the Queen's innocence, staging a procession in which an 'elegant figure of a female dressed in white satin, and richly ornamented with white ribbons' was paraded through the town. Others cast the withdrawal of the bill as a Whig victory. At Chorley, the parade of the friendly societies featured a flag in which the Queen was seen sweeping away the Bill of Pains and Penalties with a broom, a pun on Henry Brougham, the Queen's principal counsel at the trial. At Newent in Gloucestershire, someone impersonating the Whig lawyer was chaired through the village and assigned 'an appropriate speech' for the occasion.[63]

In Lancashire, however, the celebrations were replete with radical signifiers. At Middleton, the procession of the green bag was led by a man wearing a cap of liberty, a symbolic act that no doubt fed conservative fears that radicals were using the Queen's cause to subvert the monarchy. The evening's convivialities concluded with healths to Henry Hunt and to parliament reform. At Haggate, on the moors near the Yorkshire border, celebrants toasted 'The Queen—and may she advocate the cause of the people as they have done her.'[64] At Eccles, they raised their glasses to a 'Radical Reform in the representation of the People'. In Oldham, the radical message was as blunt. A cottage in Jackson's Pits displayed in one window the motto 'Non mi ricordo'. Opposite was a slogan redolent of Peterloo: 'Give us Liberty.'[65]

---

[62] *British Press*, 25 Nov. 1820.

[63] *Morning Chronicle*, 23 Nov. 1820; *Manchester Observer*, 2 Dec. 1820.

[64] *Manchester Observer*, 2 Dec. 1820.   [65] Ibid. 25 Nov., 16 Dec. 1820.

The celebrations were also contentious in a context to which I have already alluded; the control of public space. Tory magistrates sometimes refused to agree to general illuminations; or, because there was some doubt as to whether the laws pertaining to public meetings applied to 'merry-makings', did their utmost to compromise their success.[66] Troops were alerted; special constables enlisted. Publicans were threatened with the loss of their licences if they tolerated disorders; and handbills were issued forewarning demonstrators of the magistrates' determination to suppress breaches of the peace and to protect those who chose not to illuminate. These injunctions sometimes had an inhibiting effect on the celebrations, at least in respectable quarters, but they rarely closed them down. Indeed, magistrates sometimes found that their authority to authorize a general illumination was pre-empted by local committees. At Devizes, the mayor attempted to intimidate a local printer into divulging who produced handbills for the illumination; without success.[67]

In many towns it is clear that the radicals initiated the celebrations. At Colchester, where the Tory-controlled corporation attempted to prevent an illumination by recruiting 150 special constables, the organizer was a confectioner who was subsequently boycotted by some of his well-to-do customers.[68] In the northern towns the organizers tended to come from lower down the social scale. Many of them were artisans or shopkeepers. The leader of the Congleton committee was a silk throwster. The Stockport committee included two grocers, two druggists, two drapers, a baker, a shoemaker, a clogmaker, a patten-maker, and a sweep. Those at Warrington were drawn entirely from 'the working class of people'.[69] Their leadership grew out of the post-war struggles in the manufacturing districts, from the widespread strikes of 1818 and the attempt to establish a General Union of Trades, and from the rapid advance of radicalism beyond its late eighteenth-century, artisan strongholds.[70]

The demonstrations in the industrial North were also noteworthy for their relative soberness and discipline. There were few antics comparable to those at Stroud, where the inhabitants tied a green bag to an ox and pelted it with mud to signify what they felt about the Milan commission

---

[66] Magistrates at Liverpool, Leeds, and Manchester, among others, declined to sanction meetings. See PRO, HO 40/15/135; *Manchester Observer*, 18, 25 Nov. 1820. For a discussion on whether licences were required for 'merry-makings', see *Manchester Observer*, 6 Jan. 1820.

[67] PRO, HO 40/15/112–13.   [68] Brown, *Chartism in Essex and Suffolk*, 16.

[69] PRO, HO 40/15/62 and 194; *Manchester Observer*, 9 Dec. 1820.

[70] Thompson, *The Making*, 668–9; Aspinall, *Early Trade Unions*, chs. 7 and 8; Kirby and Musson, *Voice of the People*, 18–28.

(and perhaps, more covertly, a cuckolded King!).[71] Nor did one see the scenes of disorder that broke out at Bath, where a high-spirited mob attacked the house of a local clergyman and several others 'against whom they had taken umbrage' before the lancers were called in and the Riot Act read.[72] Demonstrators in the larger cotton towns were organized into parades, with banners and streamers and renditions of radical Samuel Bamford's 'God Save the Queen'.[73] They were enjoined not to give the magistrates and the specials any pretext for reading the Riot Act. 'If there should be any great mob, or any appearance of riot,' the handbill from Manchester ran, 'the radicals too well know what to expect. They have not yet forgotten the 16th of August [Peterloo].'[74]

This injunction was respected. The Bolton procession cheered as they passed the houses of well-known supporters of reform, and hissed at their enemies, but neither here nor elsewhere was there any attempt to enforce illuminations by a mob. Magistrates may have been elated that there were only partial illuminations, but they had to concede, as did the Reverend James Norris, Manchester JP, that 'throughout the whole of these populous towns not a single pane of glass has been broken offensively, nor even attempted'.[75]

If the magistrates were relieved by the absence of disorder in the industrial districts of Lancashire, they would have been unhappy with the demonstrators' reappropriation of political space. This could take very pointed forms. In Oldham the *auto-da-fé* of Majocchi and Demont, prime witnesses at the Queen's prosecution, took place on Bent Green, the site of reform meetings in the first mobilization of the mass platform in 1816. At Ashton-under-Lyne the celebrants fixed a liberty tree to the pump in Old Street where radicals had formerly received a dousing at the hands of Church and King mobs. At Hadfield, further east, a village on the borders of Derbyshire, Majocchi's effigy was ritually executed and burnt

---

[71] *Morning Chronicle*, 22 Nov. 1820.

[72] *Bath Herald*, 18 Nov. 1820, found in PRO, HO 40/15/143. The clergyman's house was attacked in an attempt to intimidate him into reinserting the Queen's name into the liturgy. At Grantham, a mob of agricultural labourers from Spittlegate and neighbouring villages used the celebrations to settle scores with the corporation. See *British Press*, 20 Nov. 1820.

[73] Printed in the *Manchester Observer*, 15 July 1820. The rendition is anti-clerical, criticizing members of the Anglican Church for refusing to include the Queen in the liturgy. The song also expresses the wish 'O may she purer rise | From the foul calumnies | Breathed by horrid spies | God save the Queen.'

[74] *Manchester Observer*, 25 Nov. 1820.

[75] PRO, HO 40/15/170–1. On Norris, see Joyce Marlow, *The Peterloo Massacre* (London, 1971), 52–3.

at the same place where Tom Paine had been twenty years earlier.[76] In this way the radicals recalled their earlier struggles for freedom and reaffirmed their determination to press on, as they did at Manchester. Here it was given out that 'Jack Ketch' would publicly burn an effigy of 'Old Hay' on the 'plains of PETERLOO'.[77] Old Hay was the Reverend William Hay, stipendiary magistrate of the Salford sessions, ultra-Tory, execrated by the radicals for his role at Peterloo but rewarded for his services with the rectorship of Rochdale, one of the wealthiest livings in the country.[78] The very thought of this champion of law and order being roasted in public sent the authorities scurrying to St Peter's Field, only to discover that they had become dupes to a radical canard.

One final aspect of the Caroline agitation must be mentioned. That is the visible role of working men and women, not simply as anonymous members of the crowd, but as members of distinct associations. At Chester and Chorley, the victory processions of the Queen featured many friendly societies, some of which were certainly covert unions.[79] At Liverpool, over twenty trades, including the cordwainers, cabinet makers, nailmakers, hatters, gunmakers, iron founders, coopers, carters, joiners, and shipwrights, marched together with gentlemen and various friendly societies (both male and female) to show their solidarity for the Queen.[80] In London a good number of trades showed common cause with the Queen by individually addressing her majesty at Brandenburg House during her trial. They also collectively addressed the Queen, either in their capacity as the 'artisans and mechanics' of London, whose address was signed by nearly 30,000; or under the banner of the 'London industrial classes'; or as part of the 4,000-strong procession of London's benefit societies representing no less than 250,000 members.[81] These spectacular processions were not without their profanities. The pseudo-royalist parade of the brass founders and braziers, for example, highlighted 'a splendid Royal Crown' suspended on two brass pillars, quickly followed and impudently juxtaposed to a representation of Majocchi in the pillory and a green bag. It also featured three cumbrous knights in their armoured regalia and a fire extinguisher, whose

---

[76] *Manchester Observer*, 25 Nov., 9 Dec. 1820. The paper cites Padfield, rather than Hadfield, but this appears to be a misprint.

[77] Ibid. 25 Nov. 1820.

[78] On Hay, see Marlow, *Peterloo Massacre*, *passim*, and Robert Walmsley, *Peterloo: The Case Reopened* (Manchester, 1969), *passim*.

[79] *Manchester Observer*, 30 Dec. 1820; *Liverpool Mercury*, 1 Dec. 1820; *British Press*, 14 Dec. 1820.

[80] *Liverpool Mercury*, 24 Nov. 1820.

[81] Prothero, *Artisans and Politics*, 138–43; *Manchester Observer*, 20 Jan. 1821.

ejaculations were greeted with 'laughing applause'.[82] At the same time these processions expressed craft pride and the dignity of labour, and were conducted accordingly. In organizing the parade of the 'Working Mechanics and Industrious Classes' in January 1821, John Gast urged his supporters to make a 'respectable appearance, with a White Favour on the left breast' and to 'bring with them any Model or Ornament of their Trade or Profession, respectable Banners or Flags, with appropriate mottos'.[83] Coordinated by a committee that met at London Wall, the massive procession to Brandenburg House was divided into regular divisions under chosen leaders. Sixty-three addresses were presented on this day, and many trades marched, adding a new dimension to popular politics and new inflections of who constituted the 'People'.[84]

The jubilations that greeted the abandonment of the Bill of Pains and Penalties, and the processions of the London trades that continued up to the reconvening of parliament in January 1821, constituted the high point of the Caroline agitation. Yet within months, the Queen's cause showed signs of faltering. Although the Whigs and gentlemanly radicals were reasonably successful in countering a flurry of loyalist petitions in favour of the King, even to the point of taking control of some of the meetings,[85] they faced setbacks in parliament. Here the government successfully fought off demands for an inquiry into the Milan commission that had mustered evidence against the Queen. With the help of country gentlemen, it refused to allow the Queen's name to be mentioned in the liturgy. When the Queen herself agreed to accept an annual pension of £50,000 in March 1821, something she had resolutely rejected some ten months earlier, she seriously damaged her credibility. Her rather pathetic attempt to attend the coronation, when she was turned back at the very doors of Westminster cathedral, signalled the end of her battle to reclaim her regal rights and the triumph of her enemies.

[82] See Huish, *Memoirs of Caroline*, ii. 614 and the *Champion*, 27 Jan. 1821; cf. Laqueur, 'The Queen Caroline Affair', 459–60, who makes much of this procession as expressing the 'deep royalist sympathies' of Caroline's supporters. In fact the braziers' procession can be read as a parody or burlesque of royal pageantry. In this context one might ponder the many meanings that the extinguisher might signify in the context of 1820. What fires were being put out? What liaisons were being celebrated or burlesqued? Was public space being consecrated or desecrated by this 'holy water'? What bodies were being cleansed by this 'royal douche'?

[83] PRO, HO 40/16/17–19.

[84] On the London trade processions and their organization throughout the Caroline agitation, see Prothero, *Artisans and Politics*, 140–6.

[85] I am not convinced by the argument recently advanced by Jonathan Fulcher that loyalist opinion overwhelmed Queenite in the early months of 1821. See Jonathan Fulcher, 'The Loyalist Response to the Queen Caroline Agitations', *Journal of British Studies*, 34/4 (Oct. 1995), 481–502.

And yet the Queen could still command some support in the country at large. Or rather, her cause could still be exploited by enemies of the King and his ministry. Although the coronation in London revealed few signs of dissidence beyond the Queen's own intervention, the same was not true elsewhere. In towns such as Bristol, Calne, Kidderminster, Leeds, and Lincoln, Queenite toasts and demonstrations sullied the proceedings. At Manchester, crowds jeered the yeomanry cavalry, and drank loyalist toasts only so long as the beer flowed, ending the festivities by singing 'God Save the Queen'. Radicals even proposed they should pass resolutions to tar and feather the JPs 'who acted so inconspicuous a part on the 16 of August, 1819 [Peterloo]', and to run the yeomanry cavalry on a skimmington ride, 'with jackets turned' and 'their faces to the horses' tails'.[86] At Tiverton, only 73 pensioners, 120 tradesmen, and 30 gentlemen could be prevailed upon to join the corporation's coronation procession, in marked contrast to the exuberant Britannia-led parade that had greeted the Queen's triumph eight months earlier. In Bungay, Queenite sympathizers destroyed every loyalist laurel and flag they could find and burnt them on the coronation bonfire.[87] At Carlisle, radicals in the working-class district of Caldewgate refused the festive fare offered by the corporation and had the audacity to crown an ass. When troops were brought in to curb the profanity, they taunted the military commander with shouts of 'Manchester, Manchester'.[88]

Carlisle was not the only northern town to reject the festive patronage of loyal corporations. At Durham and Newcastle crowds threw the chunks of roasted ox (which many believed unfit for human consumption) right back at the butchers.[89] At the Tyneside port, where the corporation had expended £1,000 for the coronation-day festivities,[90] a sailor grabbed the crown from the wine fountain and 'crowned' himself; another climbed the crane upon which the ox had been raised, and, over the crown that had been placed there, pinned a Queenite squib (*The Political Queen That Jack Loves*) to loud cheers. Not to be upstaged, another celebrant dropped his breeches before the wine fountain and washed 'his posteriors' before 'a great number of well-dressed ladies'. According to the account in the *Tyne Mercury*,

---

[86] Walmsley, *Peterloo*, 407; Mark Harrison, *Crowds and History: Mass Phenomena in English Towns, 1790–1835* (Cambridge, 1988), 256.

[87] *The Times*, 28, 31 July 1821. On Queenite sympathies, see *Leeds Mercury*, 21 July 1821; *The Times*, 24, 25, 28 July 1821; Harrison, *Crowds and History*, 184, 250–3; Ethel Mann (ed.), *An Englishman at Home and Abroad 1792–1828* (London, 1930), 190.

[88] *Champion*, 28 July 1821; *The Times*, 24 July 1821.

[89] *The Times*, 24 July 1821; Robert Colls, *The Collier's Rant* (London, 1977), 67–72; John Sykes, *A Collection of Publications Relating to Newcastle upon Tyne and Gateshead* (Newcastle, 1821), 9–12. I owe this last reference to Virginia McKendry.

[90] *John Bull* (1 July 1821), 232.

he also grabbed the spout of the wine fountain as if it was a huge penis.[91] In this lewd and farcical appropriation of festive space, the crowd was telling the Newcastle corporation of merchants and coalowners what it could do with its paternalism and royal dandy. Before the day was out, in fact, effigies of the Queen had been triumphantly paraded around the town by women, and crowds assailed the coaches of the royal mail with mud and stones.

The coronation-day revels of the Newcastle populace revealed that the Queen's cause was not entirely dead, even if the Queen herself had all but abandoned it. It was still a useful signifier of anti-ministerial rancour and contempt for George IV. Such sentiments persisted until the Queen's death from peritonitis in August 1821. On this occasion the London crowd had the last word. When it was learned that the government intended to take her body around rather than through London on its way to Harwich, London crowds blocked the procession route with barricades of carriages and carts. At Kensington Gate the cortège was forced to proceed in the direction of Hyde Park Corner, where the Horse Guards outmanœuvred the crowds and proceeded northwards towards Cumberland Gate. Here Captain Oakes had his men fire on the crowd in order to disperse it, killing two men and wounding others in the process. At this point it appeared that the government's plan to bypass the City would succeed, but further along the route the cortège again encountered barricades and even trenches cut across the road. At this point Sir Robert Baker, the magistrate in charge of the procession, conceded to popular demands and turned the cortège in the direction of the City. Here the London trades joined the procession, waving flags bearing such inscriptions as 'Power of Public Opinion', 'United We Stand', 'Justice will triumph', and 'Friends of Humanity'.[92] The re-routing of the cortège was the final symbolic seizure of the Queen's cause, a defiant restatement of the people's right to political space, a thumbing of the nose at the political establishment. As a member of the crowd told Lord Stowell: 'Ay, you gemmen thought you could carry everything your own way; but we'll show you the difference.'[93]

[91] *The Times*, 24 July 1821; Colls, *Collier's Rant*, 70. On the popularity of *The Political Queen That Jack Loves*, see Hone, *For the Cause of Truth*, 346.

[92] Huish, *Memoirs of Caroline*, ii. 770–92; Prothero, *Artisans and Politics*, 147–51; Stanley H. Palmer, *Police and Protest in England and Ireland 1780–1850* (Cambridge, 1988), 172–8.

[93] G. Pellew, *Life and Correspondence of First Viscount Sidmouth*, 3 vols. (London, 1847), iii. 356, cited in Stevenson, 'The Queen Caroline Affair', 137. The government smarted from the defeat and forced Sir Robert Baker to resign as Bow Street magistrate. It also dismissed Major-General Sir Robert Wilson from the army. Wilson, a Queenite and MP for Southwark, had remonstrated with Captain Oakes for allowing his men to fire on the crowd at Cumberland Gate without the orders of the magistrate. He had also encouraged the crowd to block the funeral route at Kensington Gardens. See Palmer, *Police and Protest*, 176–7.

The Queen Caroline affair has sometimes been cast as a trivial event, a royal soap, a diversion from the main course of popular politics if not a regression to an earlier political idiom. Comic it often was, but the satires of Benbow, Cruickshank, and Hone brought little credit to the monarchy, prompting calls for a republic in the wake of the Queen's acceptance of a pension. That demand came from ultra-radicals at a meeting in Stockport in March 1821.[94] Diversionary it was not, for the Queen's cause was always larger than the Queen. As Caroline herself remarked during her trial: 'Nobody cares for *me* in this business. This business has been more cared for as a political business than as the cause of a poor forlorn woman.'[95] This statement was only partially true, for the Queen's cause as a 'poor forlorn woman' was often inscribed within a domestic ideology that cherished connubial felicity as a staple of the social order. Equally it addressed the experiences of women for whom marital breakdown was commonplace and for whom new sexual freedom and assertiveness was a desideratum. The Queen was an unstable signifier of female purity let alone passivity, but this very instability enabled women of different sexual politics to identify with her predicament in unprecedented ways and to boost her support within her own sex.

Yet the Queen's cause also raised other issues of political and constitutional importance. The spectacle of the Queen undergoing a clearly political trial at the hands of an unreformed, venal parliament on the basis of evidence largely gathered by spies and informers was a persistent theme in the Caroline agitation. *Pace* Laqueur, the affair was not overwhelmed by 'a more compelling, . . . politically safe version of the story as domestic melodrama and royalist fantasy'.[96] It conserved the cause of parliamentary reform, for which thirty-three petitions were heard in the Commons in the aftermath of the trial.[97] It also cast the Queen's cause as a parable of political iniquity as much as a parable of royal/marital persecution and hypocrisy, one that had a particular resonance within the radical community, especially in London and Lancashire. Moreover, the groundswell of support that the Queen's agitation generated enabled the radicals successfully to repossess the political space that had been denied them by the Six Acts of 1819. The final months of 1820 not only saw the government

[94] John Belchem, *'Orator' Hunt: Henry Hunt and English Working-Class Radicalism* (Oxford, 1985), 147–8.

[95] Cited by Roger Fulford, *The Trial of Queen Caroline* (London, 1967), 243.

[96] Laqueur, 'The Queen Caroline Affair', 465.

[97] *Journals of the House of Commons*, 76 (1821), 15–16.

back down before public opprobrium; it also saw the radicals begin to revivify a political culture that had suffered serious setbacks at Peterloo and
Cato Street.

Caroline's supporters were always an uneasy and unstable alliance of
Whigs, independents, and radicals whose discourse was fundamentally
populist, pitting the 'People' against irresponsible Privilege. This lent itself
to inter-class alliances in support of the Queen. In Bristol, for example,
Whig merchants and coalowners joined forces with local radicals on behalf
of Caroline. So, too, did the leading Merthyr ironmaster, the unitarian
William Crawshay, who a decade later would be locked in a bitter struggle with his workers in what was the first proletarian rising in Wales.[98]
Elsewhere, too, the tokens of support for Caroline were clearly inter-class,
even paternalist, scenarios, with employers rallying to the Queen alongside
their workmen and subsidizing their celebrations. Yet in London and the
industrial North, the demonstrations on behalf of the Queen were intima-
tions of a working-class radicalism that was to blossom nationally in little
more than a decade. This was especially evident in the cotton towns, where
the hurly-burly of crowd intervention, with its carnival of riot and sedition, had been replaced by the mass platform and the more disciplined
language of burgeoning class solidarities.

To be sure, this language was sometimes 'producerist'. It extolled the
useful classes against the parasitical, and conceded 'fair profits to the
manufacturer' in return for 'reasonable wages to the workman'.[99] It was a
radicalism that stressed democratic reform as the central solution to the
resolution of social and economic grievances. Yet this should not detract
from its class character. In the boom and bust economy of the textile industry, amid new forms of factory discipline, loss of independence, and the
dislocation of the family economy, industrial exploitation and political
oppression were intertwined. Protesting workers were subjected to a
battery of legal and military sanctions in these years. Their unions were
outlawed; their public meetings and strikes suppressed. Their ringleaders
in the bitter strikes of 1818 were sentenced to two years in gaol. In these
circumstances workers understandably looked to political solutions as an
answer to their plight, and they seized the opportunity of the Caroline

---

[98] Jeremy Caple, *The Bristol Riots of 1831 and Social Reform in Britain* (Lewiston, NY,
1990), 96–102, 120–1; Gwyn A. Williams, *The Merthyr Rising* (London, 1978), *passim*.

[99] Such was one of the toasts given at the Bolton public meeting to celebrate the release
of the cotton spinners from Lancaster Castle in February 1821. See *Manchester Observer*,
3 Mar. 1821.

agitation to stimulate interest in reform and to restore the mass platform. It was a gamble that only partially paid off, generating divisions within the ranks about the efficacy of popular alliances with the Whigs.[100] But it was not without its moment of triumph, however symbolic. A veteran radical named John Rogers told a public meeting at Bolton that he believed the abandonment of the divorce bill would prove to be politically counter-productive. It would only divert attention away from the 'abominable deeds' of Peterloo and facilitate a coalition of Whigs and Tories.[101] Yet he continued:

> I rejoice that the Queen has overcome them [the Tories]; I rejoice that she has all along so nobly dared them to give her a fair chance. I rejoice that Borough-mongering is conquered. I rejoice that the Magistrates . . . are bound to see the Reformers Flaggs thus exhibited, thus thrown in their own teeth. On these grounds I do sincerely rejoice. But not one yard further . . . Let me see a standing army abolished. A National debt paid . . . Let me see all useless sinecures and Pensions struck off. Let me see this Nation freely represented. Let me see it ruled by wise disinterested rulers. Then I will shake hands with the Ruling Power . . . But till all this is accomplished, I will persevere in the Good Old Path of Jacobinism.

We may regard this speech as a form of radical populism, focusing as it does upon the evils of Old Corruption. Yet it was a populism charged with class rhetoric. Throughout the Caroline agitation, the plight of the Queen had been linked to Peterloo and the attempts by working men and women to secure some public space for the articulation of their political and industrial grievances; grievances that centred not only on the political exclusion of those who had sacrificed their lives and livelihoods during the French wars, but also upon the weft of political and industrial power that reduced them to the most abject immiseration. Within radical discourse this immiseration was principally attributed to unjust laws that privileged the landed gentry and the manufacturer at the expense of working people: the Corn Laws, the Combination Acts, and the heavy burden of indirect taxation that was required to pay the fundholders and a state whose pensions and sinecures still bloated its expenses. Yet radicals were also beginning to address the unequal exchange that workers received for their labour.[102] As one newspaper summarized the plight of the worker at the height of the Caroline agitation:

---

[100] Belchem, *'Orator' Hunt*, 147.   [101] PRO, HO 40/15/110–11.

[102] On this issue, see Gregory Claeys, 'The Origins of the Rights of Labor: Republican-ism, Commerce, and the Construction of Modern Social Theory in Britain, 1796–1805', *Journal of Modern History*, 66 (June 1994), 249–90.

In this country the great mass of the people . . . are doomed everlastingly to labour either with their heads or their hands—to eat the bread of carefulness, and to till the earth with the sweat of their brows; whilst such a portion of the proceeds of their toil is taken by Government, or goes to swell the overgrown wealth of the great Capitalist, that a precarious livelihood, insufficient provision for families, privations and downright pauperism . . . are their sole inheritance. Is this as it ought to be?[103]

[103] *Bristol Mercury*, 9 Oct. 1820.

Conclusion

In November 1820 Benjamin Robert Haydon was visiting Edinburgh when the news of the Queen's triumph broke. 'I had gone to bed very fatigued and had fallen sound asleep,' he recalled,

when I was awakened by Mrs Farquharson screaming and thumping at my door 'to light up'. She had a candle in her hand: I got up, scarce awake, when bump came a stone against my bed-room window and tinkle went the falling glass. The shout of the crowd was savage. They were coming out of the wynds of the old town with a hollow drum, just like the mob in the Heart of Mid Lothian. In my confusion I took the candle from Mrs Farquharson, who was screaming for her drawing-room glass, and put it against the place where the window had been broken: in came the wind and out went the candle, and bang came another shower from the rouring mob, so that I shut up the shutters and they battered till there was not a pane left. A pretty reception for me, I thought. After smashing the glass right and left of us, the drum beat, and away roared the mob into St. Andrew's Square,—certainly a more ferocious crowd than a London one.[1]

Benjamin Haydon's graphic account of the Edinburgh celebration of the defeat of the Bill of Pains and Penalties forcibly reminds us of the tremendous physical presence of the crowd on public occasions. Whether those occasions were important political trials, unpopular bills, elections, military and naval victories or defeats, or, more typically, the calendar of national and royal anniversaries, the sympathies of the crowd were important. In a society that cherished its libertarian heritage, and needed a broad audience to make its public celebrations meaningful, the disposition of the crowd was always regarded as an important index of the pulse of the people and a measure of the regime or government's popularity. This explains the tremendous time and energy that corporations and landed patrons invested in political festival and its convivialities, despite the rising

---

[1] Benjamin Robert Haydon, *Autobiography* (Oxford, 1927), 386. I thank Joanna Innes of Somerville College, Oxford, for this reference.

complaints that the rough humours of the populace were often a tonic to drunkenness and vandalism and an affront to the march of respectability. It also accounts for the politically charged manner in which the more controversial celebrations were represented in the press and the amount of space they were prepared to accord them. By the end of our period, in particular, rival newspapers would vigorously squabble over who had the more reliable narrative of what actually took place.

The street politics of the Hanoverian era drew much of their legitimacy and ritual from the annual cycle of officially endorsed public anniversaries and the public punishments that were so critical to the ideology of the law. The community at large was invited to occupy public space on these occasions, to learn and commemorate the nation's political heritage, to be edified by the ceremonial parades of the great and to be gratified by its festive paternalism, to witness the judicial terror of the gallows and be suitably deterred from a life of crime. The forms of popular politics frequently replicated those conventions. Effigies of unpopular figures were publicly punished by whipping, hanging, and burning. They were sometimes led to the gallows by mock executioners and bands playing the 'Rogue's March'. Political heroes (or their impersonators) were chaired or had their carriages drawn for them in a manner that echoed the rituals of an electoral campaign. In times of contentious anniversaries, officials could find their own processionals mimicked by those of the plebs, or deliberately snubbed by the tolling of bells, the wearing of rue and thyme, the parading of seditious emblems, and the singing of seditious airs and ballads. On those occasions when popular triumphs or anniversaries (such as those of the Pretender or John Wilkes) were not officially endorsed, the plebeian crowd could appropriate public space in dramatic ways, ringing bells, constructing bonfires, enforcing illuminations, and demanding some recompense for the festive doles that had been denied them. Street politics were replete with symbolic practices that aped and mimicked those in power, and for most of the eighteenth century they were largely defined within those parameters.

Edward Thompson suggested that we should look at the crowd interventions of the eighteenth century within an equilibrium of social relations in which the plebs prodded, negotiated, and contested the cultural hegemony of the ruling class but never fundamentally challenged its right to rule. The model was derived essentially from Thompson's own extensive research into the popular struggles over food supply, the most frequent form of plebeian intervention in the eighteenth century, and for Thompson the most paradigmatic in that it illuminated the resilient, plebeian defence of custom on the one hand and the rather contradictory stance of the landed gentry, both capitalist and paternalist, on the other. The model works best in that specific context, where the landed gentry (and their urban counterparts) were often forced to concede to the moral economy of provision in the interests of social peace and their own ideological credibility, despite the fact that the regional and national marketing of grain was necessary to feed the expanding urban centres of Britain and a boon to their own rent rolls. Yet even here, as I suggested in Chapter 2, the model does not make enough allowance for middling voices; not simply the farmers and dealers who defended the wholesale trade, but those middling groups within urban society who campaigned for a reform of the corn laws and their enforcement to buttress the moral economy at a time when Britain geared up for what promised to be a critical war with the French. In the conjuncture of 1756–7, dealers were not only seen to be anti-social but unpatriotic.

Thompson would no doubt protest that his original metaphor, a 'societal field-of-force', allows for such peripheral voices; and there is some justice to this claim. But in other contests, the power of such voices was far from peripheral. In the labour disputes of the West Country woollen industry, for example, the structure of power relations was triangular rather than dyadic, with workers appealing to local magistrates to enforce the regulatory machinery governing their trade against the incursions of the clothiers, who had cut piece rates and introduced blackleg labour and truck. Indeed, in 1757, parliament endorsed the clothiers' case despite protests from both weavers and local gentry, reversing an Act that a year earlier had endorsed compulsory labour arbitration. This reinforced the trend against industrial paternalism that, with a few exceptions, would continue into the next century.[2]

The same reservations about Thompson's model can be applied to impressment disputes, where one once again sees a triangulated struggle between the state, the shipping industry, and the seamen over labour supply in wartime situations. They apply *a fortiori* to popular political interventions, where the structural reciprocities between rulers and ruled were overlaid with partisan divisions within the propertied classes throughout much of the eighteenth century. Thompson's own work in this field, which was ancillary to his main interests, tended to focus upon those symbolic

---

[2] See John Rule, *The Experience of Labour in Eighteenth-Century Industry* (London, 1981), 113–14. At the same time that the laws regulating trades (especially apprenticeships) were being abrogated or allowed to fall into abeyance, laws against embezzlement and the policing of the labour process were being added to the statute books, as were laws against industrial combinations.

contests that epitomized a plebeian counter-theatre that was juxtaposed to that of authority; the appropriation of political idioms for the articulation of self-consciously plebeian grievances or scepticism of the status quo. This was an important insight, not only for its methodological emphasis on the semiology of the crowd, but for the way it underscored plebeian agency. It is one I have attempted to develop in Chapter 1 to counter the overly élitist definitions of popular Jacobitism. Yet one also needs to recognize that plebeian crowds could be drawn into the factional politics of their day, and that at times one sees active consenting alliances between propertied and plebeian in which the former had the upper hand, if only because they had the cultural and material resources to elicit popular allegiances, however temporary. One sees this in the popular mobilization against the Pretender in 1745; in the highly choreographed episode of Admiral Keppel, in which bourgeois radicals and Whig aristocrats mustered an impressive protest against North's ministry out of disillusionment with the American war and a tradition of anti-Gallicanism sharpened by imperial conflict. In fact, in the twenty years after the Gordon riots, when the Wilkite alliance of the 1770s collapsed in the face of a highly volatile Protestant populism that cut across traditional political alignments, it was conservatives rather than radicals who sought to woo the crowd through the traditional channels and techniques of street politics. They were less successful than historians have assumed. The popular loyalism of Reeves and company achieved rather meagre returns from the energy it expended on anti-Jacobin propaganda and effigy-burnings of Paine. None the less, loyalists were successful in halting the progress of Painite radicalism, and, in alliance with the state, in closing down radical political space.

Despite the considerable investment that conservatives made in traditional political festival, the post-war years saw a significant shift in popular politics, one that was even evident in the Queen Caroline affair. Certainly, the time-honoured traditions of the eighteenth-century mob still resonated during the Caroline agitation. The familiar repertoire of the crowd with its forced illuminations, effigy-burnings, drums, and cacophony were all present in the jubilations, as my opening quote and others in Chapter 8 have suggested. So, too, were disputes over festive rites. In Glasgow, a crowd erupted when constables put out a celebratory bonfire on the orders of the magistracy, demolishing several sentry boxes and parts of the Old Bridge before the cavalry cleared the streets.[3] At East Barnet, 'a gang of about twenty fellows' from Southgate demanded beer and money for the

---

[3] *British Press*, 18 Nov. 1820.

Queen's celebration, and when refused at the manor house 'swore they would mark it for tomorrow and broke the bell upon parting'.[4] Caroline's victory partook of the same festive licence as many others had before it.

Yet alongside these interventions were more portentous developments. Working men and women signed addresses in support of the Queen, linking her cause with that of radical reform in ways that belied a simple fascination or intoxication with the royal soap era and the politics of personality that is often associated with the eighteenth-century crowd.[5] Moreover, in London and Lancashire in particular, they mustered some impressive parades on the Queen's behalf that were noteworthy for their order, discipline, and craft pride. Certainly the distinction between the two modes of political activism can be drawn too sharply. The most dramatic intervention in London, the Queen's own funeral procession, combined elements of both; for the crowd's success in cordoning off the official route and redirecting the cortège into the City set the scene for the triumphal processions of the trades in honour of her majesty. Furthermore, the processions in celebration of the Queen's triumph sometimes culminated in effigy-burnings of her enemies. At Bury, for example, the procession featured 'a good band of music, flags, transparencies, two caps of liberty, a considerable number of blazing flambeaux, a green bag, and an effigy of Majocchi' which was burnt at Union Square. At Warrington, the procession organized by the 'working class of people' hoisted a flag of 'Union' and a transparency of Princess Charlotte, while an effigy of Majocchi 'with a green bag in one hand, and a *Courier* paper in the other' brought up the rear. When it ended, 'the enraged multitude seized the effigy and tore it instantly to pieces' before retiring 'peaceably to their own homes'.[6]

The addresses and parades of the Caroline agitation were part of a broader shift in the theatre of popular contention from 'donkeying to demonstrating', to use Charles Tilly's alliterative phrase, one that was firmly in place within little more than a decade.[7] Certainly the familiar crowd actions of the past continued to speckle the political landscape. One only needs to consider the Swing riots of 1830, the Reform riots in Bristol and Nottingham in 1831, and the Plug Plot riots of 1842, which combined massive turn-outs

---

[4] PRO, HO 40/15/106–7, 232–4. For the East Barnet incident, see also Roger Sales, *English Literature in History: 1780–1830 Pastoral and Politics* (London, 1983), 186. For a crowd threatening to burn the printer of the *Oxford Herald* in effigy, see PRO, HO 40/15/87.

[5] Cf. John Stevenson, 'The Queen Caroline Affair', in J. Stevenson (ed.), *London in the Age of Reform* (London, 1977), 144.

[6] *Manchester Observer*, 2, 9 Dec. 1820.

[7] Charles Tilly, *Popular Contention in Great Britain 1758–1834* (Cambridge, Mass., 1995), ch. 8.

with attacks upon workhouses, police courts, and the houses of stipendiary magistrates, to recognize this was so. Yet after the Reform Act of 1832, direct-action crowds became increasingly marginal to popular movements, although they were still part of the rougher working-class culture of Victorian Britain and could inject an alarming ferocity into the ethnic tensions of towns like Liverpool.[8]

The new modes of popular contention that surfaced in London and Lancashire were part of a broader change in plebeian politics that began with the creation of popular societies in the 1790s and resurfaced after 1815 with the formation of the mass platform. That platform, with its large meetings and monster petitions, was a strategy of open, constitutional confrontation with the government that stood in marked contrast to the kinds of crowd interventions that had characterized politics since the Exclusion crisis. In the first place, the mass platform was underpinned by a network of clubs and societies that served, together with an accessible radical press, as the organizational nuclei for its mass meetings. In other words, it had a different associational structure from that of the eighteenth-century crowd, whose mobilizations emerged from within the more informal networks of plebeian sociability such as the market, the pub, and the workplace. This had some important cultural implications. Eighteenth-century crowds operated within a political terrain in which property owners often had some influence and control, however much they deviated from the official writ. Platform radicals, in contrast, strove to create their own political culture, with their own heroes, martyrs, and calendar of commemoration. They often disparaged official celebration and chafed at the way in which 'turtle patriots', as Cobbett called them, made a parade of festive paternalism for the impoverished, the dependent, and the gullible. Conscious of the need to offset the blandishments of the great, they sought, like Wilkes before them, to foster a calendar that could serve as a counterpoint to the national memory of loyalism and mainstream partisanship. In 1820 this calendar was a chrysalis of what it would become, but it was already taking shape around the anniversaries of Paine, Hunt, and the tragedy of Peterloo.[9]

---

[8] See Robert D. Storch (ed.), *Popular Culture and Custom in Nineteenth-Century England* (London, 1982); Frank Neal, *Sectarian Violence: The Liverpool Experience, 1819–1914* (Manchester, 1988). See also Donald C. Richter, *Riotous Victorians* (Athens, Oh., 1981), which focuses upon some of the better-known riots in London to substantiate (and arguably exaggerate) the notion of prevalent mob violence in Victorian society.

[9] See James Epstein, 'Radical Dining, Toasting and Symbolic Expression in Early Nineteenth-Century Lancashire: Rituals of Solidarity', *Albion*, 20 (Summer 1988), 271–91. On Wilkite festival, see John Brewer, 'The Number 45: A Wilkite Political Symbol', in Stephen Baxter (ed.), *England's Rise to Greatness 1660–1763* (Berkeley and Los Angeles, 1983), 349–80, and id., *Party Ideology and Popular Politics at the Accession of George III* (Cambridge, 1976), ch. 9.

If post-war radicals sought to create a political counter-culture that was self-consciously distanced from mainstream traditions, they also strove to imbue their movement with a genuinely democratic ethos. That ethos never survived the crippling effects of gender discrimination, which became more pronounced in the wake of Owenite socialism and the decision to advance a working-class domestic ideal to safeguard male unionism, to reconfigure family values amid the quickening pace of industrial capitalism, and to wring modest industrial reforms from the state.[10] In many respects that gender differentiation was already present in radical ideology and industrial practice, and it was no doubt enhanced by the defence of the Queen in terms of male chivalry. But at its inception, at least, the mass platform was a democratizing experience in the sense that it opened up the possibility of greater political self-activism for both men and women.

Certainly radicals were keenly aware that the platform was an important strategy of mass mobilization and class solidarity. As *Sherwin's Weekly Political Register* remarked in 1818, when the question of resuming the mass platform after a period of legislative repression was once again raised, and when women's political role had only just become part of the public agenda,

Every public political meeting is calculated to produce benefit, either immediately, or ultimately. When men assemble to the amount of thirty or forty thousand, they are then capable of forming some idea of their strength as a *body*, whereas by remaining shut up in houses and workshops, each individual remains ignorant that such a unity of feeling exists among his countrymen. Public meetings likewise create discussion, and discussion when carried on fairly, invariably ends in the discovery and promulgation of correct opinions. In short, the advantages in a political point of view, that result from public meetings in a country like this, are incalculable.[11]

If the mass platform was intended to have this educative effect, it also represented the sovereignty of the People assembled. Radical men, at least, addressed the state as putative citizens who had an inalienable or historic right to their inheritance and whose service in the wars enhanced that entitlement. *Sherwin's Register* even suggested that working men possessed 'a stronger capacity for thinking than those who insolently call themselves *their betters*. Their bodies are hardened and their minds are emboldened

---

[10] On these issues, see Wally Seccombe, 'Patriarchy Stabilized: The Construction of the Male Breadwinner Wage Norm in Nineteenth-Century Britain', *Social History*, 11 (1986), 53–76; Barbara Taylor, *Eve and the New Jerusalem: Socialism and Feminism in the Nineteenth Century* (New York, 1983); Sonya Rose, *Limited Livelihoods: Gender and Class in Nineteenth-Century England* (Berkeley and Los Angeles, 1992); Anna Clark, *The Struggle for the Breeches* (New York, 1995).

[11] *Sherwin's Weekly Political Register* (25 July 1818), 189 in PRO, HO 42/178/105.

by toil and exertion, and though it does not fall to their lot to be educated in the frivolities of life, they learn how to form a proper judgment of men and things in the school of practical knowledge.' Consequently, they were 'as capable as the rich of judging who will be a fit man to guard their interests'.[12]

This unqualified rejection of virtual representation was backed up with the quite explicit rider that if universal male suffrage was not conceded, working-class radicals would revoke the social contract between rulers and ruled and repossess their rights themselves. The threat of such action was underscored by the radical commitment to constitutional arming, by the election of a legislative attorney at Birmingham in 1818, and, twenty years on, by the election of delegates to a National Convention at mass meetings attended by hundreds of thousands of working men and women. The possibility of mass resistance to the prevailing political order was taken very seriously by the politicians in power, who used every legal trick in the book to immobilize the mass platform. Even in 1848, when the state's capacity for counter-insurgency was more formidable than it had been thirty years earlier, and when the platform's capacity for insurrection was correspondingly weaker, in that fewer men had active experience of armed combat, special constables were recruited in droves to supplement the police, the army, the yeomanry, and the enrolled pensioners. What is more, the laws relating to unlawful assemblies were given a fresh airing in the press and in charges to the grand jury so that magistrates could refresh their memory.[13]

In 1848 the government destroyed the mass platform and the democratic movement with it. Henceforth working-class men would be absorbed into the mainstream of Victorian politics, into a liberal but emphatically undemocratic political order. Yet in 1820 the prospect of democratic change was still open. The shift from the demotic politics of the eighteenth century to the democratizing politics of the platform had been bridged: both in the metropolis, where older modes of associational politics coexisted uneasily with new; and in the industrial heartlands of the North, where Hampden clubs, Union societies, and strike action shaped an expanding political frontier, and where Peterloo resonated dramatically in the public memory.

[12] *Sherwin's Weekly Political Register* (25 July 1818), 178, cited in HO 42/178/100–2.

[13] John Saville, *1848: The British State and the Chartist Movement* (Cambridge, 1987). See also F. C. Mather, *Public Order in the Age of the Chartists* (Manchester, 1959), who tends to concentrate on 1839 and 1842 rather than 1848, but none the less has some interesting information on the loyalty of the troops and the Chartists' lack of expertise in training, drilling, and combativity.

Index